STUDIES IN THE BUSINESS HISTORY OF BRISTOL

STUDIES IN THE BUSINESS HISTORY OF BRISTOL

Edited by

CHARLES E. HARVEY

and

JON PRESS

BRISTOL ACADEMIC PRESS

1988

Published by
Bristol Academic Press
11 Hazelton Road
Bristol
BS7 8ER

© *Bristol Academic Press 1988*

ISBN 0 9513762 0 9

Typeset and printed in Great Britain by
J.W. Arrowsmith Ltd.
Winterstoke Road
Bristol
BS3 2NTQ

CONTENTS

ILLUSTRATIONS

TABLES

FIGURES

Preface

This collection of essays has been prepared with two sets of readers in mind: the first, the large and diverse group of people eager to know more about the history of Bristol in modern times; the second, historians and social scientists with an interest in regional economic development or the organisations, industries and issues covered in individual chapters. Readers with a fair knowledge of the history of Bristol will readily appreciate the need for detailed archival research such as that on which these studies are based. There are already many fine local histories, deeply researched, and of the highest academic quality. Examples that spring to mind are McGrath's meticulous study of the Society of Merchant Venturers, the work of Minchinton and MacInnes on the port of Bristol, and Ison's fascinating account of the city's Georgian architecture. However, it is conspicuous that while Bristol's maritime past has fired the imagination of many scholars, other aspects of the city's economic history have been sadly neglected. Comparatively little is known of local businessmen, firms or industries, and there is no satisfactory economic and social history to provide a background for more detailed studies. The nineteenth and twentieth centuries are especially neglected. With the exception of Alford's outstanding book on the Wills tobacco empire, there is not a single company study or business biography that might be considered for inclusion in a list of important works of business history. This lacuna alone gave reason enough for the editors to commission the studies presented herein.

There is a second reason, more abstract but no less compelling, for encouraging region-centred research in business history. Much of the work done in the subject involves the close study of large firms. Corporate growth, strategies, policies, leadership, performance and organisation are much favoured topics for analysis. It is acknowledged that generalising from such case studies may not always be valid, but this problem, it is often argued, might be overcome by systematically comparing the experiences of numbers of firms. This approach to business history has been strengthened, legitimised even, through the tendency of many

scholars to view the development of firms on which they are working in
relation to the 'ideal types' proposed by the doyen of American business
history, Alfred Chandler, whose main concern is with the organisational
evolution of firms that become giant, multidivisional corporations.

Few business historians would deny the inspirational nature of
Chandler's writings or the richness of the insights he provides into the
inner workings of big business. But there are evident dangers of using
the Chandler model as a standard. It is, after all, a model based on the
experience of the United States, and even then its scope is limited,
confined to selected issues and restricted in applicability to firms that
make it into the super league. It is all too easy to condemn, misunderstand
or misrepresent past actions when the standard against which judgements
are made is an inappropriate one. The business history of Britain is very
different from that of the United States. Small and medium-sized firms
predominated for longer in many British industries, and, amongst other
things, markets, labour relations and industrial finance continue to exhibit
distinctive national characteristics. If the true nature of British capitalism
is to be understood, it is not sufficient to focus on a restricted set of issues
or the activities of large firms. Alternative research paradigms must be
brought into play, to complement the case study approach.

One inviting option is to explore themes in relation to the activities of
groups of firms rather than developing multiple themes within the con-
fines of a single case study. The industry, for example, is the natural
unit of analysis for studies of competition, investment flows, technology
and profitability, and there is surely great scope for more research at
this level. But some issues cannot be investigated by way of thematic or
industry studies. Company promotion is an example. In this case,
researchers must have knowledge not just of individual businessmen but
of business communities, sometimes national or even international, but
more often regional or local. Capitalist economies are multi-dimensional,
not simply hierarchical, and the spacial dimension is one that should not
be ignored.

Recognition of the potential importance of regional business history
first led the editors to contemplate the production of this volume. Bristol
has not been home to many giant corporations nor has any single industry
ever dominated the local economy, yet what the region has lacked in
terms of size and specialisation has been more than compensated for in
terms of industrial diversity and economic flexibility. The economy of
the Bristol region may not have grown as rapidly as many others in the
nineteenth and twentieth centuries, but nor has it suffered the traumas
of retrenchment that lately have afflicted so many British towns and
cities. Ultimately we should like to explore Bristol's economic development and business community in depth, to develop a more systematic

understanding of the dynamics of the regional economy than exists at present. This collection of essays is best viewed as a starting point for a broader, more systematic programme of research rather than the final word on the business history of Bristol. Chapter one, in a very imperfect way, gives some indication of the issues and industries any such programme of research would need to cover.

The contributors to the volume were not asked to work to a master plan devised by the editors. They were in fact given a fairly free hand in selecting subjects and approaches. Only two ground rules of any significance were laid down. The first was that all studies should cover topics never previously explored in any depth by other historians; and should draw wherever possible on original documents for information and inspiration. The second was that parochialism should be avoided by setting local developments in a broader context, and relating them to debates and issues of interest to a general readership. It was hoped that in this way the book would at the very least have the merits of originality and serious purpose. At the same time, authors were encouraged to write in a narrative style, unburdened by explicit theorisation, in order to retain the interest of those readers predominantly interested in local matters rather than the academic concerns of professional historians. Readers may judge the results for themselves.

*   *   *

The production of this book has involved many others besides the contributors and editors. It has been sponsored by the Bristol & West Building Society, whose officers have at all stages given support to the enterprise. Mr Robert Coverdale, assistant general manager, Mr David Wragg, head of the press and public relations department, and Mr Ron Radnedge, head of printing services, have been especially helpful to the editors and publishers. As with other local projects sponsored by the Society, the aim has been to stimulate interest in the Bristol region – in its history, institutions, culture and traditions.

When the book was at the planning stage, the editors received valuable help from the staff of the Bristol Record Office. Anne Crawford (now on the staff of the Public Record Office), Sheila Lang and John Williams deserve special thanks. They have continued to support individual authors thoughout the project. Bristol is fortunate in having the services of archivists who recognise business records as of equal importance to those of local government and other organisations.

The pictures included in the book add much to its quality and interest. They have been drawn from a number of sources, and the editors would like to thank the following for their assistance: Andy King and Stephen

Done (Bristol Industrial Museum), Bristol Central Reference Library, Bristol City Council, Bristol Record Office, Bristol & West Building Society, British Aerospace PLC, C & J Clark Ltd., Courage Ltd., DRG plc, Imperial Tobacco Ltd., London Life Association Ltd, Mike Tozer (Historical Photograph Collection), National Westminster Bank PLC, Rolls-Royce Ltd.

Members of staff of Bath College of Higher Education have helped in various ways with the project. Maggie Collins and Caroline Deans have worked on many literature searches to the benefit of individual authors and the book as a whole. They merit a collective vote of thanks. Certain photographs and figures are the work of Peter Wilson and Chris Sarmezey, and we are most grateful for their efforts.

Production of the book has been in the hands of J.W. Arrowsmith Ltd., one of Bristol's oldest printing firms. The publishers have had the benefit of Arrowsmith's long experience and professionalism, and extend their thanks to all concerned, especially Mr Gordon Young, who expertly supervised matters from start to finish.

Our final vote of thanks goes to Jim Will, technical editor of Bristol Academic Press. Mr Will has wrestled with drafts of all chapters, and they have gained much from his expert knowledge of English grammar and literary style. The index is also his work.

Bristol, August 1988   Charles Harvey
                                                        Jon Press

Industrial Change and the Economic Life of Bristol since 1800

CHARLES HARVEY AND JON PRESS

The history of most large English cities effectively begins with the great urban expansions of the nineteenth century. This is not to deny the antiquity of the city sites themselves, but rather to assert that the essential character of places such as present-day Manchester, Leeds and Birmingham was established by industrialization – in many cases, by a single industry or group of industries. The study of the history of Bristol, however, requires a different historical perspective. Bristol did not suddenly emerge from obscurity to become a great manufacturing centre: from medieval times until the end of the eighteenth century, the city could boast that only London ranked higher as a port and trading centre. Civic pride ran high, and, during the 'golden age' of the eighteenth century, the business community of Bristol acquired an enviable reputation for shrewdness and entrepreneurial vitality. Economic growth and commercial prosperity were nourished by the substantial flow of raw materials from west to east across the Atlantic which resulted from the opening up of the Americas. Many new factories were built alongside the docks to process the bulky produce of colonial plantations. Tobacco, sugar refining, distilling and chocolate making were added to an already healthy list of long-established Bristol industries, including soap, glassware, pottery and ships. Bristol, with good links by water and road to the West Country, Midlands and south Wales, prospered at the hub of a thriving regional economy. The population of the city grew from about 27,000 in 1700 to an estimated 70,000 a century later.[1] Population growth in turn gave stimulus to a variety of trades, not least those associated with building, retailing and furniture making. The prosperity of local merchants and manufacturers, moreover, was matched by that of the bankers with whom their affairs were closely intertwined, and the existence of a strong local market for capital gave Bristol an advantage over many of its rivals. Another advantage was the ready availability of fuel from the Bristol and Somerset coalfields. Iron, lead, and later zinc, were also mined locally, and the city had many foundries noted for the production of metal wares of exceptional quality.

The whole picture is one of a clustering of highly diverse but inter-dependent industries in a flourishing and expanding local economy long before the pace of industrial change began to quicken in Britain as a whole. Yet, despite its early start, accumulated wealth and locational advantages, Bristol was never to experience industrial growth on the grand scale seen in the Midlands and North. Industry expanded, but no one industry came to dominate the city; the population continued to grow, but not much faster than in the period 1650–1800. It can hardly be said that urban growth was negligible in the nineteenth century. Bristol had more than 330,000 inhabitants by 1901, and, with municipal parks, well-lit streets, class-differentiated suburbs, local newspapers and an efficient transport network, it could claim to be a truly modern city. However, the process of economic growth was elsewhere more vigorous, with the result that Bristol moved progressively downward in the league table of British cities, to stand in tenth place at the dawn of the twentieth century.[2]

Those who have written on the economic history of Bristol in the nineteenth century generally have taken an unadmiring view of the city's declining economic standing. It is acknowledged that the Bristol region did not have sufficient natural resources or geographical advantages to stimulate industrial specialisation to the degree found in more northerly towns and cities. Even so, it is argued that the city had enough in its favour to have made a better showing. Civic and business leaders are charged with complacency, corruption and the pursuit of short term gains at the expense of long term prospects. There was, it is said, a failure to invest and keep up with the times. Many firms and traditional industries died away in consequence, and jobs were lost to other more enterprising manufacturing districts. Furthermore, the majority of surviving indus-tries remained tied to the methods of the workshop rather than the factory. Productivity levels therefore remained low, and so too did the wages and living standards of the working classes. Some historians see an improvement towards the end of the nineteenth century; others believe that the economic rejuvenation of the city was delayed until well into the twentieth century. Neither case has ever been supported by anything more than a handful of detailed case studies of individual firms or industries. Occupational, demographic and institutional studies have pre-dominated in the debate.[3]

On one thing most critics agree: that before the docks were taken over by Bristol Corporation in 1848, the port of Bristol was badly mismanaged, to the detriment of local trade and industry. Not much was done in the eighteenth century to improve facilities, and, in all essentials, the docks remained much the same as in medieval times. The winding Avon was difficult to navigate, or even, at low tide, impossible. Ships lying alongside the quays had to rest on the muddy bottom at low water. Attempts to improve matters were frustratingly half-hearted. A Floating Harbour (in which ships could float regardless of the state of the tide) was first proposed in the 1760s, but it was not until 1804 that work started, to plans prepared by William Jessop, a pupil of Smeaton. And when this was completed in 1809, the Bristol Dock Co. straightway sought to recover the cost (about £600,000) by imposing high port charges, with the result that more and more traders opted for other ports, particularly Liverpool. More competitive dues were fixed following the municipal takeover of 1848, and the city docks enjoyed a substantial trade until well into the twentieth century, even though the Floating Harbour could accept only the smaller types of steam-powered vessel. The seemingly obvious way of overcoming this limitation was to build docks at the mouth of the Avon which could accommodate the largest ocean-going ships. Not all Bristolians saw it that way, and for decades many clung to the notion that the best way forward was to improve the Avon navigation. New docks were eventually opened at Avonmouth in 1877 and Portishead in 1879, and linked to the city by rail. These were brought into municipal ownership in 1884.[4]

How much damage was done to the economy of Bristol by mistakes and vacillation on the part of the port authorities cannot be determined with any degree of precision. Some local industries must have suffered

1. Shipping in the city centre: St. Augustine's Reach around 1870.

from the high port dues, and some manufacturers no doubt fled the region for districts where goods could be imported and exported more cheaply. Yet, the Bristol port-based industries which showed a capacity to innovate and move with the times managed not only to survive but also to prosper. Two notable examples were J.S. Fry (cocoa and chocolate) and Wills & Watkins (tobacco). The latter firm was established in 1786, at an auspicious time for the tobacco industry. Demand for tobacco was growing throughout the country, and indeed doubled over the next 20 years, despite the economic difficulties caused by the interminable war with France. The firm began with a payroll of about 40 and no particular advantages over its numerous competitors, but showed what could be achieved with skilled management, aggressive marketing, and receptivity to technical innovations. After a series of name changes, takeovers and amalgamations, it became the biggest tobacco company in the area with the familiar name of W.D. & H.O. Wills. When the Imperial Tobacco Co. was formed in 1901, Wills, with a workforce of 3,000, was by far the largest and most profitable of the merging firms. It had developed the U.K. market for machine-made cigarettes after acquiring the revolutionary Bonsack machine rolling patent, and accounted for more than half of all sales.[5]

Similar success attended J.S. Fry & Sons. The founder, Joseph Fry, had started in business in the mid-eighteenth century as an apothecary. He sold chocolate as a medicinal drink, and it soon became a very fashionable delicacy. Chocolate manufacturing came to dominate his business, and the concern inherited by his widow and later his son (J.S. Fry I) was among the first to make chocolate by steam power. Demand for cocoa and chocolate soared in the nineteenth century, and, as did Wills, Frys moved to a position of market leadership. The advent of more sophisticated manufacturing methods, coupled with lower raw materials costs, enabled the firm to develop products aimed at the less affluent, and its expansion was particularly rapid in the second half of the century, when a growing population and rising real incomes brought a widening market for consumer products. In the 1850s, Frys began making eating chocolate as well as cocoa and drinking chocolate. Its celebrated Chocolate Creams appeared in 1855. Total sales rose in value from £144,000 in 1870 to £1,643,000 in 1910, and Frys, which employed 11 people in 1819, built eight new factories, accommodating a workforce which numbered 2,000 in 1893, and 4,600 in 1908. This success encouraged others to try their hand at chocolate making, but none ever matched Frys for size or profitability. Amongst these concerns was Stanton & Champion's Steam Confectionery Works, established in Lewin's Mead in 1864, which employed about 300 people (mostly girls) in 1883, and the largest was Edward Packer's Easton factory, opened in the 1880s by a former

2. Hand packing cigarettes at Wills between the wars. Although the Bonsack machine had revolutionised cigarette manufacturing from the 1880s, other processes long remained unmechanised.

employee of Frys. The business prospered, and moved to a large new factory at Eastville around the turn of the century.[6]

Of the other activities generated by the port of Bristol, mention may be made of sugar refining and shipbuilding. Sugar, like tobacco and cocoa, formed an important part of the West Indies trade, and by 1801 should have had a promising future. In that year, a record 19,000 hogsheads of sugar were unloaded at the docks, and some 20 refineries were ready to deal with it. But their owners produced no Wills or Fry to usher them into the machine age, and within about 30 years the old-fashioned, expensive refineries were virtually all gone. A worthy attempt to re-establish the industry was made by a Prussian immigrant, Konrad Finzel, who set up a steam refinery in the city in 1836. This, with some 500 workers, was then one of the largest in England, and it continued to operate until 1881. Two smaller concerns which followed Finzel's lead continued for a few more years, but with the closure of the Bristol Sugar Refinery in 1908 the industry effectively died. The main reason was the strength of competition from London, Liverpool, and Glasgow, with their lower unloading charges, though managerial failings may also have contributed something to the decline.[7]

Shipbuilding and repairing fared rather better than sugar refining in nineteenth-century Bristol. The industry had risen to an important place in the local economy by medieval times, and its fortunes continued to improve during the seventeenth and eighteenth centuries. Bristol shipowners liked to build locally because different trades had different needs. The height between decks, for instance, varied according to the type of cargo carried and its method of storage. Building in Bristol made it easier for owners to ensure that a ship had precisely the features needed for a particular trade. Many owners actually built ships for themselves or invested large sums of money in one of the yards situated on the marshy open ground along the banks of the river Avon. Several of these disappeared with the construction of the Floating Harbour, to be replaced by more substantial yards within the new docks complex. The largest was the Chatham Yard (renamed the Albion Yard in 1848), constructed for the Hilhouse family, who founded the most important and longest lasting of all Bristol shipbuilding enterprises.

The continued success of the industry down to about 1865 was ensured by an expanding local market, specialist design and construction skills, and the availability of top quality oak from the Forest of Dean. There were, of course, peaks and troughs in construction, but before that year there were enough orders for relatively small ships to sustain the industry at a healthy level. Bristol builders experienced no particular difficulty in responding to the demand for iron, and later steel, hulls, and steam-powered vessels were built in some numbers from 1813 onwards. There is no evidence to suggest that Bristol builders were wedded to outdated technologies or designs. Indeed, the achievements of engineers like Stothert, Brunel and Patterson, and the building of advanced ships like the *Great Western* and *Great Britain*, suggests quite the opposite. Yet Bristol was hardly the ideal site for a modern shipyard. The largest ships that could be built had a burden of about 3,000 tons, and iron and steel could not be had as cheaply as in the northern shipbuilding towns. Invariably, as shipowners increasingly favoured large over small vessels, iron over wood, and steam over sail, Bristol lost ground as a shipbuilding centre. The late nineteenth century saw the closure of many yards. Only Charles Hill & Sons, which had taken over the Hilhouse business in 1848, survived the acute difficulties that faced shipbuilders between the wars. The Second World War gave a final boost to the firm, but thereafter only specialist vessels like tugs, dredgers and ferries were built. Repair work, however, continued to provide employment for substantial numbers of men before the final closure of the Albion Yard in 1977.[8]

3. Charles Hill's shipyard in June 1917. The *New York City* was built for Hill's own shipping line, the Bristol City Line, which operated from 1879 to 1972.

The nineteenth century also proved to be a critical period for several older industries less obviously dependent on the port than shipbuilding. The earliest documented of these is soap making. Soap was first made for use in the textile industry, but by the sixteenth century at least, Bristol was producing high-grade toilet soap, of which it was the nation's leading manufacturer. And though Charles I, by favouring London producers in the granting of monopolies, almost annihilated the trade (the number of soap boilers in Bristol plunged from 183 to just four), a recovery began during the eighteenth century. This was lent impetus when a firm originally set up by Samuel Fripp and Joseph Fry merged with that of Thomas Thomas in 1841 (under the name of Christopher Thomas & Brothers). Other soap firms remained in existence, but none could rival the new concern. By the 1870s, Thomas's was producing about 13,000 tons of soap a year, about 8 per cent of the national total, making it one of the largest producers in Britain. The firm also produced moulded candles, and in the 1880s it developed glycerine distilling and margarine manufacturing. This was the heyday of the firm, and its 'Puritan' soap dominated the regional market. But in the later 1880s it began, like other established manufacturers, to experience increasing competition from William Lever. His aggressive marketing methods brought him quick success, and in 1910, after a period of fierce rivalry, his firm took over

Christopher Thomas & Brothers. Production continued in Bristol under the new management, but though Thomas's ornate factory – inspired by the Uffizi Palace in Florence – is still to be seen in Broad Plain, the operation in the end was too small to be viable, and production ceased in 1950.[9]

A similar fate was suffered decades earlier by Bristol's glass makers. Glass had been produced in the city for almost as long as soap, mostly in the functional form of windows and bottles. In 1800, fifteen glass-houses were operating in Bristol, and two more in nearby Nailsea. Most of the Bristol houses were engaged in bottle making, but a few produced decorative glassware of very high quality, cut, engraved, tinted or deeply coloured and decorated. The best-known of these manufacturers was Isaac Jacobs, whose characteristic work was a beautiful deep-blue translucent glass, patterned with gilt paint. Another dimension was added to the industry in the mid-1820s by W. & T. Powell, originally a pottery firm, which produced attractively elegant cut glass at the Red Lane glasshouse. However, within a decade, the total number of glasshouses in Bristol had fallen to four, through a combination of mergers, takeovers and bankruptcies. And only the Phoenix house in Portwall Lane continued to make decorated glass. Its closure in 1851, after three unprofitable years, marked the end of a comparatively short but by no means inglorious episode in the history of English art and craft. The bread-and-butter trade of bottle making, however, continued for another 70 years, concentrated now into one firm, Powell & Ricketts, of Avon Street. This house achieved notable success by staying alive in competition with the dominant new factories in the Northern and Midland coalfields until after the First World War. Depressed trading conditions and a lack of cash for investment in more productive techniques brought about liquidation in 1923.[10]

Enough has been said already to indicate the rich diversity of industrial pursuits carried on in Bristol since medieval times. But none of these industries – not excepting tobacco – ever dominated the local economy in terms of either income or employment. In his essay on the economic development of Bristol in the nineteenth century, Alford makes incisive use of census data to reveal the small scale nature of most Bristol industries throughout the period. The city, he concludes, "was a location for many industries and trades but a national centre for almost none".[11] Coal and cotton, for instance, which in northern parts developed apace, were never of similar significance in Bristol. Yet this should not obscure the importance of either to particular communities at particular times. Production from the Bristol coalfield greatly increased over much of the nineteenth century, reaching a peak in the 1870s, at about half a million tons a year; after that it steadily declined. However, because output per man fell as the seams became harder to work, the industry actually employed more labour in 1900 (about 3,000 miners) than it had done thirty years earlier. The fact that the industry kept going despite obvious geological disadvantages owed much to the efforts of Handel Cossham, a carpenter's son from Thornbury. It was the researches of this self-taught geologist and shrewd businessman that led to the discovery of many new seams, thus prolonging the life of the field for several decades. But, though the industry was still a major employer in the 1920s, by 1939 only one Bristol colliery was working – at Coalpit Heath – and that closed in 1949.[12]

The history of cotton textiles in Bristol might be told in similar terms. It was not until 1838 that cotton was produced in the city on any but the smallest scale. Two years earlier, encouraged by the exciting potentialities of steam power, a group of local industrialists had formed a company whose purpose was to introduce cotton manufacturing to Bristol on a scale comparable to the Lancashire industry. The Great Western Cotton Works (named after the ship and the railway) by the Feeder Canal at Barton Hill rivalled any in the country in size. Close links were developed with Lancashire. Expert workers from the north west were enlisted to get production off the ground, and very soon the mill employed more

4. Colliers' meal time underground at Frog Lane Colliery, Coalpit Heath. The mine was sunk in the 1850s, and worked until 1949.

than 1,500 workers, making calico and cotton goods. Liverpool and Manchester businessmen acquired substantial shareholdings in the company, and in 1864, when it was incorporated as a limited company, two of its directors were Bristolians, three were from Manchester, one from Liverpool and one from Eccleshall. Towards the end of the century Bristol interests began to predominate – the board included Albert and Lewis Fry and representatives of the Miles and Harford banking families – but the managing director, George O. Spafford, was a member of a leading Mancunian business family. Unfortunately, the concern never really throve, and was reconstructed on several occasions. Nevertheless, it did survive for nearly a century, and was largely responsible for the development of the working class districts around Barton Hill. In the last quarter of the nineteenth century it paid dividends averaging just over 5 per cent on the issued capital, and continued to earn modest profits until after the First World War. But in 1925, badly hit by recession, the firm had to go into liquidation. From then until 1929, the great mill was used by the Western Viscose Silk Co., which was attempting to develop artificial textiles, but that venture also collapsed. The building itself fell to the developers in 1968.[13]

Non-ferrous metal smelting and working are further interesting additions to the list of older industries which have made a significant contribu-

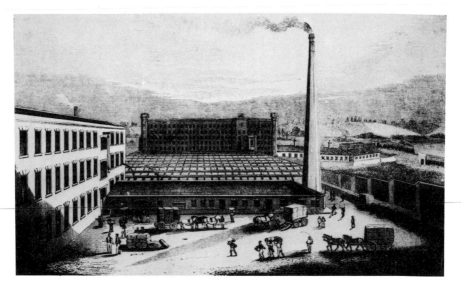

Great Western Cotton Works, Bristol.

5. The Great Western Cotton Works at Barton Hill around 1850. The largest building was the five storey spinning block.

6. William Watts' old shot tower on Redcliff Hill, in use from the 1780s until 1968.

tion to the economic life of Bristol in modern times. Lead was mined in the nearby Mendip hills up to the mid-nineteenth century, and much of it was sent to Bristol for processing. Mendip lead was generally considered of poor quality, as it was hardened by the presence of arsenic, and therefore unsuitable for pipes or sheets for roofing. It was, however, ideal for shot and bullets, which have been produced continuously in Bristol since about 1782. In that year, a plumber called William Watts patented a new method of making lead shot, which completely superseded the old method of casting shot in moulds. Watts simply poured the molten lead through a zinc sieve, whence it emerged in drops, which fell, hardening as they did so, into a vat of water, where the laws of physics preserved them as near-perfect spheres. Watts' original shot tower on Redcliff Hill was in use until 1968, when it was demolished to make way for supposedly necessary road-widening. Production continues in the Cheese Lane factory of Sheldon, Bush and Patent Shot Co., owners of the old tower since 1868. The method is still essentially that of the the original patent, though the lead is imported, and arsenic has to be added.[14]

Though not, perhaps, of greater interest, the brass industry was for a long time of greater economic significance than the lead-shot industry. Like lead, zinc was abundant in the Mendips, and, with local coal and Cornish copper readily available, Bristol was a natural centre for brass-making. The industry flourished in the first half of the eighteenth century under the leadership of Nehemiah Champion at Baptist Mills, and by the 1750s, the Bristol Brass Wire Co., founded in 1702, could claim to be the largest of its kind in Europe. The industry reached its high point with the formation and development of the Warmley Metal Works by William Champion, Nehemiah's younger son. At its peak in the early 1760s it employed 2,000 men, women and children and had a total capital estimated at £300,000. Champion was a man of extraordinary ambition, but unfortunately his grandiose plans met with stiff opposition from the Bristol Brass Wire Co. After a celebrated legal battle in 1768, William Champion lost control of his business, and was driven into bankruptcy a year later. After the closure of the Warmley works, the Bristol brass industry entered a long period of decline. It met with with ever stiffer competition from rivals in the Midlands who had close contacts with large customers like Matthew Boulton, who wished "that they may no longer be under ye arbitrary hand of the Bristoll Co." One by one Bristol's brass mills closed. By 1860, the only remaining firm, the Harford and Bristol Brass Co., was working just three, one at Saltford, and two at Keynsham. Chew Mill, Keynsham, did not survive the turn of the century; the other two lasted until the 1920s.[15]

One aspect of the general pattern of industrial change in Bristol in the nineteenth and twentieth centuries is clear enough: the older industries, though not growing rapidly, performed reasonably well for several decades, then, with a few exceptions, they entered a long and painful decline, ending eventually in liquidation. Pottery, with one notable exception, and woollen textiles (an important industry in Bristol's hinterland) had a similar history.[16] Yet, while some individuals and communities inevitably suffered from these changes, the economy as a whole did not suffer too greatly. No firm or industry was large enough for its failure to cause large-scale redundancies or induce a spiral of regional economic decline. The city was able to generate or attract sufficient new industries not only to take up the slack but also to provide fresh employment opportunities for tens of thousands of people. And, as the population of Bristol grew, so too did demand for the products – goods, services and housing – of old and new industries alike.

The most obvious need was for more housing. It is hardly a profound observation to say that the building industry, more than any other, shaped and continues to shape, the appearance of the city. Bristol grew out of all recognition in the second half of the nineteenth century, largely as a result of speculative building in districts like Cotham, Bishopston, Knowle and Southville. The city portrayed in Tallis's map of the mid-nineteenth century would have been largely familiar to a Bristolian of the Georgian era; the city by 1900 was beginning to approach its modern form. The inter-war years saw renewed growth, with the building of about 36,000 houses. Of this, about 60 per cent were constructed by private enterprise, mostly for middle class occupiers, whilst 15,000 houses were built by the council in estates on greenfield sites. Yet in spite of the importance of the subject, it is bewilderingly difficult to give a coherent account of house building, at least as far as the nineteenth century is concerned. That the buildings themselves have a degree of stylistic homogeneity is not surprising: those who built them were in general unoriginal designers, content to borrow, with or without permission, from existing designs, and if outward appearances suggest order and planning, then they are probably misleading. There were hundreds of firms engaged, one way or another, in the building industry, of which more than a half failed to last ten years. The rise of contractors after 1871 seems to have helped stabilize the industry to some extent, but even so it was clearly a high risk business to be in. Most firms were started by skilled craftsmen – masons, bricklayers, carpenters, plumbers and the like – and confined their activities to repair and small construction work which required very little capital. Some moved upward to build individual houses or groups of houses on a speculative basis, using money borrowed from a local bank, financier or, after about 1850, building society. These firms were especially vulnerable to the vagaries of the market and failure was frequent. Few had the financial resources and management skills needed to undertake large-scale construction projects. A notable exception, though, was the firm of William Cowlin & Son, founded in 1834 in Milk Street, St Pauls, and still flourishing today. Cowlins earned a well-merited reputation for modernity in both the decorative and civil engineering branches of the building trade, and its introduction of labour-saving machinery enabled the company to tender for work at very competitive prices. The firm obtained work throughout the United Kingdom, although it naturally looked first to the Bristol region for business. It carried out the restoration of Bristol Cathedral and St Mary Redcliffe; other important works included the Bristol Royal Infirmary and tobacco factories and warehouses for Wills and Franklyn, Davey & Co. Between the wars, it pioneered the use of ferro-concrete techniques, and more recently the firm has been responsible for local landmarks like Bristol's Council House on College Green (1956) and the University's Queens Building (1958).[17]

The physical growth of Bristol was made possible not just by the availability of labour and constructional skills. It was also necessary to gather the funds needed for house building. In this, the building societies eventually came to play a major part. Small societies of the 'terminating' variety (essentially savings clubs which were wound up as soon as a house had been built or purchased for each member) did sterling work in the first half of the nineteenth century. These organisations, however, were small and unstable, and it was only after 1845, with the spread of 'permanent' building societies, that housing finance began to evolve along modern lines. Even, then, most loans were made to builders and landlords rather than owner-occupiers. In Bristol, the years between 1850 and 1870 saw the establishment of at least nine permanent building societies. But none could match the Bristol, West of England & South Wales Permanent Building Society, founded in 1850. It worked on "the best principles", lending against first class securities, maintaining adequate liquidity and building substantial reserves. It gained an impressive reputation for financial strength and efficient management under the direction of leading members of the Bristol business community. By 1914, the society had total assets exceeding £290,000. In the years between the wars, a concerted effort was made to encourage owner-occupancy, especially after 1932 when low interest rates and rising real wages stimulated a boom in house building. The society shortened its name to the Bristol & West in 1935, and by 1939 its assets amounted to £4.2 million. A policy of growth through merger and the opening of new branches was followed after the Second World War, with the result that by the 1980s the society had joined the ranks of Britain's leading financial institutions.[18]

Before the twentieth-century rise of the building societies, it was the banks that dominated the market for financial services. Bristol-based banks disappeared in the amalgamations which by the 1920s had resulted in the emergence of the 'Big Five', but by then they had already played an important part in regional economic development. Stuckey's Bank, probably the most influential in the south west, was an archetypal country bank. It operated within a limited geographical area, insisted upon the close scrutiny of borrowers, and shunned requests for large overdrafts and long-term loans. Nevertheless, bankers, being part of Bristol's professional and civic elite, were in close contact with industry and commerce. The Miles and Harford families acquired substantial and diverse interests in industry and commerce, notably in brass and cotton manufacturing. There were, however, many hazards in linking the fortunes of a bank too closely with manufacturing industry, as the collapse of the West of England & South Wales District Bank in 1878 amply demonstrated. More attractive customers in many ways were the new utilities – gas, water, urban transport and electricity – primarily because of their size, predictability and the relatively secure nature of their activities.[19]

Collectively, the new public service industries of the nineteenth century changed the whole way of city life. The gas industry is a case in point. Originally, the chief use of gaslight was to keep factories open for longer hours, but its potential for illuminating city streets was soon recognised. The process, pioneered in the 1790s, was already lighting parts of London by 1810; in 1817, the first lamps of the Bristol Gas Light Co. shone in the centre of Bristol. A second supply company – the Bristol and Clifton Oil Co. – was incorporated in 1823, initially, as the name suggests, with the intention of producing gas from oil instead of coal. The two companies merged in 1853 as the Bristol United Gaslight Co., and, as the area supplied gradually widened, gasholders were constructed to supply Kingsdown and Cotham (1857), Barton Hill (1874), Bedminster (1896) and Horfield (1899). The biggest gasworks, which began production in the 1880s, occupied a 40 acre site in Eastville near Stapleton Road. The industry continued to grow rapidly in the twentieth century. In the inter-war years, industrial sales fell away, but this was more than offset by the rising popularity of gas for cooking. By 1930, when there were 101,600 consumers in the city, it was estimated that more than 90 per cent of cooking in Bristol relied on gas. The Bristol Gas Co. was nationalised in 1949. Production continued at Stapleton Road until coal gas was superseded in the 1970s by natural gas from the North Sea.[20]

A second Victorian development, possibly even more important than artificial light, was the provision of water for the city. In the Middle Ages, a population of between 5,000 and 10,000 had been adequately served by conduits bringing clean water into the city. Later generations were less fortunate. As Bristol grew, the population spilled out into nearby districts served by improvised sewerage systems, consisting largely of ghastly cess-pits and middens thick with disease. A flood or a broken drain could lead to the tainting of drinking water by sewage and thus to outbreaks of cholera and typhoid fever. In all, 584 people died of cholera in the epidemic of 1832, and 444 in that of 1849. The precise mechanics of the disease still awaited the attentions of Louis Pasteur; but an instinctive revulsion from this general squalor led to the establishment of the Bristol Waterworks Co. in 1846. Many leading local businessmen were amongst the 272 subscribers, including Konrad Finzel, Francis and Richard Fry, and members of the Thomas, Inskip and George families. Although the company experienced frequent difficulties in the early years, and it was some time before all the districts of Bristol were supplied with unpolluted water, this development saved the day, and Bristol's appalling standards of sanitation began gradually to rise. Other suppliers were taken over by the Waterworks Co., which steadily extended its catchment area into Gloucestershire and Somerset. By 1945, it was supplying 110,000 houses with 420,000 inhabitants, over an area of 78 square miles.[21]

The introduction of an effective system of urban transport brought a further improvement in the quality of city life. The hilly character of Bristol prevented the development of a local rail network, and, before the 1870s, unless they were 'carriage folk', people walked to work, or caught a slow and overcrowded omnibus. The solution eventually found to the transport problem, and in turn inner city overcrowding, was tramways. The Bristol Tramways Co. was founded in 1874 by a group of local businessmen, and at first operated a few miles of track with horse-drawn vehicles. Horse trams proved popular, but the real break-through came with the electrification of the system in the late 1890s. At last, the city had a rapid, cheap and clean urban transport system. Bristolians made 27 million journeys in 1900. Not content with this, the Tramways Co., under the leadership of Sir George White, further improved local transport services through the introduction of motor omnibuses, charabancs and taxis. The public responded with enthusiasm to the new services; city centre shopping, visits to relatives and pleasure trips were just some of the activities enjoyed by large numbers for the first time. By 1914, the number of passengers carried had more than doubled to 58 million.[22]

In Bristol, the supply of gas, water and urban transport services was the province of private firms, and, in contrast to most large cities, little success was experienced by those who tried to bring these enterprises into municipal ownership: 'gas and water socialism', as the movement was known, did not prevail, although attempts were made at intervals to take over the operations of the Tramways Co. Electricity, however, the last of the great nineteenth century public utilities, was from the outset in the hands of the local authority. In this case, the council, which, with some justification, felt that it had been consistently outmanoeuvred by the Tramways Co., resolved that the public interest would be best served if the local electricity supply monopoly was owned by the community. The concept of municipal ownership had come of age. In 1883 the necessary legal powers were obtained under the Electrical Lighting Act of 1882. An Electrical Committee was set up in 1884, and the eminent engineer William Preece was hired as a consultant. The committee, ably guided by Preece, did sterling work. It kept the economics of power generation and supply to the fore, and avoided costly mistakes like building power stations that had unproven technology or a capacity far in excess of local demand. The first power station, built at Temple Back, was not begun until 1891 and electricity did not light Bristol streets and homes until 1893. However, the superiority of electricity over gas for lighting was soon recognised; by 1900, 128 miles of cable had been installed and the number of private customers had risen to 1,200. A second power station was commissioned in 1902. The Avonbank station was located on a ten acre site alongside the Feeder canal, and it continued in service until 1955. Demand continued to grow, and by 1931 more than 50,000 of the 113,000 households in the Bristol area were connected to the electricity supply. The greater part of demand was satisfied from a large new generating station built at Portishead between 1926 and 1929. In 1948, the Portishead station and all other assets of Bristol Corporation's electricity department were taken into national ownership.[23]

The availability of gas, fresh water, local transport and electricity did much to improve the quality of life for many citizens. That more and more Bristolians could afford these services highlights the fact that both employment opportunities and wages were on the increase. Many found employment in the mass production factories that began to displace craft-based occupations in the later nineteenth century. Large employers like Wills and Frys, with their roots in the eighteenth century, have already been mentioned. But there were many more. One example is the packaging firm of E.S. & A. Robinson. The founder of the company, Elisha Smith Robinson, came to Bristol in 1844 from Tewkesbury in Worcestershire, and having acquired premises in Redcliff Street, began selling wrapping paper to grocers. The firm consistently widened its scope during the rest of the century, to include all kinds of packaging from paper bags to paper sacks, stationery and colour-printed posters. The most modern machinery was employed, and by 1914 the firm had two factories in Bedminster in addition to the rebuilt premises in Redcliff Street. By 1914, the firm had over 2,500 employees, many of them women and girls. The period also saw the emergence of Mardons as the leading supplier of printed packaging to the tobacco trade. Its expertise in high quality colour printing led to rapid growth once Wills began to sell cheap, machine-made cigarettes. It became a subsidiary of Imperial Tobacco in 1902, and was employing around 3,800 by the outbreak of the First World War. These developments led in turn to the establishment in 1912 of St Anne's Board Mills, as a wholly-owned subsidiary of Imperial Tobacco. The factory, on a nine acre site on the south bank of the Avon, was built to meet the growing demand for paperboard, for the industry was demanding a stronger packaging material for cigarettes than the paper packets hitherto used. Plentiful water supplies were required for the manufacturing processes, and coal and woodpulp – both bulky items – could be brought to the works by barge. Production started in 1914, and by 1938 annual output was 38,000 tons of paperboard a year. Twenty years later, it had risen to over 100,000 tons a year, and the works covered more than 100 acres. Output far exceeded the requirements of the tobacco industry, and about half the total was used for packaging chocolates, pharmaceutical products, cereals and other foodstuffs. In 1980, however, the Board Mills were closed down, with the loss of 1,700 jobs. This was

7. Inspecting packets for John Player's Navy Cut cigarettes at Mardon, Son & Hall, 1950.

the result of declining tobacco sales and competition on the part of foreign rivals which benefited from heavy fuel subsidies.[24]

Other sectors of the printing industry experienced less sweeping changes. New techniques were introduced more gradually, and old technology persisted for some time, alongside the new. As a result, letterpress printers and newspaper publishers retained more of a 'craft' atmosphere. To prosper, though, a firm had to keep abreast of new developments and exploit the new opportunities provided by an emerging consumer society. In newspaper publishing, the key development was the advent of the Linotype typesetting machine at the end of the nineteenth century; this led to the gradual decline of hand compositing, and, together with the introduction of large, fast presses, facilitated the transformation of the newspaper into an item of mass consumption. In Bristol, the lead was taken by a young Scot, Peter Stewart Macliver, who established the first daily paper in the west of England, the *Western Daily Press*, in 1858. It was soon followed by other daily papers, the *Bristol Daily Post* (1860) and the *Bristol Times & Mirror* (1865), but they never succeeded in overhauling Macliver, who had a head start on his rivals, and led in the adoption of new technology. In the beginning, the *Western Daily Press* was published on a hand-fed press, capable of turning out less than 2,000 newspapers an hour. By the early years of the twentieth century, its equipment could produce 120,000 copies an hour.[25]

In the footwear industry too, for many decades, traditional hand methods continued alongside new machine technologies. From the third quarter of the nineteenth century the industry was mechanised, and factories replaced cottage workshops. Yet it was a very gradual process. There were a few substantial employers in Bristol and Kingswood (notably Derham Brothers with 1,500 employees in 1883), and these tended to take the lead in the adoption of new methods. But most businesses – and there are known to have been at least 119 in operation in 1901 – were very small concerns, producing for local or regional markets. Most remained wedded to the old ways and the manufacture of a single staple product – heavy boots. In the depression which hit footwear manufacturers after 1918, Bristol firms suffered badly, and many went into liquidation. Even after this, however, few of the survivors could muster the resources or imagination needed to move into the manufacture of lighter footwear, which had better long-term prospects. When the pace of technological change began to accelerate after 1945, and the heavy boot market collapsed, many more firms went out of business. Only Brittons, which invested heavily in new technology, had the vitality to pioneer products and increase its market share. It remains as the sole survivor – albeit as part of a multinational conglomerate – of a once flourishing local industry.[26]

The displacement of small firms by more heavily capitalised ventures has been a feature of many Bristol industries covered in this book. In brewing, for instance, the weak began to give way to the strong quite early in the nineteenth century. The principal beneficiary was the firm of Georges & Co., which in 1788 took control of the Bristol Porter Brewery. Sound management, good beers and aggressive marketing enabled the firm to push gradually ahead of its rivals. It already had a large share of the Bristol market when in 1888 it acquired limited company status. A large amount of money was raised to finance the purchase of other brewers and scores of public houses. By the 1920s Georges had more than 700 tied houses in the Bristol region. More mergers followed, until in 1962, having acquired a very profitable local monopoly, Georges itself fell victim to a takeover by Courages.[27]

The process of industrial change, of new industries rising to prominence as others decline, is nowhere better illustrated than in the metalworking and engineering sector of the Bristol economy. Brassworking and shipbuilding faded, but as they did so brand new industries rose to the fore. One of these was the production of galvanised iron (and later steel) sheet. John Lysaght Ltd. began operations in 1857. Lysaght, a young Irishman, acquired a small Bristol factory which made galvanised buckets, and soon started to specialise in galvanised and corrugated iron sheet. The firm moved to bigger premises at St. Philips in 1869, and took on a structural engineering works at Netham seven years later. In 1878, Lysaght decided to begin rolling his own iron sheet, and acquired a factory at Wolverhampton. About 400 men were employed in Bristol, and 700 in Wolverhampton. A second rolling mill was built at Newport in the late 1880s. After John Lysaght's death in 1895, his nephews carried on the business, which continued to grow; by 1908, total employment had reached nearly 5,000. In 1913, the Newport works alone employed 3,000 people and produced 175,000 tons of rolled sheet a year, of which 140,000 tons was sent to Bristol for galvanising. The company became part of the G.K.N. group in 1920.[28]

The railway age offered an abundance of opportunity for the entrepreneurially-minded. One man who responded to the challenge was Henry Stothert of Bath who in 1837 established in Bristol the Avonside Ironworks. Avonside built steam powered ships and a range of machinery, but its speciality was steam locomotives. The Bristol locomotive building industry never achieved the production levels of Glasgow, Leeds, Newcastle or Manchester – even after the founding in 1867 of a second important factory, Fox, Walker & Co.'s Atlas works – but the city ranked for many decades as a centre of international importance, building robust engines for railways in all parts of the world. The Avonside locomotive works was a victim of the depression of the 1930s, and in 1958 the closure of the Atlas locomotive works, after years of struggle and decline, marked the end of steam engine building in the city.[29]

Bristol's involvement in railway engineering was not confined to locomotive manufacturing. The city also had a substantial interest in wagon and carriage building. Prominent amongst local firms was the Bristol Wagon & Carriage Works Co. (B.W.C.W.), formed in 1866 "to acquire the business of Agricultural Implement and Machine Makers, Wheelwrights, and Ironfounders, carried on in partnership by Messrs Albert and Theodore Fry at Temple Gate in the City of Bristol." The Fry brothers were sensitive to the rapid growth in the market for railway wagons, trucks and carriages, and wished to raise, through the medium of the company, enough cash to build a factory that, in terms of equipment and efficiency, would be second to none in Britain. Albert Fry became managing director, and within a decade the issued share capital of B.W.C.W. had risen to £110,000. The firm's Lawrence Hill works covered 12 acres by 1883, when 900 men and boys were in regular employment. Carriages of the most elaborate kind were built, mainly for export; while

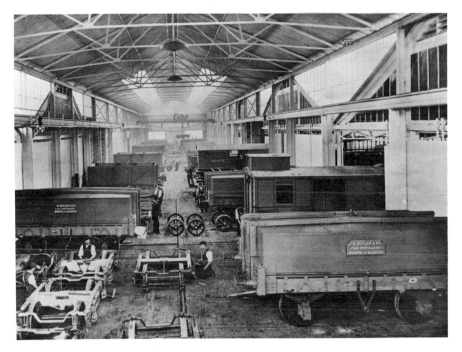

8. The packing shop at the Bristol Wagon & Carriage Works in Lawrence Hill. The photograph is one of a number contained in a superb catalogue of 1906. The Bristol chemicals firm of William Butler & Co. was an important customer. Other wagons were for export.

basic wagons were turned out in large numbers for the coal trade. Agricultural vehicles and machinery remained a speciality of the firm. The business continued to prosper until after the First World War, paying regular dividends and keeping abreast of new technology, but in 1920, for reasons not known to the authors, it was taken over by the Leeds Forge Co. Three years later, this company amalgamated with Cammell Laird, which closed the Bristol works.[30]

The engineering and metalworking trades, however, did not die with the railway age. Indeed, engineering work of various kinds, from the highly sophisticated to the prosaic, remains the region's principal employer in manufacturing. The *Engineering Directory*, published since 1945 by the Bristol Engineering Manufacturers' Association, provides a clear indication of the great volume and variety of work undertaken by Bristol firms. In 1951, for example, the Association had 260 members (about 96 per cent of the engineering firms in Bristol), employing more than 50,000 people. Their products included pumps, welding equipment, diecastings, structural steelwork and buildings, chains and pulleys, wire rope, machine tools, industrial fans, pipework, lifts and conveyors, and domestic appliances. Industrial machinery was a speciality of a number of the region's leading firms. Most local brewers bought their equipment from the Bristol firm of George Adlam & Sons, which until recently was one of the country's foremost brewers' engineers. Strachan & Henshaw, since 1920 a subsidiary of Robinsons, has by degrees become a market leader in the production of machinery for the printing and packaging trades, besides making specialist handling equipment to deal with coal, quarry materials, and the like. The Thrissell Engineering Co. produced a wide range of machines for the box-making, printing, packaging and allied trades. It was founded in 1805, and production continued until 1982, when its Easton factory finally closed.[31]

Diversity in production has been one important factor of Bristol's engineering sector in the twentieth century; another has been the continuation of the ninteenth-century tradition of transport engineering. At the very time when railway engineering was beginning to fade, newer forms of transportation were coming to the fore. Bus and lorry manufacture was begun by the Bristol Tramways & Carriage Co. in 1908, and four years later the firm built a Motor Construction Works at Brislington. The new business did well for the Tramways Co., enabling it to keep pace with the rapidly changing technology of the interwar years. Immediately after the Second World War the outstanding Lodekka design was introduced, which allowed operators to run high-capacity double deckers on routes previously restricted to single deckers. Standard models were also provided for the bus and freight companies controlled by the British Transport Commission. The Brislington works was transferred to a new company, Bristol Commercial Vehicles Ltd., in 1943, and placed under separate management in 1955. In the 1970s, however, following its acquisition by the Leyland Bus and Truck group, the Bristol works was closed in one of those agonisingly familiar bouts of rationalisation that in recent times have progressively eroded Britain's vehicle manufacturing capacity.[32]

Motor cycle manufacture is another industry to have risen to prominence and disappear within a single lifetime. In Bristol, the banner was carried by Douglas Engineering of Kingswood, a firm set up in 1882 to manufacture bootmaking equipment. Motor cycles were first assembled in 1907, and production remained at the low level of 10 machines a week until 1914. The outbreak of war brought a War Office order for 300 a week, and the finance for a massive expansion programme. Stationary engines, pumps and motor cars (from 1913) also sold well, and in the 1930s Douglas built aero engines for the Bristol Aeroplane Co. and Supermarine. But it is for motor cycles that Douglas will always be remembered; victories in numerous speed trials and races boosted sales in all parts of the world. After World War Two, the company experienced financial difficulties, only alleviated in the early 1950s when it began making Vespa scooters under licence. Production continued until 1964, providing employment for a workforce of 2,000 people. In 1956, the company was acquired by Bendix Westinghouse, the world leaders in air braking systems, and gradually air brakes have taken over as the principal business of the Kingswood factory, supplying manufacturers like Scania, Volvo, Leyland and E.R.F.[33]

Motor cycles, like steam locomotives, have about them an aura of romance that attaches to few products of industry. So too does aviation, which has become the most economically significant of all Bristol's transport industries. It began in 1910, when Sir George White of tramways fame founded the British & Colonial Aeroplane Co. (better known under its later title, the Bristol Aeroplane Co.) It was claimed as the first aviation company in the world to be launched on a proper financial footing. The company's reputation was made with its first production model, the Boxkite. More advanced designs followed, notably the Scouts and Fighters which were among the First World War's outstanding aircraft. Like other British aircraft makers, the firm was badly hit by the market collapse which came with peace in Europe. It nonetheless retained an enterprising outlook. Engine construction began in 1920, and within a decade Bristol had emerged as the national centre for air-cooled engines. Rearmament and war led to rapid expansion; the number of workers on the books leapt from 4,300 in 1935 to 52,000 in 1942. Relations with the Air Ministry were often strained, but the Bristol firm nevertheless made an important contribution to the war effort. It produced a total of 101,000 engines between 1939 and 1945, and large numbers of aircraft, principally Blenheims, Beauforts and Beaufighters. After the war, the company developed the ill-fated Brabazon, the largest passenger airliner of the age and a technical *tour de force*, but one which was soon overtaken by the rapid development of jet airliners. By the end of the 1950s, it was apparent that the day of the independent aircraft manufacturer was over, and the Bristol Aeroplane Co. merged with other leading manufacturers to form the British Aircraft Corporation (now British Aerospace). Its engine division became part of Rolls-Royce's Bristol Engine Division. Bristol remains one of the main locations of the British aerospace industry, having had responsibility for technically advanced projects such as Concorde, built at Filton and Toulouse, and the Pegasus vectored thrust turbofans used in the Harrier jump-jet. Since the war, aerospace has grown to become the biggest employer of industrial labour in the region, accounting for over a third of male employment in manufacturing in Bristol and surrounding districts in the 1980s. It has also generated

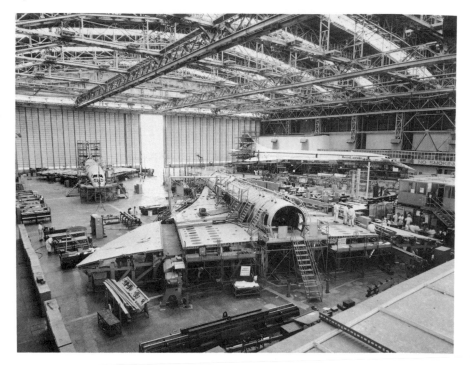

9. Concorde under construction at Filton in the massive hangar originally built to house the Bristol Brabazon.

employment in many subsidiary industries, notably electrical engineering concerns such as G.E.C. Avionics at Nailsea.[34]

Another technologically advanced industry with its roots in the nineteenth century is chemicals. Crew's Hole, an area to the east of Temple Meads, which in the 1830s lay outside the Bristol conurbation, was the original location of the Bristol tar works. In the early days, under the name Roberts & Daines, the principal product was creosote, sold as a preservative for the wooden sleepers of the Great Western Railway. The raw material was coal-tar, the residue from gas production. Later, under the name of William Butler & Co., the firm diversified into the production of all kinds of oil-based chemicals, ranging from the relatively primitive (lamp black) to the highly sophisticated (ingredients for plastics). Its tar distilling interests were sold out to the gas boards in 1962, and it was later relocated at Avonmouth, producing disinfectants, antiseptics and preservatives. It is now a subsidiary of an American company, Tenneco Organics.[35]

Crew's Hole must have been a place to avoid in the nineteenth century. The tar distillery was just one of several chemical factories emitting unpleasant fumes into the atmosphere. Most notable was the Netham Alkali works, originally opened in the 1840s, which produced sulphuric acid, and other chemicals such as sal ammoniac, washing soda and superphosphates. By the late nineteenth century it had between 400 and 500 men on its payroll. The firm provides yet another example of the interlocking interests so typical of business in Bristol; its chairman was the soap manufacturer Charles Thomas, and the board included Joseph Wethered, a leading coal-owner. The company was eventually taken over by I.C.I., which closed the factory after the Second World War. I.C.I. remains the most important manufacturer of chemicals in the region, with an enormous complex at Severnside for the production of ethylene oxide, glycol, ammonia and fertilisers. Work began on the 1,000 acre site in 1960. This, as in the case of the Imperial Smelting Corporation's Avonmouth Works, is best seen as a development quite independent of older industries, now defunct, in Bristol itself.[36]

The building of the vast Avonmouth zinc complex between 1917 and 1923, at a cost of more than £800,000, was a result of the exigencies of war. Before 1914, a large part of the zinc concentrates produced in Australia were sent to Germany for refining. Britain in turn imported a large part of the refined metal needed by industry. When war broke out with Germany, government initiatives led to the formation of the National Smelting Co. and the decision to build a massive smelting works and sulphuric acid complex at Avonmouth. It is not clear why the Avonmouth site was chosen, though it seems certain that the availability of cheap land close to the government munitions factory and the advantage of a deep water port were important factors. After the war, demand plummeted and National Smelting ran into difficulties. The business was rescued by a team of eminent British industrialists with interests in metals and chemicals, and it progressed steadily in the 1920s before being taken over by the newly formed Imperial Smelting Corporation in 1929. Imperial was from the first controlled by the Zinc Corporation of Australia, and that connection remains down to the present, although it should be borne in mind that the Australian owners themselves are controlled by yet more powerful British interests. Over the years, smaller British zinc plants have been closed down by Imperial in order to concentrate production at Avonmouth. It is here that the famous Imperial Smelting Process was developed. From 1967, the Avonmouth Works was home to the largest and most efficient zinc blast furnace in the world.[37]

The manner in which the Imperial Smelting Works at Avonmouth was commissioned and developed is illustrative of an important trend in British business in the twentieth century: the tendency for impersonal

10. An aerial view of Imperial Smelting's Avonmouth works.

forces to predominate in determining the location of manufacturing plants and offices. Before 1914, there existed in Bristol a close-knit business community with a commitment to the economic well-being of the city. The leaders of this community – men like Sir George White, Albert Fry, Christopher Thomas and Joseph Wethered – formed an economic elite with powerful social and political connections. They jointly promoted many companies, held many directorships, and controlled a large number of major enterprises. This was not so much family capitalism as community capitalism. It persists today in a much diluted form, and, of course, even in the nineteenth century, this form of economic leadership was never monolithic or static. We cannot point to a particular time when community capitalism ended, eroded to the point of inconsequence by the rise of powerful national and international firms. However, we may note the tendency and recognise its long term significance. Large firms nowadays come to Bristol mainly for financial reasons, not because their owners were born in the city.

Most of the firms with operations at Avonmouth fall into this category of enterprise. Likewise, the recent influx of insurance, banking and financial institutions into the city – the Clerical, Medical & General Life

11. The London Life Association's new headquarters in Temple Street, completed in 1983. London Life currently employs 520 people in Bristol.

Society, the London Life Association, the Sun Life Assurance Co., and divisions of Lloyds Bank and the National Westminster Bank are examples – is a reflection of comparative cost thinking on locational matters in the boardrooms of major organisations. There is no special sense of attachment to the city. At the same time, many of the more successful Bristol-based companies have lost or are rapidly losing their local identity. Many have been gobbled up by national concerns in one of the periodic merger waves that have swept British industry in the twentieth century. W.D. & H.O. Wills was absorbed into the Imperial Tobacco Co. as early as 1901, and Imperial itself has since been incorporated into the Hanson Trust. Frys joined Cadburys in 1918. Georges & Co., the brewers, after a long period of sustained growth was acquired by Courages in 1962, and Courages in turn was later taken over by the Imperial Group. G.B. Britton joined the Ward White footwear group in 1973. Many other examples could be given, and by the same token it is possible to identify Bristol-based firms that have grown big through the acquisition of others. The most notable of these is Robinsons which between the wars embarked on a policy of diversification through acquisition. Members of the Robinson family continued to run the firm for many years, but today, having joined forces with John Dickinson & Co. to form the Dickinson Robinson Group, it is one of the few multinational companies based in Bristol, employing about 2,000 people in the city.

Corporate growth, multi-plant operation and merger have all made it progressively more difficult to think in terms of Bristol firms and Bristol businessmen.[38] The regional economy is now the concern of planners and local politicians who compete with their opposite numbers elsewhere in Britain and Europe to attract new investment to the city. Thus the decision of the American computer firm Hewlett Packard to build a plant in north Bristol, which created over 500 jobs by the end of 1986, was hailed as a triumph by city bureaucrats. Unfavourable location decisions pass without much comment. Bristol must compete as a city or suffer decline; it can no longer rely on the enterprise of individuals to sustain its economy. Favoured by its proximity to London, and the excellence of its communications, Bristol has weathered the economic storms of recent years much better than most urban communities. Although manufacturing jobs in the region fell by 35 per cent between 1971 and 1986, the service sector – stimulated by the relocation of firms from London – has grown rapidly, accounting for 67 per cent of all jobs in October 1986. At that time the unemployment rate stood at 10.6 per cent of the workforce, compared with figures of 13.9 per cent for Manchester and 16.1 per cent for Birmingham. All in all, the city has done well, reinforced in its traditional role as a regional administrative and distribution centre.[39]

The thrust of this short survey of industrial change in Bristol, though limited in scope and inconclusive in nature, has been to assert that the city has long been much more than a maritime centre in decline. On the contrary, Bristol has for a long time enjoyed a diversified economy which has proved adaptable, resilient, and responsive to national trends. It has been able to weather, without too much suffering, catastrophic changes in the fortunes of individual industries. Bristol may never have been the centre of an industrial revolution – first, second or third – but it has grown and prospered, steadily and in robust fashion. Economic historians have for long recognised the dangers of regional specialisation, and more recently they have come to see that the history of the British economy in the nineteenth and twentieth centuries cannot be told simply in terms of coal, cotton, iron, railways, shipping and shipbuilding. Even at the height of Britain's industrial expansion, the country as a whole retained a diversified economic structure, and a strong commitment to commerce, finance and light industry. This feature of the British economy has endured. It has endured too in Bristol, as it has elsewhere in other of the more prosperous towns and cities of western Europe.

NOTES

1. B. Little, *The City and County of Bristol: a Study in Atlantic Civilisation* (1954), pp.326–7.

2. Ibid. B.W.E. Alford, 'The Economic Development of Bristol in the Nineteenth Century: an Enigma?', in P. McGrath and J. Cannon, eds. *Essays in Bristol and Gloucestershire History* (Bristol, 1976), p.258. B.R. Mitchell and P. Deane, *Abstract of British Historical Statistics* (Cambridge, 1962), pp.24–7. H.A. Shannon and B. Grebenik, *The Population of Bristol* (Cambridge, 1943), pp.5–11.

3. See especially Alford, 'Economic Development of Bristol', pp.252–83. A.J. Pugsley, 'Some Contributions towards the Study of the Economic History of Bristol in the Eighteenth and Nineteenth Centuries' (unpublished M.A. thesis, University of Bristol, 1921). S.J. Jones, 'The Growth of Bristol', *Transactions of the Institute of British Geographers*, 11 (1946), p.77.

4. R.A. Buchanan, 'The Construction of the Floating Harbour in Bristol, 1804–9', *Transactions of the Bristol and Gloucestershire Archaeological Society* (hereafter *Trans. B.G.A.S.*), 88 (1969), pp.184–204. R.A. Buchanan and N. Cossons, *The Industrial Archaeology of the Bristol Region* (Newton Abbot, 1969), pp.31–4, 55–6. Little, *City and County of Bristol*, pp.163–5, 252–5. W.E. Minchinton, *The Port of Bristol in the Eighteenth Century* (Bristol, 1962). Pugsley, thesis. C.Wells, *A Short History of the Port of Bristol* (Bristol, 1909). A.F. Williams, 'Bristol Port Plans and Improvement Schemes of the Eighteenth Century', *Trans. B.G.A.S.*, 81 (1962), pp.138–88.

5. B.W.E. Alford, *W.D. & H.O. Wills and the Development of the U.K. Tobacco Industry, 1786–1965* (1973). Idem, 'Penny Cigarettes, Oligopoly and Entrepreneurship in the U.K. Tobacco Industry in the Late Nineteenth Century', in B. Supple, ed. *Essays in British Business History* (Oxford, 1977), pp.49–68.

6. See below, S. Diaper, 'J.S. Fry & Sons: Growth and Decline in the Chocolate Industry, 1853–1918'. Also see *Bristol Times & Mirror, Work in Bristol* (Bristol, 1883), pp.136–43. Little, *City and County of Bristol*, pp.260, 313.

7. Public Record Office (hereafter P.R.O.), BT31 17066/77966, Bristol Sugar Refinery Ltd., Extraordinary General Meeting, 22. Jan. 1909. *Bristol Times & Mirror, Work in Bristol*, pp.54–61. Buchanan and Cossons, *Industrial Archaeology*, pp.67–9. Little, *City and County of Bristol*, p.259. G. Measom, *Official Illustrated Guide to the Great Western Railway* (1860), pp 819–31 contains an illustrated account of Finzel's refinery.

8. *Bristol Times & Mirror, Bristol's Many Industries* (Bristol, 1922), unpaginated. J.C.G. Hill, *Shipshape and Bristol Fashion* (Liverpool, 1951). G. Farr, *Shipbuilding in the Port of Bristol* (1977). Idem, *Records of Bristol Ships*, Bristol Record Society, XV (1949). Buchanan and Cossons, *Industrial Archaeology*, pp.48–50. Little, *City and County of Bristol*, pp.257–8. C.M. MacInnes, 'The Port of Bristol', in H.A. Cronne, T.W Moody and D.B. Quinn, eds. *Essays in British and Irish History* (1949), pp.200–17.

9. S.J. Diaper, 'Christopher Thomas & Brothers Ltd: the Last Bristol Soapmakers: an Aspect of Bristol's Economic Development in the Nineteenth Century', *Trans. B.G.A.S.*, 105 (1988). *Bristol Times & Mirror, Work in Bristol*, pp.20–30. *Bristol Times & Mirror, Bristol's Many Industries*. T. O'Brien, 'Christopher Thomas & Brothers Ltd.', *Progress*, 40 (1949), pp.43–8.

10. B.W.E. Alford, 'The Flint and Bottle Glass Industry in the Early Nineteenth Century: a Case Study of a Bristol Firm', *Business History*, X (1968), pp.12–21. F. Buckley, 'The Early Glasshouses of Bristol', *Journal of the Society of Glass Technology*, 9 (1925), pp.36–61. A.C. Powell, 'Glassmaking in Bristol', *Trans. B.G.A.S.*, 47 (1925), pp.211–57. C. Weeden, 'The Bristol Glass Industry: its Rise and Decline', *Glass Technology*, 25 (1983), pp.241–56. C. Witt, C. Weeden and A.P. Schwind, *Bristol Glass* (Bristol, 1984).

11. Alford, 'Economic Development of Bristol', p.281.

12. H. Cossham, *The Bristol Coalfield* (Bath, 1876). W. Ashworth, *The History of the British Coal Industry, volume 5: 1946–82* (Oxford, 1986), pp.14, 17, 234. J. Cornwell, *Collieries of Kingswood and South Gloucestershire* (Cowbridge, Glamorgan, 1983), p.4. Buchanan and Cossons, *Industrial Archaeology*, pp.78–96. Little, *City and County of Bristol*, pp.262–4. There was a brief renaissance in the 1950s, when a drift mine was worked at Harry Stoke by the N.C.B.

13. P.R.O., BT31 14801/9175, Great Western Cotton Co. Ltd., Memorandum of Association, 13 June 1885; Summary, 20 Oct. 1885; Register of Directors, 23 Jan. 1901; Prospectus, 4 July 1904; Extraordinary General Meeting, 16 April 1925. *Bristol Times & Mirror, Work in Bristol*, pp.90–9. Buchanan and Cossons, *Industrial Archaeology*, pp.137–9. S.J. Jones, 'The Cotton Industry in Bristol', *Transactions of the Institute of British Geographers*, 13 (1947), pp.66–79. J. Latimer, *Annals of Bristol in the Nineteenth Century* (Bristol, 1883), p.237. W.T. Sanigar, *Leaves from a Barton Hill Notebook* (Bristol, 1954), pp.22–4, 49–50.

14. H.C. Salmon, 'Lead Smelting in the Mendips', *Mining and Smelting Magazine*, 6 (1864), pp.321–8. *Bristol Times & Mirror, Work in Bristol*, pp.177–94. Buchanan and Cossons, *Industrial Archaeology*, pp.102–15. Another long-lived lead firm was Capper Pass & Son, which manufactured high quality solders at Bedminster from 1866 to the 1960s. At its peak, it employed 200 men in Bristol. B. Little, *Capper Pass: the First One Hundred and Fifty Years* (1963).

15. H. Hamilton, *The English Brass and Copper Industries to* 1800 (1926). R.A. Buchanan, 'Industry', in J. Moore, ed. *Avon Local History Handbook* (Chichester, 1979), p.50. J. Day, *Bristol Brass: a History of the Industry* (Newton Abbot, 1973). R. Jenkins, 'The Zinc Industry in England: the Early Years up to about 1850', *Transactions of the Newcomen Society*, 25 (1945–7), pp.41–52.

16. The exception was Pountney & Co.'s Bristol Pottery. The business was originally established in 1662 by Edward Ward, making Bristol Delft from local clays. It changed hands many times, but by the beginning of the nineteenth century was firmly established, and was renowned for its hand-painted pottery ware. Many other firms tried to emulate its success, although only Pountneys survived into the twentieth century. It moved to a modern factory at Lodge Causeway, Fishponds, in 1906, and utilised a combination of hand and machine methods. In more recent times, the firm manufactured a range of table ware, and also produced sinks and sanitary ware. Pountneys finally moved to Cornwall in the 1960s, thus breaking a link with Bristol which had lasted for over 300 years. *Bristol Times and Mirror, Bristol's Many Industries*. W.J. Pountney, *Old Bristol Potteries: being an Account of the Old Potters and Potteries in Bristol and Brislington, between 1650 and 1850* (Bristol, 1920). *Western Daily Press*, 21 July 1952. Buchanan, 'Industry', p.52. On woollens, see J. de Lacy Mann, *The Cloth Industry in the West of England from 1640 to 1880* (Oxford, 1971). J. Morris, 'The West of England Woollen Industry, 1750–1840', *Bulletin of the Institute of Historical Research*, 13 (1935), p.106–10. K.G. Ponting, *The Woollen Industry of South-West England* (Bath, 1971).

17. M. Dresser, 'Housing Policy in Bristol, 1919–30', in M.J. Daunton, *Councillors and Tenants: Local Authority Housing in English Cities, 1919–1939* (Leicester, 1984), pp.155–216. R. Jevons and J. Madge, *Housing Estates: a Study of Bristol Corporation Policy and Practice between the Wars* (Bristol, 1946), pp.9–13. Latimer, *Annals of Bristol in the Nineteenth Century*, p.512. Anon, *Ports of the Bristol Channel*, p.195. William Cowlin & Son Ltd., *A Record of Building* (Bristol, 1928). M. Dresser, 'Sir Francis Nicholas Cowlin', in D.J. Jeremy, ed. *Dictionary of Business Biography*, vol.I (1984), pp.809–12. K. Mallory, *The Bristol House* (Bristol, 1985), pp.47–55. C.G. Powell, 'Case Studies and Lost Tribes: the Bristol Firm of James Diment and Stephens, Bastow & Co.', *Construction History*, 1 (1985), pp.25–35. Idem, 'He that Runs against Time: Life Expectancy of Building Firms in Nineteenth-Century Bristol', *Construction History*, 2 (1986), pp.61–7. R.D. Savage, *History of Famous Firms: Bristol Survey*, vol.I (1959), pp.24–5.

18. See below, C.E. Harvey, 'Old Traditions, New Departures: the Later History of the Bristol & West Building Society'.

19. See below, P. Ollerenshaw, 'The Development of Banking in the Bristol Region, 1750–1914'.

20. *Bristol Times & Mirror, Bristol's Many Industries*. H.Nabb, *The Bristol Gas Industry, 1815–1949* (Bristol, 1987).

21. Sir H. de la Beche, *Health of Towns Commission: Report of the State of Bristol and Other Large Towns* (1845). F.C. Jones, *Bristol's Water Supply and its Story* (Bristol, 1946). D. Fraser, *Power and Authority in the Victorian City* (Oxford, 1979), pp.116–8.

22. See below, C.E. Harvey and J. Press, 'Sir George White and the Urban Transport Revolution in Bristol, 1875–1916'.

23. L. Hannah, *Electricity before Nationalisation: a Study of the Development of the Electrical Supply Industry in Britain* (1979), p.8. P.G. Lamb, *Electricity in Bristol, 1863–1948* (Bristol, 1981).

24. See below, D. Bateman, The Growth of the Printing and Packaging Industry In Bristol, 1800–1914'. On the Board Mills, see R.D. Savage, *History of Famous Firms: Bristol Survey*, vol.II (1960), pp.5–8. Bristol City Council, *Bristol: an Employment Profile* (Bristol, 1987), p.13.

25. A.A. Allen and A.G. Powell, *Bristol and its Newspapers, 1713–1934* (Bristol, 1934). E. Averis, *Hold the Front Page* (Bristol, 1984). A.P. Woolrich, *Printing in Bristol* (Bristol, 1986).

26. See below, J. Press, 'G.B. Britton and Footwear Manufacturing in Bristol and Kingswood, 1870–1973'.

27. See below, G. Channon, 'Georges and Brewing in Bristol'. Also see Anon, *Ports of the Bristol Channel*, p.192. Bristol United Breweries Ltd., *A Century of 'Good Health'* (Bristol, 1932). L. Richmond and B. Stockford, *Survey of the Records of 1,000 of the First Registered Companies in England and Wales* (1986), no.596.

28. J. Lysaght & Co., *The Lysaght Century* (Bristol, 1957). *Proceedings of the Institution of Mechanical Engineers*, July 1908, p.752. *Bristol Times & Mirror, Work in Bristol*, pp.3–8. Savage, *History of Famous Firms*, vol.II, pp.24–5.

29. See below, P. Davis, C.E. Harvey and J Press, 'Locomotive Building in Bristol in the Age of Steam, 1837–1958'.

30. *Bristol Times & Mirror, Work in Bristol*, pp.46–53. P.R.O., BT31 14381/21976, B.W.C.W., Memorandum of Association, 21 July 1864; Form E, 10 July 1876. Railway wagons were also built by the Bristol & South Wales Railway Wagon Co. and the Western Wagon Co., both established in 1860 to exploit the demand for 'private owner' wagons from colliery companies. Many other concerns produced road carriages and carts – notably John Fuller & Sons (St. George's Road), John Barton & Sons (St. Augustine's Back), Melhuish & Dew (Maudlin Street) and Perry & Co. (Stokes Croft). *Bristol Times & Mirror, Work in Bristol*, pp.153–5. Anon, *Ports of the Bristol Channel*, pp.194, 201, 205. *Bristol Times & Mirror, Bristol's Many Industries*. T. Skinner, *Stock Exchange Year-Book* (1881), pp.280–1; (1889), p.602.

31. Bristol Engineering Manufacturers' Association, Engineering Directory, 1945-. A.B. Cooper, 'Mechanical Engineering around Bristol', *Proceedings of the Institution of Mechanical Engineers*, 166 (1952), pp.278–82. B. Darwin, *Robinsons of Bristol, 1844–1944* (Bristol, 1945). Savage, *History of Famous Firms*, vol.II, pp.14–5.

32. Bristol Omnibus Co. Ltd., *The People's Carriage, 1874–1974* (Bristol, 1974). M. Curtis, *Bristol: a Century on the Road* (Falmouth, 1977).

33. Bendix Ltd., *100 Years of Engineering Achievement at Kingswood* (Bristol, 1985).

34. See below, G. Stone, 'Rearmament, War and the Performance of the Bristol Aeroplane Company, 1935–45'. *Flight International*, 'Rolls-Royce, Bristol, 1920–1980', 26 July 1980, pp.245–8. J. Lovering, *The Development of the Aerospace Industry in Bristol, 1910–1984* (Bristol, 1984). C.E. Harvey and J. Press, 'Sir George White, 1854–1916: a Career in Transport', *Journal of Transport History* (forthcoming, autumn 1988). Total employment in aerospace and related industries is currently estimated at 21,000.

35. Anon, *Ports of the Bristol Channel*, p.193. T.H. Butler, *The History of William Butler & Co. (Bristol), Ltd., 1843–1943* (Bristol, 1954). J.E.L. Bowcott, 'The Industrial Background of the Bristol Area', *Chemistry in Britain*, II (1966), pp.68–9. Bristol City Council, *American-Owned Companies in the Bristol Area* (Bristol, 1987).

36. *Bristol Times & Mirror, Work in Bristol*, pp.109–113. *Bristol Times & Mirror, Bristol's Many Industries*. R. Holland, 'The Netham Chemical Co. Ltd: Alkali Production in Bristol', *Chemistry and Industry*, 3 June 1985, pp.366–71. J. Davidson, 'The Initial Development of Severnside Works', *Chemistry and Industry*, 28 Nov. 1964, pp.1968–77. Bowcott, 'Industrial Background', pp.67–8.

37. E.J. Cocks and B. Walters, *A History of the Zinc Smelting Industry in Britain* (1968). Bowcott, 'Industrial Background', p.68.

38. A notable exception is the Bristol United Press, which publishes the region's leading newspapers, the *Evening Post* and the *Western Daily Press*. It successfully fought off takeovers by outside interests in the 1930s and again in the early 1980s, and continues to identify strongly with the local community.

39. Bristol City Council, *Employment in the Bristol Area* (Bristol, 1987), pp.10–4. S. Baskett et al., *Why are Financial Institutions Moving to Bristol?* (Bristol, 1981), pp.4–8. M. Boddy, J. Lovering and K. Bassett, *Sunbelt City? a Study of Economic Change in Britain's M4 Corridor* (Oxford, 1986).

J. S. Fry & Sons: Growth and Decline in the Chocolate Industry, 1753–1918

STEFANIE DIAPER

The chocolate and cocoa making firm founded by Joseph Fry in Bristol in the early 1750s played a significant part in the city's economic development over the following 150 years.[1] It became one of the largest employers in Bristol by 1914, contributing to the city's renewed prosperity in the second half of the nineteenth century, whilst emerging as an important force in the industry nationally. The company was owned and controlled by successive generations of the Fry family down to the First World War, after which the firm was effectively taken over by its great rival Cadburys. J.S. Fry & Sons is an interesting example of a successful, growing organization in an expanding industry, which, however, failed to adapt to changing conditions in the closing years of the nineteenth century and so went into decline. This allows us the opportunity to examine some aspects of business failure, as well as of business success.

Joseph Fry was born in 1728 into a devout Quaker family, and his religion had a lasting effect on the business he founded. He was brought up in the Quaker tradition, which a number of successful businessmen emerged from, and which saw trade and industry as a form of service to the community and firmly believed in hard work and fair dealing. Quaker (and nonconformist businessmen generally) played a disproportionately large part in British economic life during the eighteenth century. They were denied access to the English universities and the learned professions by the Test and Corporation Acts and therefore tended to go into trade to earn their living, where their frugality and industry and the support of their fellow believers helped many of them, including Joseph Fry, to succeed.[2]

Fry was educated at a Quaker boarding school and then learned the trade of apothecary as apprentice to another member of the Society of Friends. At the end of his apprenticeship in 1753, he settled in Bristol, which was close to his family in Wiltshire and had a thriving Quaker community.[3] His practice quickly began to prosper, thanks to his "affable and courteous manner and sound Christian principles".[4] As well as making up medicines, he began to sell chocolate, which he and other

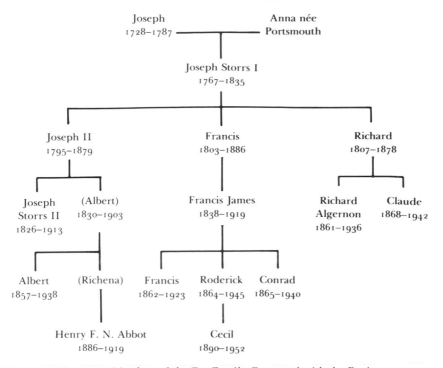

Figure 1. *Members of the Fry Family Connected with the Business.*

medical men of the day recommended for its supposedly health-giving properties. Like tea and coffee, chocolate first appeared in England in the middle of the seventeenth century as a drink, introduced from Spain where it had become popular after its discovery by the Conquistadores in Central America. Chocolate was an acquired taste, but it caught on as an expensive, fashionable delicacy, in addition to its use as a medicine.[5]

Joseph Fry was following in the footsteps of other apothecaries (most notably Sir Hans Sloan in London) when he began to manufacture chocolate, and though for many years he ran this side of this business alongside his medical practice, it quickly came to predominate. Chocolate manufacture in the middle of the eighteenth century was essentially a small-scale process. Cocoa beans were roasted over an open fire to bring out their flavour; then crushed and winnowed by hand to remove the outer shell, leaving the cocoa nibs, which were ground to a paste. Flavourings such as sugar, vanilla and spices were added to the paste, which was then formed into cakes for sale. The customer made up his chocolate at home by scraping some of the cake into a jug, and then boiling it with milk or water. Chocolate was not soluble, however; particles were held in suspension in the liquid, and the finer the beans were ground the more palatable the drink would be. Fry extended his manufacturing activities in 1761 when he took over Churchmans, a Bristol firm whose founder had patented a water-powered machine that enabled him to produce chocolate much more finely ground than most producers could do by hand. Fry exploited this technical advantage to the full, and Churchman's chocolate became one of the mainstays of his business, although he continued to produce a range of cheaper chocolates using his own recipes in order to reach the widest possible market.[6]

No figures survive to show the size of the business during the second half of the eighteenth century, but it was clearly growing, since Fry moved to larger premises and had enough money to invest in other business ventures. Chocolate was an expensive product at that time, and its consumption was limited to the relatively well-to-do. Fry's location in the thriving port of Bristol was a great advantage, as it gave him ready access to imported raw materials and to a prosperous local market for his products. The Hotwell Spa provided an additional, though seasonal, local market, as did Bath with its fashionable visitors. Fry, however, quickly

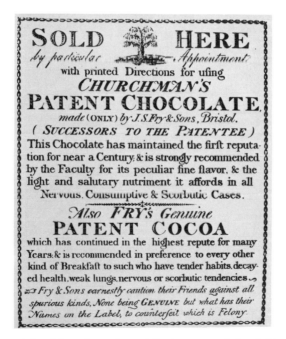

12. Advertisement for Churchman's and Fry's cocoas, late eighteenth century, emphasising their medicinal qualities.

moved beyond reliance on local markets and by the early 1760s he was operating on a larger scale than most other chocolate manufacturers, advertising his products throughout the country. By 1764 he had built up a network of agents in 53 towns, and demand in London was great enough to justify his opening a warehouse there, managed by his younger brother William. Increasing production meant that the firm needed larger premises, and in 1777 Fry moved to Union Street, where the firm remained for the next 150 years.[7]

Joseph Fry also entered on a series of other business ventures over the years, some of which played a significant part in Bristol's economic development, although it was the manufacture of chocolate that engaged most of his time and enthusiasm. He set up a printing and typesetting business with a Bristol man named William Pyne in the mid-1750s; took an interest in a chemical works in Battersea; invested in Richard Champion and William Cockworthy's attempts to make china in Bristol; and became a partner in one of the largest firms of soap manufacturers in the city. The investments in the chemical and china industries were short-lived, but the soap and printing businesses were great successes, and the latter provided lifelong employment for Fry's two eldest sons.[8]

Fry ran his chocolate business until his death in 1787 at the age of 59. The firm passed to his wife, and, after her retirement in 1795, to their youngest son, Joseph Storrs Fry, who embarked upon a policy of expansion and mechanical improvement. He developed a new roaster, which could roast larger quantities of beans more rapidly, and installed his machine in a purpose-built factory, erected next door to his existing building in Union Street. He called in specialists to overhaul the firm's steam engine, and his advertising began to stress the improvements that had been made as evidence of his technical superiority and commitment to producing quality goods.[9]

After this initial burst of energy, however, the business had a difficult time under J.S. Fry's leadership. His building work was expensive, and in the same period he and his cousin (Gawen Bell) bought the Queen Street brewery. This was an additional drain on Fry's resources, and a few years after taking control of the family firm he had to find a partner who would put money into the chocolate business. His Quaker connections proved useful: in 1805 he went into partnership with a young Quaker businessman named Henry Hunt. Initially Hunt put just over £1,000 into the business, but this gradually increased until by 1814 he and Fry had roughly equal capitals of about £6,800. Though the business prospered with this injection of funds, Fry and Hunt seem not to have got on, and in 1822 the partnership was dissolved. Surprisingly, Hunt's departure had little impact on the scale of the firm's operations. Sales in fact went up from £10,228 in 1822 to £12,072 in 1823 while the proportion of the

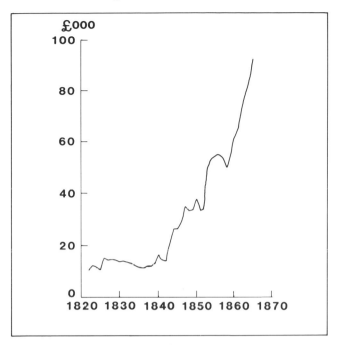

Figure 2. *J.S. Fry & Sons: Sales, 1822–65*
Source: Fry's Archive, General Trade Account, 1822–65.

cocoa imported into Britain used by the firm also went up, from 36 to 39 per cent.[10]

After Hunt's departure Fry brought his three sons, Joseph II, Francis and Richard, into the partnership, and the firm underwent its final change of name, becoming J.S. Fry & Sons. The next few years, which were a time of general recession in the British economy, were not easy ones for the firm. Sales fell between 1826 and 1836, and, far from ploughing profits back into the business, the partners actually withdrew capital. (The partnership capital fell from £18,683 in 1826 to roughly half that by 1834.) The reasons for this are unclear, but it may have been that Fry was providing for his children. His four daughters married during the 1820s, while the boys were also growing up, taking on domestic responsibilities, and finding other business interests. For example, Joseph II invested in a series of coal mines in the Bristol area in the late 1820s, and the money to buy them must have come, at least in part, from the family firm. Furthermore, the firm probably suffered from a lack of leadership during the early 1830s, for Joseph Storrs Fry was in poor health, yet retained control of the business until his death in 1835.[11]

When they inherited control, his three sons set about trying to improve the firm's performance, and embarked upon a successful sales drive. They continued with periodic newspaper advertisements, and opened a new warehouse in London to supply their valuable trade there. Sales rose almost tenfold between 1836 and 1867, from £11,041 to £102,747. Growing revenue allowed the brothers to begin work in 1840 on a new factory on the site of the original Frys workshop in Union Street, and this greatly increased the firm's productive capacity. This growth was achieved during a time of increasing prosperity for many, and increasing demand for chocolate and cocoa. Consumption of cocoa per capita in Britain doubled between 1841 and 1868, and with the new factory Frys was well placed to take advantage of this increasing market. Not only did the firm's production increase in absolute terms over this period, but its share of the U.K. market also began to recover. The firm had used over 30 per cent of the cocoa beans imported into Britain in the 1820s, but during the decline in the 1830s this slipped to around 15 per cent. The sharp increase in sales after 1842, however, meant that the figure recovered to around 23 per cent in the 1840s and early 1850s.[12]

Fry's range of products grew as the nineteenth century wore on, and the partners continued their past practice of introducing new lines to keep pace with developments in consumer tastes and to keep up with the activities of their competitors. The firm produced 11 different types of chocolate and cocoa in the mid-1820s; by 1843 this number had increased to 28, and increased still further in later years. Public taste began to shift from drinking chocolate, which was very sweet, towards cocoa, which was made in much the same way as chocolate but with far less sugar. The first detailed production figures to survive date from 1839, and by then cocoa had overtaken drinking chocolate as the main branch of the business. The firm produced a range of cocoas during the 1840s and 1850s, designed to appeal to as much of the potential market as possible. These ranged from the cheaper 'rock' and 'flake' cocoas, which contained cocoa shell as well as cocoa nibs, to Soluble Cocoa, which was made from finely ground cocoa nibs to give a drink smoother than the cheaper, grittier, cocoas. The partners also introduced two new cocoas in this period, both of which became best-selling lines: Homeopathic Cocoa in 1843, which was sold as a nutritious health food (to take advantage of growing concern about health), and Pearl Cocoa in 1856, which was flavoured with sugar and molasses, and contained arrowroot to reduce its oiliness. Being moderately priced, it was aimed at the emerging working-class market for cocoa, and quickly became one of the firm's largest-selling lines. This expanding market was the result of falling prices, thanks to lower rates of duty on cocoa, improved raw material supplies and more sophisticated manufacturing techniques, together with rising real incomes, which allowed a growing proportion of the population to spend money on more than the absolute necessities of life. In 1771 Frys sold its best quality chocolate for 7s. 6d. per pound (37½p.), which was only a little less than the average agricultural labourer's weekly wage at the time. By the 1850s Homeopathic Cocoa was sold for 11d. (4½p.) per pound wholesale, and, with other brands cheaper still, the potential market was obviously much increased.[13]

The middle of the nineteenth century saw a great innovation in the cocoa industry in Britain, with the introduction of eating chocolate, copied from French manufacturers who were already producing prettily wrapped chocolates with a variety of flavours and centres. Most of the sweets eaten in Britain during the first half of the nineteenth century were sugar confectionery in one form or another, produced by small, specialist producers, not cocoa manufacturers. Frys first produced eating chocolates around 1850, beginning with simple chocolate sticks and drops, and later progressing to more complex items: these included nuts and crystallized fruits coated with chocolate, and chocolates with cream fillings. Frys introduced Chocolate Creams in 1855, and this became one of the firm's most famous and long-lived lines. Like other English chocolate manufacturers at the time Frys copied the style of French competitors, giving French names to many products to take advantage of the prestige that French chocolates had for British consumers at the time. The chocolates were sold in presentation boxes and the cheaper lines were also sold individually – the customer who could not afford a box of chocolates might still be able to afford a chocolate stick at a penny or halfpenny.[14]

During the 1850s the three Fry brothers began to plan for the future management of their firm. In 1854 Joseph Fry II's eldest son, named Joseph Storrs Fry after his grandfather, was made a partner, followed by Francis' son Francis James four years later. Joseph Fry II retired in 1867 at the age of 72 and, with Francis then in his 60s and Richard taking less interest in the business, control of the firm was clearly passing into the hands of the younger men. Francis Fry remained technically the senior partner until his retirement in 1878 at the age of 75, but when Richard Fry died in the same year Joseph Storrs Fry II and his cousin inherited sole control of the firm. Francis Fry left capital in the firm for several years after his retirement and Richard Fry's executors followed the same policy, so the changes in partnership of 1878 did not have a serious impact on the firm's capital structure and ability to continue trading. The remaining partners clearly felt that they needed a larger management team, however, and in 1880 they made Joseph Storrs II's nephew Albert a partner, thus bringing the fifth generation of the family into business.[15]

No figures have survived for Fry's capital for most of the second half of the nineteenth century and profit figures are fragmentary, so that the only available guide to the firm's development over this period is the volume of its sales. They rose from £102,747 in 1867 to £1,866,395 on the eve of the First World War. This growth was achieved against the background of a growing market for consumer goods, with an increasing population and generally rising real incomes. Consumer expenditure rose in real terms from just under £1,000 million a year in the early 1870s to about £1,850 million by 1914, and this expansion allowed the development of not just the cocoa and chocolate industry, but a whole range of consumer industries from soap to meat extract. Fry's growth in the second half of the nineteenth century was partly the result of the policies adopted by the partners, but they were greatly assisted by the favourable market situation.[16]

Most of the increased production during this time was for home consumption, but the proportion exported also increased. Exporting was not a new development for the firm. Frys had exported its merchandise on a very small scale since its earliest days, much of it to Ireland, where Bristol merchants had extensive trading connections; and the firm cherished the memory of Fry's chocolate being drunk at an investiture in Dublin Castle. From the mid-1850s Frys began to record details of its exports systematically, although they still accounted for only a small part of the firm's output. They were worth less than £5,000 a year before 1870 – a few per cent of the firm's sales - but increased rapidly thereafter to reach £352,226 (19 per cent of total sales) in 1913. Like most other British exporters at the time Frys sold its products abroad through agents. By the end of the nineteenth century the firm sold cocoa and chocolate throughout the world, but the major overseas markets were in the Dominions or countries like India with large expatriate communities. Fry's cocoas were particularly popular in Canada, where they dominated the market before the First World War, while English winter visitors to Tenerife and Madeira ensured a steady market on the islands. Frys found business in Europe more difficult to come by, however, as this entailed competition with continental manufacturers which were used to producing cocoas to suit local tastes, and which were increasingly protected by tariffs designed to keep out foreign producers.[17]

The dramatic increase in sales over the second half of the nineteenth century required Frys to increase productive capacity and staff. Numbers of employees went up from 193 in 1867 to around 5,000 by 1914, and over the same period Frys undertook an extensive building programme which made its premises a prominent feature of the city centre. The firm built eight new factories, converted a series of existing buildings, and bought a dockside timber yard in Canon's Marsh to store wood needed for packaging. Each of the new factories was carefully designed by Fry's own experts to make it as efficient as possible, but working on so many sites clearly caused problems. Space was always at a premium, and Joseph Storrs Fry II regretted that this made it impossible to provide the sort of recreation facilities for the staff that he would have liked. Despite their recognition of the problems inherent in their position in the centre of Bristol, the partners seem not to have considered the solution, adopted by many other manufacturers at the time, of moving out of the city to a greenfield site. Cadburys and Rowntrees both did this, but Frys was content to soldier on in cramped and fragmented sites.[18]

The growth in Fry's sales in the second half of the nineteenth century came partly from increased sales of existing lines and partly from the introduction of new types of cocoa that proved popular with the public. The most successful of these were Caracas Cocoa (introduced in 1868) and the highly roasted Flag Cocoa that the firm put on the market in 1877, but others were also developed to exploit significant niches in the market. As Quakers, the partners were happy to produce cocoa for the British Workman cocoa houses that were built as part of the temperance movement, and, encouraged by the popularity of malted drinks, they introduced a malted cocoa in 1880. The new lines did not mean that older products were abandoned, and by 1880 Frys was producing nearly 50 different types of cocoa and drinking chocolate. Batch production

13. J.S. Fry's factories in central Bristol.

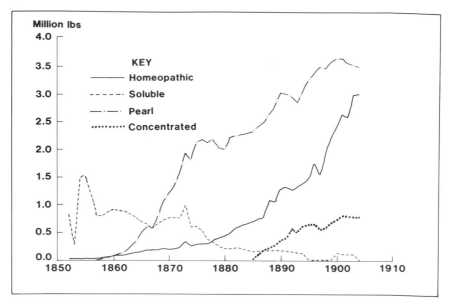

Figure 3. *Cocoas produced by J.S. Fry & Sons, 1852–1904*
Source: Fry's Archives, Stock and Makings Book, 1852–1904.

methods made it practicable to continue manufacturing items that had only a limited sale, but eventually some lines were dropped as hopelessly uneconomic, and by 1900 the product range had been slimmed down to about 40 different types of cocoa and chocolate.[19]

The most significant innovation in the British cocoa industry during the second half of the nineteenth century came in 1866, when a British manufacturer introduced a new type of cocoa based on an earlier Dutch invention. In 1828 a Dutch cocoa manufacturer named Van Houten developed a method of pressing out part of the cocoa butter contained in cocoa, thus producing a pleasanter, less oily drink which no longer needed the addition of farina to make it palatable. The innovation was doubly useful, since the excess cocoa butter could be used in the production of eating chocolate. Cadburys, after recovering from near bankruptcy a few years earlier, decided to produce a Van Houten type cocoa, and in 1866 introduced Cocoa Essence which was advertised as "Absolutely Pure: Therefore Best". Cocoa Essence came on the market at a good time, as it coincided with public concern about the adulteration of food. Cadburys played up the purity of the new product, to the irritation of other reputable cocoa manufacturers, like Frys, which argued quite fairly that adding flour to their products to reduce oiliness was not adulteration in the same sense as unscrupulous producers who added dangerous bulking agents like red lead to their cocoa.[20]

Cadbury's Cocoa Essence quickly caught on with the public, and formed the basis of the firm's recovery and subsequent growth after 1866. Frys appears to have been taken by surprise by this development, allowing Cadburys to be first into the field, and being slow to respond after Cadburys had taken the initiative; perhaps Frys felt secure in the growing sales of existing products and failed to recognise the importance of this new type of cocoa. In 1870 Frys introduced Cocoa Extract, a name which suggests that it may have been intended as a response to Cocoa Essence, but it was not given the sort of advertising support that Cadburys gave to Essence, and although sales reached respectable levels during the 1880s it did not become one of the firm's leading lines. Far more successful was Fry's Concentrated Cocoa, introduced in 1883. This was advertised vigorously with the same approach that Cadburys had used for Cocoa Essence, emphasising the purity and wholesomeness of the product. Sales increased rapidly, and within six years Fry's Concentrated Cocoa was established as one of the firm's fastest selling lines, although it was still a long way from rivalling the importance to the firm of the cheaper Pearl and Homeopathic Cocoas.[21]

The demand for eating chocolate also grew rapidly during the second half of the nineteenth century as real incomes rose. Mechanization and the availability of cocoa butter as a by-product of Van Houten-style cocoas brought down the prices of chocolate, so that a growing proportion of the population could afford it. Fry's sales of eating chocolate rose from

Table 1. *J.S. Fry & Sons, Output of Cocoa and Eating Chocolate, 1852–1904*

	Total Output 'ooolbs	Output of Cocoa and Drinking Chocolate 'ooolbs	Output of Eating Chocolate 'ooolbs
1852	995	975	20
1855	1,951	1,904	47
1860	1,675	1,566	109
1865	2,233	1,949	285
1870	3,667	2,988	679
1875	6,455	4,470	1,986
1880	6,759	4,260	2,500
1885	11,116	5,196	5,920
1890	21,260	8,161	13,099
1895	24,325	8,510	15,816
1900	37,233	9,643	27,589

Source: Fry's Archive, Stock and Makings Book, 1852–1904.

9 tons in 1852 to over 12,000 tons in 1904, and continued to grow thereafter as consumption of eating chocolate in Britain rose by 45–50 per cent between 1900 and 1914. Chocolates were originally a sideline for the firm, but this changed as demand for them grew more rapidly than that for cocoa, and after 1885 Frys produced more chocolates than cocoa each year.[22]

British chocolate manufacturers faced stiff competition towards the end of the nineteenth century from Swiss producers. The Swiss firms had a new product to offer: milk chocolate. This was developed by Daniel Peter of Vevey in Switzerland in 1876, and was made by mixing cocoa, sugar, and milk solids condensed by evaporation. Peter exported his chocolate to Britain himself and within a few years it was taken up by other Swiss manufacturers which became a powerful influence in the business. In contrast to the situation with Van Houten cocoa 40 years earlier, J.S. Fry & Sons was the first British firm to produce milk chocolate of its own to rival these imports, although the quality was poor. It was put on the market for the first time in 1902, when just over 29 tons were sold. The new chocolate was introduced as Five Boys Milk Chocolate to link it in the public mind with the dark chocolate which Frys already produced. This was well known through an advertisement showing a

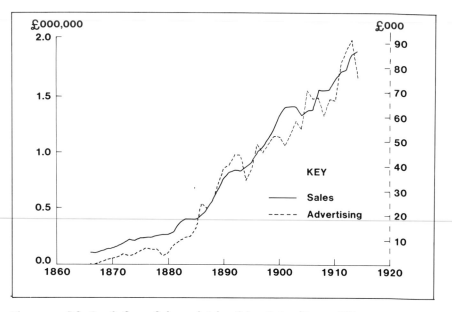

Figure 4. *J.S. Fry & Sons: Sales and Advertising Expenditure, 1866–1914*
Source: Fry's Archives, General Trade Account and Table of Advertising Expenditure, 1865–1914.

young boy's face passing through five expressions, from sorrow to joy, as he ate Fry's chocolate. Cadburys subsequently responded to Fry's initiative with its Dairy Milk Chocolate, introduced in 1905. This was a better quality chocolate than Five Boys, and quickly became a market leader, despite Cadbury's late entry into the field.[23]

Fry's sales had always been built up and sustained by advertising. This was limited in extent in the firm's early years, but increased in amount and sophistication over the course of time, paralleling developments in the food and consumer goods industries generally. Frys laid great stress on the supposedly health-giving properties of chocolate and cocoa in early newspaper advertisements, and this continued to be a major theme in the firm's advertising throughout the nineteenth century. Advertisements frequently carried testimonials from members of the medical profession, and as late as the 1880s Frys advertised that its Malted Cocoa had been "specially introduced at the request of the medical profession". Two other themes were prominent in Fry's advertising in this period – the royal warrants held by the firm as evidence of the quality of its products, and the 375 medals won at various trade exhibitions at home and abroad between 1851 and 1912. These exhibitions, which became popular after the Great Exhibition in London in 1851, were a useful form of publicity in themselves, and Fry's displays became increasingly elaborate. The firm's earliest advertisements were short, with just a few lines of text describing where Fry's products could be bought, but they too became more complex as time went on and the firm took advantage of improvements in printing techniques to produce first illustrated, then coloured,

Table 2. *Sales of J.S. Fry & Sons, Cadbury Brothers and Rowntree & Co., 1870–1910*

	Frys £	Cadburys £	Rowntrees £
1870	143,750	–	7,384
1875	236,075	70,396	19,177
1880	266,285	117,505	44,017
1885	404,189	274,342	63,974
1890	761,969	515,371	114,529
1895	932,292	706,191	190,328
1900	1,326,312	1,231,789	463,199
1905	1,366,192	1,354,948	903,991
1910	1,642,715	1,670,221	1,200,598

Sources: Fry's Archive, Home and Export Sales Ledgers, 1870–1910. Cadbury's Archive, Sales Book Quarterly Returns, 1874–1910. Rowntree's Archive, Continuous Yearly Record of Sales.

advertisements. This was not achieved alone. Advertising became an increasingly professional business in the closing years of the nineteenth century, and like other companies in the consumer goods industries Frys began to take expert advice, notably from the prominent London advertising agents Mather & Crowther.[24]

Fry's advertising expenditure rose from just under £2,000 a year in 1866 to more than £180,000 in 1913. The firm needed to increase its advertising expenditure to protect its position from growing competition, not just from Swiss manufacturers of eating chocolate, but also from domestic producers of cocoa and chocolate, in particular Cadburys and Rowntrees. These two competitors were growing rapidly during the last 30 years of the nineteenth century, and Frys was losing its earlier dominance in the industry. Cadbury's growth over this period was founded on the success of its Cocoa Essence, while Rowntree's growth was based on the popularity of its fruit pastilles and on the success of its Van Houten cocoa, Elect, introduced in 1887. At first, Elect Cocoa was slow to catch on with the public, and after eight years of limited sales Rowntrees decided to target its advertising on this product. This policy bore fruit and sales began to pick up rapidly, demonstrating the value of advertising to the industry. In 1906, not only did Rowntree's advertising expenditure exceed Fry's but its advertising campaigns (devised by S.H. Benson), also appear to have attracted much more attention. This trend continued, and in 1910 Frys spent £69,000 on advertising whilst Cadburys spent £119,000 and Rowntrees £127,000. In the years before the First World War, then, Frys was not spending as much money on advertising, or putting as much effort into marketing as Rowntrees or Cadburys; as a result, its share of the market declined, despite steadily growing sales.[25]

The Fry family's attitude to advertising, as with everything relating to business affairs, was influenced by religion. No details of the planning behind the firm's advertising have survived, but the partners' views were summarised in an article in the Quaker magazine *Truth* in 1910. They explained that although it was possible to build a business on advertising, this was not a solid foundation in itself. To survive and prosper, a firm must make good products, and the public must trust them to do so. This echoed the traditional Quaker concern for truth and fair dealing, and formed the basis of their advertising philosophy. They were not alone in their views. Joseph Rowntree, who was also a convinced Friend, took a lot of persuading to advertise at all, but when his firm did begin to do so, it had the same emphasis on quality and dealing fairly with the public.[26]

The founder of the Fry family business was a devout member of the Society of Friends, who took his religious convictions very seriously throughout his life. So too were his son and grandsons, all of whom married women who shared their convictions. They played an active part in the life of their Meetings and in the social and educational work of the Society. Joseph's son, Joseph Storrs Fry I, became active in the provision of education for the poor; his daughter-in-law became a minister in the Society, working for the welfare of French prisoners of war held in Bristol during the Napoleonic Wars, and later preaching to the colliers of the villages around Kingswood, including the notorious group of hooligans known locally as the Cock Road Gang. Their sons followed in their footsteps as active members of the Society; Francis became a member of the Anti-Slavery Society, Richard served on the committee of management of Sidcot School, near Bristol, and both were warm supporters of the British and Foreign Bible Society.[27]

The family's religious tradition continued into the next generation, but there were changes in the family in the second half of the nineteenth century that mirrored changes within the Society as a whole. Increasing wealth caused problems of adjustment for many Quakers, as they tried to reconcile their traditional values of simplicity and plain living with the way of life that their financial position allowed. Reactions varied considerably. Some, like the Barclays and Gurneys, left the Society altogether, while others remained 'plain'. A third group, however, tried to find a middle way, becoming 'worldly' Quakers. This process of 'conformity to the world' was encouraged by the Society itself, partly as a result of worries over recruitment and partly because it was becoming harder and harder for successful businessmen to remain apart from the world. In 1859 the rules of the Society were changed to allow members to marry out without being disowned, and after 1860 peculiarities of speech and dress were made optional. The Fry family contained examples of all three responses to the changes that were taking place. Joseph Storrs Fry II and his cousin Francis James remained 'plain' Quakers, while his brother Edward abandoned the old-style dress and speech to become a successful barrister and finally a Lord Justice of Appeal, even accepting a knighthood on the way. He remained within the Society, however, unlike their younger brother David, who left after his second marriage.[28]

Despite these changes, the partners' Quakerism continued to influence their attitude to their staff, as it did that of other Quaker employers. They shared a dislike of exploitation and an abhorrence of conflict, together with a concern for the individual with his own "spark of the light of Christ". The general view of Quaker employers towards the end of the nineteenth century is one of benevolent paternalism, coupled with a sense of moral duty towards their staff that led them to introduce welfare benefits ahead of many other companies. The Frys were typical of this general picture, although they were not as innovative in their management thinking as either the Cadburys or the Rowntrees. Edward Cadbury and Seebohm Rowntree were leading forces in the initial development of welfare work and personnel management, setting up works councils and suggestion schemes in their firms, but the Frys were followers rather than leaders in this field.[29]

The Frys' concern for the welfare of their staff manifested itself in wages that were good by local standards, and in the provision of dining rooms, night-school teachers and facilities for clubs and societies to meet. Their concern for the individual was also clear. Like George and Richard Cadbury, the Fry partners were very proud of the close relationship between themselves and their staff; Joseph Storrs Fry II did what he could to keep this alive during the second half of the nineteenth century, although it became more and more difficult as the size of the workforce grew. He continued to interview new staff personally and gave a copy of Mrs Beeton's *Book of Household Management* to girls leaving to marry. He also led a religious service at the works each morning, in an effort to provide for his employees' spiritual welfare, and left gifts amounting to £42,000 to them in his will. Unlike Edward Cadbury, who was a stong supporter of trade unionism, the Frys believed that unions interrupted their personal relationship with employees. They argued that unions were unnecessary because the firm provided good conditions and fair wages, and, in a company that employed a large number of women, unionism was not a major force. The attitude of the partners towards

14. Weighing and filling packets of cocoa, 1884. Frys was a major employer of women and young girls.

their staff was summarised in the house magazine in the 1920s. It was "ingrained in the Frys not to look upon their employees as so many cogs in a machine for producing dividends, but as human creatures possessed of immortal souls, for whom they were very largely responsible": a classically Quaker view.[30]

By the early years of this century J.S. Fry & Sons was in an equivocal position. The firm's sales were growing rapidly and profits were respectable, but at the same time it was losing market share to its younger rivals in Birmingham and York. Cadburys and Rowntrees were more aggressive in their marketing and were prepared to spend more on their advertising to increase their market share. Both had moved away from city centre sites to locations which allowed them to expand, while Frys remained in the centre of Bristol, with all the disadvantages of cramped conditions and multi-site operations. The firm had also taken the decision to concentrate on producing for the cheaper end of the market where profit margins were low. To complicate matters still further, the cocoa and confectionery sides of the business were administered as separate entities, and the members of the family running them were hardly on speaking terms. Egbert Cadbury (who joined Frys after the First World War) summarised the firm's problem as one of complacency. It had been in business successfully for over 150 years, and the men running it had simply not thought that their position could be challenged. In these circumstances Fry's relative decline was hardly a surprise, and it was the final recognition of its weakened position that prompted the firm to agree in 1917 to Cadbury's proposal for a merger.[31]

Fry's relative decline in the years before the First World War was largely the result of a lack of vigour and entrepreneurial skill in the leadership. This lack of dynamism contrasted with the energy evident at Cadburys and Rowntrees in the same period, and inevitably weakened Fry's position. Much of the problem lay with the interests and attitudes of Joseph Storrs Fry II, who dominated the firm's management from 1867 until his death in 1913. He never married, and religion and business were his main interests. He was a plain Quaker and according to a relative "extraordinarily conservative in his habits". He worked hard for a series of good causes, and he was active in the work of the Society of Friends, serving as Clerk to the Yearly Meeting (the Society's highest position) for 15 years in the 1870s and 1880s.[32]

Joseph Storrs Fry II took his work in his family business very seriously, and in keeping with his religious views he regarded it "not only as a source of profit but as entailing great responsibility".[33] He was not an innovator in his business life, however, and given his personality it would perhaps have been surprising if he had been. Furthermore, it was the employees rather than any other aspect of the business that engaged his interest. He never retired from the business, and despite age and failing eyesight he remained chairman until his death at the age of 87. This limited the power of the younger generation to introduce new policies, particularly over the firm's relocation away from the centre of Bristol, and made it more difficult to respond to the challenge posed by Cadburys and Rowntrees.[34]

The initiative for a merger of interests between Cadburys and Frys grew out of a long tradition of co-operation as well as competition. Frys, Cadburys and Rowntrees had entered into a series of agreements on pricing and advertising policy in the years after 1889, and they drew closer in the difficult trading conditions of the First World War, as they faced the same problems over the shortages of imported raw materials.[35] The suggestion for a merger came from Edward Cadbury. He was convinced that such a move was necessary because of the damaging level of competition in the industry, particularly with the arrival on the scene of Nestlé. His partners had qualms about the morality of a merger, but he argued that it would be entirely ethical if it was done for the right reasons:

> My view is that not only are we out to make profits, but also out to serve the community and a joint concern can obviously give better service than two competing ones with the great wastage caused by their competition. It all depends on the point of view as to the morality of the transaction, it is immoral if it is done in order to overcharge the public, or cut down the rate of wages of our employees, but it is right and continued competition wrong, if it is done to give better service to the public and better conditions to our workers.[36]

The suggestion of a merger came at an opportune time for the Frys, who were also worried about the level of competition in the industry. They agreed to go ahead with an amalgamation, and both firms took advice from outside experts on how this should be done. Frys consulted City accountants Deloitte, Plender & Co., who had been involved in the formation of Imperial Tobacco more than a decade earlier, while Cadburys went to another leading City firm, Price Waterhouse. The first plan was for a complete amalgamation of the two firms, but there were technical problems involved in deciding how to rank their assets, and in the end it was agreed to form a holding company that would take over them both. Agreement on all the details of the plan was reached during the summer of 1918, and in October that year the two firms announced the merger of their interests through the intermediary of the British Cocoa & Chocolate Co., with an initial capital of £2.5 million. Both firms continued in business in their own names, but now as subsidiaries of the new holding company, which was dominated by Cadburys. The Frys directors had entered into the negotiations knowing that Cadburys had grown considerably in recent years, but they were still surprised to find that the younger firm's assets were roughly three times as large as theirs. They had expected a much smaller difference in size between them. Barrow Cadbury became chairman of the new holding company and Richard A. Fry vice-chairman; but as the larger firm at the time of the merger, there was never any doubt that control rested with the Bournville directors, however careful they were to preserve appearances and to spare the Frys' feelings. This company structure was retained during the 1920s but then the directors decided to recognise the reality of the relative positions of the two companies, and in 1935 Frys became a wholly-owned subsidiary of Cadburys, ceasing formal independent life after 182 years in business.[37]

J.S. Fry & Sons grew from small beginnings in Bristol in the middle of the eighteenth century, to become one of the largest companies in the city by the time of the First World War. The firm's location was an important factor in its early development because of the ready availability of raw materials and a prosperous local market, but it soon began to sell its products throughout the country, and its location became increasingly incidental to its growth as communications improved. The firm became important to the city as it grew and became a large employer during the second half of the nineteenth century, thereby contributing to the prosperity of the local economy. The Fry family were also important locally because of their other business activities, and their work for local charities and education.

Fry's growth took place against the background of an expanding market for its products, particularly during the second half of the nineteenth century, but it was not without setbacks. The firm's sales fluctuated from year to year with changing market conditions, and, more importantly, its prosperity also varied with the skill and enterprise of the members of the family who ran the business. The firm went through a difficult period during the 1820s and early 1830s under Joseph Storrs Fry I's leadership, but recovered when his sons took over and adopted a more expansionist policy. The firm once again began to experience problems towards the end of the nineteenth century as Joseph Storrs Fry II grew older, this time with more serious consequences. He was not an innovator in his business life and his conservative attitudes were not well suited to meeting the growing challenge from Cadburys and Rowntrees. J.S. Fry & Sons remained an old-fashioned firm, content to rest on its laurels, at a time when its main rivals were vigorously trying to increase their share of the market. The firm suffered as a result, and was eventually taken over by Cadburys which was growing much faster in the early years of this century, thus ending an era in the history of chocolate making in Bristol.

NOTES

1. I am grateful to Cadbury Schweppes Plc for permission to study the records of Frys and Cadburys on which this chapter is based. I was also granted access to Rowntree's archive at York, and I would like to thank the archivists of both firms for their assistance. I am also especially grateful to Mr Basil Murray, who kindly continued to take a keen interest in this project after retiring as Cadbury's archivist. Fry's records are now held by the Bristol Record Office, while Cadbury's records are at Bournville. Much of the research for this paper was undertaken while I was E.S.R.C. Research Fellow in Business History at the University of Bath, and I am grateful to the E.S.R.C. for its support.

2. Society of Friends' Library, Friends House, London (hereafter S.F.L.), biography of John Fry (1701–75), and Joseph Fry (1727/8–87). M.W. Kirby, *Men of Business and Politics: the Rise and Fall of the Quaker Pease Dynasty of North East England, 1700–1943* (1984), pp.4–6.

3. A. Fry, *A Memoir of the Rt. Hon. Sir Edward Fry* (Oxford, 1921), p.11. M.F. Pease, 'Notes on the Fry Family of Sutton Benger and Bristol, 1627–1921' (unpublished typescript, 1951), pp.2–6. (A copy is held by Bristol Central Reference Library.). Obituary of Joseph Fry, *Gentleman's Magazine*, May 1787.

4. T. Fry, *A Brief Memoir of Francis Fry, F.S.A.* (1887), p.10.

5. A.W. Knapp, *Cocoa and Chocolate: the History from Plantation to Consumer* (1920), pp.7–11.

6. J.S. Fry & Sons Archive (hereafter F.A.), 38538/1/3, Churchman's will (proved 1761) and letters from the Secretary of the Bristol Law Society about Churchman; Letters Patent no. 539, 1733. *Felix Farley's Bristol Journal*, 24 Oct. and 21 Nov. 1761.

7. F.A., 38538/11/5, Folder of Newspaper Advertisements, 1693–1856 (contains a series of advertisements in a variety of provincial and metropolitan newspapers from this period, including *St. James's Chronicle*, 7 July 1764). W.E. Minchinton, 'Bristol, Metropolis of the West in the Eighteenth Century', *Transactions of the Royal Historical Society*, 5th ser. IV (1954), p.86. *Idem*, 'The Port of Bristol in the Eighteenth Century', in J. Cannon and P.V. McGrath, eds. *The Port of Bristol in the Eighteenth Century* (Bristol, 1972), pp.132–3. J. Walters, *Splendour and Scandal: the Reign of Beau Nash* (1968), pp.31, 48, 63. J. Haddon, *Portrait of Bath* (1982), pp.78, 88. J. Latimer, *Annals of Bristol in the Eighteenth Century* (Bristol, 1893), p.177.

8. S.H. Steinberg, *Five Hundred Years of Printing* (1959), p.143. P.H. Emden, *Quakers in Commerce and Industry: a Record of Business Achievement* (1940), p.190. A Raistrick, *Quakers in Science and Industry* (Newton Abbot, 1968), pp.215–6. S.F.L., biographies of Henry Fry (1756–1817) and Edmund Fry (1757–1835). Pease, 'Notes', p.7. J.S. Fry, *An Essay on Wheeled Carriages* (1820), p.117. F.S. McKenna, *Champion's Bristol Porcelain* (Leigh-on-Sea, 1947), pp.17–20. S.J. Diaper, 'Christopher Thomas & Brothers: the Last Bristol Soapmaker', *Transactions of the Bristol and Gloucestershire Archaeological Society*, 105 (1988).

9. Joseph Fry's will, 3 June 1783 (retained by firm). F.A., 38538/11/2, Patent Application by Joseph Storrs Fry, 1795; 38538/11/1, Joseph Fry to Matthew Boulton, 29 April 1783. Pease, 'Notes', pp.9, 21. S.F.L., biographies of Ann Fry née Allen (1764–1829) and Joseph Storrs Fry (1767–1835). *Morning Chronicle*, 19 June 1798.

10. F.A., 38538/5/36–7, Fry, Ball & Co., Account Books, 1802–9; 38538/5/1, Trade Stock Ledger, 1799; 38538/1/3, Note of Meetings between Fry and Hunt, 13–14 Sept. 1822, and Deed of Dissolution of Partnership, 11 Nov. 1822. S.F.L., biography of Henry Hunt (1780–1862). Pease, 'Notes', pp.7–9.

11. F.A., 38538/6/1, Stock Book, 1824–47; 38538/6/2, Stock and Account Book, 1825–46. S.F.L., Biographies of Joseph Fry (1795–1879), Francis Fry (1803–86) and Richard Fry (1807–78). T. Fry, *Memoir of Francis Fry*, p.13.

12. F.A., 38538/5/2, General Trade Account Book, 1822–66; 38538/6/2, Stock and Account Book, 1825–46; 38538/6/58, Cocoa Statistics – Consumption U.K. and Frys, 1821–1925; 38538/3/43, Notebook on Building of the Factories and Stacks, etc., kept by Thomas Denford;

38538/11/1, Agreement between J.S. Fry & Sons and Thomas Wilcox & Sons, 1 July 1841. J. Holm, *Cocoa and its Manufacture* (1874), p.24. A. Fry, *Memoir of Edward Fry*, p.19.

13. Volume of Manufacturing Recipes, n.d., early 19th century; J.S. Fry & Sons, *A Concise Description of the Characteristics of the Different Varieties of Chocolate and Cocoa Manufactured* by J.S. Fry & Sons (mid-1860s); advertisement in *Public Advertiser*, 23 Dec. 1871 (retained by firm). F.A., 38538/11/1, Trade Circular and Table of Amount Made, Stock Held and Sold, 1839–45; Price List, 1851; 35838/6/31, Receipe Book, 1868; 38538/6/35, Cost Office Note Book and Recipe Book, 1840–75; 38538/6/5, Stock and Makings Book, 1851–1904; 38538/7/1, Tasting Room Book, 1851.

14. Price Lists, 1850s; J.S. Fry, *Concise Description* (retained by firm). F.A., 38538/6/5, Stock and Makings Book, 1851–1904. J.B. Jeffries, *Retail Trading in Britain, 1850–1950* (Cambridge, 1954), p.253. B.W. Minifie, *Chocolate and Cocoa Confectionery: Science and Technology* (1970), p.318.

15. F.A., 38538/5/18, Private Ledgers, 1854–76. Private Ledgers, 1877–86 (retained by firm). Joseph Fry's younger son Albert founded the Bristol Carriage and Wagon Works, which employed around 1,000 men building railway locomotives and rolling stock and agricultural machinery by the end of the nineteenth century. 'The Bristol Wagon Works', in *Western Daily Press, Work in Bristol* (Bristol, 1883), pp.46–53.

16. F.A., 38538/5/2, General Trade Account, 1822–66. B. Supple, 'A Framework for British Business History', in B. Supple, ed. *Essays in British Business History* (Oxford, 1977), p.16.

17. F.A., 38538/5/2, General Trade Account, 1822–66; 38538/7/10, Home and Export Sales, 1896–1914. Export Sales Ledgers, 1910–30 (retained by firm). G. Jones, 'Multinational Chocolate: Cadbury Overseas, 1918–39', *Business History*, XXVI (1984), p.62.

18. F.A., 38538/11/1, Copy of Report to H.M. Inspector of Factories, 20 Sept. 1867; Joseph Storrs Fry II to staff, Feb. 1891. 38538/3/43, Denford's notes on Factory Building; 'History of the Building of the Works', *Frys' Works Magazine*, Jan.-Sept. 1923. 'A Historic House: a Visit to Bristol the Cocoa Metropolis', *Grocery*, July 1908. I.A. Williams, *The Firm of Cadbury* (1931), pp.54–7. B.G. Murray, 'George Cadbury' in D.J. Jeremy, ed. *Dictionary of Business Biography*, (hereafter D.B.B.)., vol.I (1984), pp.549–51. M. Higham, 'Joseph Rowntree', in Jeremy, *D.B.B.*, vol.IV (1985), pp.966–7.

19. F.A., 38538/6/5, Stock and Makings Book, 1851–1904; 38538/6/33, Makings Book, 1887–1905; 38538/11/1, Historical Records, vol.I, p.59, 'Observations on the use of Cocoa for British Workman Public Houses' (booklet, n.d.).

20. Knapp, *Cocoa and Chocolate*, p.15. Murray, 'George Cadbury', p.549. Williams, *Cadburys*, p.41.

21. F.A., 38538/6/5, Stock and Makings Book, 1851–1904. File of Nineteenth Century Advertisements (retained by firm). Murray, 'George Cadbury', p.549.

22. F.A., 38538/6/5, Stock and Makings Book, 1851–1904. Price Lists and Advertisements, 1850–1914 (retained by firm). Jeffries, *Retail Trading*, pp.253–4.

23. Text of lecture given by Major Egbert Cadbury (n.d., retained by firm). F.A., 38538/11/3, Press Release, 17 Jan. 1962; 38538/6/5, Stock and Makings Book, 1851–1904. Knapp, *Cocoa and Chocolate*, pp.154–5. Murray, 'George Cadbury', p.551. J. Heer, *World Events, 1866–1966: the First Hundred Years of Nestlé* (1966), pp.78–87.

24. List of Grands Prix, Diplomas of Honour, Gold Medals, etc. awarded to J.S. Fry & Sons, 1851–1912 (retained by firm). F.A., 38538/4/7, Box of Correspondence re Royal Warrants; 38538/11/1, Correspondence re Warrants and Endorsements. S. Piggott, *O.B.M: A Celebration, One Hundred and Twenty-Five Years in Advertising* (1975), p.11. T.R. Nevett, *Advertising in Britain: a History* (1982), passim.

25. F.A., 38538/7/10, Home and Export Sales Ledger, 1896–1914; 38538/6/58, Cocoa Statistics – Consumption U.K. and Fry, 1821–1925. Cadbury's Archive (hereafter C.A.), Sales Book Quarterly Returns, 1874–1910. Rowntree's Archive, Continuous Yearly Record of Sales. Murray, 'George Cadbury', pp.549–51. F. Goodall, 'Marketing Consumer Products

before 1914: Rowntrees and Elect Cocoa', in R. Davenport-Hines, ed. *Markets and Bagmen: Studies in the History of Marketing and British Industrial Performance, 1830–1939* (1986), pp.16–56.

26. 'The Test of Time', *Truth*, 1910–11 (retained by firm). Goodall, 'Marketing Consumer Products'.

27. S.F.L., biographies of Joseph Fry (1727/8–87), Joseph Storrs Fry (1767–1835), Joseph Fry II (1795–1879), Francis Fry (1803–86), Richard Fry (1807–78) and Ann Fry (1764–1829). Pease, 'Notes', pp.7, 10–21. T. Fry, *Memoir of Francis Fry*, pp.16–55, Appendix B.

28. Kirby, *Men of Business*, pp.xiv, 47–8. T.A.B. Corley, 'How Quakers Coped with Business Success: Quaker Industrialists, 1660–1914', paper given at the Christianity and Business Seminar, London School of Economics, March 1982. D.J. Jeremy, *Business and Religion in Britain* (1986), passim. T. Fry, *Memoir of Francis Fry*, passim. A. Fry, *Memoir of Edward Fry*, passim. Pease, 'Notes', pp.37, 45. 'Sir Edward Fry (1827–1918)', *Dictionary of National Biography* (Oxford, 1975), p.2642.

29. J. Child, 'Quaker Employers and Industrial Relations', *Sociological Review*, 12 (1964), pp.294, 300–7. S. Keeble, 'Benjamin Seebohm Rowntree', in Jeremy, *D.B.B.*, vol.IV (1985), pp.961–2.

30. Joseph Storrs Fry's will and Reminiscences of Laura Cella and Francis Green (retained by firm). 38538/11/1, Report to H.M. Inspector of Factories, 20 Sept. 1867; *Fry's Works Magazine*, bicentenary issue, 1928, p.28. 'J.S. Fry & Sons', in Anon, *The Ports of the Bristol Channel: Progress, Commerce* (1893), p.188. Williams, *Cadburys*, pp.49–50. E. Cadbury, *Experiments in Industrial Organisation* (1912), pp.269–72.

31. Memo, 'Proposals for Putting J.S.F. on a Profit Earning Basis'; Text of lecture given by Major Egbert Cadbury; Frys Board Minute Book, 24 Oct. 1917 (retained by firm). F.A., 38538/4/5, R.J. Fry Letter Book, R.J. Fry to Manufacturing Confectioners' Alliance, 4 Jan. 1917.

32. Pease, 'Notes', pp.35–7. S.F.L., biography of Joseph Storrs Fry (1826–1913).

33. A. Fry, *Memoir of Edward Fry*, p.38.

34. G. Wagner, 'Joseph Storrs Fry', in Jeremy, *D.B.B.*, vol.II (1984), pp.436–7. Pease, 'Notes', pp.35–7. Corley, 'Business Success'.

35. Papers relating to the Cheltenham Conference meetings between Fry, Cadbury and Rowntree, and File of Conference Agreements (retained by firm).

36. C.A., Envelope CF936, Edward Cadbury to Barrow Cadbury, 18 July 1917.

37. Memo, 'Proposals for Putting J.S.F. on a Profit Earning Basis'. C.A., Board Minute Book 2, Fry to Cadbury, 2 Aug. 1917; Board Minute Book 3, 7 May 1918; Board Minute Book 3, Notice to Staff, 9 Oct. 1918; Envelope CF936, 'Rough Notes on Holding Company versus Amalgamation'.

The Development of Banking in the Bristol Region, 1750–1914[1]

PHILIP OLLERENSHAW

At the beginning of the nineteenth century the banking system in England and Wales consisted of the Bank of England and hundreds of small localised banks restricted by law to no more than six partners. Many of these so-called 'private' banks did not have the resources to withstand major downturns in economic activity and the collapse of several dozen of them between 1815 and 1825 was regarded as both arising from and contributing to economic instability. In an effort to promote stability the government in 1826 removed the restriction on the permissible number of bank partners, and thus enabled banks to attract large numbers of shareholders, each of whose property was liable to be sold if the bank failed. Private banks did not disappear immediately but in the long-term they were superseded by the joint-stock concerns which, especially from the mid nineteenth century, often developed large regional and eventually even national branch networks. In the fifty years or so before 1920 the banking system tended strongly towards amalgamation, which resulted in the emergence of the 'Big Five': Barclays; Lloyds; London County Westminster and Parr's; London Joint City and Midland; and National Provincial and Union Bank of England. Clearly then a revolution had taken place in the structure of English banking.[2]

This chapter examines how the Bristol region was affected by national developments and considers the role of banks in this economically diversified region. The first part contains a brief discussion of the private banks and some business connections of their partners. This is followed by an examination of the emergence of joint-stock banks with special reference to Stuckeys, which was one of the leading English provincial banks in the nineteenth century and had its origins in late eighteenth-century Somerset. We then turn to explain patterns of competition and amalgamation in the south west and conclude with a survey of bank lending before 1914.

The point of departure for any assessment of the banks' structure and function is an appreciation of the economy in which they operated. The position of eighteenth century Bristol as the second port in the kingdom

after London is well known, as is the fact that relative decline was a
feature of the next century.[3] The port not only provided the trade to
sustain a complex industrial base within the city itself but also served as
an entrepôt for produce within a large part of the Midlands, south west
of England and south Wales. This role was fully appreciated by Daniel
Defoe who visited the city in the 1720s:

> The Bristol merchants as they have a very great trade abroad, so they have
> always buyers at home, for their returns, and that such buyers that no cargo
> is too big for them. To this purpose the shopkeepers in Bristol who in general
> are all wholesale men, have so great an inland trade among all the western
> counties, that they maintain carriers just as the London tradesmen do, to all
> the principal counties and towns from Southampton in the south, even to the
> banks of the Trent north; and though they have no navigable river that way,
> yet they drive a very great trade through all those counties.[4]

It is evident that such extensive trading connections, both inland and
overseas, implied a sophisticated credit structure and made it likely that
Bristol would play a pivotal role in that structure. Indeed, overseas trade
was probably the most important factor in leading to the emergence of
formal banking facilities in Bristol from the 1750s. Banking developed
in other west coast ports for the same reason, for example in Glasgow
from 1750 and Liverpool from 1770.[5]

There is substantial evidence that Bristol businessmen and bankers
were important providers of capital and credit in other areas such as
south Wales and Shropshire from the earliest stages of industrialisation.
During the early eighteenth century and after, Bristol merchants "provided, directly or indirectly, a good deal of the capital, technical and
industrial leadership which was to develop Welsh industrialism".[6] Many
early iron works, including the large-scale enterprise at Dowlais, obtained
finance from the city, and in the coal industry too there is evidence of
a similar migration of capital and entrepreneurship from Bristol. As for
the city's links with Shropshire, many of them involved Quaker businessmen. Abraham Darby, who revolutionised iron production through his
substitution of coke for charcoal in the smelting process, was active in
several different businesses in Bristol during the very late seventeenth
and early eighteenth centuries and, with other Quakers, became a partner
in the Bristol Brass Wire Co. Darby leased the Coalbrookdale blast
furnace in 1708 and from this time onwards it is clear that Bristol
merchants, many of whom were Darby's relatives or friends and fellow
Quakers, provided a great deal of the capital for the impressive development of the Shropshire iron industry.[7] Bristol itself became both a market
and entrepôt for ironware produced in Shropshire.

Just as overseas trade depended on increasing sophistication of credit and payment facilities so industrialisation in the eighteenth and nineteenth centuries depended on the easy transfer of funds from net saving to net investing regions, and strongly influenced the emergence of country banks. Typically, partners in country banks pursued other active business and/or civic careers at the same time. The 'Old Bank', for example, Bristol's first bank (established in 1750) had the maximum number of partners permissible (six). The senior partner, Onesiphorus Tyndall, was a West Indies merchant and dry salter; another, Isaac Elton, was a partner in the Bristol Copper Co. and Sheriff in 1743, Mayor in 1761 and Master of the Society of Merchant Venturers in 1764–5. Thomas Goldney, the senior partner of Miles Bank, established in 1752, was a partner in the Coalbrookdale Iron Works and a Quaker; another partner, Morgan Smith, was a sugar refiner. Most of the partners in the Exchange Bank, established about 1766, were members of the legal profession. Two further examples among many were the Harford and George families. The former included Joseph Harford (1741–1802), a partner in Ames, Cave & Co., a bank founded in 1786, who had been an original partner in the Bristol China Works in 1768 and in the 1790s became a major force in the Bristol Brass Company. Several other Harfords were partners in the Harford Bank, established in 1769. The George family, best known for its brewing enterprise, became connected to the banking business through James George, an original partner in the Castle Bank, founded in 1810.[8]

Bristol bankers in the later eighteenth and early nineteenth centuries were thus very firmly part of the city's industrial, professional and civic elite. Banks themselves were controlled and managed by their owners and, before the 1820s, were arguably in closer direct contact with industry and trade than they have ever been since. There were, of course, problems such as commercial crises and the strains of war (1793–1815) and its aftermath. In the crisis which accompanied the outbreak of war in 1793, for example, nineteen Bristol merchant houses failed for around £1.1 million, and the same crisis produced a regional cluster of bank failures – at Bristol, Bath, Chepstow and Worcester.[9] The commercial crisis of 1825 was on an even greater scale, bringing down about 70 banks in England and Wales, with one failure in Bristol and two suspensions of payment by banks in both Bath and Cheltenham.[10] In Bristol itself other banks voluntarily stopped business or amalgamated so that by 1826 the number of banks was only half that of the previous year (see Table 1). This crisis, and the number of ensuing bank failures, finally persuaded the government to permit the formation of larger, stronger joint-stock banks and in 1826 the six partner rule was abolished.

There were two ways in which joint-stock banks might emerge. The first was for one or more private banks to be converted to the joint-stock form, enabling maximum continuity of business and leadership and thereby maintaining the bank's reputation. The second was for an entirely new concern to be established, in which case the bank had to find shareholders, directors, staff, premises and business and begin to compete with established banks in its chosen territory. The Bristol region offers examples of both of these and it is relevant here to examine one of each in order to emphasise the contrasts between the two.

Our examples are Stuckey's Banking Co. (1826) and the West of England & South Wales District Bank (1834). Stuckeys was formed from four private banks in which Vincent Stuckey was a partner, and it had the distinction of being only the second joint-stock bank to be founded under the new legislation. Its founder and driving force, Vincent Stuckey of Langport in Somerset, became chairman in 1826 and remained so until his death in 1845. The Stuckey family, together with their business partners the Bagehots (with whom they were connected by marriage), dominated the commercial life of Langport from the mid-eighteenth to the end of the nineteenth century. The family's first banking venture about 1770 developed out of its extensive business in the coasting trade at Langport. In 1806 Stuckeys opened offices in Bridgwater and Bristol, where the bank was styled the Bristol and Somersetshire Banking Co. Between then and 1814, further offices were opened at Taunton and Wells.[11] Vincent Stuckey himself became a partner in 1807 having spent several valuable years at the Treasury. Family wealth, large business interests and government connections all helped to make Vincent Stuckey one of England's foremost bankers in the 30 years before 1845, as is

Table 1. *Banks in Bristol in 1825*

Name	Remarks
The Old Bank	Amalgamated with Ames, Cave & Co., 1826
Ames, Cave & Co.	Amalgamated with The Old Bank, 1826
Miles, Harford & Co.	Amalgamated with The Old Bank, 1877
The Bullion Bank	Failed 20 December 1825
Haythorne & Wright	Taken over by Northern & Central Bank of England, 1834
Pitt, Powell & Fripp	Relinquished business, 1826
The Castle Bank	Taken over by Stuckey & Co., 1826
Savery & Co.	Relinquished business, 1828
Stuckey & Co.	Taken over by Parr's Bank, 1909
The Exchange Bank	Relinquished business, 1828.

Source: C.H. Cave, *A History of Banking in Bristol* (Bristol, 1899), passim.

evidenced by the frequent invitations he received to submit evidence to parliamentary enquiries. One of Vincent Stuckey's main business interests was the manufacture of salt, and his banking concerns complemented this business, by facilitating the remittance of the enormous sums payable in salt duty. As he explained in 1819:

> we pay £1,000 a day duty; the amount of our duty last year was near one-fifth of the whole duty on salt. How are the payments made? Devonshire, Somerset-shire, Gloucestershire, and other parts, are supplied from our works, and the payments are made in bills of exchange and cash notes, and the amount of currency which passes through our hands is of course very considerable; our remittances to London last year were upwards of £12,000,000.[12]

When Stuckeys was converted to a joint-stock bank, it had a head office at Langport and three other offices including Bristol where in 1826 it took over the business and office of the Castle Bank. Although head office was at Langport, Bristol was described as the "chief office"[13] since the volume of business there was far greater than at any of the bank's other branches. Stuckeys was a county bank *par excellence*; until late in the nineteenth century virtually all its offices were in Somerset, as were almost all its shareholders. Wherever possible, its strategy of expansion for many years after 1826 was to take over the business of private banks which were offered for sale, or whose partners wished to retire and whose business and goodwill were bought for cash, shares in Stuckeys, or both.[14] In both cases Stuckeys preferred to retain the expertise of former partners and staff as local directors, managers or clerks. The main reason for this strategy was clearly spelled out in 1833:

> at each place of business a director, manager or agent (one of the former if it can be done) should be resident, who is well known in the neighbourhood and well acquainted with its wants and means – By acting thus you have the strength of a joint stock with the knowledge of a private banker.[15]

Vincent Stuckey also identified additional ingredients for his bank's success: a small number of shareholders of known wealth; a limited geographical area for the company's business; and a high denomination share (at least £100),[16] presumably to ensure that only those with substantial wealth would apply.

However desirable the above characteristics were, they were no guarantee of survival. Stuckeys, like other English banks, operated in an economy subject to chronic instability (see Figure 1), and the Bristol business was for this bank both the largest and the most unpredictable of any of its branches. This state of affairs continued throughout the nineteenth century. There were few years before 1860 in which the directors did not feel the need to stress to managers the need for close scrutiny of

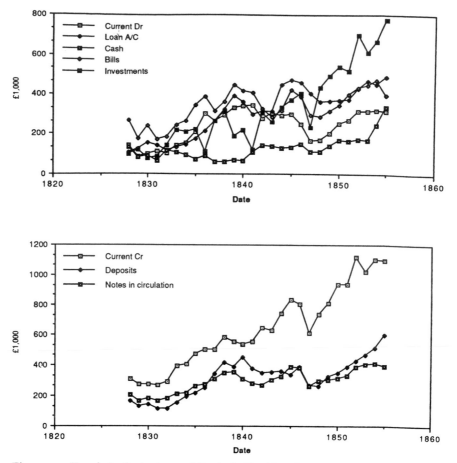

Figure 1. *Trends in the business of Stuckey's Banking Co. 1828–1855*
Source: Stuckey's Bank MSS Balance Sheets (31 Dec), National Westminster Bank Archives.

advances and, above all, to avoid long-term loans. It was noted in 1837, for example, that:

> a permanent overdrawn account is contrary to the true principle of banking and where an advance of this kind is required the overdrawn account should be converted into a loan and a note taken for it, and no overdrawing afterwards permitted ... all cheques beyond that amount will be refused payment unless proper communication is previously made and assented to.[17]

This comment conforms well with the conclusions of recent research into English country banking in the early nineteenth century: that overdrafts should not be 'permanent', and that fixed period loans were preferable. Indeed, as Figure 1 shows, fixed period loans were almost always greater than overdrafts, and sometimes loan accounts were more than double those overdrawn in the period 1828–55.

Between its conversion into a joint-stock bank and the arrival of new competitors in the mid-1830s, the most pressing problem facing Stuckeys was the combination of developments most feared by bankers everywhere: economic depression, political agitation and widespread social disorder, lasting from the end of 1830 to the passing of the first Reform Act in June 1832. By December 1830 Stuckey's board of directors noted the "serious and alarming state of the country" which had shaken public credit and rendered "all banking operations" uncertain.[18] Somerset was on the western fringes of the wave of agrarian violence which swept through southern England in 1830–1, but neighbouring counties such as Wiltshire were badly affected.[19] At about the same time economic depression resulted in the failure of two important West India merchant houses in Bristol together with the stoppage of Payne & Co., bankers at Wells. So serious were these that in July 1831 Stuckeys felt it necessary to sell "a large portion" of its government securities so as to provide the necessary gold with which to increase liquidity at branches. Six months later, however, political agitation arrived on Stuckey's own doorstep with the riots in Bristol which, together with less serious riots at Derby and Nottingham, marked the most violent phase of the Reform Bill period. Once again the bank was forced to sell "a considerable number of the Stock and Exchequer Bills" and tried to call in outstanding debts, warning of the need to avoid "permanent and dead advances".[20] A refusal to lock up funds in illiquid loans was a hallmark of Stuckey's policy throughout its existence and became paramount during periods of crisis. As far as Bristol was concerned there was not only a contraction of bank lending in the early 1830s; the uncertainty seems also to have unnerved investors generally and retarded specific projects such as the Clifton Suspension Bridge.[21]

Every storm successfully weathered added to Stuckey's already high reputation, and by 1833 business was increasing significantly, especially at the Bristol and Wells branches.[22] The upturn in the British economy between 1833 and 1836 represented a sharp contrast with the previous three years and was a promising context for another wave of joint-stock bank promotion in England and Wales which in turn had permanent significance for the Bristol region. For Bristol itself the most important development was the formation of the West of England & South Wales District Bank with its head office in the city, opened in December 1834. This bank, as is evident from its title, chose a much larger area for its operations than county-bound Stuckeys. Indeed, the spread of its network

Table 2. *Two Branch Networks in South West England in 1837*

(a) Stuckey & Co.

Langport (Head Office)	Ilminster
Axbridge	Martock
Bridgwater	Shepton Mallet
Bristol	South Petherton
Bruton	Taunton
Castle Cary	Wellington
Chard	Wells
Crewkerne	Wincanton
Frome	Yeovil
Glastonbury	

(b) West of England & South Wales District Bank

Bristol (Head Office)	Glastonbury
Axbridge	Merthyr
Bath	Newport
Barnstaple	Somerton
Bideford	Swansea
Bridgwater	Taunton
Cardiff	Wells
Exeter	Williton

Sources: P.T. Saunders, *Stuckey's Bank* (Taunton, 1928). *Select Committee on Joint Stock Banks*, (P.P. 1837, XIV), Appendix 1 nos. 13 and 29.

Note: All Stuckey's branches except Bristol were in Somerset and none was more than 40 miles from head office; the West of England Bank had branches in four counties with one (Bideford) 110 miles from head office.

by 1837 (see Table 2) shows it to have been one of the more geographically adventurous of the new English banks.

In common with many of the latter formed in the mid-1830s its share denomination (£20) was relatively low compared to Stuckeys and most of the earlier joint-stock banks. Low denomination shares appealed to a wider cross section of society and permitted new sources of investment to be tapped, particularly since they tended to be only partly paid-up.[23] They were also more marketable. Unlike Stuckeys, the West of England & South Wales District Bank had no roots in private banking. It was floated by what Sayers has described as "professional promoters of joint-stock banks" from Manchester and Leeds. Its deed of settlement was signed in February 1835 by 414 people.[24] The vast majority, however, had addresses in south west England and of its six original directors three were from Bristol and one each from Swansea, Bodmin and Exeter.[25] One of the Bristol directors, Thomas Richard Guppy, became the first chairman. He was a partner in a Bristol sugar refinery, and was also an important local figure in the promotion of the Great Western Railway between 1833 and 1835.[26] During the early stages of the bank's promotion it became clear that the demand for shares was strong and for this reason the directors felt able to become more selective as to whom shares were allotted, and the price paid. In October 1834 it was announced that "all future applications for shares must be accompanied by the promise of an account or important influence on behalf of the Bank and that in every other case a premium will be required".[27]

While Stuckey's staff were recruited largely from the Somerset area, the West of England & South Wales District Bank cast its net far and wide in an effort to secure high quality officers. To this end the bank advertised for officers and clerks in all the Bristol newspapers, one Edinburgh paper, *The Times*, *Globe*, *Standard*, *Morning Post* and *Morning Herald*. The key post was that of general manager and in October 1834 the bank appointed John Bates at an annual salary of £800 subject to "the Board's approval of the sureties proposed by Bates to guarantee his

15. The West of England & South Wales District Bank in Corn Street. By William Bruce Gingell and T.R. Lysaght, 1854–8, and based on Sansovino's St. Mark's Library, Venice. The lavish symbolic decorations are by John Evan Thomas.

faithful management to the amount of £10,000". Bates was clearly a highly experienced bank officer. He had "from early youth" worked in banking and spent ten years at Spooner, Attwood & Co. in Birmingham. Thereafter – in 1827 – he went to the Provincial Bank of Ireland and successively worked as accountant at its Cork branch, manager at Youghal and assistant inspector at Dublin.[28] The high degree of mobility of many bank officers within the United Kingdom in the 1820s and 1830s has long been recognised by historians, and Bates is a good example of it.

The West of England Bank's policy of offering shares at favourable prices in return for prestigious accounts was a method of poaching business. As bank promotion in the Bristol region proceeded rapidly in the mid-1830s, it is clear that competition for lucrative business intensified. Typically, this was reflected in levels of interest rate for deposits and credit. In Bristol, competition faced by old-established banks came not only from the West of England Bank, but from the new branch of the Bank of England which opened in 1827, and the Northern & Central Bank of England, which took over the Exchange Bank in 1834 and whose Bristol business was itself taken over by the National Provincial in 1836. In a broader regional context other important new banking companies included the Gloucestershire (1831), the Gloucester County & City (1834), and the Cheltenham & Gloucester (1836). The second of these merged in 1836 with a private bank at Cirencester to become the City of Gloucester Banking Co. Like Stuckeys, it proceeded to take over private banks and indeed swallowed the Cheltenham & Gloucester in 1856. Two important banks emerged in Wiltshire. The Wilts & Dorset was established at Salisbury in 1835 and the North Wilts, an older private concern at Melksham, became a joint stock bank in the same year. Both developed by a typical combination of absorption and opening entirely new branches. The Wilts & Dorset had about a hundred branches in five south western counties by 1914, having opened its first branch in Bristol in 1872.[29]

Bank promotion and expansion of branch networks meant of course that local monopolies were eroded or disappeared altogether, and banks could no longer depend on geographical isolation to secure their business. One result of this was that interest rates tended to become more competitive as banks sought to retain accounts. There is some evidence to suggest that before 1850 customers in larger towns were more likely than rural customers to react to uncompetitive rates by moving their accounts. When Vincent Stuckey was asked by the Select Committee on Banks of Issue (1841) if his bank had followed a recent move by the Bank of England in raising interest on deposits to 6 per cent, he replied that in some cases it did but "not generally". The convention was to give 3 per cent and the bank had held some deposits at that rate for 50 years. The move by the Bank of England had led to some withdrawal of Stuckey's deposits but not in rural areas because "our depositors in the agricultural districts" did not respond to the possibility of a higher rate, "but in Bristol and Bath people understand the matter better, and withdraw the deposits in some cases".[30] This is not only an interesting observation on the relative sophistication of urban customers, it also helps to explain why uniformity of interest rates throughout the branch network was never achieved during the nineteenth century. In the early 1830s, when it became apparent that new joint-stock banks were poised to enter the Bristol region, Stuckeys prepared a new scale of charges with the aim of achieving maximum possible uniformity between branches and at "the lowest rate consistent with the interest of the proprietors".[31] Shortly afterwards, senior officers were reminded "of the necessity of transacting the business with liberality as one of the best means of preventing competition".[32] This pre-emptive move by an established bank to a threatened invasion of its territory by newcomers was perfectly logical. No bank welcomed competition, but Stuckeys was not at all certain that in the long term every new bank would succeed because the available amount of good banking business seemed inadequate to support them all. Moreover, Stuckeys criticised the low demonination of shares in both the Northern & Central and the West of England Bank and the fact that only a small fraction was paid-up on each. In Stuckey's judgement "the coalition of a number of persons, as bankers, residing in various and distant parts of the Country, who in their individual capacities are not entitled to credit and who can bring little business to any concern is merely extension without strength".[33]

It would seem that Stuckeys underestimated both the market for banking services in the mid-1830s and the rate at which that market would expand in the long term. It also failed to appreciate fully that the need to raise large amounts of capital quickly, together with fierce competition in the capital market from other enterprises such as railways, would inevitably lower share denominations. Stuckey's views on shareholders and share denominations were the product of long experience, and in an age of unlimited liability no doubt had much to commend them but the new banks simply could not afford to take the same view. In the long run, of course, the vast majority of new banks in the region survived and grew, but all banks had to be constantly on guard against a sudden deterioration of confidence in them. Distrust might derive from local or national causes; correspondingly, its impact might be highly localised or geographically widespread. The fact was that bank customers, especially depositors and noteholders, had no way of knowing the state of a bank's finances because accounts were not normally published until the later nineteenth century. Vincent Stuckey was unusual amongst English country bankers in advocating regular publication of figures for assets and liabilities of individual banks. Advertising financial strength in this way, he argued, would tell to the advantage of proven concerns because shareholders "would see that their private property cannot be called on, and they will also have an opportunity of ascertaining whether it will not be more profitable to become shareholders in an old established Company than joining a new one".[34] Such enlightened self-interest was rare. This was unfortunate because publication of assets and liabilities in the early nineteenth century might well have helped to dampen distrust in English country banks.

Stuckeys did learn from the mistakes of others and from its own experience and frequently strengthened its own position. At the end of the 1830s, for example, it became clear that fraud had been committed at Miles & Co.'s bank in Bristol and this demonstrated to Stuckeys "the necessity of peculiar vigilance and attention on the part of directors and managers in their several offices and of frequent investigation".[35] Stuckeys also made continued efforts to ensure that it could quickly convert its securities held in London with its agents as well as with the Bank of England. The need for vigilance was amply demonstrated in 1841, when unfounded rumours circulated about the solvency of Stuckey's Bank and these, occurring in the trough of depression and after two decades of instability for bankers everywhere, led to demands on the bank's deposits and notes for £150,000 within a few days.[36] Holding enough cash to meet such contingencies may have been sensible, but it was not profitable, whereas lending or investment was. Every banker had to choose between liquidity and profitability and would always prefer the lowest cash ratio consistent with safety. In a clear statement of the art of managing a bank's reserve, Vincent Stuckey declared in 1840 that the "great object to accomplish is with how little *Dead Weight* in the Country we can carry on our business and at the same time stand fully prepared to meet sudden emergencies".[37] He concluded on this occasion that £5,000 in Bank of England notes, gold and silver should be kept at the head office in Langport and £10,000 at the most important branch in Bristol beyond what the bank needed for "current and daily operations". All other branches were instructed in case of need to communicate with one or other of these two offices. A few weeks after these instructions were issued the sudden failure of the Old Bank of Hobhouse & Co. at Bath "again threw affairs (particularly in the eastern half of the county) into confusion".[38] Stuckeys had opened a branch in Bath in 1838 and Hobhouse's failure was yet another reminder of how the stoppage of a reputable bank (Hobhouse himself was chairman of the Committee of Country Bankers) could affect others in the region. Later the same year Stuckeys strengthened its position in this lucrative city by taking over the private bank of Falkner, Falkner & Reynolds.[39]

It was noted above that Bristol was, from an early stage in Stuckey's life as a joint-stock bank, the most important of its branches. This branch not only served as a regional reserve of gold and silver for emergency use by other branches, but was itself subject to considerable stresses and strains. This latter feature of business at Bristol became very obvious in the 1840s and 1850s. The city's position as a major provincial financial centre was well established by the 1820s and 1830s and was further strengthened by the formation of a stock exchange in 1845. This exchange, like so many others in England, was created largely to cater for the burgeoning market in railway shares which accompanied the second and greatest railway mania of 1844–7.[40] The impact of railway investment on Bristol banking will be examined later in this chapter. The growth and instability of business at Stuckey's Bristol branch proved a perpetual strain on the management and this strain surfaced in 1853 when the directors instructed the Bristol management not to permit further advances and discounts. During the fifteen months to the end of 1853 discounts at Bristol has increased from £170,000 to £290,000 and the latter figure represented about two-thirds of the bank's total discounts.[41] Overdrafts at Bristol too gave cause for concern and, in June 1854, the directors ordered that they be "materially lessened".[42] General apprehension about the Bristol branch increased still further in August of the following year as rumours of alleged mismanagement and heavy losses there spread. It was decided to strengthen the management structure at Bristol and add another manager to the existing two. Until one could be found an interim committee of three would attend at Bristol every fortnight "or as aften as may seem desirable" for three months to assist managers with their advice.[43] A painstaking investigation into business at Bristol concluded that the need to recruit an extra manager "was more than confirmed, it being also clear that not only have the funds of the Company been much mismanaged, but that there is an absence of co-operation and a neglect of discipline in the establishment which is very injurious and calls for an early remedy".[44]

Not until May 1857 was business at Bristol deemed to be on a satisfactory footing. One notable result of the review of the Bristol Committee of Management was the appointment of Walter Bagehot as its secretary in 1855 at the age of 29. Son of the bank's vice-chairman, Bagehot had graduated from London University and gone on to take an M.A. there, winning a gold medal in philosophy. Having been admitted to the Bar in 1852 he then rejected a career in law and took a post in Stuckey's Bank.[45] By 1857 he took a major role in the management at Bristol as well as helping to run head office at Langport. Two years later he began his involvement in the management of the *Economist*, founded by his father-in-law Edward Wilson. He split his time between Bristol and

London (where he undertook business on behalf of Stuckeys) but editor-
ship of the *Economist* occupied more and more of his attention. Although
Stuckey's directors agreed to his resignation from the Bristol management, they thought it desirable that he be retained in a supervisory
capacity "of a substantial and not a nominal kind" at that branch.[46] In
fact Bagehot continued his connection with the bank throughout his later
years when he became an economist, writer and critic of international
stature with works such as *The English Constitution* (1867) and *Lombard
Street* (1873). In addition to these and other literary works Bagehot was
the inventor of the Treasury Bill. He continued to attend directors'
meetings in Bristol and elsewhere until shortly before his death in 1877,
aged 51. Stuckey's decision to bolster its Bristol management was a timely
one in view of the many problems thrown up in the 1840s and early 1850s.

As far as banking at city, regional and indeed national level was
concerned, however, the 50 years after 1860 were a great deal smoother
than the 50 years before. For the Bristol region, the one great exception
to this picture of relative stability was the banking crisis of 1878 which
has always been most closely identified with the massive failure of the
unlimited City of Glasgow Bank on 2 October. The historian of Lloyds
Bank has argued that this was probably the greatest banking crisis since
1825.[47] In the south west, the crisis was symbolised by the failure of the
West of England & South Wales District Bank on 9 December – the
greatest bank failure the region has ever seen. It would appear that the
bank had been involved in lending ever-increasing sums to a small number
of iron firms in South Wales since the 1840s, and when the iron industry
went into severe depression at the end of the 1870s the firms' position,
and that of the bank, became unbearable.[48] A summary of its financial
position in December 1878 is provided in Table 3.

So it would seem that the West of England Bank had made the mistake
of becoming too closely involved in long term industrial lending; this
was a market which Stuckeys never entered, and indeed believed that
no bank should enter. Moreover, Vincent Stuckey's warnings about the
modest means of shareholders in the new joint-stock banks of the 1830s,
including the West of England Bank, were at least partially vindicated
in 1878. The Bristol agent of the Bank of England noted that about
two-thirds of the West of England Bank's 2,100 shareholders were widows
and spinsters; the rest were "a very mixed lot" and included domestic
servants, labourers, railway guards and "great numbers of yeomen". This
list of shareholders "gives one the idea of weakness" with only a few
names of substance.[49] Many individuals and families were ruined by the
failure and other banks were immediately affected. Between the failure
of the City of Glasgow and that of the West of England, Stuckeys felt it
desirable to 'keep strong' at the Bank of England,[50] and to allow its

Table 3. *Approximate Statement of Affairs, 7 December 1878*

West of England & South Wales District Bank — Approximate Statement of Affairs, 7th December 1878.

Liabilities :—	£	s	d
Current Accounts	1,472,340	0	2
Deposit Receipts	1,602,349	11	9
Notes in circulation	64,420	·	·
Current Drafts and Advices	136,133	9	4
Dividends due to Shareholders	1,792	19	3
Creditors holding Security £107,725.9.1 (deducted from Amounts on other side)			
	3,364,506	1	1
Deduct:— Claims by the Crown & others to be specially provided for	16,240	3	5
£	3,353,265	17	8

Assets :—	£	s	d
Cash in hand & at Bank of England	211,822	13	9
Bills current in hand £747,112.9.1 Estimated to produce	691,112	9	1
Remittances to London for collection	58,284	11	3
Balances due to Bank Considered good £1,486,183.2.0 less estimated on realization 40,000.0.0	1,446,183	2	·
Doubtful & Bad Debts and Overdue Bills £388,804.0.0 Estimated to produce	249,498	·	·
Bank Premises Furniture &c	107,462	11	·
Investments £776,925.4.10 Estimated to produce	189,645	7	8
Government Securities and Bills Deposited £529,475.13.10 Less Claims thereon 438,723.9.1	90,752	4	9
Balances in suspense between Head Office & Branches	27,742	14	8
Stamps on hand	2,683	15	5
	3,085,187	14	7
Deduct:— Amount required to meet Preferential Claims	16,240	3	5
	3,068,947	11	2
Estimated Deficiency	304,318	6	6
£	3,353,265	17	8

Source: Bristol Record Office, Veale Benson Collection.

holding of Bank notes and gold to accumulate, the directors reporting
that the failure at the West of England Bank "caused much distrust at
Bristol and our various branches and large amounts [were] ... withdrawn
by our customers from running accounts and deposits".[51] In addition
to the £40,500 of Bank and railway stock sold in November 1878, Stuckeys
was forced to sell a further £186,000 of public securities shortly after the
West of England Bank failure "to meet the demand on us at our various
branches especially at Bristol and Bath".[52]

Out of the wreckage of the West of England Bank a new limited liability
concern, styled the Bristol & West of England Bank, began business early
in 1879 with a paid-up capital of nearly £110,000 and 700 shareholders.[53]
Some of the failed bank's branches were taken over by other banks in
the region, but the new bank immediately set about constructing a branch
network and by March 1879, in addition to its Corn Street head office
in Bristol, had opened two in Monmouthshire, two in Glamorgan and
two in Devon. The chairman of the new bank, C.J. Thomas, told a
shareholders' meeting that "notwithstanding the numerous banks they
had in Bristol" there was still room for another; but he also struck a
cautionary note about over-rapid expansion:

> He did not himself wish to force the business of the bank at all, and they had
> the experience of other banks which made large lock-ups and so on, but they
> would endeavour, to the utmost of their power, to adhere to strict and
> legitimate banking (hear, hear); rather to have a sound business than to aim
> at a big business (hear, hear). If the business was to grow, let it grow naturally.[54]

The new bank did indeed progress, and had opened 22 offices by 1892.
However, it had only a short life, being taken over that year by Lloyds.[55]
Failure of large banks with unlimited liability persuaded many of the
older banks to become limited companies in order to protect themselves
and their shareholders. The National Provincial, for example, followed
this course in 1880, the Wilts & Dorset in 1883. Stuckeys, more confident
of its unlimited status and its financial position, took much longer to
register as a limited company, and did so in 1892 only after a great deal
of debate.[56]

One of the most notable features of banking in Bristol between 1880
and 1914 was the proliferation of suburban branches. This process was
slow to start, but accelerated in the very late nineteenth century as banks
began to provide more convenient facilities for the increasing number
of people with accounts. For example, the new Bristol & West of England
Bank opened offices at St. Philips and Stokes Croft in 1881, Kingswood
(1885), Temple Gate (1888), St. George (1889) and Staple Hill (1892). In
the early twentieth century there were more than 60 branches in the
city;[57] Stuckeys had opened 13 branches in Bristol by 1909.[58] Amalgama-

tion was another important trend in the late nineteenth century, and a large number of the region's banks lost their independent existence through amalgamation with larger banks based elsewhere. An example of this process is provided in Figure 2, which charts the emergence of the modern National Westminster bank group at Bristol. Even Stuckeys, which for nearly 140 years had symbolised the proud independence of English provincial banking, was taken over in 1909 by Parr's Bank, which had originated in Warrington. At this time Stuckey's network included 47 branches and about two dozen part-time agencies. A small number of other banks in the region retained their independence a little longer. The most important of these, the Wilts & Dorset and the Capital & Counties (formerly the Hampshire & North Wilts Banking Co.) were taken over by Lloyds in 1914 and 1918 respectively. In 1921 Lloyds also took over Fox, Fowler & Co., based in Wellington, Somerset, the last English country bank to issue its own notes.[59]

The revolution in the structure of banking in the Bristol region before 1914 should not be allowed to obscure the fact that the basic range of services offered by banks remained much the same: deposit taking and providing credit by way of fixed period loans, overdrafts or discounted bills. Many banks issued their own notes before the 1850s, but this practice declined as the government made a determined effort to eliminate the issue of paper currency in England and Wales by any bank other than the Bank of England. In any case the use of cheques became more widespread with the development of branch banking and the popularisation of the banking habit, thus economising on the use of notes and coin.[60]

It is unsafe to generalise about the nature of banking business throughout the United Kingdom in the nineteenth century, since there were so many local variations. This was recognised by bankers in the Bristol region who sometimes contrasted conditions there with those prevailing in other places such as Lancashire. There were important imbalances between regions in the demand for, and supply of, funds. As Walter Bagehot told the Select Committee on Banks of Issue in 1875:

> Somerset is an accumulating district where we have more money than we can employ, and Lancashire is a great employing and borrowing district where they have less money than they can employ, and therefore it is reasonable that in Lancashire the banks should offer more for money, and also that they should charge higher rates for money than we do in Somersetshire.[61]

In short, Somerset was a saving area and Lancashire an investing area. Channelling funds from saving to investing areas, usually via London, has long been recognised as a notable contribution made by banks to the process of industrialisation in Britain. Until the 1870s, most banks were

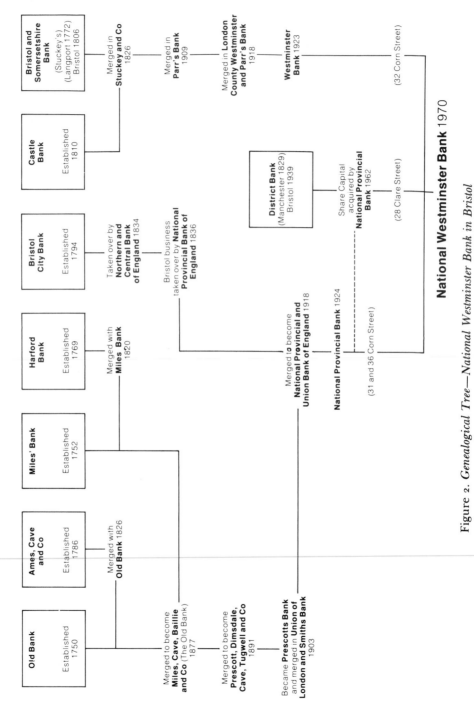

Figure 2. *Genealogical Tree—National Westminster Bank in Bristol*

16. Banknotes issued by Stuckey's Banking Co., 1818 and 1908. The earlier note features an illustration of Stuckey's branch on Broad Quay, Bristol.

local or regional concerns operating either in saving or investing areas. Only with the amalgamation movement did banks emerge which typically operated in both. As far as Stuckeys was concerned, total advances (loans, overdrafts and discounts) were always less than investments. Between 1878 and 1908 deposits increased by 94 per cent, investments by 116 per cent and total advances by 38 per cent. The ratio of advances to deposits was much lower in Stuckeys (57 per cent in 1878, 41 per cent in 1908) than in Parrs (91 per cent in 1878, 57 per cent in 1908).[62] One striking feature of Stuckey's business before 1909 was the decline of its note issue. On the eve of its amalgamation with Parrs, Stuckey's circulation was only £79,500, whereas in 1845 it had been £357,000 and in the latter year Stuckeys issued more notes than any bank in England and Wales apart from the Bank of England.[63]

The right to issue notes was extremely important in the early decades of joint-stock banking because it promoted the banking habit, contributed to profits and was a valuable method of advertising. According to Walter Bagehot, "the whole system of banking in Somersetshire" was based upon Stuckey's circulation.[64] Confidence in this bank's notes rarely wavered; indeed in the political crisis of the early 1830s, some people brought in Bank of England notes to exchange them for Stuckey's in which they had greater trust.[65] In Lancashire the position was different for several reasons, including a shortage of small denomination currency together with an unhappy history of note-issue which not only undermined confidence in local paper currency but led to the widespread practice of circulating bills of exchange as a substitute for bank notes. However, as Vincent Stuckey put it in 1832, "the County of Somerset has always been used to a Country bank circulation ... we never circulate in the County of Somerset a bill of exchange as they do in the North".[66]

In the area around Bristol the state of agriculture was the principal determinant of the number of notes issued, and downturns in agriculture such as those in 1849, and 1861 significantly depressed circulation.[67] West Country farmers clearly depended on banks to provide them with credit during the lean summer months. In Somerset in the early 1840s, for example, Stuckeys typically advanced between £40,000 and £50,000 to the county's farmers between March and October:

> Every gentleman here knows that at this time farmers are generally poor; they having sold everything off they want money for the seed time and to buy cattle; and ours having been more an agricultural bank than anything else, and a great portion of its business being agricultural now, we assist farmers in that way; the money advanced at that season is generally replaced in the winter. At one season of the year we have their money, at another they have ours, and I always consider that legitimate banking, if it were not for that I am sure their rent would not be paid.[68]

Since landlords and farmers were important as circulators of Stuckey's notes and as sources of deposits, the bank valued their custom highly. When rival banks opened in primarily agricultural areas, Stuckeys sought to protect its business by reducing commission and other charges. Again in 1864 Stuckey's Bristol branch was authorised "to hire an office near the cattle market in order to accommodate our customers who wish to pay in money and to avoid the trouble of going into the city".[69] Stuckeys also made several subventions to large meetings of the Royal Agricultural Society in the south west.[70] The bank assisted agriculture in other ways, for example by occasional lending to the Somerset Drainage Co. Thus in February 1880 this company requested and received "a further advance of £4,000" secured by the rates, totalling some £12,000, "payable by the owners of more than 100,000 acres of Somersetshire land". The advance, required to pay surveyors' fees, would be repaid within six months following collection of the rates.[71]

Of indirect assistance to agriculture was Stuckey's frequent provision of large, short-term credit for Bristol-based merchants involved in importing guano. Guano became a major item in fertilisers from the mid-nineteenth century, and Bristol was an important point of import for South America guano. A typical advance of this nature occurred in September 1871 when it was agreed to lend a Bristol firm of merchants:

> the sum of £100,000 on the security of guano, to be deposited in our names at warehouses in Bristol and Plymouth, the margin of security to be 25 per cent in excess of the advances and the debt to be paid off, at stated periods, between this day and next Lady Day.[72]

Bristol grain merchants also received large short-term credits. The grain trade was revolutionised in the later nineteenth century with a massive rise in imports which followed the opening of large new territories overseas such as the North American prairies, and the great improvements in ocean transport. The trade became more sophisticated with the development of futures buying and in 1889 Bristol followed Glasgow, Liverpool and Hull by forming a Corn Exchange Association.[73] This was an unstable, potentially risky business and bankers, as in the example of guano noted above, normally insisted on a substantial margin between the value of cargoes and the level of an advance. On many occasions Stuckeys advanced up to about £100,000 to Bristol grain traders and corn brokers from the 1880s until 1909.[74]

Within the Bristol region, as in so many other parts of the country, one of the most potentially lucrative new lending opportunities in the nineteenth century was the railways. Indeed, because of their impact on the regional economy, railways influenced the business of banking in several respects – not all of them positive. It soon became obvious that railways would have an impact on the business of nearby canals. The contribution of banks to the financing of canals is generally agreed to have been modest, but bankers did often act as treasurers of canal companies. Bankers were usually appointed to this position from the 1780s because they facilitated the canal company's task in securing loans and overdrafts.[75] An important, if fairly unusual, example of extensive bank finance was the case of the Kennet & Avon Canal whose treasurer Samuel Worrall had provided a credit of £6,000 by 1797 through his bank, Worrall Blatchley (The Exchange Bank) in Bristol. A subsequent refusal to extend credit further led to the transfer of account to Harford, Davis & Co. at Bristol. It was in credit between 1801 and 1807 but continually overdrawn from 1807 until 1815, by which time the overdraft had reached the very substantial figure of £60,631. This debt was paid off in 1816.[76]

Stuckeys was likewise treasurer to the Bristol & Taunton Canal almost from its inception in 1822,[77] and remained so when the title and scope of this scheme was changed to the Bridgwater & Taunton Canal in 1824. By the early 1830s the debt to Stuckeys was about £10,000 and remained obstinately high, but the bank had no doubts that the loan was safe.[78] However, when the debt had risen to about £22,000 in 1844 some doubts began to be voiced. Reviewing the history of this account, Vincent Stuckey pointed out in 1844 how the prospects for the canal had originally been considered excellent, but that unforeseen competition from the railway had led to a review of this projection. The following analysis by Vincent Stuckey must have been shared by bankers in many parts of Britain whose advances to canal companies suddenly appeared less secure:

> ... a few months ago there was the best ground for believing that our debt would have been paid by this time – since then, however, a competition has arisen between the canal company and the Great Western Railway and, in consequence the Canal Co. have been forced to reduce their tolls, which has materially lessened their income. Every step has been taken for placing the Company's debt on as safe a footing as it can be but the opposition still continues, and the railway in this instance as well as others may permanently influence the welfare of older modes of conveyance.[79]

This tentative, but accurate, prediction became more definite over the next few years and Stuckeys eventually wrote off a large proportion of the canal company's debt in 1847 and 1851.[80] The bank was subsequently a party to the negotiations which led to the sale of the canal to the Bristol & Exeter Railway in 1866.[81]

As far as railways themselves were concerned, the most significant development in the region was of course the construction of the Great Western. Most business enterprises in nineteenth century Britain had only one banker, but the Great Western Railway was a very large concern and it originally had no fewer than four bankers, one in London and three in Bristol: Miles, Harford; Elton, Baillie, Ames; and Stuckeys. Bankers as well as merchants and manufacturers with banking interests were well represented on the Bristol Committee of the Great Western, they included James Lean (of Stuckeys), John Cave, Thomas Guppy and John Harford for example.[82] Stuckeys itself bought £5,000 worth of Great Western shares in 1835.[83] The evidence suggests that until the end of the nineteenth century the relationship between Stuckeys and the Great Western was a highly erratic one; sometimes the bank lent large sums at short notice for short periods, and at other times the railway was cash-rich, and able to place some £50,000 on deposit with the bank.[84]

There is no doubt that Stuckeys regarded this as a valuable account both at Bristol and Bath, but during the railway mania of the mid-1840s the bank became generally cautious about lending to railway companies. At the height of the boom in 1845 all bank staff were urged "to abstain from proceedings in railway shares which might lead the public to regard them as speculators".[85] By the end of that year Stuckey's board noted that a "very large" sum was now held by railway companies, shareholders and brokers especially at Bristol, and the board was clearly concerned that although it had £570,000 in cash or at call, a period of tight money might have serious consequences. For this reason it "seemed necessary to be especially watchful against lending money on shares and for railway purposes and to avoid it in all cases, except such as came within the regular course of our business".[86] As Figure 1 shows, having increased strongly between 1843 and 1845, lending fell steeply for the next three years.

When share prices fell in 1846, several railway companies, including the Great Western, approached Stuckeys for "large loans to enable them to make their deposits for new lines",[87] but the bank declined all these requests since it would have necessitated selling stock, or borrowing on it, and this was something the bank refused to do. Not even prestigious customers, then, could persuade Stuckeys to alter its time-honoured policy of "liquidity first". The bank again refused to make an advance to the Great Western just after the financial crisis of 1857.[88] At other times, Stuckeys provided large short-term credit on flexible terms. Indeed, in 1855 the bank was well aware that its lending to the Great Western had hitherto always been without security and in an "undefined manner", and was anxious to ascertain the conditions on which the railway company's other bankers provided credit. It was told that the railway could offer no security and that none was required by their other bankers.[89] Shortly after the financial crisis of 1866, however, Stuckeys became more insistent on some form of security for advances, and was happy to take Great Western preference stock or debentures for this purpose.[90] The relationship between Stuckeys and the Great Western was long and cordial, and it would appear that by the end of the nineteenth century the latter, so far from requiring credit, was more often asking what interest rate the bank could give on sums of £50,000 deposited for definite periods of several months. This happened at least three times in the 1890s.[91]

With regard to other railways in the Bristol region Stuckeys sometimes invested directly, acquiring, for example, 25 shares in the newly promoted Somerset Central Railway from Highbridge to Glastonbury in 1852, a similar number in the Yeovil & Salisbury Railway four years later, and stock worth £2,000 of the Bristol & Clifton Railway in 1861 with interest at 4 per cent guaranteed by the Great Western. At other times the bank lent to firms in the normal way, for example £10,000 to the Mid-Somerset Railway for 6–12 months in 1854. By 1861 the West Somerset Railway owed Stuckeys £30,000.[92]

The opportunities for bank lending in the region before 1914 were not, of course, confined to agriculture, trade and transport. A substantial difficulty facing the historian, however, is that the banks did not assemble data on sectoral lending so that one can do little more than to multiply individual examples in order to demonstrate the range of customers who received credit. One attractive area for the banks was public utilities, primarily because of their size and the predictable and relatively secure nature of the activity. In 1898 Stuckeys lent £100,000 for up to a year to the Bristol Sanitary Authority. This advance had been sanctioned by the Local Government Board and secured by a mortgage on the rates and also on the seal of Bristol Corporation.[93] Similarly in 1908 the bank lent £25,000 for a year to the Bath and District Electric Supply Co. Ltd. "to enable them to pay the first instalment of the purchase money for the Bath Corporation Electric Light Works".[94] Another bank in Bristol, the National Provincial, was involved in public utility finance, holding the important account of the Bristol Water Works. In the Edwardian period the latter requested and received credit usually twice a year for sums between £14,000 and £50,000 which were required for the payment of dividends and which were secured by collection of the rates.[95] Generally, it was riskier to lend to the manufacturing sector than to public utilities and there could be dangers in long-term industrial finance as the failure of the West of England & South Wales District Bank in 1878 had shown. The available evidence indicates that the vast majority of firms requested and received short-term assistance though this was not necessarily restricted to one year. Thus in 1897 Stuckeys lent up to £10,000 for two years to Stothert & Pitt, the important Bath engineering firm. This sum was needed to help the firm complete a £50,000 Admiralty contract for work at Gibraltar and was secured by the promissory note of three directors. In 1907 the bank lent £75,000 for eight months to the Bristol & South Wales Railway Wagon Co. Ltd. and two years later provided a facility of £25,000 to C. & J. Clark Ltd., the shoe manufacturers.[96] The Bristol branch of the National Provincial Bank provided credit to some large firms in the city before 1914. Thus in 1911 Georges' Brewery requested up to £50,000 for four years to be repaid by four equal annual instalments plus interest. This account, which had been open for more than 20 years, was obviously a prestigious and lucrative one. In 1911 the brewery had about £45,000 on deposit but needed a similar additional sum to buy 48 licensed premises which were valued at between £85,000 and £90,000, the title deeds to which would be lodged as collateral. As the branch manager noted "From a private source they have the money offered at 4 per cent therefore they would not listen to the suggestion of a higher rate from us. It is a perfectly safe advance, and seeing that they keep a large credit with us it is recommended".[97] On another occasion, in 1907, the National Provincial lent up to £40,000 to Charles Hill & Sons, the shipowners and shipbuilders, and in 1912 this firm requested and received a renewal to the extent of £15,000 secured by deeds to freehold property.[98]

National Provincial also provided credit to the city's burgeoning hotel industry. Both the Clifton Hotel Co. and the Grand Hotel Co. received regular credit for sums up to £20,000 before 1914, mainly for the purchase of new land and property or upgrading existing buildings.[99] Hotel outfitting was an expensive business. Thus in 1907 Stuckey's branch at Bath was asked by Bath Cabinet Makers Ltd. for a loan of up to £10,000 "to enable them to complete a contract for the furnishing of the new hotel to be built on the site of Exeter Hall, Strand". The loan was granted and secured by directors' guarantee.[100]

In this chapter it has been argued that all sectors – primary, manufacturing and service – received credit from banks in the Bristol region. Most customers sought, and received, short term credit, but there were instances where longer term (i.e. more than a year) credit was provided. Every banker knew the risks of extensive long-term lending to industry, though in the case of the West of England & South Wales District Bank those dangers appear not to have been heeded. More generally this chapter has indicated our very considerable ignorance of agricultural, manufacturing and mercantile finance in this period: even the most comprehensive history yet written of a Bristol firm has virtually nothing to say about its finance.[101] Further research in banking history cannot fail to improve our understanding of the dynamics of regional economic development before 1914, and to add much-needed detail to what we already know about the position of Bristol as the financial metropolis of the south west.

NOTES

1. Much of the research for this chapter was undertaken in the archives of National Westminster Bank Head Office in London. I am greatly indebted to Mr R.H. Reed, the bank's archivist, for his hospitality and help. I am also grateful to Dr John Booker, archivist at Lloyds Bank for his assistance, and to staff at Bristol Record Office for access to the Veale Benson Collection.

2. For the national background see L.S. Pressnell, *Country Banking in the Industrial Revolution* (Oxford, 1956). P.L. Cottrell, *Industrial Finance, 1830–1914* (1980). W.A. Thomas, *The Finance of British Industry, 1918–76* (1978).

3. Anon, *Industrial Rivers of the United Kingdom* (1891), pp.142–57. R. Davis, *The Rise of the English Shipping Industry* (Newton Abbot, 1962), pp.36–7. B.W.E. Alford, 'The Economic Development of Bristol in the Nineteenth Century: an Enigma?', in P. McGrath and J. Cannon, eds. *Essays in Bristol and Gloucestershire History* (Bristol, 1976), pp.252–83.

4. D. Defoe, *A Tour Through the Whole Island of Great Britain*, (1724–6, Penguin edn. 1983), p.362.

5. P. Mathias, *The Transformation of England* (1979), p.98.

6. A.H. John, 'Glamorgan 1700–50', in A.H. John and G. Williams (eds), *Glamorgan County History, volume V: Industrial Glamorgan, 1700–1970* (Cardiff, 1980) p.3.

7. B. Trinder, *The Industrial Revolution in Shropshire* (Chichester, 1981), pp.13–17.

8. C.H. Cave, *A History of Banking in Bristol* (Bristol, 1899), passim. J. Day, *Bristol Brass: the History of the Industry* (Newton Abbot, 1973), pp.112–3, 125, 132.

9. Pressnell, *Country Banking*, p.457.

10. Sir J. Clapham, *The Bank of England: a History, volume II,' 1797–1914* (Cambridge, 1944), p.102.

11. P.T. Saunders, *Stuckey's Bank* (Taunton, 1928), chs.1–3.

12. Ibid., p.15.

13. *Select Committee on Renewal of the Bank Charter* (P.P. 1831–2, VI), Q.931.

14. See, for example, National Westminster Bank Archives, Stuckey's Banking Co., Directors' Minute Book (hereafter S.D.M.B.), 6 Sept. 1828; 3 Dec. 1841; 25 Nov. 1848.

15. Ibid., 27 July 1833.

16. V. Stuckey, *Thoughts on the Improvement of the System of Country Banking in a Letter to Viscount Althorp* (2nd edn. 1836), pp.6–7.

17. S.D.M.B., 18 Oct. 1837.

18. Ibid., 23 Dec. 1830.

19. E.J. Hobsbawm and G. Rude, *Captain Swing* (1969), pp.116–33, 304–5, 308–9.

20. S.D.M.B., 17 Jan, 1832.

21. G. Channon, *Bristol and the Promotion of the Great Western Railway* (Bristol, 1985), p.2.

22. S.D.M.B., 29 Jan. and 24 July 1833.

23. See generally S.E. Thomas, 'The First English Provincial Banks', *Economic History*, II (1934).

24. R.S. Sayers, *Lloyds Bank in the History of English Banking* (Oxford, 1957), p.20. *Select Committee on Joint Stock Banks* (P.P. 1837, XIV), Appendix 1, no.29.

25. Lloyds Bank Archives (hereafter L.B. Archives), West of England & South Wales District Bank, Directors' Minute Book, (hereafter W.E.D.M.B.), 9 Oct. 1834.

26. Channon, *Great Western Railway*, pp.3, 19.

27. L.B. Archives, W.E.D.M.B., 10 Oct. 1834.

28. Ibid., 25 Sept. and 23 Oct. 1834.

29. Sayers, *Lloyds Bank*, pp.17–19.

30. *Select Committee on Banks of Issue* (P.P. 1841, V), QQ.636–8.

31. N.W.B. Archives, S.D.M.B., 10 Oct. 1834.

32. Ibid., 26 Nov. 1833.

33. Ibid., Half-yearly Report, July 1834.

34. Ibid., Half-yearly Report, July 1835.

35. Ibid., 10 Oct. 1838; 30 Jan. 1839. The latter also notes embezzlement at Elton, Baillie & Co. in Bristol.

36. Ibid., 29 Oct. 1841.

37. Ibid., 30 July 1841.

38. Ibid., 29 Oct. 1841.

39. Ibid., 3 Dec. 1841.

40. See in particular M.C. Reed, *Investment in Railways in Britain, 1820–1844* (Oxford, 1975), passim.

41. N.W.B. Archives, S.D.M.B., Report of Head Office to Directors, 14 Dec. 1853.

42. Ibid., 14 June 1854.

43. Ibid., 10 Aug. 1855.

44. Ibid., 17 Dec. 1855.

45. See the excellent biographical sketch in T.E. Gregory, *The Westminster Bank through a Century*, vol.II (1936), pp.237–73.

46. N.W.B. archives, S.D.M.B., 13 March 1861.

47. Sayers, *Lloyds Bank*, p.211. For new evidence on this crisis see M. Collins, *The Banking Crisis of 1878* (University of Leeds School of Economic Studies, Discussion Paper, Series A, 87/9, 1987).

48. J. Latimer, *Annals of Bristol in the Nineteenth Century* (Bristol, 1887), pp.505–6.

49. R.O. Roberts, 'Banking and Financial Organisation, 1750–1914', in John and Williams, eds. *Industrial Glamorgan*, p.387.

50. N.W.B. Archives, S.D.M.B., 16 Oct. 1878.

51. Ibid., 18 Dec. 1878.

52. Ibid., 28 Jan. 1879.

53. Bristol Record Office, Veale Benson Collection, Advertisement for Bristol & West of England Bank Ltd., October 1879.

54. *Bristol Mercury and Post*, 21 May 1879.

55. Sayers, *Lloyds Bank*, p.20.

56. N.W.B. Archives, S.D.M.B., 23 April 1879; 21 June 1882; 15 Sept. and 17 Nov. 1886; 1 June 1891.

57. *Arrowsmith's Dictionary of Bristol* (2nd edn. Bristol, 1906), pp.11–13.

58. See, for example, *Bristol Daily Mercury*, 30 Oct. 1909.

59. Sayers, *Lloyds Bank*, pp.299–300.

60. Stuckey, *Country Banking*, pp.21–3. *Select Committee on Banks of Issue*, 1841, Q.456.

61. *Select Committee on Banks of Issue* (P.P. 1875, IX), Q.7970.

62. Gregory, *Westminster Bank*, vol.II, pp.94–6, 320–3.

63. The highest note issue reached by Stuckeys was £415,326 in June 1853. See N.W.B. Archives, S.D.M.B., Balance Sheet.

64. *Select Committee on Banks of Issue*, 1875, Q.7998.

65. *Select Committee on Banks of Issue*, 1841, Q.503.

66. *Select Committee on Renewal of the Bank Charter*, 1831–2, Q.1180.

67. N.W.B. Archives, S.D.M.B., 25 July 1849; 31 July 1861.

68. *Select Committee on Banks of Issue*, 1841, Q.485. See also Q.473.

69. N.W.B. Archives, S.D.M.B., 3 May 1864.

70. See for example ibid., 19 Nov. 1873; 18 April 1877.

71. Ibid., 14 Feb. 1880.

72. Ibid., 20 Sept. 1871. See also 15 Nov. 1882; 15 Aug. 1883.

73. G.L. Rees, *Britain's Commodity Markets* (1972), pp.138–9.

74. N.W.B. Archives, S.D.M.B., 20 Aug. 1890; 18 Feb. 1891; 16 Feb. 1893; 22 Jan. and 18 Feb. 1896; 21 March 1900; 18 Aug. 1903; 21 Oct. 1907; 13 April 1908.

75. J.R. Ward, *The Finance of Canal Building in Eighteenth Century England* (Oxford, 1974) pp.109–11.

76. Ibid., 66–9, 112–19, 188.

77. *Taunton Courier*, 25 Feb. 1824.

78. N.W.B. Archives, S.D.M.B., 28 Jan. 1831.

79. Ibid., 26 Jan. 1844. See also 30 April 1844.

80. Ibid., 30 July 1847; 25 July 1851.

81. C. Hadfield, *The Canals of South West England* (Newton Abbot, 1967), pp.61–4.

82. Channon, *Great Western Railway*, pp.19, 22.

83. Reed, *Investment in Railways*, p.156.

84. See, for example, N.W.B. Archives, S.D.M.B., 29 Jan. 1840; 28 April 1852; 26 Oct. 1853; 19 Nov. 1855.

85. Ibid., 30 July 1845.

86. Ibid., 29 Oct. 1845.

87. Ibid., 30 Jan. 1846.

88. Ibid., 28 Oct. 1857.

89. Ibid., 17 Dec. 1855.

90. Ibid., 19 Sept. and 31 Oct. 1866; 13 March, 3 April, 22 May 1867.

91. Ibid., 18 April 1894; 14 Oct. 1895; 22 June 1898.

92. See, for example, ibid., 28 Jan. 1852; 28 April 1854; 14 Dec. 1856; 13 March 1861; 13 Nov. 1861.

93. Ibid., 22 June 1898.

94. Ibid., 13 April 1908.

95. N.W.B. Archives, National Provincial Bank Loan Book (Bristol Branch) 1912–22, 2 March 1912; 25 Aug. 1912; 24 Feb. and 25 Aug. 1913; 2 Feb., 23 June and 12 Aug. 1914.

96. N.W.B. Archives, S.D.M.B., 24 Aug. 1897; 21 Oct. 1907; 15 March 1909.

97. N.W.B. Archives, National Provincial Loan Book (Bristol Branch) 1912–22, 2 May 1911.

98. Ibid., 6 May 1912.

99. Ibid., 13 Sept. and 17 Dec, 1911; 7 March, 3 July, 20 Aug., 18 Dec. 1912; 11 and 18 June 1913; 3 Jan. 17 June 1914.

100. S.D.M.B., 19 Aug. 1907.

101. B.W.E. Alford, *W.D. & H.O. Wills and the Development of the U.K. Tobacco Industry,* 1786–1965 (1973).

The Growth of the Printing and Packaging Industry in Bristol, 1800–1914[1]

DONALD BATEMAN

A typical printing office in Bristol at the opening of the nineteenth century consisted of half a dozen hand compositors working at wooden frames. They set type by hand in a wooden setting stick from cases made locally by a printer's joiner. They no longer cast their own type but bought it from a founder, and they bought their hand-made paper from a local manufacturer. These were the only significant changes made since the day of William Bonny who had brought printing to the city in 1695.[2] Standing in the corner of the print shop would be a large and cumbersome wooden press, braced to the ceiling for rigidity. The hand-made paper was damped before printing and hung on strings or racks to dry after printing. The iron printing press was invented by Stanhope in 1800, but is unlikely to have reached Bristol until fifteen or twenty years later.[3] The presswork, although regarded as a menial task, was done by compositors. Printers' ink was made in the office by mixing oils, waxes and carbon pigment to formulae regarded as a trade secret. The work was local in origin, the customer brought it in by hand and often collected it personally. The run-length was short and the master-printer worked alongside his journeymen, often doubling up his office with that of bookseller, vendor of artists' materials or some other retail activity.

This picture of a small-scale handicraft industry was to change fundamentally over the course of the nineteenth century. All over Britain forces were at work which progressively transformed the scale and character of the industry, especially after about 1850. The most powerful of these forces were technological change and rising markets for printed and packaged goods. The expansion of the market, it might be argued, was the more important of the two. Traditional sectors of the industry – newspaper and book publishing – were stimulated by rising real incomes and the spread of literacy.[4] Moreover, as society grew richer, new mass markets developed for printed and packaged goods. Rather than serving the consumer directly, printing was an increasingly important secondary activity serving other industries. Mechanisation and volume production in factories made it possible for the industry not only to meet the challenge of rising markets, but also to drive unit costs ever downward. Thus the printing industry expanded in size and scope. As it did so, it became highly sectionalised. Specialisation – greatly encouraged by the creation of an efficient national transport system – became the order of the day, and by the late nineteenth century the industry was divided into four main branches: the printing of newspapers, the printing of books, jobbing printing, and large-scale manufacturing of stationery, bags and packaging. The industry was neatly divided into market sectors, and to some extent this was matched by differences in the technology employed in each branch of the trade. The largest firms were those specialising in the mass production of printed stationery, bags and cartons; the smallest were the jobbing printers who still met purely local needs and produced a wide range of printed matter in short runs.

An important consequence of the later-nineteenth-century boom in printing and packaging was the emergence of rivals to London as the 'natural' centre of the industry. In 1851 just under half of the 22,000 printers in England and Wales were Londoners, and in highly skilled trades like lithography and copper plate engraving more than two thirds of the adult workers and about half the apprentices worked in the metropolis.[5] London's pre-eminence was due to its position as the economic, administrative, social and cultural centre of Britain, as well as to its large population; the government, for example, was an important customer of the printing industry. At mid-century, London firms had an annual gross output of £800,000 out of a national total of about £1,500,000.[6] From the 1850s and 1860s, however, much of the growth in employment took place in provincial towns and cities. London remained the hub of the industry, but it experienced relative decline with the advance of the industry in places like Bristol, Reading and Oxford. Lower rents and labour costs, improved communications, specialisation and volume production often meant that provincial firms could undercut their metropolitan rivals. By 1911, when gross output had reached £23 million, the number of printers and lithographers in England and Wales had grown to 152,666, and another 21,873 people were employed in the printing industry in ancillary occupations, including clerks, messengers and commercial travellers. About 70 per cent of the total labour force now worked outside London.[7]

Bristol was one of the main beneficiaries of these changes. Printing in the city grew more rapidly than elsewhere, and by the end of the nineteenth century the most vigorous Bristol firms had achieved national standing. Growth was most rapid in the packaging sector, but letterpress printing was also expanding fast. This chapter examines the growth of printing and packaging in Bristol, both of the industry as a whole and of some of its larger firms. It also examines the birth and death rates of printing houses, and the reasons why a small minority of firms achieved enormous success whilst most failed or remained small-scale producers. The lack of sound statistical series for employment, production or capital investment in Bristol printing makes it difficult to chart the rise of the local industry with any precision. However, some idea of the general pattern can be formed by an examination of local trade and commercial directories.[8] Table 1 provides a summary of the number of printing offices in Bristol between 1775 and 1911.

The use of data from directories does have to be treated with caution; one problem is that the classifications used changed from year to year, and care must be exercised to avoid recording the same firm more than

Table 1. *Number of Printing Enterprises in Bristol, 1775–1911*

Year	Number of Firms (excluding newspapers)				Newspapers D = Daily W = Weekly M = Monthly	New Firms Launched in the Previous Decade†
	Letter Press	Copper Plate	Litho	Total*		
1775	n.a.	n.a.	n.a.	7	n.a.	n.a.
1801	15	3	–	18	n.a.	n.a.
1811	n.a.	n.a.	n.a.	n.a.	n.a.	n.a.
1821	23	6	–	29	5W	n.a.
1831	25	12	3	40	4W	17
1841	27	13	3	43	6W	16
1851	39	16	7	62	6W	27
1861	40	15	12	67	2D;6W;1M	22
1871	42	14	12	68	4D;4W	24
1881	44	‡	19	63	4D;4W	25
1891	49	‡	15	64	5D;4W	21
1901	72	‡	10	82	5D;7W	29
1911	§	§	§	92	4D;7W	27

Sources: Trade Directories. D.F. Gallop, 'Chapters in the History of the Provincial Newspaper Press, 1700–1855' (unpublished Ph.D. thesis, University of Bristol, 1954).

* Some of the firms appear in more than one category in the directories for certain years and the final totals have been adjusted to deal with this. Similarly, towards the end of the nineteenth century some firms based in other towns (e.g. Petty of Leeds) maintained a sales representative in the town and his address was entered in the directory. Such an instance has not been included as a *bona fide* firm.
† An allowance has been made for name changes by checking addresses.
‡ Included under lithography (which was gradually superseding copper plate printing).
§ The 1911 directory entered all firms as "printers" without differentiation.

once under different headings. Yet, despite such deficiencies, the general trend is clear. The number of printing establishments in operation in Bristol roughly doubled in the second quarter of the nineteenth century to reach 62. The total then remained fairly static until 1891, but there followed a sudden surge in the next two decades, reaching a total of 92 by 1911. This represented almost a 50 per cent increase over 1881.

The growth of the industry is also reflected in employment totals, although it is not easy to obtain an accurate picture from ten-year censuses. There are no details for Bristol before 1841, and matters are complicated further by changes in occupational classification in later surveys. Alterations to Bristol's boundaries add another difficulty. Nonetheless, Table 2 gives a fair indication of the general trend. Again, there is evidence of a surge in the late nineteenth century.

The figures refer solely to people whose occupations were given as 'printer', 'lithographer' or 'copper plate printer', and not total numbers employed in the industry. Yet many people were employed in ancillary trades and occupations. Indeed, the printing industry increasingly employed less-skilled workers. This was particularly true of the 'spurt' in Bristol of the late nineteenth and early twentieth centuries, associated with the development of packaging firms. The changed composition of the labour force in 'printing' following the packaging boom is shown in Table 3. These figures are drawn from the 1911 Census, which was far more detailed than earlier occupational surveys.

By 1911, the printing industry in Bristol had completely changed; it was no longer a microcosm of the London industry, but had acquired a distinctive character of its own. There were many new jobs for women,

Table 2. *Employment of Printers in Bristol, 1841–1911*

	Males			Females			Total Employed
	Over 20	< 20	Total	Over 20	< 20	Total	
1841	154	38	192	2	0	2	194
1851	188	85	273	0	0	0	273
1861	273	150	423	9	5	14	437
1871	n.a.	n.a.	444	n.a.	n.a.	2	446
1881	n.a.	n.a.	882	n.a.	n.a.	35	917
1891	n.a.	n.a.	1,121	n.a.	n.a.	75	1,196
1901*	958	946	1,904	152	18	170	1,974
1911*	1,884	1,328	3,212	427	71	498	3,710

Sources: Censuses of Population: England and Wales, 1841–1911.
*1901 and 1911 include Bedminster (previously included in figures for Somerset).

Table 3. *Employment (by Occupation) in the Bristol Printing Industry, 1911*

	Males			Females			Total
	Over 20	< 20	Total	Over 20	< 20	Total	Total Employed
Paper box, bag manufacturers, stationery manufacturers	291	275	566	1,755	1,813	3,568	4,134
Paper bag makers	41	34	75	303	338	641	716
Cardboard box makers	105	151	256	1,054	1,333	2,387	2,643
Printers, lithographers	1,022	1,762	2,784	183	315	498	3,282
Bookbinders	123	31	154	68	179	247	401
Other workers	106	48	154	47	75	122	276
TOTAL	1,688	2,301	3,989	3,410	4,053	7,463	11,452

Source: *Census of Population*: *England and Wales*, 1911, vol. 10 pt. 1, p.166.

whose dexterity brought higher productivity, and whose lower wages kept down costs. Operations like making up and glueing cartons after they had been cut and creased were highly labour-intensive, and were largely done by girls in the 15–20 age group and unmarried women. There is also evidence of 'de-skilling' in more traditional printing occupations. In lithography, large numbers of boys were taken on when they left school to feed the machines which by 1911 had taken over from hand work. The 1911 Census data confirm that in the late nineteenth and early twentieth century Bristol became an important centre of commercial printing and packaging. Though Bristol accounted for only about 7 per cent of the total number employed in the U.K. printing industry, it had almost one third of those employed in bag and box making. Employment in Bristol in the cardboard box and paper bag sector had risen by a staggering 93.5 per cent between 1901 and 1911, and on the eve of the First World War the printing and packaging industry had become the biggest employer of labour in the city.[9]

Underpinning the growth of the printing industry were important changes in markets. Localisation characterised the first half of the century, as printing firms were tightly clustered in the commercial centre of Bristol whence most of their custom came. Thus, they rarely advertised their services, relying upon personal contacts and recommendations for their work. The later decades of the nineteenth century, however, saw the emergence of new opportunities which enabled printers to tap regional or national markets, bringing the benefits of increased output and long production runs. Particularly important in Bristol was the growing demand for packaging and wrapping materials. These products were

17. Paper bag making at E.S. & A. Robinson. Like Frys and Wills, Robinsons employed large numbers of women and girls.

outside the sphere of traditional printing, but they were a powerful stimulus to Bristol firms. By 1888, for example, seven firms were listed as 'paper bag makers' in the trade directories. Four of them, including Mardon, Son & Hall, had developed from established printing houses, but there were three new specialist firms.[10] Packaging developed as an effective advertising medium, and paper bags and cartons had to be printed (often in colour) as well as being cut out and glued up. Printing houses could also meet a growing demand for other types of advertising material, such as showcards or posters. Opportunities for specialisation appeared. Edward Everard's printing house in Broad Street, for example, became the official publisher to the Bristol Stock Exchange, and published illustrated timetables and guide books for the Bristol Tramways & Carriage Co. Account books and ledgers were sold in large numbers to Bristol businesses, and in 1911 the firm secured a contract to supply aircraft logbooks to the British & Colonial Aeroplane Co.[11]

Newspaper and book publishing benefited from rising standards of literacy in British society. The number of daily and weekly newspaper titles published in the United Kingdom, for example, rose from 267 in 1821 to 563 in 1851 and an astonishing 2,491 in 1901.[12] The first daily

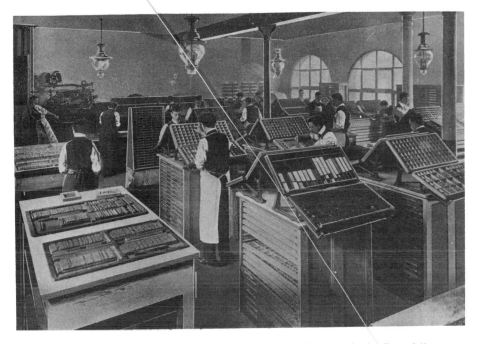

18. Compositors at work in Edward Everard's printing works in Broad Street, built in 1901. The facade, designed as a monument to the printer's craft, survives.

papers in Bristol were the *Western Daily Press* (1858) and the *Bristol Daily Post* (1860). Furthermore, newspapers were becoming more substantial; extra pages were added, and there was a growing volume of advertising material. In book publishing too there were new opportunities which could be exploited. Nationally, the average number of new books published each year rose from about 580 in the first quarter of the nineteenth century to about 2,600 by 1850, then rocketed to 6,044 in 1901 and 12,379 in 1913. A widening of the reading public created a growing demand for both cheap and specialist literature. Urban growth led to a demand for street and trade directories, and the development of railway and steam packet services created a lucrative market for timetables, maps and other travel information. In the world of fiction, the 'railway libraries', sold in large numbers by railway booksellers like W.H. Smith and John Menzies in the second half of the nineteenth century, were among the first of the modern pocket editions.[13]

Technological developments helped the printing industry to respond to these opportunities. The iron hand press underwent considerable development in first half of the nineteenth century, but could not exceed about 250 impressions per hour. Two operators were needed, one to ink the type and the other to feed in the paper and operate the press. Various ideas were put forward to increase output, and by the middle of the century other types of printing press were coming into use. One of these was the platen machine, which was ideally suited to jobbing work. As with the hand press, the type was quoin-locked into a flat forme, but ink was applied automatically. The paper, which lay on a flat plate, was then brought into contact with the type. The main advantages over hand presses were that all but the smallest platen presses could be power-driven, and they could be operated by one man instead of two. Typically, they offered a fourfold increase in the rate of production. A somewhat earlier development was the cylinder or 'Wharfedale' machine. Like the platen press, it was power-driven, and ink was automatically applied to the forme. However, a cylinder rather than a flat plate was used to hold the paper. As it rotated, the type bed was moved back and forward by a simple crank arrangement. The printed material was neatly stacked by a delivery mechanism. Wharfedales were widely used to print packaging as well as newspapers and books, and they offered something like an eightfold increase in output, compared to hand methods. However, these platen and cylinder machines printed on one side of the paper only, and the needs of book and magazine publishers led to the development, from the 1840s, of the perfecting machine. It did not print on both sides at once, but contained two impression cylinders and a double inking mechanism, together with an arrangement of rollers and guides to transfer the paper from one set of type to the other. However, it was not suited to very long production runs, and the first truly rotary press was introduced by *The Times* in the mid-1850s (platen and cylinder types used a reciprocating motion rather than a rotary one). The rotary press printed from curved plates, and it was soon coupled with the use of a continuous roll of paper to speed production. It was fitted with devices to cut the printed material into sheets and collate it. Though unreliable at first, the rotary press became increasingly efficient and sophisticated, and facilitated the rapid rise in newspaper circulations which took place towards the end of the nineteenth century.

The needs of firms which specialised in printing packaging and wrapping materials were rather different from more traditional printers. Design and graphics were much more important than typesetting. A suitable process was lithography, invented by Aloys Senefelder of Prague in 1796. Based on the principle that oil and water do not mix, it originally involved drawing a design on a slab of fine-grained stone with a greasy pen. The stone was then wetted, and when ink was applied it would adhere to the design and not the background. The master could then be used directly, or to make multiple copies for more rapid production. In the 1850s and 1860s it was realised that zinc plates could be used, and this led to the development of litho machines. The offset litho process was commercially developed in America in the 1900s. It was called 'offset' because the design was transferred to the paper via an intermediary rubber-blanket covered roller. It was found that the quality was better than when printing direct from the master, partly because of the flexible image carrier and partly because it was no longer necessary to draw the design in reverse. Packaging companies were also amongst the first to adopt colour printing machines, and ancillary tasks such as cutting and creasing became mechanised.

Unlike the printing process itself, composition (assembling the individual letters and characters in the required sequence) was very difficult to mechanise. There was a prolonged search for fast, mechanical means of setting type, but it was not until the 1880s and 1890s that the real breakthroughs were made with the invention in America of Linotype and Monotype machines. These were operated from a keyboard, and could set type between five and ten times as fast as hand methods. Molten lead alloy was cast into moulds, and the use of fresh type for each job ensured high quality results. The Linotype cast a line of type in a single 'slug' and was particularly suited to newspaper work, whilst the Monotype

19. E.S. & A. Robinson's lithography department. Designs were drawn upon slabs of polished limestone with a greasy ink.

cast individual characters, and was preferred for book printing. Not surprisingly, they were complex and expensive.[14]

These machines brought about a revolution in the printing of books and newspapers. The old system of hand-setting was highly labour-intensive, especially in the case of newspapers, where speed was of the essence. It was also skilled work, and compositors had become the elite of the printing industry. Most were employed by local newspapers, and before their position was undermined by the arrival of Linotype machines, the compositors were a favoured group of workers. Their interests were represented at local level by the Bristol Typographical Society, a branch of the National Typographical Association (founded in 1844 by the federation of local societies in all the major centres of the printing industry).[15] But the existence of an elite, represented by a long-established trade society, did not mean that organised labour had the power to resist changes in technology and working practices. In fact, Bristol firms were largely able to ignore trade unionism until the early twentieth century. Successful firms were able to expand through the employment of juvenile labour. In 1861, for example, 48 per cent of the printers recorded in the Census of England and Wales were apprentices. Similarly, in 1881 49 per cent of the printers and 38 per cent of the lithographers were aged less than 20. The Bristol Typographical Society often complained about the hordes of young lads employed as cheap labour, but was powerless to do anything about it.[16] Furthermore, much of the nineteenth-century growth in the printing industry was in lithography or the printing of packaging and wrapping materials, and these sectors of the industry were poorly unionised in comparison with letterpress printing. The Bristol Typographical Society remained a 'craft' society; it sought to exclude printers who had not been formally apprenticed, women, and manual workers. Consequently it neglected the areas of the industry which were growing most rapidly. Not until the end of the First World War did a majority of the workers in the Bristol printing industry belong to a trade union.[17]

The favourable labour, technological and market conditions prevailing in Bristol were not in themselves a guarantee of commercial success for local firms. It was noted earlier that many new firms were launched throughout the period. But whilst birth rates were high, so too were death rates. Table 4 is based upon trade directory entries, and indicates the survival rates of printing concerns in Bristol.

Between 1831 and 1911 a total of 208 new firms were established, but in the same period 156 closed down. Many of them were decidedly short-lived. Only one concern survived from the late eighteenth century to the end of the period under review. This was a family firm established by Philip Rose in 1777, which became Rose & Harris in 1866. It survived until the end of the First World War, when it was taken over by another Bristol firm, Partridge & Love.[18]

The survival pattern of firms shown in Table 4 reflects the national picture. It was relatively easy to set up in printing in a small way. The great majority of Bristol firms were jobbing printers, which were increasing in numbers all over the United Kingdom at this time. Typically, they were very small, employing a handful of people; most had 10–20 workers. There was plenty of work about of the sort which the 'instant print' shop does today. This consisted of business cards, letter-headings, handbills and a whole range of short run work. Very cheap machines, such as small platen presses, became available for this type of work. A 13 by 9 inch platen press by Hatton cost £35 in 1891, and £2 extra if steam-powered facilities were needed. A foolscap folio ($13\frac{1}{2}$ by $8\frac{3}{4}$ inch) National Platen made in Stockport was even cheaper in 1892 at £28 and £2 extra for steam drive fittings. In the same year a London firm advertised "The Model Platen Press" even cheaper at £19 10s. for a 9 by 6 inch model and £25 for an 11 by 7 inch one.[19] High rates of failure in the industry ensured that there was also a thriving market in secondhand equipment. All this meant that a tradesman with enough ambition and a modest capital could secure his independence. This was true for most of the

Table 4. *Printing Firms in Bristol: Number and Survival Pattern, 1775–1911*[*]

| Year | No. Of Printing Offices | Survival Pattern No. of Firms existing from; | | | | | | | | | | | |
		1775	1801	1811	1821	1831	1841	1851	1861	1871	1881	1891	1901
1775	7												
1801	18	4											
1811	n.a.	n.a.	n.a.										
1821	29	0	2	n.a.									
1831	40	0	2	n.a.	19								
1841	45	0	2	n.a.	11	25							
1851	62	0	2	n.a.	11	15	24						
1861	67	0	?	n.a.	10	10	17	30					
1871	68	0	1	n.a.	6	8	13	25	27				
1881	63	0	1	n.a.	3	5	10	13	19	31			
1891	64	0	1	n.a.	2	3	9	10	13	25	33		
1901	82	0	1	n.a.	2	2	6	9	10	19	22	38	
1911	92	0	1	n.a.	1	2	4	8	10	15	22	33	54

Source: Trade Directories, 1775–1911.
[*] All figures have been adjusted to avoid double counting firms engaged in more than one sector of the trade.

nineteenth century, and as late as 1894 one writer could refer to "the comparative ease with which a pushing man can become a small master".[20]

Many of them, however, were doomed to failure; of the 84 firms operating in 1914, 48 were set up after 1900, and only 21 could trace their origins as far back as 1875. Growing competition for work and the rapid changes taking place in the industry put small firms under pressure. Effective exploitation of the new opportunities of the post-1850 period required a much larger capital and better organisation than hitherto, and made greater demands upon management. A few large firms began to exert a disproportionate influence in the industry. This was particularly true of the packaging sector: by 1900 the largest firms in packaging were approaching 1,000 employees, whilst only a handful of letterpress firms employed 250 or more.

The qualities needed to take advantage of favourable market, techno- logical and labour conditions – to prosper, while so many competitors went to the wall – can best be illustrated by the experiences of of leading firms in the industry. First amongst these was Mardon, Son & Hall. The firm was founded in 1846 when James Mardon moved to Bristol from South Molton in Gloucestershire and entered into partnership with his brother-in-law, John Harris. The new firm opened an office at 39 Broad Street, in the middle of Bristol's banking and legal quarter. It did not do conventional printing of the letterpress variety, but concentrated upon copper plate and steel engraving.[21] Its initial success was based upon headed business notepapers. Attractive designs featuring picturesque local views proved popular, and the firm's clientele soon extended into south Wales. It engraved cheque books for Stuckey's Bank – only a stone's throw away – and produced share certificates in large quantities.[22] The largest and most profitable part of its business, however, soon came to be the printing of packaging materials. An important early client was Robert Charlton, a Quaker pin maker who had a factory at Two Mile Hill, Kingswood, for whom the partners engraved pin papers. This was a lucrative business, for Charlton sold large quantities of pins to London wholesalers, which made for long printing runs. Packaging for other consumer products followed – notably engraved tobacco wrappings for the Bristol firm of Franklin, Davey & Co.[23]

The partners soon added lithography to their existing business. This was a natural step from engraving; copper plate dies could be used to produce multiple images on the litho stone, thus speeding up the rate of production. They acquired two flat-bed litho presses in 1850 from a local firm which had failed, and expanded into label printing, dealing mostly with druggists and wholesale chemists.[24] Some idea of the range of services offered at this time can be gained from an engraved trade card of 1853:

Old-established engraving lithographic and general printing office. Wholesale stationery and account book manufactory. Die sinking, embossing and copying presses of the best manufacture. Wedding, visiting and mourning cards &c. executed in the best style on the shortest notice.[25]

In 1854 Harris retired due to ill health, and James Mardon took over. By 1860, when the firm moved to larger premises in nearby Clare Street, it had further diversified into letterpress printing, using steam-powered presses bought secondhand from a failed Gloucester firm. It was a decade of rapid development for the firm. James's son, Heber, who was to be largely responsible for the firm's rapid growth in the later nineteenth century, became a partner in 1860. In 1863, he was joined by his brother-in-law, George Hall, and the firm became known as Mardon, Son & Hall. Throughout his career, Heber Mardon ensured that the firm was to the fore in the adoption of new machinery and techniques. An interest was acquired in paper mills in Bath and Pensford, and in 1866–7 a new purpose-built factory was constructed in Milk Street.[26] A surviving engraving of this factory shows the mezzanine floor; for letterpress work, there were six composing frames, three hand letterpress proofers and three powered printing machines. Six litho transfer presses, eight powered litho machines and a range of copper plate presses can be also be seen.[27] In addition, the new factory produced cardboard boxes for many local firms, including makers of collars, corsets, boots and shoes, drapery and tailoring.[28] But the crucial factor in the firm's development was its association with the tobacco firm of W.D. & H.O. Wills. In 1883 Wills acquired the rights to the Bonsack cigarette-making machine, and in the next few years sales of cheap cigarettes rose sharply.[29] Cigarettes were packed in cardboard boxes or paper packets, and Mardons, which already supplied labels and showcards to Wills, became its biggest supplier. Extra factories were opened in Rupert Street and Dighton Street, and some years later Heber Mardon stated that:

No one could have conceived to what an enormous extent that branch of the trade [cigarettes] would grow, but I date from that day the first insertion of the wedge that led us on to become to a great extent the printers for the tobacco trade in England.[30]

As Wills' sales grew, Mardons began to experience difficulty in keeping up with the demand for cigarette packets, and in 1890 the two firms jointly developed a machine to replace hand work. In 1895, they began to sell machine-made cases to other tobacco manufacturers.[31] Mardons was also one of the first firms (if not the first) to manufacture cigarette cards. To give added protection, a stiffening card was inserted in paper cigarette packets, and it was realised that this had great advertising potential. It is uncertain whether Wills actually pioneered the cigarette card, but its first series was produced by Mardons in 1887, and replicated the showcards supplied to tobacconists. Subsequent series, such as the 'Kings and Queens' series of 1897, were produced in vast quantities, and were avidly collected by the public.[32] Mardons was able to meet this demand because it had invested heavily in high-class colour printing at a time when it was a new and intricate operation. Another new factory was constructed at Temple Gate for lithography and the highly specialised facsimile printing process of Collotype.[33] In 1898, the growth of this work led to a doubling of capacity, and in the following year Mardons claimed to be the first firm in Europe to install a rotary lithographic machine. This used aluminium plates, and was much faster than the earlier flat bed machines.[34] The workforce grew rapidly, from 200 in the 1880s to about 500 in the following decade.[35]

When James Buchanan Duke's American Tobacco Co. launched a frontal attack on the British market in 1901, Wills called together the other British tobacco companies to fight off the invasion, and the Imperial Tobacco Company (of Great Britain and Ireland) Ltd. was formed on 3 October. Wills decided that Mardons was vital to the interests of the new company: its work was of a high quality, and it possessed a number of patents for packaging machines which could not be allowed to fall into the hands of the Americans. Negotiations began, and in 1902 Mardon, Son & Hall became part of Imperial Tobacco.[36] Its expansion continued, and eight new factories were opened between 1902 and 1915, by which time the firm was employing 3,800 people. It had become efficient and profitable; when Heber Mardon died in 1925 he left a fortune of £399,518.[37] Its success was largely due to its enterprise in applying new production techniques and developing products that found a mass market.

A second firm which rose to prominence in the later nineteenth century is that of E.S. & A. Robinson. Elisha Smith Robinson came from Overbury near Tewkesbury, where his father owned a paper mill. After an apprenticeship in the paper trade, he moved to Bristol in 1844 and set up in business with a capital of £190, dealing in wrapping papers for the grocery trade. It was the practice at that time to wrap up tea, sugar, flour and other items in sheets of paper, twisted under the eyes of the customer with great skill and flourish by the shopkeeper. Robinson saw the virtues of selling ready-made paper bags – especially ones printed with the name of the dealer or the commodity. He began by hand-making paper bags, and made a profit of £400 in his first year's trading. By 1846 the business was doing so well that he moved into larger premises in Redcliffe Street, where the Dickinson Robinson Group offices stand today. His younger brother Alfred joined him two years later and by 1850 they had diversified into account book making for the thriving business community.[38] In the same year they began hand lithography and six years later mechanised their processes for printing on paper bags and wrapping papers.[39] Lithographic artists drew the image directly on the stone or transferred it down from work produced on special paper. An advertisement of 1860 emphasised the importance of consumer packaging:

TO GROCERS AND TEA DEALERS.

At Robinsons the best and largest stocks of paper and paper bags, bill heads and circulars, tea and tobacco papers, may be procured at moderate prices, the latter articles printed in that clear and superior manner, to be obtained alone from steam power. Warehouse and lithographic printing office, at 2, Redcliffe Street, Bristol; steam press in Thomas Street.[40]

Another 1860 advertisement boasted that the firm possessed 11 litho presses and two litho machines, and stocked "200,000 reams of the most useful sizes in brown and shop paper and a larger assortment of paper bags than any other House in Great Britain". It went on to mention every conceivable variety of paper for the wrapping of consumer goods, and indicates that the firm was now beginning to dominate the market in the Bristol region.[41]

In 1860 Robinsons began to use machines for making paper bags, although hand made products continued to predominate for some time. By 1873 the rate of progress had quickened again, for an American visit had led Elisha to a machine which made paper bags at high speed. More important still, they incorporated a gusset, which was necessary for the mechanical filling of bags. Elisha paid £1,000 for the British rights, and although at first he was criticised for profligacy, he was soon praised for his far-sightedness. Wholesalers and retailers welcomed the arrival of cheap, machine-made bags, and demand soon outstripped the firm's capacity to supply them. Further properties were bought and rebuilt in Redcliffe Street and Victoria Street to house more machines. The company was not slow to exploit its golden opportunity.[42]

The harnessing of new technology to the new consumer market continued apace, and in the 1870s and 1880s the firm began to use colour lithography in the production of calendars and almanacks. Elisha hit upon the revolutionary idea of sending out large numbers of travellers to persuade even small firms that they should have colour calendars and almanacks overprinted with their name and address for distribution to customers. By 1876 the firm was offering a range of 25 different coloured subjects per year, printed by litho in 12 colours or more, and the more popular titles were selling 200,000 copies. By 1882 the firm was also turning out 685,000 almanacks annually, in full colour at an average cost of 6d. ($2\frac{1}{2}$p.) each.[43] These staple products made a fortune for the firm. Its prosperity and ambition were reflected in its decision in 1887 to build a spacious new factory at Bedminster, two miles distant from the city centre.

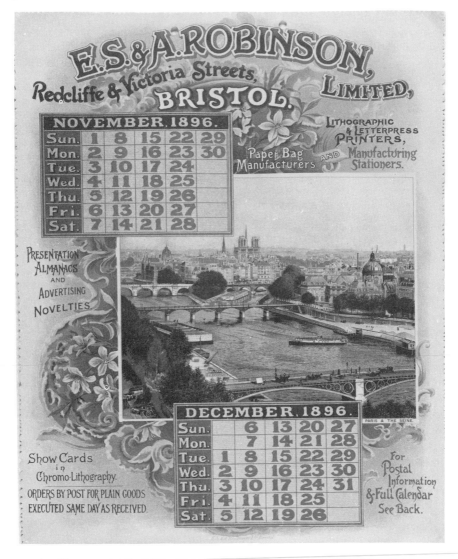

20. An illustrated calendar of 1896, listing the services offered by Robinsons. Colour printing of this type became a speciality of the firm.

In 1885 Elisha Robinson died, and his sons, Edward and Arthur, took control. When Elisha's younger brother Alfred retired in 1893, E.S. & A. Robinson became a limited company. The workforce had reached 800, including 30 full-time commercial travellers to sell the company's products.[44] In the next 12 years nine new factories were built, and in 1911 a new paper bag factory was built at Bedminster, with an initial capacity of 11 million bags a week. By then, the company had 2,500 employees, and factories covering ten and a half acres.[45] In the early twentieth century, the Robinsons pioneered the adoption of offset lithography to replace the direct process. An American 'Potter' machine was acquired in 1908, and the firm installed the first colour offset machines in Britain in 1913.[46]

Like Mardons, Robinsons was a 'paternalistic' employer. As early as 1889 its workers had been granted a week's fully paid holiday in addition to the customary Bank Holidays.[47] In 1908, the working week was reduced to 50 hours, commencing at 8 a.m. each day. This compared well with other firms: with newspaper publishers, a 51-hour week was normal, and many printing firms worked for 52 or 54 hours.[48] However, Elisha and his sons insisted on dealing directly with their workers, and refused to grant them collective bargaining rights. Mardons and Robinsons pursued aggressive 'free market' philosophies which made them antipathetic to trade unions. Attitudes gradually softened, but as late as 1899 Robinson's directors posted a public notice stating that while they did not forbid union membership, they would not recognise the right of trade unions to represent their workers. Recognition was not granted to the Bristol Typographical Society until 1910.[49]

Although the printing of packaging and wrapping materials was the sector which experienced the most rapid growth in Bristol, the period under review also saw important developments in more traditional sectors of the industry. Whereas the packaging sector did not really get under way until the 1870s and 1880s, the book and periodical market had been growing since the 1840s. Two Bristol letterpress firms, John Wright & Sons and J.W. Arrowsmith, rose to prominence. John Wright was born in Tewkesbury, and was brought to Bristol in 1817 at the age of 12. His father was in business at various times as a hosier, tallow chandler and soap maker. None of his ventures prospered, and in 1821 he left Bristol and went to live in Cheltenham. John, however, was apprenticed at the age of 16 to one of their Bristol neighbours, John Wansbrough, Printer and Bookbinder, of 142 Redcliffe Street. This was a rather superior form of apprenticeship – the Bristol Apprentice Books reveal that a very high premium of £130 was paid – which led to Wright's being elected as a Freeman of the City after completing the seven-year term of indenture.[50] By 1828, he was in business on his own account as a printer and bookseller in Bridge Street.[51] The source of his starting capital is unknown, but his family were Quakers, and he may have received assistance from the strong Quaker community in Bristol. Little is known of his early years in business, but there is some evidence that he was already beginning to gain a reputation for printing and publishing medical treatises and textbooks – which later become an important and profitable part of the firm's work. Bristol University's Medical Library possesses a copy of a pamphlet entitled *Plain Observations on the Management of Children during the First Month*, which was published by Wright in 1829. The quality of the work is indicative of a well-appointed firm. So too are other early publications, such as the *Friends' Monthly Magazine*, published under the imprint of Wright and Bagnall. (Wright was in partnership with Bagnall during the early 1830s. It is thought that he may have been a medical man.)[52] A good proportion of Wright's early publishing consisted of temperance tracts, some written by himself. He had witnessed the Bristol Riots of 1831, and been appalled by the scenes of mass drunkenness. He became a keen supporter of the Bristol and Clifton Temperance Society, to which he gave the proceeds of some of his pamphlets. Politically, he was a Whig, and supported electoral reform as a means of elevating the masses. In 1842 he and his family left the Society of Friends and joined the Church of England, but he never lost his evangelical zeal and the firm became known for the printing of nonconformist works, including large hymn sheets for public gatherings.[53]

Between 1828 and 1845, Wright took on 12 apprentices; like other enterprising printers, he used boy labour to expand his business. Indenturing apprentices could also serve as a means of obtaining capital. The parents of two of his apprentices paid premiums of £29, and payments of £10–15 were paid by charities in respect of three others. Other premiums, however, were much more modest, and Wright accepted three boys whose parents were unable to pay anything at all.[54] By the early 1840s, the volume of business was growing fast, and Wright left Bridge Street for Avon Street, near Temple Meads. Most of the firm's business was book printing, and in 1841 he acquired the first steam printing press in Bristol. Four years later he announced the purchase of the first perfecting press in the west of England.[55] Evidently Wright was now able to raise large amounts of capital. The source is obscure, but it is believed that he was financed by a fellow Quaker, Arthur Albright, who encouraged the development of the religious publishing side of the business.[56]

Wrights advertised itself as "Publishers of cheap books for Sunday Schools, gratuitous distribution and colonial missions. Merchants and societies supplied on advantageous terms for exportation".[57] Religious reformers were very conscious of the prevalence of illiteracy. The Bristol Statistical Society reported in 1841 that 2,535 children in the city between the ages of three and fourteen did not attend school, and of the 3,394 who did, nearly 1,500 attended only on Sundays.[58] The Sunday School movement was expanding fast at that time, and there was an urgent need for simple reading material of a more or less devotional nature. Wright helped to meet the demand, and also produced a wide range of tracts and other literature which reflected his own interests and beliefs. One which achieved a wide circulation was an anti-Catholic work entitled *A Few Plain Words about Popery by a Plain Man to Plain People*. The firm took another big step forward with the publication of *Wright's Steam Packet and Railway Monthly Timetable* (1853) and the takeover in 1870 of *Mathews' Bristol and Clifton Directory*. The directory soon grew to 1,000 pages, and was divided into residential, trade and professional sections. It was followed by similar directories for Weston-super-Mare, Clevedon and Cardiff, and this business proved very profitable. In 1904, it was sold to Kelly's, the national leader in directory publication, and the proceeds from the sale were used to develop the medical publishing side of the business, which had become the firm's main interest.

In the early 1880s control passed to John Wright's sons, Hartland and Reginald, and it was mainly to Hartland Wright that the firm owed its subsequent worldwide reputation as a medical publisher. He began to publish the highly successful *Medical Annual* in 1887, and in 1913 he launched the *British Journal of Surgery*.[59] Like his father, he made use of the most up-to-date machinery,[60] and like other leading Bristol businessmen he was hostile to trade unionism. The wages paid were good, but there were constant battles about the right of the Bristol Typographical Society to speak for its members, and about Hartland Wright's desire to introduce piecework. By 1914, the firm employed about 150 workers – large for this sector of the printing industry – but only 15 were members of the Typographical Society.[61] Hartland Wright showed little interest in diversification. The firm was a committed letterpress house. Wright took part in the establishment of the Bristol Association of Master Printers in 1905, and became its first chairman, representing the employers in their dealings with the union. Later generations of the family held important positions nationally in the employers' federation.[62]

The firm of J.W. Arrowsmith began in 1854 with the move to Bristol of a Worcester printer and publisher, Isaac Arrowsmith. He was 54 years of age when he entered into a partnership with a bookseller named Evans in Clare Street, and commenced publishing a penny timetable of steam packets and railway trains "For Bristol, Bath, the Western Counties, and South Wales".[63] The partnership did not last long, however, and Isaac Arrowsmith soon moved to new premises at 11 Quay Street, about a hundred yards from John Wright's offices. Arrowsmiths remained there for 97 years before moving to a site in Winterstoke Road, Ashton Gate, which it still occupies. When Isaac died in 1871 he was succeeded by his son, James. J.W. Arrowsmith was a man of great drive, vision and business acumen, who became a well-known and popular figure in Bristol. He took advantage of the demand for cheap literature which resulted from

the growth of railway travel, and in the late nineteenth century Arrowsmiths became the largest supplier to railway bookstalls in Britain. Some
of its more durable and successful publications were Jerome K. Jerome's
Three Men in a Boat (1889), George and Weedon Grossmith's *Diary of a
Nobody* (1892), and *The Prisoner of Zenda* (1894) and *Rupert of Hentzau*
(1898) by Anthony Hope. Surprisingly, though, it was a now long-
forgotten 'shilling shocker', *Called Back* by Hugh Conway, which proved
most successful of all; published in 1883, it sold 350,000 copies within five
years.[64] The rich profits from these best sellers provided the capital
needed to expand the business. With new and faster machines the firm
began to print books for other publishers.

Large profits also enabled Arrowsmiths to treat its employees generously. Wages were set at or above the rates which the Bristol Typographical Society was trying to establish as industry standards, and in
1894 the firm introduced a 48-hour week. This did not endear James
Arrowsmith to his fellow employers at a time when many printing offices
worked a 54-hour week, but it won him the respect and loyalty of his
workers.[65] James Arrowsmith was also much more favourably inclined
towards trade unionism than many of his contemporaries. He believed
that craft unions promoted the highest standard of craftsmanship and a
more reliable kind of worker. The firm was able to employ the cream of
local craftsman-printers, and thereby gained a reputation for high quality
work. Like Wrights, Arrowsmiths published detailed railway timetables
and from 1883 it moved into the medical field, publishing the *Bristol
Medico-Chirurgical Journal* and its successor, *the Medical Journal of the
South-West*. Educational works later became a major part of Arrowsmiths'
business. James Arrowsmith was an enlightened Liberal, and wished to
provide an alternative to the Technical College run by the Conservative-
dominated Society of Merchant Venturers. He became a leading figure
in the campaign for a University College, and joined other prominent
Liberals such as the Frys and the Wills who pressed the Liberal Government for a full-blown University.[66] When the new University buildings
were built, his work was commemorated by the Arrowsmith Tower on
Woodland Road, and a bronze plaque in the entrance hall reads:

By leave of Council the workpeople of James Williams Arrowsmith of 11 Quay
Street Bristol Printer and Publisher and others connected with him in his
business set up this tablet as a mark of their esteem and regard as well as to
record that on the 22nd day of September 1911 Council resolved in commemor-
ation of the distinguished services rendered by him to the University that this
tower should henceforth be known as the Arrowsmith Tower.

In view of J.W. Arrowsmith's work, it was natural enough that the firm
should become printers to the University College and the University,

producing a wide range of learned papers, journals and books. By the end of First World War it employed about 100 workers, most of whom were highly skilled in letterpress processes. When J.W. Arrowsmith died in 1913, his obituaries paid tribute to his civic and charitable work, and to the loyalty he displayed to the trade and to the people in his employ. The union officials also acknowledged:

> the readiness with which he adopted any measures that had been introduced by the Typographical Association for the benefit of its members, thereby setting an example that we trust may be closely followed, not only by his successors, but also by other employers of labour.[67]

It can be argued that he could afford to act in such a manner because he had the support of a very successful firm. Whatever the truth of that, the firm was successful because he had percipiently moved into the growth areas for letterpress printing: transport, higher education, and the new mass market for cheap literature. Moreover, profits had been ploughed back into the business, keeping it abreast of technological developments and increasing its efficiency. Perhaps even more importantly, he had encouraged the best craftsmen to work for him by paying them well and by viewing their trade union as an institution which raised standards, both of the men and of the industry in which they worked.

The business achievements of the Arrowsmiths, Wrights, Robinsons and Mardons were noteworthy by any reasonable standard. Their firms were at the forefront of the Bristol printing 'revolution' of the second half of the nineteenth and the early twentieth centuries. They took advantage of fresh market opportunities to build flourishing enterprises whilst many others suffered the ignominy of business failure.

Their success may be attributed to several factors. Firstly, they were responsive to the requirements of the market. Increased purchasing power expanded the market for printed matter of all kinds. Many semi-luxury items such as cigarettes, tobacco, chocolate and cocoa were produced in Bristol, and all created work for the printing and packaging industry; and with the creation of a fast and efficient national transport system opportunities arose to cater for a much expanded market. There was a spirited growth in the market for newspapers and books, both technical and for the general reader. Literacy was good for business, as was the appetite of professional men for scientific and commercial information. Those capable of discerning market trends and producing the right product had the advantage over their rivals. This is borne out by the evidence of this chapter: Mardon's cultivation of Charlton and later Wills; Robinson's assault on the grocery trade; Wright's directories, journals and religious books; and Arrowsmith's popular novels.

Secondly, these firms had a progressive attitude to new technologies and methods of working. Operating in expanding markets on a national scale meant volume production and longer runs. Machine printing became a necessity, as did manufacturing in factories rather than cramped workshops. Only businessmen with plenty of confidence and foresight were willing to take risks and raise the funds needed for the large investments dictated by new technologies and rising markets. A spectacular example of bold innovation is Elisha Robinson's acquisition in 1873, for what was then a princely sum, of exclusive access in Britain to highly efficient American paper bag making machinery. This gave the firm an advantage over its competitors, as did the swift adoption of many other machines and processes. Mardons displayed similar boldness in opening new factories and introducing new systems, such as the introduction of high-class colour printing and rotary lithography. Wrights and Arrowsmiths likewise kept abreast of the times.

Thirdly, and perhaps even more important than market or technological factors, was the sound leadership which the firms enjoyed. Many printers were as ambitious as the men who founded Mardons, Robinsons, Wrights and Arrowsmiths, but few managed to stay the course. The high incidence of business failure in printing clearly demonstrates the unsparing operation of market forces. Wrong decisions when times were difficult often proved fatal. To avoid disaster and rise above the pack required a steady stream of good decisions, and the firms examined in this chapter were well-blessed in this respect. James Mardon, Elisha Robinson, John Wright and James Arrowsmith built on sound foundations. Quality and attention to the needs of the customer counted, as did good relations between management and workers. In very different ways, they created a 'corporate style', establishing distinctive ways of doing things that persisted long after control had passed to later generations. It may further be observed, more speculatively, that the architects of the printing revolution in Bristol had much in common: they were Noncomformists, leaned towards Gladstonian liberalism, and were men who had moved to Bristol in search of fortune. The importance or otherwise of these characteristics remains to be explored elsewhere.[68]

The rise of large firms with forward-looking managers and directors progressively changed the character of the printing and packaging industry in Bristol. Before the second half of the nineteenth century, most printing houses were based in workshops, employing at most tens of people rather than hundreds. Such enterprises continued to exist right down to 1914, and indeed actually increased in number.[69] However, by the end of the period they had been eclipsed by a handful of large firms which employed the majority of workers in the industry and accounted for the greater part of capital investment and value of production.

Industrial dualism had become the order of the day. It remains so today.[70]

NOTES

1. I should like to acknowledge the ready help afforded by the staffs of the Bristol Record Office and the Bristol Central Reference Library. The valuable advice given by Dr June Hannam and Dr Geoffrey Channon of Bristol Polytechnic throughout my whole programme of research has been of inestimable value, and I have profited greatly from the assistance of the editors of this volume.

2. J. Latimer, *Annals of Bristol in the Seventeenth Century* (Bristol, 1900), p.471. D. Knott, 'Aspects of Research into English Provincial Printing', *Journal of the Printing Historical Society*, 9 (1974), pp.6-19.

3. H. Hart, *Charles, Earl Stanhope and the Oxford University Press* (1966), pp.398-404. Also see W.T. Berry, 'Printing and Related Trades', in C. Singer et al, eds. *A History of Technology, volume V: the Late Nineteenth Century* (Oxford, 1958), p.691.

4. On the growth of literacy, see R.K. Webb, *The British Working Class Reader, 1790-1834* (1955).

5. *Census of Population, England and Wales*, 1851, vol.2 pt.I, *Occupational Abstracts*, pp.ccxxii-ccxxvi, 11-4.

6. P.M. Hanover, *Printing in London* (1959), p.192. B.W.E. Alford, 'Government Expenditure and the Growth of the Printing Industry in the Nineteenth Century', *Economic History Review*, 2nd ser. XVII (1964), pp.96, 111-2. *Idem*, 'Business Enterprise and the Growth of the Commercial Letterpress Printing Industry, 1850-1914', *Business History*, VII (1965), p.1. G. Stedman Jones, *Outcast London* (Oxford, 1971), p.25.

7. *Census of Population, England and Wales*, 1911, vol.X pt.I, pp.xcii-xciii. Because of frequent changes in the classifications used, there are problems in making comparisons between data from different censuses. Nevertheless, the figures cited are clearly indicative of the general trend. Also see Alford, 'Government Expenditure', p.112.

8. Sketchley's *Bristol Directory* of 1775 was the earliest, and *Mathews' Bristol and Clifton Directory* was published annually from 1789 to 1873. The latter was taken over by John Wright & Sons in 1870, and was published as *Wright's Bristol Directory* until 1910, although it had been sold to Kelly's in 1904.

9. *Census of Population, England and Wales*, 1911, vol.X pt.I, pp.xcii-xciii. Also see *Census of Production*, 1907, pp.596, 615-6.

10. *Wright's Bristol Directory*, 1888, p.423.

11. See, for example, C. Challenger and E. Everard, *Illustrated Guide to Bristol* (Bristol, 1911). Bristol Tramways & Carriage Co., *Pictorial Bristol: and Handbook of the Bristol Tramways & Carriage Co.* (Bristol, 1897). Bristol Record Office (hereafter B.R.O.), George White Papers, 35810/3, Bristol Stock Exchange Monthly Lists, 1876-1903. Everard was exploiting family connections; he was the brother-in-law of Sir George White (q.v.).

12. *Newspaper Press Directory*, 1861, 1901.

13. M. Plant, *The English Book Trade* (1939), pp.445-9. Alford, 'Business Enterprise', p.4.

14. On technological change, see C. Clair, *A History of Printing in Britain* (1965), pp.205-91. W.T. Berry, 'Printing and Related Trades', pp.683-716. *Encyclopaedia Britannica* (11th edn. 1911), vol.XXII, pp.350-9.

15. B.R.O., 34463/2-7, Bristol Typographical Association, Minute Books, 1869-1907. Also see A.E. Musson, *The Typographical Association* (1954).

16. *Census of Population, England and Wales*, 1861, vol.II, p.xlvi; 1881, vol.III, p.xiii. B.R.O., 34463/6, Bristol Typographical Association, Minutes, 4 April 1891. 34463/84, Report of Typographical Association Delegate Conference, Manchester, 21 Sept. 1891.

17. D. Bateman, 'An Examination of the Organisation and Policy of the Bristol Typographical Society in the Second Half of the Nineteenth Century' (unpublished M.A. thesis, Bristol Polytechnic, 1985), pp.60–71.

18. *Mathews' Bristol Directory*, 1867. *Bristol Times & Mirror, Bristol's Many Industries* (Bristol, 1922/3), unpaginated. Partridge & Love Ltd., *A Brief Record of Over 50 Years of Progress* (Bristol, 1951), p.3.

19. Advertisements in the *British Printer*, 1889–92.

20. B. Jones, *Co-operative Production* (1894), p.572.

21. Harris had been in business as a copper plate engraver since 1823. H. Mardon, *Landmarks in the History of a Bristol Firm* (Bristol, 1918), p.15. *Mathews' Bristol Directory*, 1829, p.231.

22. Mardon, *Landmarks*, pp.7, 9.

23. Mardon, Son & Hall, 'Further Landmarks in the History of a Bristol Firm', *Caxtonian*, III (1957), p.109. *Mathews' Bristol Directory*, 1826, p.251.

24. Mardon, *Landmarks*, p.15.

25. *Caxtonian*, I (1949), p.102.

26. R.D. Savage, *Histories of Bristol Firms*, vol.I (Bristol, 1959), p.12.

27. Reproduced in Mardon, *Landmarks*, p.32.

28. Anon, 'A Century of packaging', *Tobacco*, Aug. 1949, p.71.

29. B.W.E. Alford, *W.D. & H.O. Wills and the Development of the U.K. Tobacco Industry, 1786–1965* (1973), pp.148, 169.

30. Mardon, *Landmarks*, p.44.

31. Alford, *Wills*, p.232.

32. Ibid., pp.169–70.

33. The Collotype process was invented in France, and used photosensitive materials to prepare the plates.

34. Mardon, *Landmarks*, pp.55–60.

35. Obituary of Heber Mardon, *Bristol Times & Mirror*, 16 June 1930.

36. Alford, *Wills*, pp.256–262.

37. Savage, *Histories of Bristol Firms*, vol.I, p.13. *The Times*, 30 May 1925. Obituary of Heber Mardon, *Bristol Times & Mirror*, 16 June 1930.

38. *Bristol Times & Mirror, Work in Bristol* (Bristol, 1883), p.62. Anon, *The Ports of the Bristol Channel: Progress, Commerce* (1893), p.189. Anon, *The Dickinson Robinson Group Ltd.* (Bristol, 1977), p.5.

39. Savage, *Histories of Bristol Firms*, vol.II (Bristol, 1960), p.2.

40. Anon, *The Dickinson Robinson Group Ltd.* (Bristol, 1977), p.6.

41. *Mathews' Bristol Directory*, 1860. Every line of the advertisement was set in a different typeface – which by modern standards would imply both versatility and bad taste.

42. Anon, *Ports of the Bristol Channel*, p.189. *Bristol Times & Mirror, Bristol's Many Industries* (Bristol, 1922/3), unpaginated. Savage, *Histories of Bristol Firms*, vol.II, p.2

43. Anon, *Ports of the Bristol Channel*, pp.189–90.

44. The total number employed in 1883 had been 668. *Bristol Times & Mirror, Work in Bristol*, p.67.

45. B. Darwin, *Robinsons of Bristol, 1844–1944* (Bristol, 1945), p.33.

46. *Bristol Times & Mirror, Bristol's Many Industries*.

47. Anon, *Ports of the Bristol Channel*, p.190.

48. *E.S & A. Robinson Annual Review*, 1909, p.22. B.R.O., 34463/53, Bristol Typographical Society, Rules, 1900, p.12.

49. *Typographical Circular*, Dec. 1899, p.9. B.R.O., 34463/1, Bristol Typographical Society, Annual Report, 1911, pp.4–6.

50. J. Wright & Sons Ltd., *A Centenary Souvenir, 1825–1925* (Bristol, 1925), pp.25–6. *Idem,*

150 *Years of Printing and Publishing* (Bristol, 1975), p.7. B.R.O., 04356/19, City of Bristol Apprentice Books, 31 Jan. 1821.

51. *Mathews' Bristol Directory*, 1828.

52. Wright, *150 Years*, p.7.

53. Wright, *Centenary Souvenir*, p.27. *Idem, 125 Years of Printing and Publishing, 1825–1950* (Bristol, 1951), p.4.

54. B.R.O., 04356/19–20, City of Bristol Apprentice Books, 1820–49.

55. *Mathews' Bristol Directory*, 1841 and 1845, end paper advertisements.

56. Albright was a successful chemist and druggist who was later to become famous for his work on the manufacture of phosphorus. Wright, *150 Years*, p.11.

57. Ibid.

58. E. Bromby and A Biggs, *Statistics of Education in Bristol* (Bristol, 1844), p.10.

59. Wright, *150 Years*, p.15.

60. An early Monotype machine was acquired in 1901. The first Monotype machine in Britain had been installed by Wyman & Sons of London in 1898. E. Howe, *The British Federation of Master Printers, 1900–1950* (1950), p.10. Also see Anon, 'A Printing House Centenary', *Monotype Recorder* XXV (1926), unpaginated.

61. B.R.O., 34463/15, Bristol Typographical Society, Fees Books and Membership Lists.

62. M. Sessions, *The Federation of Master Printers: How it Began* (York, 1950), pp.104–7. Howe, *Master Printers*, p.13.

63. Anon, *Arrowsmith, 1854–1954* (Bristol, 1955), p.2.

64. Anon, *Ports of the Bristol Channel*, p.209.

65. The society tried to persuade other firms to follow suit, but none complied. B.R.O., 34463/6, Bristol Typographical Society, Committee Minutes, 7 April 1894; Annual Report, 1894. 34463/7, Minutes of Meeting of Bristol Master Printers, 26 Nov. 1901.

66. B. Cottle and J.W. Sherborne, *The Life of a University* (Bristol, 1951), p.15.

67. B.R.O., 34463/67, Bristol Typographical Society, Minutes of Special Meeting, 20 Jan. 1913.

68. The author is currently preparing a thesis on printing in Bristol at Bristol Polytechnic.

69. There were 7–8,000 printing firms in Britain by 1911, compared with perhaps 1,200 sixty years earlier. Alford, 'Business Enterprise', p.10. W.T. Berry, 'Printing and Related Trades', p.708.

70 A review of statistical sources relating to concentration in the printing industry is to be found in W.D. McClelland, *Reviews of U.K. Statistical Sources, volume XXII: Printing and Publishing* (Oxford, 1987).

Locomotive Building in Bristol in the Age of Steam, 1837–1958

PETER DAVIS, CHARLES HARVEY AND JON PRESS

When most people think of locomotive building, whether in the great age of steam or in the more prosaic years of diesels, they tend to think of high speed locomotives like the Great Western Railway's *King George V*, or the *Flying Scotsman* and *Mallard* of the London & North Eastern Railway, or British Railways' *Deltics*, which were built for main line passenger traffic. Little thought is given to the thousands of workaday locomotives that were built for goods or commuter traffic, for private industrial railways or to meet the needs of overseas customers in India, Africa, Latin America and elsewhere. It is, however, with these markets that Bristol was mainly concerned, though large engines for main line passenger and goods work were in fact produced in some numbers from 1837 until the later 1870s. Thereafter, as competition in this sector grew fiercer, Bristol firms specialised in small shunting engines for industrial and commercial use. These locomotives remained Bristol's staple product until the very end of the age of steam. When the last engine left Pecketts' Atlas Works in 1958, approximately 4,200 locomotives of all types had been built in the city. Local firms may never have risen to the heights of their giant northern competitors, clustered in Glasgow, Manchester, Leeds and Newcastle, yet for more than a century Bristol ranked as a centre of international importance in locomotive engineering (see Table 1).

The first man to build locomotives in Bristol was Henry Asprey Stothert (1797–1860), the son of George Stothert, ironmonger and foundry owner of Bath. Henry was a practically trained engineer of enquiring disposition, fascinated by steam technology. His technical authority was soon recognised, and in 1827 he was placed in charge of the family iron foundry.[1] The business prospered under Henry's management, encouraging him to think more ambitiously. In 1837, having patented a number of mechanical inventions, he formed a partnership with his brother John and the Bristol maritime engineers, Robert Bruce and George Lander, announcing the purchase of "land in the neighbourhood of Bristol for the establishment of a manufactory of locomotive engines as well as iron machinery of all descriptions".[2]

Table 1. *Output of Leading British Independent Steam Locomotive Manufacturers,*
1825–1961*

Firm	Location of Main Works	Period of Building	Number of Locomotives
North British Loco. Co. (1)	Glasgow	1903–1958	11,318
Beyer, Peacock & Co.	Manchester	1855–1958	7,911
Neilson, Reid & Co.	Glasgow	1838–1903	6,354
Vulcan Foundry Co.	Newton-le-Willows	1833–1956	6,210
Kitson & Co.	Leeds	1838–1938	5,405
Sharp, Stewart & Co.	Glasgow	1833–1903	5,088
Dübs & Co.	Glasgow	1865–1903	4,485
R. Stephenson & Co.	Newcastle	1825–1937	4,190
Hawthorn, Leslie & Co.	Newcastle	1831–1937	2,783
Hudswell Clarke & Co.	Leeds	1861–1960	2,600
Hunslet Engine Co.	Leeds	1865–1964	2,235
Andrew Barclay & Co.	Kilmarnock	1859–1962	2,210
Peckett & Sons (2)	**Bristol**	**1864–1961**	**2,166**
Avonside Engine Co. (3)	**Bristol**	**1841–1935**	**2,078**
Kerr, Stuart & Co.	Stoke	1892–1930	2,020
W.G. Bagnall	Stafford	1876–1960	1,660
Nasmyth, Wilson & Co.	Manchester	1839–1938	1,650
Armstrong, Whitworth & Co.	Newcastle	1919–1937	1,439
R. Stephenson & Hawthorn (4)	Newcastle	1937–1959	1,000

Sources: J.W. Lowe, *British Steam Locomotive Builders* (Cambridge, 1975). J.O. Slezak, *The Locomotive Works of Europe* (Vienna, 1962). The figures given by Lowe and Slezak vary somewhat, and not consistently in the same direction. The rule applied here has been to take the highest figure of the two. Thus the figures *generally* represent upper-bound estimates, and probably exaggerate total production to a small degree. Only in the case of W.G. Bagnall was the lesser of the two figures taken, as the figure of 3,000 given by Slezak does not conform with what is generally known about the company.
*   Firms which manufactured 1,000 locomotives or more.
(1)   Formed in 1903 through the amalgamation of Nielson, Reid & Co., Sharp, Stewart & Co. and Dübs & Co.
(2)   Includes locomotives built by Fox, Walker & Co. between 1864 and 1878.
(3)   This is the total for the two firms named the Avonside Engine Co., and the predecessors of the first firm of that name.
(4)   Formed in 1937 through the merger of R. Stephenson & Co. and Hawthorn, Leslie & Co.

Henry Stothert had every reason to be thrilled by the prospects for his new business venture. The whole nation was in the grip of railway fever, and Bristol was no exception. The Great Western Railway (G.W.R.) had received the Royal Assent for its line between Bristol and London in 1835, and local businessmen had promoted the Bristol & Exeter Railway in the same year.[3] Construction of both lines was pressing ahead under the supervision of Brunel. Stothert, as an engineer respected throughout the south west, must have believed that his firm could win substantial orders. His personal knowledge of steam gave the fledgling concern an advantage that other local firms simply could not match.

The site chosen for the new engine works at Cuckold's Pill (later known as Avonside Wharf) was ideal for a heavy engineering establishment. On one side was the terminus of the Bristol & Gloucestershire Railway's line, which brought coal to the city, and on the other was the Floating Harbour. Access to a major port and an important network of inland waterways was extremely valuable, for high-quality pig iron and other essential materials were not produced locally. Furthermore, finished engines could be dismantled and crated for shipment by coaster or barge – which had some significance before the completion of a national rail network. Other advantages of the site were less tangible but no less important. The Avonside works was close to the terminus of the G.W.R. and the headquarters of the Bristol & Exeter, with which a substantial trade was expected. In the early days of steam, close collaboration between the engineers employed by railway operators and engine contractors was necessary, and proximity therefore was a decided business advantage. So too was the availability in Bristol of skilled engineering and metal workers trained in the shipyards and metal factories which had flourished since medieval times.

The foresight and ambition which Henry Stothert showed in building the Avonside Ironworks was rewarded by early success. The first locomotives built by the new firm were two *Firefly* class locomotives, *Arrow* and *Dart*, to designs by Daniel Gooch, the locomotive superintendent of the G.W.R. They were delivered in time for the opening of the railway's Bristol to Bath section on 31 August 1840.[4] More locomotives for the G.W.R. followed, including eight *Sun* class engines delivered between July 1841 and January 1842. There were also many locomotives for the G.W.R.'s 'satellite' broad gauge lines, the Bristol & Exeter and the South Devon Railway, which remained Avonside customers until the mid-1870s. Of the 28 locomotives operated by the Bristol & Exeter in 1849, 18 came from Avonside. Like other firms in the industry, Stotherts was the beneficiary of a market expanding at a tremendous pace. At the height of the second railway boom in 1847, 256,509 men, about 4 per cent of the entire male workforce, were engaged upon building Britain's railway network. By 1850, Britain had 6,084 route-miles of railway, operated by 180 independent companies.[5]

Yet, favourable as market conditions were, survival in the locomotive building industry was never assured. Badly managed concerns were frequently forced into liquidation. Most of the 245 firms known to have tried their hand at engine building failed, and vanished without leaving much of a trace.[6] The main problem was that whilst orders might be won at low prices, it was very much more difficult to make a profit and deliver at a quality acceptable to customers. The firms that survived were those with the shrewdness not to become overstretched, that could cost their products accurately, and had sufficient flexibility to weather periods when the engine trade was depressed. Stotherts displayed these characteristics. The firm quickly won a reputation for quality work at low prices. In December 1841, for example, Brunel informed one client that the best work was done by Fenton, Murray & Co. and Stephensons, both of which charged high prices, but that "Stothert of Bristol have made excellent engines for us and at low prices".[7] That the firm won the approval of an engineer as talented as Brunel speaks highly of Stothert's management.

The sudden growth of a national rail network brought in its wake a host of business problems as well as opportunities. Management and engineering skills were in short supply, and if the Avonside venture failed to attract leadership of the right calibre, it could not expect to compete with firms like Robert Stephenson & Co. of Newcastle which were already capable of producing locomotives in quantity. Henry Stothert was astute enough to recognise this, and in 1839 he took the bold step of engaging a brilliant young man, aged just 25, as his managing partner. Edward Slaughter (1814–91) had been educated in London and Paris before serving for five years as an engineering apprentice to John Seaward of the Canal Ironworks, Limehouse. In 1837 he joined the G.W.R as an assistant engineer, and, two years later, having won the admiration of colleagues, found himself in charge of the Avonside Ironworks; the original partnership was dissolved, and the name was changed to Stothert, Slaughter & Co. Slaughter was the leading figure in the Bristol locomotive industry for the next 30 years, developing Avonside as an innovative, high quality builder for the home and overseas markets. His grip on the business was consolidated in 1852 when Henry Stothert retired. The founder of the Avonside Ironworks was replaced by his son, John Lum Stothert (1829–1891), who had served an apprenticeship at the Avonside Ironworks "under Mr Slaughter's strict but admirable rule".[8]

All the signs are that, until Stothert's retirement, he and Slaughter made a strong management team. Slaughter designed engines and other machines, ran the works and scheduled production. Stothert was general manager, financier and salesman. They used family, personal and business connections to the full in securing credit and winning orders. In 1846, for instance, the firm signed a contract for 14 large passenger engines at £2,300 each with the London, Brighton & South Coast Railway, whose resident engineer, Robert Jacomb-Hood, was married to Henry Stothert's sister Catherine.[9] Other work of various kinds was secured at times when the demand for locomotives was slack. One of the first jobs the firm undertook was to supply Brunel-designed point capstans and switches for the Great Western.[10] Steam pumping equipment and marine engines were also built, and in 1844 two iron screw steamers were built to Slaughter's design. Other iron steamships were constructed at Avonside Wharf before the firm of Stothert & Fripp was set up to take over this side of the business.[11]

The need for sidelines and factory fillers faded as Stothert's position in the market became more secure. In 1856, a new partner, the engineer Henry Grüning, was persuaded to join the firm, and its name was changed to Slaughter, Grüning & Co. Between 1841 and 1856, an average of 22 engines a year had been turned out by the Avonside Ironworks.[12] Over the period, the average price for an Avonside locomotive appears to have been £2,300-£2,400. In 1846, two tender engines cost the London, Brighton & South Coast Railway £2,300 apiece,[13] and in the same year Slaughter quoted the Bristol & Gloucester £2,500 apiece for two broad gauge engines.[14] The available evidence suggests that Avonside was able to tender at lower prices than more prestigious rivals. In 1858, for example, the Norwegian Government Railways received a quotation from Robert Stephenson & Co. of £1,160 for a small tank engine, while Stothert, Grüning & Co. quoted £1,020 for a six-wheeled goods engine and £920 for a four-wheeled tank engine. In the following year, Beyer Peacock quoted £1,420 per locomotive, which also compared unfavourably with the Bristol company's prices.[15]

It is, of course, difficult to make direct comparisons between the prices charged by different makers. Specifications varied considerably, despite the fact that there were just a few basic types of locomotives. There were express passenger engines, generally with a single pair of large driving wheels; freight engines, typically with an 0-6-0 wheel arrangement; and small shunters, generally 0-6-0s or 0-4-0s, often tank engines rather than with tenders to facilitate running in either direction. In all types, leading or trailing bogies might be added for increased stability, or to spread the weight of the locomotive over more axles.[16] Nevertheless, whilst there may have been few basic engine types, a lack of standardisation in design became a feature of the British locomotive industry. This was partly due to the great numbers of railway companies, which favoured many different operating standards. Variations in maximum axle weights and loading gauges naturally resulted. Besides this, there were many locomotive superintendents and chief mechanical engineers, often of an autocratic bent, and each with his own ideas about maximising the performance of locomotives.[17]

The Avonside Ironworks apparently responded to this market situation by specialising from an early date in a limited range of standard locomotives suitable for the traffic demands of most English railways. Whilst there was as yet little standardisation of individual parts, fittings and decoration, over three-quarters of the locomotives built at the Avonside Ironworks between 1837 and 1864 were of three basic types: a 2-2-2 express passenger engine; a 2-4-0 mixed traffic type; and an 0-6-0 goods engine. Moreover, as time went by, the firm increasingly came to specialise in goods locomotives. Most of its passenger engines were built in its early years, and as early as 1861 Slaughter wrote to Daniel Gooch stating that he preferred to make goods engines, as he now had "improved facilities for this class". Partly in consequence of this initiative, the G.W.R. placed an order in 1862 for 12 0-6-0 standard gauge goods locomotives at £2,880 each, despite seven competing bids ranging from £2,500 to £3,140 per locomotive.[18]

However persuasive an advocate for his firm Slaughter may have been, he had little power to resist the dictates of market forces. Locomotive building was a highly competitive business. Contractors were under constant pressure to reduce prices, and more and more customers began to insist upon penalties for late delivery. This is demonstrated by Stothert, Slaughter & Co.'s dealings with the Monmouthshire Railway & Canal Co. (M.R. & C. Co.). In January 1853, Stothert received an inquiry concerning the supply of six tank engines. After a good deal of haggling, a price of £2,200 per engine was agreed, leaving Slaughter to complain that much better prices had recently been obtained for his company's products. A few months later, however, when a second batch of six engines was wanted, he was obliged to reduce the price to £2,160, whilst agreeing to a penalty clause of £10 a month for each engine not delivered within three months.[19] Unfortunately, Stotherts experienced a string of difficulties. Increased iron and copper prices during the course of 1853 added £120 to the cost of each locomotive, and materials were in short supply. Skilled men were hard to find and could only be hired at high rates of pay. In June 1854, when the locomotives were six months overdue, Slaughter wrote to the company secretary of the M.R. & C. Co., George Harrison, apologising for the delay, and appealing to him to ignore the penalty clause, which would have cost the Avonside Ironworks upwards of £400. He argued that the fault lay with his suppliers, stating that "although I had represented to the various parties my engagement with your Company the times have been such that no Locomotive House in the Kingdom has been able to keep faith with the Public".[20] Extended guarantees were offered on the locomotives, which were finally delivered by September 1854, and eventually the railway agreed to waive the penalty.[21]

It is evident that the Bristol firm, like other locomotive manufacturers, felt the pressure of heightened competition which followed the downturn of railway building in Britain after the commercial panic of 1847.[22] Profit margins were eroded, and increasingly railway companies demanded guarantees from contractors. A contract of 1864, between Slaughter, Grüning & Co. and the South Eastern Railway reveals that payment on each of 10 tank engines, priced at £2,160 each, was not made until they had run 3,000 miles to the buyer's complete satisfaction.[23] An even more worrying development for independent locomotive builders, however, was that railway companies started to build engines on their own account. Steam engines of all types needed regular repair and maintenance, and railway operators had to set up workshop and servicing facilities to keep their locomotives running. Once these operators could handle the heaviest repairs and rebuilds, it was but a short step to building new locomotives. After the opening of Swindon works in 1843, for example, Gooch and Brunel convinced their directors that they could build better locomotives there than could be obtained from outside suppliers.[24] This tendency was encouraged by the fact that the private firms charged fairly high prices in the early years when demand was buoyant, and the quality was not always of the best. Other railways followed suit. The Bristol & Exeter Railway opened its own works in 1852 at Bath Road, Bristol, and its first new locomotive was completed in 1859. A total of 35 locomotives was built at Bath Road before amalgamation with the G.W.R. in 1876 led to closure.

The internalisation of locomotive construction by the large railway companies was in general a gradual process. The biggest railway in Britain, the London & North Western, built all its own locomotives at Crewe after 1862, whereas the Great Western, which absorbed a great many 'satellite' lines in south Wales and the West Country, continued to buy some locomotives from contractors until the 1870s. In 1865, for example, the Avonside Ironworks supplied 26 *Hawthorn* class passenger locomotives to Gooch's designs. The general practice on the Midland, the Bristol & Exeter, the Great Northern and many other railways was for the company workshop to undertake rebuilds and the construction of replacement engines (which were charged to revenue account), while additions to stock (charged to capital account) were ordered from contractors.[25]

The independent manufacturers, therefore, came increasingly to rely upon orders from smaller railway companies like the Taff Vale Railway or the East Lancashire Railway, which were not in a position to build

21. *Melling*, one of a batch of 26 passenger locomotives built by the Avonside Engine Co. in 1865 for the Great Western Railway.

their own engines. Once established, a relationship between a small railway company and a manufacturer often became self-supporting: there were obvious advantages to operators in going to the same supplier when a further batch was required, if only to achieve a degree of standardisation and avoid the task of retraining engine crews and maintenance staff. Unfortunately for the independents, this market too was gradually eroded by the progressive amalgamation of railway companies into ever larger concerns. Although frowned upon by parliament and closely regulated by government,[26] there was a seemingly irresistable logic to the emergence of powerful regional and national operators like the Midland Railway, the London & North Western, and the North Eastern. By 1870, the 15 largest railway companies accounted for 83 per cent of the gross traffic revenue of Britain's railways, and 80 per cent of the paid-up capital. Only a handful of the smallest railways in Britain remained tied to the private locomotive builders.[27]

As the manufacturers lost ground at home, they turned their attention to overseas markets. The second half of the nineteenth century saw the promotion and construction of railways throughout the world, and large numbers of these were British-built, British-owned and British-managed. British firms were active in Europe and the United States, besides dominating railway construction in Africa, Canada and Australia. In addition, Britain was "almost solely responsible for the South American rail network, and for initial developments in Asia and the Middle East as well". India was particularly important. The East India Railway was opened in 1857, the first major section of what was to become the largest rail network in Asia.[28]

Slaughter and his partners took full advantage of export opportunities to develop the business. The Avonside factory first built for export in 1847, supplying six engines to the Maria Antonia Railway in Tuscany, for which Brunel acted as consulting engineer, at a cost of £2,300 each.[29] But it was in the 1850s that the export trade really assumed importance, as Table 2 indicates. India was the prime target for Slaughter's drive for sales, and his efforts were well rewarded. The pioneering East India Railway took 93 Avonside engines in a series of major purchases between 1857 and 1880. Other Indian concerns followed suit, notably the Great Indian Peninsular Railway, the Indian State Railways and the Oudh & Rohilkund Railway. Responsiveness to the needs of customers was vital in winning orders abroad. Gauge, traffic volume, and climatic and topographic variations all demanded a sensitivity to particular and often unique requirements. Judging from the Avonside order book, Edward Slaughter was a master of the game. The firm was content to supply whatever gauge or type of engine was required, even if a special engineering effort was demanded. The result was a stream of orders from distant parts of the world: India, New Zealand, Australia, South Africa, Chile, Brazil, Mexico, Canada, Spain and Portugal being foremost among them.

Successful as the export sales drive was, home sales remained important; in the 1850s and 1860s more than half of the engines produced by the Avonside Ironworks were still destined for British railways. After a quiescent period in the 1850s, railway investment in Britain recovered fast, culminating in the third 'railway mania' of the mid-1860s. The Bristol company was profitable and expanding, ranking as one of the biggest locomotive builders in Britain at this time. If the works numbers are to be believed, over 550 locomotives were built between 1841 and 1864, averaging 24 a year.[30] The Avonside Ironworks was an important supplier of 7 ft. broad gauge locomotives. Of the 661 locomotives known to have been produced for broad gauge lines in Britain, the Swindon works built 240, Avonside 141, and the third largest supplier, Rothwell & Co. of Bolton, just 39.[31] Of course, the decision of the Gauge Commission in favour of standard gauge meant that this was not a platform for long-term growth, but for a while at least it remained a profitable corner of the market.

In 1864, with a growing order book, the partners decided that the concern should be reconstituted as a limited company to obtain access to additional capital. The Avonside Engine Co. Ltd. was incorporated on

Table 2. *Large Customers of the Avonside Engine Co., 1837–82* *

Customer	Country	Period of Supply	Number Supplied	Gauge**
East Indian Railway	India	1857–80	93	B
New Zealand Govt. Railway	New Zealand	1874–80	79	N
South Devon Railway	Britain	1859–75	59	B
Great Western Railway	Britain	1841–65	42	B/S
Great Indian Peninsular Railway	India	1866–67	40	B
Indian State Railways	India	1870–81	40	N
Bristol & Exeter Railway	Britain	1849–73	32	B
Great Northern Railway	Britain	1865–67	32	S
Great Eastern Railway	Britain	1864–73	25	S
Oudh & Rohilkund Railway	India	1870–76	25	B
Northern Railway	Spain	1861–65	22	B
Cape Government Railways	South Africa	1875–78	22	N
Chilean State Railways	Chile	1865–76	21	S
South Eastern Railway	Britain	1864–76	20	S
London, Brighton & South Coast Railway	Britain	1848–68	19	S
Finland Government Railways	Finland	1864–74	18	?
Grey & Bruce	Canada	1870–72	18	?

Source: P.R.O., ZSPC 11/446B, Avonside Engine Co., Building List 1841–1935, compiled by W.E. Hayward.

* The details given in this list are intended as indicative rather than definitive. Customer details are not known for scores of Avonside locomotives, and thus some large customers may have been excluded and others understated. The definition of large customers as those purchasing 18 or more locomotives is purely arbitrary.

** B = broad gauge, S = standard gauge, N = narrow gauge.

11 April 1864, with an authorised capital of £150,000 in shares of £10. Initially, the paid-up capital was £70,000 (10,000 shares, on which £7 was paid), but over the next five years the remaining 5,000 shares were issued, increasing the paid-up capital to £105,000 in 1870. There were six ordinary directors, including Henry Grüning and the soap manufacturer Christopher Thomas. William Bevan became chairman of the new company. Edward Slaughter was appointed managing director at an annual salary of £1,200, plus bonuses. He was the final authority both in engineering matters and general management. A young protégé, Alfred Sacré, was appointed works manager, at a salary (£1,000 per annum in 1872) which reflected the directors' high regard for his technical ability.[32]

The performance of the Avonside Engine Co. in its early years was very encouraging. In 1865, a £13,580 profit was earned on a turnover of about £100,000, and a 15 per cent dividend declared. In the following year, when a similar dividend was paid, the chairman emphasised that the key to the company's success was the great experience and ability of Edward Slaughter, and he received a bonus of £500 in addition to his salary of £1,200. At this time, the company employed 8–900 people, and total production rose from 29 locomotives in 1864 to 66 in 1867.[33]

Favourable market conditions in the 1860s were the result not only of the third railway boom, but also of a vigorous industrial demand for cheap, robust shunting engines. Civil engineering projects, mining, docks and heavy industry all required small locomotives of this type. The 1860s in consequence saw the formation of several firms specialising in industrial locomotives built to standard designs, requiring less capital investment than main line engines. This market was especially cultivated by engine builders in Leeds and Bristol. In Leeds, Manning, Wardle & Co. was organised in 1859, Hudswell Clarke & Co. in 1861 and the Hunslet Engine Co. in 1864.[34] In Bristol, the first specialist manufacturer of industrial locomotives was the firm of Fox, Walker & Co., established in 1864.

Francis William Fox was born in 1841 at Kingsbridge, South Devon, into a Quaker banking family. In 1857, he entered his father's Kingsbridge branch to learn the principles of banking and accounts. Little is known of his early career, which presumably was not much to his liking, for two years later he went to Bristol to be trained as an engineer. He was articled to his cousin, Francis Fox, a protégé of Brunel who had become engineer-in-chief to the Bristol & Exeter Railway in 1854. Fox was an able pupil, and in 1863 he was trusted to survey the projected Taunton & Chard Railway. A year later, he joined forces with Edwin Walker (1840–1917), another engineer with a Quaker background. Walker had been apprenticed to Hewitson & Kitson, engineers, of Leeds, and later worked in India. He moved to Bristol in the early 1860s, where he met Fox at the Society of Friends' Meeting. The two men surveyed the opportunities before them and decided to enter industrial locomotive building on their own account: Fox would provide the bulk of the capital injected into the partnership, whilst Walker brought with him a thorough understanding of the market and formidable engineering knowledge.[35]

The site chosen for their new works was to the east of Bristol, at Deep Pit Road, St George, adjacent to a branch from the Midland Railway's main line. From 1864 to 1878 the Atlas Engineering Works, as the factory was called, turned out large numbers of small tank engines. Many of these were built to standardised designs for industrial undertakings and civil engineering projects in the United Kingdom, but about 40 per cent of production was exported, mainly to supply narrow gauge railways in Europe, Scandinavia and South America. The most numerous type was an o-6-o tank engine, of which 121 are known to have been built, and the firm also produced 35 smaller o-4-o engines.[36]

With the formation of Fox, Walker & Co. and the prosperity of Avonside, locomotive building in Bristol had come of age. In the mid-1860s, things could hardly have looked better, with the simultaneous blossoming of the overseas and industrial engine markets. Yet, for anyone who cared to think carefully about the future, there was also cause for anxiety. The internalisation of engine construction by the leading British railway companies has already been mentioned, and, more immediately, it must have been apparent that the third British railway boom, like those its predecessors, could not last forever. And so it proved. The collapse in home railway construction which followed the Overend Gurney banking crisis of 1866 soon took its toll on Avonside. The total number of locomotives built for the home market, which had peaked at 36 in 1866, averaged just six a year between 1867 and 1871. No dividend was paid between 1868 and 1871, and a loss of £3,181 was made in 1868.[37]

Avonside weathered the storm. The home market gradually picked up, peaking again in 1874/5. Between 1873 and 1876, when dividends gradually rose from $2\frac{1}{2}$ per cent to 6 per cent, 18 engines a year were supplied to British customers. In 1876, a profit of £9,088 was made on a record turnover of £140,000.[38] A full order book, however, was not achieved without cost. In the late 1860s and early 1870s over two-thirds of the locomotives built at the Avonside Ironworks were destined for railways overseas, and, as their home sales fell, the independent locomotive manufacturers competed ever more fiercely for overseas sales. This battle for sales was all the keener for the fact that in the 1870s foreign markets were themselves in a period of contraction (Table 3). Orders could only be won at prices which left little or no room for profit.

One effect of cut-throat competition was to heighten the growing tension between the independent locomotive builders and the railway companies with manufacturing capacity. Ever since the G.W.R. erected its Swindon works in 1843, a debate initiated by Gooch and Brunel had raged as to the economics of engine building. The independent manufacturers refused to accept the oft-repeated claim of the operating companies that their workshops could build better-quality locomotives more cheaply than contractors. They argued that competition obliged the independent sector to keep down prices and keep abreast of technical developments, whereas the railway companies, without the stimulus of competition, only managed to make a profit on locomotive building through 'creative' accounting practices. Essentially, they claimed, operating revenues were used to subsidise construction.

The anger of the private sector against what was regarded as 'unfair' competition was raised to fever pitch in the early 1870s, when the London & North Western Railway actually began selling to those British railways

Table 3. *Overseas Sales by British Locomotive Manufacturers, 1855–1939*[*]

Date	Average Annual Value of Sales £[**]
1855-1859	968,461
1860-1864	940,624
1865-1869	922,906
1870-1874	793,235
1875-1879	713,138
1880-1884	1,084,868
1885-1889	1,186,009
1890-1894	1,208,343
1895-1899	1,168,496
1900-1904	1,997,276
1905-1909	2,764,764
1910-1914	2,554,997
1915-1919	1,651,888
1920-1924	4,748,861
1925-1929	2,932,987
1930-1934	1,360,441
1935-1939	1,218,812

Source: Parliamentary Papers, *Annual Statement of the Trade of the U.K. with Foreign Countries and British Possessions* (1855-1899). *Statistical Abstract of the United Kingdom* (1900-39). *Railway Gazette*, 10 March 1944, p.235.
* Railway locomotives and parts thereof. Road locomotives, agricultural and stationary engines are excluded.
** Current prices.

without manufacturing capacity; thus posing a new threat to an already troubled industry. Between 1871 and 1874, the L.N.W.R.'s Crewe works supplied 101 locomotives to the Lancashire & Yorkshire Railway, at a total cost of £225,000. Direct competition on this scale could not be ignored by the independent manufacturers. A meeting was held at Leeds in April 1875 at which 13 companies, employing a total of 9,600 workers, were represented, including Avonside and Fox Walker. It was agreed to "take steps for the protection of Engineers and others against the competition of Railway Companies as manufacturers for sale". The Locomotive Manufacturers' Association was formed, and included on its Committee

of Managment were J.L. Stothert and Alfred Sacré, then the general
manager of the Yorkshire Engine Co. Legal action followed, and in March
1876 an injunction was served upon the L.N.W.R. preventing it from
manufacturing engines or rolling stock for sale or hire to other railway
companies. This had the effect of preserving the export market and what
remained of the home market for the private manufacturers.[39]

Collective action to prevent railway workshop encroachment was one
way of limiting the effects of industrial depression. Each company was
also obliged to think hard about business policy. In Bristol, concentration
on the more lucrative sectors of the market requiring specialist expertise
was judged to be the best way of securing the future. One such sector
was narrow gauge locomotives, for which demand was increasing, following the successful application of steam power to the Festiniog Railway in
the 1860s. Avonside and Fox Walker both offered narrow gauge versions
of their engines, and in 1871 Avonside began to build articulated locomotives to the designs of Robert Fairlie.[40] On many railways, particularly in
Latin America, South Africa and Australasia, track was lightly laid, and
steep gradients and tight curves created severe problems. Operators
began to demand larger and more powerful locomotives which could
haul heavy loads without exceeding weight restrictions. The Fairlie
locomotive was the most successful of the solutions adopted in the 1870s.
In essence, it was two locomotives joined back to back, mounted on two
0-4-0 or 0-6-0 bogies to which steam was supplied through flexible steam
pipes. It met the requirements of high power combined with a low axle
weight, and could negotiate tight curves. Fairlies were very successful
and some remained in service for many years, although later superseded
by other articulated locomotives, notably the Mallett and Beyer Garratt.[41]
Other manufacturers, including Neilson & Co. of Glasgow and the Vulcan
Foundry, produced a few engines under licence from Fairlie, but Avonside was by far the most important builder. Records survive of some
hundred or so double Fairlies built in Bristol, together with 30 of a later
single-ended design. Some degree of standardisation was achieved, Avonside's largest design being supplied to lines in Mexico, Peru, Chile and
Russia. In all, 52 examples of this design were constructed in the early
1870s. Smaller designs were supplied to narrow gauge railways in
Venezuela, Brazil, Uruguay, Burma, South Africa, Western Australia,
and, nearer home, to the 2 ft. Festiniog Railway in north Wales.

Similarly, Fox Walker, having concentrated upon industrial locomotives in its early years, began to exploit the new opportunities in narrow
gauge, and also developed a locomotive for use on severe gradients. The
'Steep Gradient Locomotive' patented by Henry Handyside in 1873 used
a locking system which gripped a centre rail, and was able to climb
gradients as severe as 1 in 10, albeit at very slow speeds. Fox and Walker
were the principal shareholders in the Handyside Steep Gradient Co.

Ltd., registered in 1875. Prototypes were tested in the construction of Avonmouth Docks and on the High Peak Railway in Derbyshire, but, although there was a good deal of interest in the Handyside locomotive, various rack systems were generally preferred, and it was never marketed successfully.[42]

Despite the emergence of new opportunities and the upturn in the market of 1874–5 the 1870s were a difficult time for locomotive builders. Production costs increased fast early in the decade. Coal roughly doubled in price between 1870 and 1874, and in January 1873 Avonside agreed to adopt the 'nine hours system', reducing the working week from $58\frac{1}{2}$ to 54 hours. Soon afterwards, a six per cent wage increase was agreed, and this had a significant impact upon manufacturing costs.[43] Towards the end of the 1870s, the locomotive building industry entered a serious recession. There was little demand from home railways, and British locomotive exports fell to £556,429 in 1879, the lowest level for more than 30 years.[44] In Glasgow, Dübs & Co. was forced to lay off 300 workers, and production at Beyer Peacock's was cut by 40 per cent in 1878–9.[45] Avonside suffered more than most; there were few large orders, and a very competitive market forced prices sharply downward after 1876. Locomotives were built on slender profit margins, or even at a loss, in the knowledge that returns were generally better on spares and repeat orders. Loss leading was common practice in the locomotive industry, but obviously could not be sustained for any length of time. In 1877, Avonside made a loss of £11,500 on a turnover of £95,000. J.L. Stothert, who had replaced Bevan as chairman, insisted that the firm was sound, but many shareholders expressed their dissatisfaction with the management.[46] Early in 1878, Avonside's directors announced that wages would be cut by $12\frac{1}{2}$ per cent:

> To the Workmen of the Avonside Engine Co. Ltd., Bristol. The Directors very earnestly call your attention to the depression which exists in the locomotive trade generally and more particularly in these works. The result of last year's trading has been most unsatisfactory; instead of earning money the concern has lost heavily ... These works cannot be kept open simply for the benefit of the workpeople at a loss to the shareholders. The Directors have therefore, after a most careful consideration of the subject, concluded to reduce wages and piece work prices all round, and that this reduction shall be $12\frac{1}{2}$ per cent.[47]

Only 50 men out of the total workforce of about 800 were prepared to accept the reduction in wages. The result was a lockout which lasted for several months. Severe production delays resulted, and one customer, the Dungarvan & Lismore Railway in Ireland, refused to accept delivery of engines which were delivered late. Avonside's trading difficulties were thus exacerbated, with losses of £7,160 in 1878 and £5,000 in the following year.[48]

At the same time as Avonside was struggling for survival, Fox Walker too entered a period of crisis. For a while at least, it appeared that locomotive building in the city would cease for good. In the 1870s, Fox Walker's industrial locomotives were selling in quantity, and the firm developed a substantial business with overseas railways, exhibiting at the Vienna Exhibition of 1873 and the Paris Exhibition of 1878. Engines were supplied to the Dutch government for the Java railways, and were also built for the Argentine and various French and Italian lines. In all, the firm built 424 engines between 1864 and 1878, with a workforce of about 200.[49] However, the firm's attempted diversification was not a success. The Steep Gradient Locomotive did not generate profits, and investment in steam tram technology likewise proved a failure, largely due to the restrictive regulations imposed by the Board of Trade.[50] Trading losses began to accumulate, and in December 1878 it was decided that the partnership should be wound up. There is little evidence to determine whether the concern had been badly managed, although Walker's technical adventurousness was perhaps not best suited to the times, and after Fox's death it was suggested that "his special qualities, which included to a marked degree impulsiveness and optimism, were not in all ways best fitted to ensure commercial success". Moreover, his attention had already turned to the philanthropic and public works which occupied his later life.[51]

Management failings certainly compounded Avonside's difficulties. The key figure in the firm's development, Edward Slaughter, had retired in 1874, due to ill health and increasing deafness. He was without question a talented engineer and successful businessman. His network of influential business associates extended through the railway industry. As a member of both the Institute of Civil Engineers and the Institute of Mechanical Engineers, he was well aware of the importance of visiting railway companies to gain experience of the operating conditions which they faced. In 1854, for example, he made two trips to Holland and Belgium before tendering for locomotives for the Antwerp & Rotterdam Railway. He later visited the United States to learn about locomotive design, at a time when most English engineers believed they had little to learn from American practice.[52] After his retirement, and the simultaneous departure of Alfred Sacré, the company began to lose direction. Although John Lum Stothert was highly respected in the engineering world, he was not Slaughter's equal in technical or business matters. Possibly, too, he devoted a disproportionate part of his time to other interests, having become managing partner in the general engineering firm of Stothert & Pitt. The day-to-day management of Avonside was left in the hands of John C. Wilson, until his replacement in September 1879 by John J. Platts. Both men were pilloried for the company's failings.

A statement published in the *Bristol Times & Mirror* in June 1881 spitefully denounced Platts for the inaccurate and inefficient manner in which estimates had been made, and the losses that had resulted.[53] Orders had been obtained, but at prices that condemned the business to failure and liquidation.

In May 1879, the impending crisis was precipitated by the failure of the West of England & South Wales District Bank. Its liquidators applied to Avonside for repayment of an overdraft of £11,738, and the board decided that the company should be wound up "on account of a want of orders at prices which would yield a reasonable rate of return".[54] However, J.L. Stothert, William Bevan and Henry Grüning subsequently proposed a reconstitution, arguing that "it would be unwise to dissolve the company when ... there are decided indications of a revival in trade", and this was approved at a meeting of the shareholders in September 1879. As from 11 January 1880 each £10 share (of which £9 was paid), was exchanged for one fully-paid £5 share, the issued capital thus being written down to £75,000, of which £59,253 had been received by 23 March 1880. The debenture holders, who included the shipbuilder Charles Hill, agreed that they would not enforce payment until the end of 1886, provided there were no defaults on payment of interest.[55]

Following its reconstitution, Avonside won several large orders. The Fairlie Engine Co. ordered 17 locomotives for Burma and another seven for New Zealand. Even more substantial orders were placed by the East India Railway for 25 0-6-0s, and by the Indian States Railway for 20 2-6-0s. In June 1881, the company brought in Edwin Walker as general manager to spearhead a drive for efficiency.[56] But it was too late in the day. Debts had continued to mount since 1879, and on the petition of creditors a liquidation order was issued against the company on 8 July 1881. The liquidator, Henry Spain, applied for powers to continue running the factory until the outstanding orders had been completed, and this was approved by the High Court and the debenture holders. In all, there were 149 creditors, of which the largest was the Bristol & West of England Bank. Another major creditor was Christopher Thomas, who had made strenuous efforts to save the company. He was the largest shareholder, and had made loans totalling £4,000. Many of the company's suppliers were hurt by the failure, although creditors eventually received 15s. in the pound by way of compensation. The Avonside Engine Co. was offered at auction on 29 March 1882. The auctioneers valued the concern at £81,000, and stated rather optimistically that it was capable of producing 75 locomotives a year, but there were no takers.[57]

It was unfortunate for Fox Walker and the first Avonside company that they failed to survive the recession of the late 1870s, for the next decade saw a great improvement in the market. The private manufacturers were practically excluded from the U.K. market, except at times of unusually high demand, but overseas markets were generally strong in the 1880s and 1890s (Table 3), and there was a big improvement in trade after 1896. Between 1875 and 1885 the biggest customers were the Indian railway companies, but thereafter the export market was sustained by orders from railways in South America and South Africa.[58]

The recovery of the market in the 1880s proved to be the salvation of locomotive building in Bristol. Industrial traditions die hard, and following the collapse of Fox Walker and Avonside moves were soon afoot to reconstruct the local industry. The existence of plant, skilled labour and management were powerful attractions to enterprising businessmen who were sensitive to market developments and ready to expand their interests. The Atlas Engineering Works of Fox Walker was taken over by Thomas Peckett (1834–91), a Birmingham engineer, in 1881. He was joined by his four sons, George, John, Thomas Jnr and Richard, and the business continued as a family concern until the final days of steam. In this case, the rescue operation was a complete one, for Peckett & Sons continued the Fox Walker policy of building industrial locomotives to

22. The office of Thomas Peckett & Sons in 1905. The large drawing over the fireplace is of Fox, Walker & Co.'s Steep Gradient Locomotive.

standard designs. Such good fortune did not favour Avonside, and most of the works was lost to other uses. However, Edwin Walker had decided to set up in business on his own account, and in August 1882 he acquired Avonside's machinery, patterns and spares for around £20,000.[59] He also leased part of the site from its new owner, John Mardon. Cannily, and amidst some controversy, he decided to trade under the name of the Avonside Engine Co. Walker only had the capacity to operate on a modest scale, but he hoped that loyal Avonside customers would be drawn to him in the belief that they were dealing with the same concern that had satisfied their needs in the past. In his advertising literature he even carried the pretence so far as declaring that the firm had been "established in 1837". This led to trouble with the official liquidator, and it was not until 4 February 1887 that the Avonside Engine Co. Ltd. was finally liquidated, the Court of Chancery ordering that "the Books and Papers of the said Company be destroyed by being torn up and cut in such a manner as to be incapable of being used as a means of information".[60] Walker, however, survived, building just two locomotives in the 1880s and accepting a wide variety of general engineering work to keep the business going.

It was the market for small, robust engines for industrial and narrow gauge lines that attracted both Peckett and Walker's Avonside Engine Co. The industrial market expanded rapidly towards the end of the nineteenth century, and there was hardly a gas works, dock, mine, quarry or large factory anywhere in Britain that did not run at least one small steam locomotive. Bristol became nationally famous for small engines, and the name Peckett in particular was almost synonymous with the industrial tank engine throughout the first half of the twentieth century. Avonside produced very similar engines – both firms used designs developed from Fox Walker's industrial engines of the 1860s and 1870s – but showed more interest in the overseas market. More than half of Avonside's output of new locomotives went to foreign railways, mostly narrow gauge.

The collapse of the later 1870s left the Bristol industry much reduced in size. In the early 1890s, Avonside produced an average of four locomotives a year, and Peckett eleven. But from 1897 they grew vigorously, and in the 1900s they were producing 16 and 25 engines a year respectively. Growth was made possible by the expansion and modernisation of production. Pecketts' Atlas Works acquired a large new machine shop and the boiler shop was rebuilt. Buildings occupied five acres of a 13 acre site. In 1905, a publicity brochure claimed that the works was "what an up-to-date engineering establishment should be … The engines are manufactured by skilled workmen in buildings especially designed and erected to obtain the maximum amount of light and convenience for the proper execution of the work. The machinery installed is of the most modern type, and additions to the plant are constantly being made."[61] Avonside, meanwhile, had outgrown its premises in central Bristol. In 1904 Edwin Walker went into partnership with Ronald Murray, who provided the capital to build a superb four acre factory at Fishponds on the outskirts of the city. Extensive re-tooling took place. There was a machine shop, a smithy, a boiler shop, a pattern shop, an erecting shop and a paint shop. 300 people were employed at the new works at times of peak demand.[62]

By the early years of the twentieth century, the steam locomotive had achieved technological maturity. According to Kirby, standardisation had become "a meaningful concept in the engineering sense due to the innovation of improved machine tools, new methods of workshop organisation, and developments in metallurgy. Handicraft methods of production were by then as obsolete as the use of wrought iron as a construction material".[63] Pecketts certainly stressed the value of standardisation and

23. The erecting and paint shop at the Avonside Engine Co.'s new Fishponds works in 1905. On the right is a saddle tank for the Burry Port & Gwendraeth Railway. Behind it are two railmotor power units for the Great Northern Railway. Repair work was very important, and several locomotives are stripped to the frames for heavy repairs.

specialisation in its promotional literature: "Specialisation and standardisation, the advantage of which has only lately been recognised, have been for years a distinctive feature of our productions. Being built to standard designs and templates, worn parts can always be replaced at the shortest notice by duplicates which will fit with utmost accuracy." A small range of tank engines was available from stock, and was advertised as "eminently suitable for branch lines, mineral lines, steel and iron works, gas works, tinplate works, collieries and all kinds of contractors' work".[64]

Avonside's advertisements, in contrast, emphasised the firm's "large and varied experience". Although small tank engines made up the bulk of production, the catalogues also illustrated a range of medium-sized tender engines. It was noted that "we have always made a speciality of narrow gauge engines" which were suitable for "light railways, sugar plantations, tea estates, timber, mining, nitrate works, and other Colonial work where practically only native labour is obtainable, roads are bad and the engine must be subjected to hard use". The South American market was particularly important, so catalogues were printed in Spanish as well as English. Avonside emphasised the combination of build quality and constructional simplicity; all materials were "of the highest class throughout, and of British Standard Specification quality", and "the general design of all our engines is made as simple as possible without diminishing efficiency, and every part is made for as easy access as possible for overhauling and repairs".[65]

24. A Peckett advertisement of 1921 (the locomotive is of an earlier vintage).

In many ways – small engines, simple construction, standardisation, quality materials – Pecketts and Avonside evolved along very similar lines, to the extent that 'Bristol' had a single meaning in the minds of railway engineers around the world. At the same time, however, in the minds of directors, management and employees, the two firms were like chalk and cheese. Thomas Peckett & Sons was a sound, straightforward concern with a strong sense of its own identity, content with its niche in the market. Avonside was none of these things. It may in the prosaic world of reality have been largely confined to the production of 'lesser' engines, but there was a constant urge to diversify, to build 'bigger and better', more novel and technically innovative locomotives. Avonside's publicity material bulged with pictures and drawings of large, exotic engines – few of which were ever built for customers. It was one of the first companies to develop steam railcars for commuter traffic or lightly-used branch lines. The firm had high hopes of bulk orders from the south east and other densely populated areas, and indeed several railcars were built for the Taff Vale and the Great Northern Railways. In practice, however, the claim that railcars could reduce costs per train by between 30 per cent and 70 per cent and were an attractive alternative to electric trains could not be sustained. Like many other bright ideas to emerge from Avonside, railcars did not herald the commercial breakthrough that was so actively sought. More successful was the development of an internal combustion engine in 1913, an 0-4-0 shunter with a Parsons petrol/paraffin engine. This was the prototype for large numbers of 2 ft. 6 in. gauge engines which were built for the War Department during the First World War.[66] The essential character of Avonside was not much changed even after Edwin Walker's retirement in 1905. He was replaced by others of similar disposition: his son, Edwin Webster Walker, took over as senior partner until his early death in 1909. The firm then became a private limited company, controlled by Ronald Murray and the hotelier Vivian Gordon. Pecketts' character likewise changed little; its conversion to a limited company just before the outbreak of war in 1914 having no practical significance.

Unlike many locomotive builders, the Bristol firms did not abandon locomotive work in favour of armaments production with the advent of war in 1914. Both were kept busy with repair work and new orders. Pecketts' output of new engines fell somewhat to an average of 17 a year in 1914–8, compared with 24 in 1900–13, but Avonside did rather better, averaging 31 locomotives a year during the war years, compared with 17 in the earlier period. In addition to its internal combustion engines for the War Department, Avonside built 0-4-0 tank engines for the 1 ft. 6 in. railways which the Allies built behind the Western Front, and did a substantial amount of work for the Admiralty and for dock railways.[67]

The Port of Bristol Authority, which had 30 miles of track at Avonmouth and Portishead, bought all its engines from Pecketts and Avonside. The war saw an increase in the volume of shipping using the port, and to handle this six new engines were purchased from Avonside and one from Pecketts.

The end of the war in 1918 brought boom conditions to the locomotive industry. Inadequate maintenance and replacement programmes were the norm during the war, and railway operators were now anxious to secure new engines and rolling stock. Export markets, particularly in India and South Africa, likewise generated many orders. Moreover, the market remained buoyant for much longer than was the case in other industries. Although the peak of 1920 was not maintained, orders remained at a high level throughout the rest of the decade.[68] This was partly the result of the 1921 Railways Act, which grouped Britain's 100 or so railway companies into four new companies, the London, Midland & Scottish, the London & North Eastern, the Southern and the Great Western. The new companies absorbed large numbers of locomotives from their constituent railways, many of which were in a poor state of repair, and needed rebuilding or replacement. Avonside received a large amount of repair work from the G.W.R., and, in 1926, when the Swindon works was especially busy, the firm received an order for six powerful shunting engines for work in Swansea Docks.[69] This was just one of many orders received from port managers; the Mersey Docks & Harbour Board, Devonport Dockyard, and the Calcutta Port Commissioners were other large customers.

The fact that the 1920s were prosperous years for Bristol's locomotive builders makes the industrial collapse which followed all the more tragic. Financial figures often disguise rather than illuminate reality, but this is not the case here. Sales by independent manufacturers to the four British railway companies totalled £402,289 in 1929, plummeting to £10,323 in 1932, and over the same period the value of exports dived from £3,275,153 to £366,875.[70] Distress spread throughout the industry, and before 1936 there was little sign of recovery. Even the giant North British Locomotive Co. built only 13 engines in 1931, and seven in 1936.[71] Inevitably, some firms were driven to the wall, and the Avonside Engine Co. was one of them.[72] It went into liquidation on 29 November 1934, and the Fishponds works closed after the final order was delivered early in 1935. In July 1935 Avonside's goodwill, drawings, patterns and spares were acquired by the Hunslet Engine Co. of Leeds.

Thomas Peckett & Sons managed to weather the industrial storm of the early 1930s. The firm was financially sound, and it reaped the reward of its past conservatism. The labour force had to be slashed, but the works was kept 'alive' on repair work and a handful of small orders accepted

25. One of the last large locomotives manufactured by the Avonside Engine Co.: a metre gauge 2–8–0, built for a Bolivian railway in 1930.

on the basis of little or no profit.[73] Recovery began in the later 1930s, but only after the outbreak of the Second World War in 1939 did the Atlas Locomotive Works regain its old sense of vitality. Several large orders were placed by the Royal Ordnance Department, and production remained fairly steady until 1945 at around 12 locomotives a year.

The Allied victory did not bring prosperity to Pecketts. The recovery of locomotive building was hampered by shortages of materials and machine tools.[74] Only five new locomotives left the works in 1947, and part of the factory was engaged in stripping salvaged aeroplane engines. What was worse, however, was the threat facing the firm from diesel power. Many industrial users were changing to more cost effective diesel units. Firms like the Hunslet Engine Co. had anticipated this development, acquiring experience in internal combustion locomotives as early as the 1920s, but Pecketts, dogged by technological blindness, made no investment in the new technology until the 1950s. The firm had passed into the hands of George Peckett's sons, Frank, Wilfred and Roy. Frank and Wilfred Peckett, like most British locomotive builders, were reluctant to build diesels. Only after Frank Peckett's retirement in 1954 and British Railways' pronouncement of the end of steam traction in 1955 did the company make a belated attempt to switch to the new technology, too late to make an impact upon the market. Its first diesel mechanical locomotive, with a 200 h.p. Crossley engine, was not completed until 1956, and only five were made before the works closed. The last steam engine to be manufactured in Bristol was an o-6-o tank engine for a sugar estate in Mozambique, which left the works in June 1958.[75]

The closure of the Atlas Works marked the end of a long chapter in the industrial history of Bristol: a chapter full of interest, and not a little romance. It must have been gratifying for men like Henry Stothert, Edward Slaughter, Francis Fox, Edwin Walker and Thomas Peckett – entrepreneurs of some vision – to think of their locomotives in operation in all parts of the world, working in all kinds of environments. These were the machines that helped unify nations, develop 'frontier' economies, create a new social consciousness and promote the economic wellbeing of entire continents through the stimulation of trade and financial flows. This, of course, is a rosy view of the 'railway revolution', long since deflated by students of the historical accounting school of thought. But more than a grain of truth remains. Locomotive building was not an easy business. Under constant competitive pressure, British firms turned out engines of remarkable inventiveness and durability at prices that hundreds, if not thousands, of railways could afford. Bristol locomotives – main line and industrial – were numbered amongst the best, and examples still survive in the hands of museums and preservation societies.[76] How delightful it is to see these old workhorses cared for, given new life, preserved to stimulate the imaginations of generations of young people yet to come.

NOTES

1. H. Torrens, *The Evolution of a Family Firm: Stothert & Pitt of Bath* (Bath, 1978), pp.8, 23–4.

2. *Bath and Cheltenham Gazette*, 24 Jan. 1837.

3. G. Channon, *Bristol and the Promotion of the Great Western Railway*, 1835 (Bristol, 1985). R.A. Buchanan and N. Cossons, *The Industrial Archaeology of the Bristol Region* (Newton Abbot, 1969), pp.207–11. E.T. MacDermot and C.R. Clinker, *History of the Great Western Railway* (Revised edn. 1964), vol.I, pp.54–8, 64–6, 104–5.

4. *Bath and Cheltenham Gazette*, 1 Sept. 1840.

5. T.R. Gourvish, *Railways and the British Economy, 1830–1914* (1980), p.20. Idem, 'Railway Enterprise', in R.A. Church, ed. *The Dynamics of Victorian Enterprise: Problems and Perspectives to 1870* (1980), p.126.

6. Public Record Office (hereafter P.R.O.), ZLIB29/765, J.O. Slezak, *The Locomotive Works of Europe* (Vienna, 1962).

7. University of Bristol Archives, Brunel Papers, Letter Book 2b, p.237, I.K. Brunel to Maudsley, Sons & Field, London, 20 Dec. 1841.

8. *Proceedings of the Institute of Civil Engineers*, 105 (1891), pp.316–7, obituary of Edward Slaughter. H. Torrens, 'John Lum Stothert', in D.J. Jeremy, *Dictionary of Business Biography*, vol.V (1986), pp.367–8.

9. Torrens, *Stothert & Pitt*, p.37.

10. MacDermot and Clinker, *History of the Great Western Railway*, vol.I, p.310. Torrens, *Stothert & Pitt*, p.36.

11. Torrens, *Stothert & Pitt*, pp.43–7. G. Farr, *Bristol Shipbuilding in the Nineteenth Century* (Bristol, 1971), p.22. *Clifton Chronicle*, 30 August 1854.

12. P.R.O., ZSPC11/446B, Avonside Engine Co., Building List, 1840–1935.

13. Torrens, *Stothert & Pitt*, p.46.

14. P.R.O., RAIL74/3.

15. North Western Museum of Science and Technology, Manchester, Beyer Peacock Archives, correspondence between C.F. Beyer and C.Pihl, Norwegian State Railways, quoted in R.L. Hills and D. Patrick, *Beyer Peacock: Locomotive Builders to the World* (Glossop, Derbyshire, 1982), pp.49–50.

16. The standard Whyte locomotive classification is used throughout this chapter. Three figures are used to describe a conventional engine; the first digit refers to the leading wheels, the second to the number of powered wheels, and the third to any trailing wheels. An o-6-o, for example, would only have driving wheels (three on each side).

17. On the factors making for a proliferation of designs, see M.W. Kirby, 'Product Proliferation in the British Locomotive Building Industry, 1850–1914: an Engineer's Paradise?', *Business History*, XXX (1988), pp.287–305.

18. P.R.O., RAIL1008/3, E. Slaughter to D. Gooch, 4 Sept. 1861.

19. P.R.O., RAIL500/33, E. Slaughter to G. Harrison, M.R. & C. Co., 17 Jan. 1853; 15 Sept. 1853.

20. Ibid., 30 June 1854.

21. P.R.O., RAIL500/34, E. Slaughter to G. Harrison, 14 Sept. 1854.

22. On the railway investment boom and the panic, see D. Morier Evans, *The Commercial Crisis of 1847* (1849). H. Boot, *The Commercial Crisis of 1847* (Hull, 1984), pp.3–24.

23. P.R.O., RAIL635/225, Slaughter, Grüning & Co. to South Eastern Railway, 9 Feb. Similarly, see RAIL635/228, Avonside Engine Co. to South Eastern Railway, 5 April 1876.

24. G. Channon, 'Sir Daniel Gooch', in Jeremy, ed. *Dictionary of Business Biography*, vol.II (1984), p.599. Also see MacDermot and Clinker, *History of the Great Western Railway*, vol.I, pp.74–7.

25. See, for example, J.B. Radford, *Derby Works and Midland Locomotives* (1971), p.37. F.A.S. Brown, *Great Northern Locomotive Engineers, volume I, 1846–81* (1966), p.138.

26. Gourvish, *Railways and the British Economy*, p.49.

27. Ibid., p.10. Kirby, 'Product Proliferation'.

28. L.E. Davis and R. Huttenback, *Mammon and the Pursuit of Empire: the Political Economy of British Imperialism* (Cambridge, 1986), pp.56, 97.

29. Bristol University Archives, Brunel Papers, Letter Book 5, pp.293, 297.

30. P.R.O., ZSPC11/446B, Avonside Engine Co., Building List, 1840–1935. The evidence suggests that this is a maximum figure; some numbers were undoubtedly allocated to orders which were subsequently cancelled.

31. Railway Correspondence and Travel Society, *Locomotives of the Great Western Railway, volume 2: Broad Gauge* (1952).

32. P.R.O., BT31 928/1161C, Avonside Engine Co., Articles of Association; Annual Returns, 1865–70.

33. *Clifton Chronicle*, 28 March 1866. *Bristol Observer*, 23–4 March 1866. P.R.O., ZSPC11/446B, Avonside Engine Co., Building List, 1840–1935.

34. See L.T.C. Rolt, *A Hunslet Hundred* (Newton Abbot, 1964), pp.11–32.

35. J. Marshall, *A Biographical Dictionary of Railway Engineers* (Newton Abbot, 1978), p.88. J.E.G. De Montmorency, *Francis William Fox: a Biography* (Oxford, 1923), p.7. Society of Friends Library, London, *Digest of Births*, 1840. *Annual Monitor*, 105 (1917), p.160; 107–8 (1919–20), pp.114–5, obituary of Francis William Fox.

36. Stephenson Locomotive Society, Locomotive Building List no.2377.

37. P.R.O., ZSPC11/446B, Avonside Engine Co., Building List, 1840–1935. *Bristol Observer*, 20 March 1869.

38. Skinner, *Stock Exchange Year-Book* (1876), p.218. *Bristol Observer*, 23 March 1872; 29 March 1873. *Clifton Chronicle*, 21 March 1877.

39. North Western Museum of Science and Technology, Beyer Peacock Archives, Locomotive Manufacturers' Association, Minutes. B. Reed, *Crewe Locomotive Works and its Men* (Newton Abbot, 1982), p.84. O.S. Nock, *The Premier Line: the Story of London & North Western Locomotives* (1952), p.58. *Railway Gazette*, 10 March 1944, p.235.

40. *Clifton Chronicle*, 4 Oct. 1871.

41. 'Fairlie's Improvements in Locomotive Engines', *Engineer*, 2 Dec. 1864, pp.341–2. R.A.S. Abbot, *The Fairlie Locomotive*, (Newton Abbot, 1970).

42. T.J. Lodge, 'Handyside Locomotives', *Industrial Railway Record*, 53 (1974), pp.205–19. *Clifton Chronicle*, 29 March 1876.

43. *Bristol Observer*, 29 March 1873.

44. P.P., *Annual Statement of the Trade of the U.K. with Foreign Countries and British Possessions*, 1879.

45. Hills and Patrick, *Beyer Peacock*, p.283.

46. *Clifton Chronicle*, 10 April 1878.

47. *Bristol Observer*, 12 Jan. 1878.

48. *Clifton Chronicle*, 16/23 Jan. 1878; 9 April 1879; 21 Jan. 1880. P.R.O., ZSPC 11/446B.

49. De Montmorency, *Francis William Fox*, p.7. Stephenson Locomotive Society, Locomotive Building List no.2377.

50. C. Klapper, *The Golden Age of Tramways* (1961), pp.47–9.

51. De Montmorency, *Francis William Fox*, p.7. *Annual Monitor*, 107–8 (1919–20), pp.117–21.

52. *Clifton Chronicle*, 24 March 1875. *Proceedings of the Institute of Civil Engineers*, 105 (1891), p.317.

53. *Bristol Times & Mirror*, 28 June 1881. Also see Clifton Chronicle, 24 March 1875; 8 Oct. 1879.

54. *Clifton Chronicle*, 28 May 1879. *Bristol Observer*, 24 May 1879. P.R.O., BT31 928/1161C, extraordinary general meeting, 28 May 1879.

55. *Clifton Chronicle*, 28 May, 1879; 24 Sept. 1879. Skinner, *Stock Exchange Year-Book* (1881), p.280. P.R.O., BT31 928/1161C, extraordinary general meeting, 3 Oct. 1879.

56. *Clifton Chronicle*, 21 Jan. 1880. *Bristol Observer*, 28 June 1881.

57. P.R.O., C26 40, Papers relating to the Liquidation of the Avonside Engine Co. Ltd. *Clifton Chronicle*, 14 Jan. 1880; 29 June 1881. *Bristol Observer*, 1 April 1882.

58. Skinner, *Stock Exchange Year-Book*, 1876 and 1913. Saul, 'Engineering Industry', pp.199–200.

59. *Clifton Chronicle*, 5 April 1882; 9 August 1882. P.R.O., C26 40.

60. P.R.O., J15 1829. BT31 928/1161C, Liquidation Order, 4 Feb. 1887.

61. P.R.O., ZLIB29/272, Thomas Peckett & Sons, Catalogue, c.1905.

62. *Proceedings of the Institute of Mechanical Engineers*, July 1908, pp.725, 752. P.R.O., ZSPC11/446B, Avonside Engine Co., Notes by W.E. Hayward.

63. Kirby, 'Product Proliferation'.

64. P.R.O., ZLIB29/272, Thomas Peckett & Sons, Catalogues, c.1905–14.

65. P.R.O., ZLIB29/272 and Bristol Central Reference Library, Avonside Engine Co., Catalogues, c.1909–22.

66. Rolt, *Hunslet Hundred*, p.113.

67. Ibid.

68. R.H. Campbell, 'The North British Locomotive Co. between the Wars', *Business History*, XX (1978), p.205. Rolt, *Hunslet Hundred*, p.76.

69. *Locomotive Magazine*, Sept. 1906.

70. P.R.O., RAIL424/5, Papers of Sir James Milne, 'Home Railways Manufacturing Policy', Oct. 1943. *Railway Gazette*, 10 March 1944, p.235.

71. R.H. Campbell, 'North British', p.206.

72. The number of locomotive building firms in Britain fell from 16 in 1914 to 10 in 1937. *Railway Gazette*, 10 March 1944, p.235.

73. See, for example, R.A. Wheeler, 'Peckett in Retrospect', *Industrial Railway Record*, 53 (1974), p.202.

74. C.I. Savage, *Inland Transport* (Official History of the Second World War, Civil Series, 1957), p.638.

75. M.J. Lee, 'Peckett & Sons Ltd: a Brief Memoir', *Industrial Railway Record*, 53 (1974), pp.195-7.

76. Peckett engines in particular were robust and hard-wearing, and as many as 60 have survived in the hands of museums and preservation societies. Three locally-built engines can be seen at the Bristol Industrial Museum.

Sir George White and the Urban Transport Revolution in Bristol, 1875–1916[1]

CHARLES HARVEY AND JON PRESS

The modern city, sprawling, sectionalised and socially gradated, is a creation of surprisingly recent origin. Until the last decades of the nineteenth century, most city and town dwellers lived cheek by jowl with their neighbours in compact and densely populated localities. Urban congestion was an unhappy fact of life. There were some elegant commuter settlements on the peripheries of larger conurbations, but suburban development, the obvious answer to overcrowding, had not progressed very far. The great majority of citizens, unable to contemplate the luxury of a private carriage or travel by cab, walked to and from work and shopped, socialised, and worshipped within easy reach of home. Only when, from the 1860s onwards, innovations in urban transport – suburban railways, tramways and motor omnibuses – slashed the cost of commuting, was a general solution found to the problem of urban population growth. Thereafter towns and cities spread outward rapidly as agricultural land was gobbled up in a succession of housebuilding booms. Landowners, speculators, builders and house agents prospered as new estates, of varying degrees of substance, were laid out for skilled workers, clerks and middle class professionals. Immigrants and other poor members of society remained amidst less salubrious surroundings in the old, unfashionable inner city districts.

Limited suburban growth before the second half of the nineteenth century was, as already suggested, largely a consequence of transport technology and economics. Only in the 1830s had horse-drawn omnibuses begun regular operation in Britain, and even then the services, being costly beyond the means of most ordinary people, made little impact on the day-to-day pattern of city life. Eventually, sizeable omnibus networks were established in London and some provincial cities, but high capital and operating costs restricted their expansion.[2] Engineers, politicians and businessmen were aware of the limitations of omnibus travel, and, as the problem of urban congestion went from bad to worse, the search intensified for a more efficient form of urban transport. A simple and promising solution, which emerged in the 1850s and 1860s, was to run horse-drawn carriages on iron rails instead of across irregular cobble-stones or potholed dirt roads. It was widely appreciated that tramlines reduced friction between wheel and track to the extent that "a team of horses could pull [on tramlines] double the weight of most omnibuses".[3] Thus cheaper fares and a smoother, faster, less noisy ride would be made possible. Moreover, the success of tramways in the United States confirmed that theoretical operating economies could actually be realised in practice.[4]

In Britain, however, conditions did not favour the rapid spread of tramways. Narrow streets were common, and many local authorities were not prepared to give private operators control of already congested public highways. Tramway pioneers like the flamboyant American G.F. Train, who opened lines in London, Birkenhead and Darlington in 1860–1, came to grief after clashing with the authorities.[5] Parliamentary approval was needed for new lines, and, as obtaining it was an expensive, risky and time-consuming business, promoters often lost heart and abandoned their plans. Things changed for the better in 1868, when the Liverpool Tramways Co. succeeded in getting its plans approved by parliament. This established a precedent and signalled that the time was ripe for the advance of new schemes. Businessmen in many towns and cities now began to think hard about local possibilities. The government, anticipating a surge in company formation, passed enabling legislation in the form of the Tramways Act of 1870. The process of gaining official approval was standardised. A promotional boom followed, and by the time this had ended in 1877 there were in Britain "40 tramway companies operating on 343 km. of track and providing transit facilities in all the major towns of the country".[6]

The city of Bristol was one beneficiary of the tramways boom of 1870–6. Only months after the 1870 Act had come into force, two rival consortia were vying to build lines in the city. The first, represented by an enterprising firm of Bristol solicitors, Stanley & Wasbrough, laid before the council a plan to connect Temple Meads railway station with Clifton and Hotwells. The second, led by London-based railway contractors Waring Brothers, unveiled a more grandiose plan involving the expenditure of £120,000 on the construction of an entire network of lines.[7] There followed a prolonged debate in newspapers and council chamber over the merits of the rival schemes and the wisdom of allowing either to go ahead. Similar debates were then going on in nearly all British towns and cities. In essence, opinion divided between advocates of municipal ownership of public services and those who believed, almost as an act of faith, that private individuals should control business ventures, whatever the nature of those ventures. The municipalists reasoned that tramways, like water or gas, were 'natural monopolies'; and should not be entrusted to private concerns because of the danger of high fares and low safety standards. Their opponents countered that transport undertakings involved high risks and that under council ownership, without the discipline of market forces, tramways might well lapse into unprofitability and become a charge on the rates. In the event, Bristol councillors, possibly swayed by local hostility to the London speculators rumoured to be behind both the Waring and Stanley & Wasbrough schemes, sided with the municipalists and rejected both schemes. Instead, it was agreed that the council should construct tramways in the city, and parliamentary approval was sought for two lines, from St. Augustine's Parade to the foot of Black Boy Hill, Redland, and from Old Market to Lawrence Hill, at an estimated cost of £14,000.[8]

The council soon began to regret its decision. Iron prices rose sharply in 1872–3, causing a minor financial crisis and a major loss of nerve. It became clear that the local authority's authorised borrowing limit was insufficient to fund the building of both lines, and plans were hurriedly revised to leave just a section of the proposed Redland line intact. When the line was completed in the spring of 1874, and the council sought a lessee, as it had to do under the 1870 Act, it had the embarrassment of advertising one of the shortest and least promising tramways in the country.[9] The response to its national search for a trustworthy operator was duly disappointing and it was left to local interests to sort out local difficulties. Stanley & Wasbrough, tenacious in the cause of tramway development in Bristol, again came forward with serious proposals. In October 1874, they offered, as representatives of a group of Bristol businessmen, to lease the existing line for 21 years, provided permission was given to build further lines from Old Market to St. George and Fishponds, together with a connection to the Redland line. The council gave way, leaving private interests responsible for the transport needs of the Bristol public.[10]

The Bristol Tramways Co., vehicle of the urban transport revolution in Bristol, was registered as a limited company on 23 December 1874. Behind it were men of substance with a vested interest in improving the infrastructure of the city. They were not speculators, as were many of those involved in tramway promotion elsewhere, but seasoned businessmen, keen to encourage the growth of the regional economy. William Butler, first chairman of the Tramways Co., had already made a fortune in tar-distilling and chemicals, and was diversifying his interests in Bristol and south Wales, as were entrepreneurs like coal magnate Joseph Wethered and the prosperous wholesaler Henry Gale Gardner. In sponsoring tramways, these men were not merely looking for short term profits but commercial involvements and urban development from which they might benefit in the longer term. As members of an ambitious elite group with many financial interests in common, power and knowledge ranked high in their list of priorities. Control of urban transport initiatives was what mattered to them, not the ownership of the new company. Hence their decision to purchase relatively few Bristol Tramways Co. shares themselves, whilst recommending them as a sound investment to the public of Bristol at large. Of the initial 5,000 £10 ordinary shares, the promoters took just 20 each, and, by 1880, William Butler, with 160 shares (1.6 per cent of the 10,000 shares then issued), was the only director with a substantial holding in the company. Bristol Tramway shares were from the beginning quite widely distributed (its 417 shareholders had a mean shareholding of 24 £10 shares in 1880), with ownership concentrated in the hands of the lawyers, accountants, clerks, retailers, merchants, manufacturers, widows and clerics who lived in the more prosperous areas in and around Bristol.[11]

The effective separation at an early stage of ownership and control had immediate and important consequences for the Bristol Tramways Co.; the most striking of these being the fact that the company was able to forge ahead with its schemes unfettered by a lack of capital. A large number of shareholders meant access to a large pool of savings and this in turn meant that Butler and his fellow directors could plan on a scale

26. Bristol's first horse tram in August 1875, at the junction of Perry Road and Colston Street.

that would have been imprudent if they had been reliant on their own resources. The Redland line, which opened in 1875, was an immediate success, carrying half a million passengers in the first six months of operation. Eastville and St. George, densely populated working class districts, were connected to the city centre in the following year. In 1878 Bristolians made some 3,379,000 journeys by tram.[12] Public enthusiasm for the system was such that "urgent solicitations" were made for new lines by "the inhabitants of various districts". In March 1879, the company, "greatly encouraged by many influential members of the Town Council", responded by proposing "a scheme which would have the effect of consolidating the Company's working and making a complete system for Bristol".[13] By the early 1880s, as Table 1 shows, Horfield, Hotwells and Bedminster had been incorporated into an integrated, though not fully developed, tramway network. This, with all the supporting facilities of offices, carriages, depots, horses and stables, had been financed by the shareholders to the tune of £115,000, and a further £19,200 had been raised through the issue of $4\frac{1}{2}$ per cent debentures (see Appendix for fuller financial details).

The expansion of the Bristol tramway system between 1875 and 1881, while not hampered by a shortage of funds, was not achieved without difficulty. The Tramways Act of 1870 was intended to balance public, municipal and private interests, and throughout the history of tramways in Britain tension and struggle were rife between these competing interest groups. This was as true in Bristol as in any other major city. New lines required the sanction of the Board of Trade, and local and county councils had the power to impose constructional standards and operating conditions before granting approval. Moreover, opposition from a third or more of directly affected residents and tradespeople, referred to as 'frontagers', was enough to block a scheme. At every stage of planning, therefore, the Bristol Tramways Co. had to win the support of local communities and city worthies without making so many concessions as to render the proposed development uneconomic. Each and every scheme brought forward involved countless hours of negotiation and the drafting and redrafting of technical and legal papers. Tramway promotion was thus time-consuming and costly – far more than it needed to be, according to its proponents, who argued that regulation seriously handicapped the growth of urban transport.[14]

Yet out of these thorny and frustrating complexities a young man, destined to become one of Britain's great transport entrepreneurs, developed a career. George White was 15 years of age when, in 1869, he began work as a junior clerk in the offices of Stanley & Wasbrough. Over the next few years, he worked mainly on bankruptcy cases, commending himself to his employers by his application and his command of detail.

Table 1. *The Bristol Tramways System, 1876–1916*

	Date of opening
Perry Road – Black Boy Hill	1875
Perry Road – St. Augustine's Parade	1875
Old Market – Eastville	1876
Perry Road – Old Market	1876
Old Market – St. George	1876
Bristol Bridge – Totterdown (Three Lamps)	1879
St. Augustine's Parade – Hotwells (Dowry Square)	1880
Bristol Bridge – Bedminster	1880
Horsefair – Horfield (Egerton Road)	1880
Old Market – Bristol Bridge (via St. Philip's Bridge)	1881
St. Augustine's Parade – Bristol Bridge (via Baldwin Street)	1881
Horsefair – St. Augustine's Parade	1888
St. George – Kingswood	1892
Stokes Croft – Ashley Road (Sussex Place)	1892
Horfield (Egerton Road) – Horfield Depot (Ashley Down Road)	1892
Bedminster – Ashton Gate	1896
Eastville – Fishponds (via Stapleton Road)	1897
Fishponds – Staple Hill	1897
Ashley Road – Stapleton Road	1898
Totterdown (Three Lamps) – Arnos Vale	1898
Horfield Depot – Horfield Barracks	1900
Bedminster – Bedminster Down	1900
Totterdown (Three Lamps) – Knowle	1900
Arnos Vale – Brislington	1900
Zetland Road – Durdham Down (via Redland Green)	1900
St. George – Hanham	1900
Horfield Barracks – Filton	1907
Black Boy Hill – Westbury-on-Trym	1908

Sources: B.R.O., 35810/23, Bristol Tramways & Carriage Co. Reports and Accounts. 28787/1, Tramways Committee, Minutes. *Western Daily Press*, 1870–1908.

When the firm began its adventures in tramway promotion, White was set the task of mastering the legal aspects. He distinguished himself in this and was rewarded by appointment as first company secretary of the Bristol Tramways Co. on a part time basis at a salary of £150 per annum. It seems that White had impressed the 'tramways set' – Butler, Gardner, Wethered, Henry Wasbrough, Charles Hoskins Low and Thomas Davey –

by his charm and cool intellectual authority. Complex legal and political wranglings of the kind facing the tramways company could not have been inviting to men accustomed to command, and White, with his patient shrewdness, must have appeared an ideal junior officer to install as day-to-day administrator. The appointment was of great importance to White: it allowed him to leave Stanley & Wasbrough and embark on a career in business. In 1875 he founded the stockbroking firm of George White & Co., which, along with the Bristol Tramways Co., formed the platform on which he created a personal transport empire; an empire which included the Imperial Tramways Co., London United Tramways, and, ultimately, the British & Colonial Aeroplane Co. (predecessor of the Bristol Aeroplane Co.).[15]

27. Sir George White (1854–1916).

William Butler and his associates had not misplaced their confidence in their young protégé. Through the 1870s, White worked diligently behind the scenes preparing the ground for each advance in Tramway Co. business. He was not yet a public figure, but it was he who presented the case for new lines to the Board of Trade, the city council and residents' associations. He was firm and forthright in his dealings, often threatening that the company would abandon its plans unless they were approved in full. He used this tactic to good effect in 1879, when the council threatened the viability of the major expansion scheme announced in that year by insisting that passengers should not be charged more than a penny a mile, even if their journey involved changing trams. This would have involved the issuing of transfer tickets, and White obstinately resisted the imposition of 'unworkable' regulations, claiming that the council was trying to run the company's affairs. He produced evidence to show that the Bristol Tramways Co.'s practice was in line with that of all other tramways in the country, declaring that the entire scheme of extensions then under way was jeopardised by the council's demands.[16] By the late 1870s, the need for cheap urban transport was more widely accepted than had been the case at the beginning of the decade, and White was able to win the support of the local press. *The Bristol Times & Mirror* commented that

> The Company have expended nearly £2,000 in promoting the Bill, the extensions are looked forward to with the greatest eagerness by the inhabitants of the various districts to which the lines would go, and it is to be hoped that no mere technicality will be allowed to stand in the way of what would obviously be a great public benefit.[17]

The council gave in.

Another contentious issue was that of Sunday working, and here White was less successful. Following a motion proposed by James Inskip, a prominent local solicitor and leading sabbatarian, the council voted in November 1875 that extensions to the system should only be permitted if the company agreed to cease working during the hours of Sunday services. White argued that, apart from interfering with general traffic, this would prevent "the large industrial population of the city" – especially that of St. Philips and Bedminster – from visiting Clifton and Durdham Downs, which had been bought by the city for their benefit.[18] On this occasion, however, the council refused to back down, and several years passed before the restrictions were eased.[19]

Meetings were also held to enlist the support of residents in the districts affected by the proposed extensions. Usually the company's schemes were favourably received. In Bedminster and Horfield, for example, public meetings concluded that, although a few local tradesmen might suffer, the coming of the tramways would benefit the population as a whole.[20] In Clifton, however, the Bristol Tramways Co.'s experience was very different. Although some Clifton businessmen were in favour of improved communications with the city centre, the majority of the inhabitants were very hostile to the scheme. This matched the experience of tramway promoters elsewhere in the British Isles; in general, tramways were welcomed by the inhabitants of lower class or lower middle class districts, but not by residents of the more well-to-do suburbs.[21] In Clifton it was feared that trams would bring in hordes of undesirable visitors, depress property values, encourage jerry-building, and cause residents to shop in Bristol, to the detriment of local traders.[22] The attitude of Clifton society towards Bristol and its tramways was unambiguously stated in the following vitriolic letter, published by the *Bristol Mercury* in October 1878:

> Sir – is it not something terrible and most wicked that the disgusting tramway is to bring the nasty, low inhabitants of Bristol up into our sacred region? We have nothing common or unclean amongst us at present. Poor people do not walk about on Clifton streets ... And now here are those money-making plebeians of Bristol talking of running tramcars through our beautiful and lovely Clifton! ... Why is this to be? Why must the common people be allowed to walk about here? They should stay in their own homes. They would feel more comfortable, surely, among their own houses and streets than here. The policemen should stop it.[23]

This, presumably, was not a particularly eccentric view: residents' objections led the council to reject the Clifton extension. White, however, was never disconcerted by a setback of this kind. Indeed, his confidence in the scheme was such that he felt entitled to resort to subterfuge. In November 1880, when a second application was made for the Clifton extension, together with a new line from the top of Park Street to College Green and St. Augustine's Parade, he informed the council that the inhabitants were now in favour of the proposals:

> I would mention that the Company are being much pressed by influential citizens of Clifton to connect that district with the Tramways System and also that of the one hundred houses in Park Street and College Green the occupants of ninety have memorialised the Company to run through those streets.[24]

Opponents of the scheme quickly made it clear that this statement was misleading, to say the least, and at the next meeting of the council's Tramways Committee Alderman Warren presented a memorial from 277 inhabitants of these same streets "requesting the Committee would not sanction the construction of a line up Park Street".[25] The company's proposals were again rejected, and, although White continued to apply pressure to the council, his bluff had been called. The Clifton route was subsequently served by horse omnibuses.

Defeat in Clifton was not a serious blow for the Bristol Tramways Co. All remaining plans were approved and by 1881 seven key routes were operational along with a number of connections. The original Redland line was bought from the council for £8,000, and was quickly relaid in heavier gauge double tracks.[26] There followed a long period of consolidation, lasting into the early 1890s, during which the company tightened its grip on passenger transport in Bristol. In 1881 an agreement with the Great Western Railway and the Midland Railway granted it the sole right to "ply for hire public vehicles of all kinds at the Bristol Joint Railway Station". Temple Meads station was "the base of all passenger carrying operations in Bristol", and this justified the payment of a hefty rental to the railway companies. Most of this, however, was recouped through subletting the right to operate cabs to and from the station to parties which in 1886 formed the Bristol Cab Co. – a concern with the same directors and officers as the Bristol Tramways Co. This agreement, and others of a similar nature, effectively preserved the monopoly of the Temple Meads trade, free of cost.[27] Budding competitors suffered the inevitable consequences. The Bristol General Omnibus Co. and the Bristol Omnibus & Carriage Co. both failed during the 1880s, leaving the Tramways Co. free to develop omnibus routes wherever a tramway line was not an economic proposition.[28] With the opposition thus dispatched, the assets of the Bristol Cab Co. were merged in 1887 with those of the Tramways Co. to form a new concern, the Bristol Tramways & Carriage Co.[29] Over the next few years the new company enjoyed a steady growth in traffic and income. In 1886, the year before the merger, the Tramways Co. carried 5.5 million passengers (20 journeys per head of population), whilst in 1891 the combined tramways, cab and omnibus company carried 11.2 million passengers (38 journeys per head of population).[30]

Despite their rapid spread and popularity, however, horse-drawn tramways were never a complete solution to urban congestion, and as the years went by their shortcomings became increasingly apparent. Operating companies complained about the high costs of stabling and feeding hundreds of horses (the Bristol company had 876 horses in 1899). Horses had a working life of only four to five years, and, because they could pull for just a few hours daily, a team of five to seven horses was needed for every tramcar. Horse costs typically absorbed 50 per cent of revenues. In Bristol, in the 15 years between 1876 and 1890, forage alone accounted for 34 per cent of operating expenses, compared with 35 per cent for wages and salaries; veterinary fees and stabling accounted for a large part of the rest. Moreover, while companies suffered high operating expenses, the public and local authorities increasingly complained of high fares and a poor standard of service. Tramways gained an unenviable reputation with their dirty, crowded carriages and slow services.[31] Added to which the horses fouled the streets and broke up roads with the incessant pounding of hooves. Severe gradients aggravated matters in Bristol: trace horses were frequently needed, and James Clifton Robinson, the company's first general manager, commented that "The Bristol Tramways Co. own a series of lines which have the reputation of being the most difficult to work of any in the United Kingdom".[32]

The board of the Bristol Tramways Co., like those of many other companies, was well aware of the problems of horse-drawn transportation. In December 1877, the company began experiments with a steam tram built by the Bristol firm of Fox, Walker & Co. for Rouen's tramways. The company was sufficiently encouraged to experiment with steam on the Horfield line.[33] Seven engines were leased for a trial period from the Hughes Locomotive and Tramways Co. of Loughborough and fitted with passenger trailers, but the hoped for economies did not materialise. Although they cost less to run than horse-drawn trams, the saving had to be set against greater rail wear and higher wages for skilled drivers and engineers. Furthermore, steam trams were noisy and dirty, and were generally disliked by the public. They were returned to the manufacturer after a year, and horse trams took over.[34] Elsewhere in Britain, steam proved more enduring, but even the most advanced steam trams had problems meeting strict Board of Trade anti-pollution standards, and, with speeds limited to 10 miles per hour, unit costs remained too high for a severe challenge to be mounted against the horse.[35]

But the search for alternatives to horses went on. In 1883, the company became interested in cable cars, which were in use in San Francisco, Chicago and other American cities. Clifton Robinson, who had left Bristol in 1882, had become general manager of the English patent holders, the Hallidie Patent Cable Tramways Corporation Ltd. He drew the attention of his former colleagues to the advantages of cable traction. Its appeal was its particular suitability for steep hills (with which Bristol is well endowed), and its relatively low working costs of 7d. (3p.) per mile.[36] In September 1884, William Butler told the shareholders:

> The cable system of working tramways continues to engage the attention of the Directors who are at present in negotiation with the Patent Cable Tramways Corporation with reference to the conversion of the Redland line.[37]

In the event, however, the company decided not to proceed. Low working costs were offset by high capital costs. Extensive road excavation was required, and, at £10,000 per mile of single track, a cable line cost roughly twice as much as a horse tramway.[38]

The technical solution was eventually found in electric traction; the adoption of which inspired in Britain a second tramways boom beginning in the mid-1890s and involving a rapid multiplication of capital invested in the industry. Most of the development work on electric tramways had been done in the 1880s in the United States. The first commercial electric street railway was opened in 1884, but it was only with Frank Sprague's development of an efficient overhead conductor and powerful motors that the real breakthrough was made. Following the success of the 12-mile Richmond Street Railway, opened in 1887, electric tramways became "one of the most rapidly accepted innovations in the history of technology".[39] Larger, double-decked carriages, improved speeds and faster turnaround times (vehicles could reverse direction) meant immediate increases in carrying capacity. Electric trams were also quiet, clean, reliable and able to negotiate steep gradients. Above all, they were sufficiently fuel-efficient to allow lower costs and fares despite the considerable capital outlay needed to electrify lines. It is little wonder that the American electric tramways boom of the later 1880s and early 1890s excited so much attention this side of the Atlantic.[40]

In Bristol it was George White who became the enthusiastic promoter of the new technology. He had matured as a businessman during the 1880s, engaging in the affairs of many companies and making a substantial personal fortune. He was widely respected for his commercial acumen and by 1890 had virtually taken over the running of the Bristol Tramways & Carriage Co. His reputation and resources were such that in 1892 he was able to gain control of the Imperial Tramways Co. which operated sizeable networks in Dublin, Middlesbrough and Reading.[41] At Imperial he installed his old friend James Clifton Robinson as managing director. Robinson had worked extensively in the United States since the mid-1880s, and had become, through his work on major projects, one of the world's leading authorities on cable and electric tramways.[42] The two men, close friends with a common enthusiasm for technological innovation, determined to bring the advantages of electric tramways to Britain.

Bristol was an ideal place to start: the topography of the place indicated that major operating economies could be made, and the sound financial record of the Tramways Co. (see Appendix) made it likely that funds would be available from the investing public. In 1893, Robinson was invited, at White's behest, to report on the "advisability of adopting electricity as the motive power of the present lines from Old Market to St. George and the proposed extension to Kingswood".[43] Robinson's report, which pointed out the advantages of the overhead trolley system of current collection and the suitability of electric power for the gradients of the Kingswood route, concluded that "in electric traction we have the means provided by which an enormous extension of tramway enterprise may profitably be undertaken".[44] The directors, in recommending the report to shareholders, noted that the Kingswood district, with 60,000 inhabitants, was "not only a very populous one, but an important manufacturing one" that had long "suffered from want of communication with Bristol".[45] Work began almost immediately under Robinson's supervision. Most of the equipment was supplied by the British subsidiary of the American General Electric Corporation, British Thomson-Houston. The line was completed in October 1895 at a total cost of £49,981, and Bristol became the first city to operate electric trams under the newly published Board of Trade regulations.[46] According to Barker and Robbins, the opening of the Kingswood line "marked the real beginnings of electric tramway operation in Britain", and heralded the start of the nation's second tramway investment boom.[47]

The public responded to the speed and sheer novelty of the new trams with enormous enthusiasm. On opening day, 14 October 1895, east Bristol schools and factories were closed, and crowds lined the streets, cheering the trams on their way. The City & Kingswood Electric Tramway was an instant success. Within the first four months of its opening the number of passengers exceeded one million. The public, appreciative of "improved facilities and lower fares", clamoured for the conversion of old lines and the building of new ones. White, who had been elected managing director of the Tramways Co. in 1894, in "recognition of the

28. An electric tram in Old Market, around 1910.

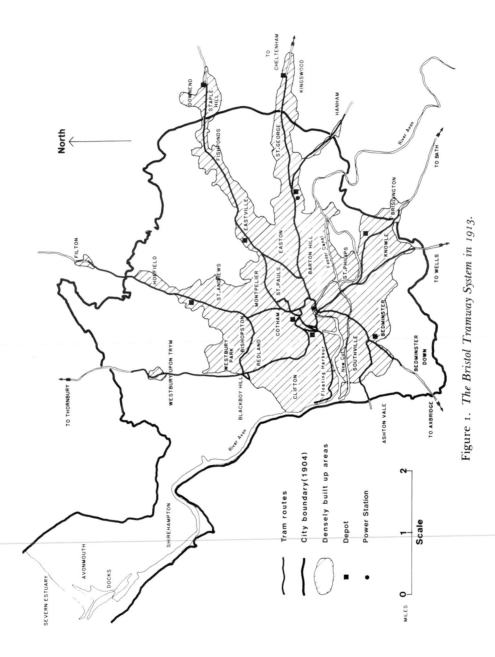

Figure 1. *The Bristol Tramway System in 1913.*

valuable services made by him during the last 20 years", responded with alacrity to these demands.[48] Plans were made to electrify the entire system and extend existing lines to outlying districts like Fishponds, Bedminster Down, Knowle, Brislington and Hanham (see Table 1). The whole operation was completed by 1900, and entailed the building of 10.5 miles of new lines, the conversion of 16.5 miles of horse tramways, the commissioning of a centrally located generating plant and the erection of a new depot and car building works on a five acre site at Brislington.[49]

The electrification programme completely changed the character of the Bristol Tramways & Carriage Co. A simple technology was superseded by one that was capital intensive and sophisticated. Huge amounts of money were expended in the process. Between 1896 and 1902 the paid up capital of the company increased fourfold to £1 million, whilst the total capital employed in the business increased at a similar rate to £1.5 million. And this was not the end of it. Almost before the novelty of electric trams had worn off the motor bus had appeared on the scene.[50] Buses which carried their own power source could operate anywhere without the need to lay tracks or put up cables, so that routes could be

29. A charabanc on an excursion, at Ashton Court. This was one of the first vehicles built at the tramways company's Brislington works, in 1911.

created in a day or discontinued without loss of fixed capital. Although the early buses were inefficient and unreliable, their potential was obvious to White. In 1905, right at the start of the motor bus boom in Britain, 12 double-decker buses were bought from Thorneycroft to replace horse-drawn vehicles on tramway feeder routes and to open new country services. Thornbury, Saltford, Kelston, and Westbury were thus brought within commuting distance of Bristol, and within the space of a few years motor bus depots were opened at Bath, Cheltenham, Gloucester and Weston-super-Mare.[51]

The development of more efficient petrol engines brought other business opportunities to the Bristol Tramways & Carriage Co. A large fleet of motor taxis was purchased after White's visit to Paris in 1908 had convinced him of their commercial potential. Early models were imported, though many had their bodywork built in the company's workshops.[52] Full scale vehicle production soon followed, including the manufacture of buses and lorries for sale or hire. In 1912 White reported that "leading firms in London and the provinces are already hiring motor vehicles for commercial purposes from the Company, and a further number of such vehicles are now being built to supply the growing demand".[53] A new and well equipped motor construction works was built at Brislington in 1912. White informed shareholders that "the installation, comprising machinery and automatic tools of the most recent invention, is designed to yield an output of about 300 new motor omnibuses, cabs and other vehicles each year as well as to enable all repairs to the Company's rolling stock and privately owned cars to be executed under the most economical conditions".[54] By 1914 the company was an established vehicle manufacturer, the operator of 17 distinct tramway services and 15 omnibus services, and the owner of a fleet of 169 tramcars, 44 buses, 29 charabancs, 124 taxis, and assorted vans, lorries and commercial vehicles. It was one of the biggest employers in Bristol, with a full time workforce of over 2,000 and an annual wage bill in excess of £110,000, total capital of more than £2 million, and a yearly income of £455,000 (53 per cent from trams and the remainder from other sources).[55]

The impressive growth of the Tramways Co. following George White's appointment as managing director in 1894 had important consequences for the people of Bristol. Public transport already had a place in the lives of many people before electrification, but thereafter trams, and later buses, became a vital part of the city's life. People caught the riding habit in a very big way, as can be seen from a glance at Table 2.

At a time when real wages were steadily rising, fares moved downward as a result of electrification (from about 1d. per mile to about 0.75d. per mile) and especially cheap fares were available to those travelling to and from work (about 0.33d. per mile).[56] Lifestyles changed. Men rode to

Table 2. *The Population of Bristol, Tramway Company Passengers, and Journeys per Head, 1876–1916*

Year	Population*	Passengers Carried	Journeys per Head
1876	237,215	2,014,255	8.5
1881	260,408	6,092,678	23.4
1886	277,821	5,565.870	20.0
1891	296,405	11,179.325	37.7
1896	317,058	17,456,406	55.0
1901	339,150	36,714,906	108.3
1906	348,035	46,096,257	134.8
1911	357,173	49,561,001	138.8
1916	366,961	60,628,342	165.2

Sources: Population data are taken from H.A. Shannon and E. Grebenik, *The Population of Bristol* (Cambridge, 1943), p.6; traffic data is taken from B.R.O., 35810/23, Bristol Tramways & Carriage Co., Annual Reports and Accounts, 1876–1916.
* The tramways network extended beyond the old city boundaries into districts which did not become part of the City of Bristol until 1904. The population figures given here are standardised to include those resident in the city as defined in 1904. The figure given for non-census years are estimates based upon ten-yearly rates of population growth.

work, housewives travelled to specialist shops, children were relieved of the walk to school, social visits to friends and relatives became common-place, and weekend excursions to the Downs and other beauty spots became part of the recreational diet. Once the new motor bus routes were operating, Bristol families travelled even further afield. Demand rose to such an extent that just before the First World War George White reported to shareholders that "a large and additional number of pleasure Charabancs are also being constructed as this branch of the business is rapidly developing".[57]

The introduction of electric trams and motor buses had other more subtle, and in some ways more profound, effects upon urban lifestyles. Suburban development proceeded much faster as tram lines and bus routes extended outwards from central districts to villages or small town-ships like Kingswood, Hanham, Westbury and Filton. In the era of horse tramways, Bristol Tramways Co. policy had been to extend the system through "thickly populated districts" so that "traffic will be immediately developed".[58] Although the early tramways therefore cannot be credited with initiating the growth of inner suburbs, they certainly aided the process. For example, numerous small, speculative builders moved into Redland, St. George and Horfield following the opening of tram lines.

From 1895, because commuting distances were greatly increased and a vast amount of land was made accessible for building, the whole suburban movement was given a tremendous stimulus. Speculators and property dealers built new houses in set price ranges to suit the pockets of aspiring home owners. Whole areas of Bristol took on a particular social character, and within these areas there were drawn even subtler local distinctions. Social gradation in housing gave concrete meaning to expressions like 'moving up in the world'. The social legacy of the urban transport revolution was, in Bristol as elsewhere, very great indeed.[59]

Despite the success of the Bristol Tramways & Carriage Co. in extending its operations, yielding major benefits for the local population and fresh business opportunities for local capitalists, neither the company nor George White were universally popular in the city. The school of thought which held that local transport should be in municipal, not private, hands had never been completely silenced, and the post-1894 expansion, at a time when municipalisation was proceeding apace elsewhere in Britain, almost inevitably revived opposition to the company and its plans. Local rivalries also worked to heighten tensions. White, once referred to as "the Napoleon of Bristol", was viewed with suspicion in some quarters. As his business empire had grown, he had on occasion clashed with civic leaders like James Inskip, and the memory of such disputes was bound to promote opposition to schemes promoted by White.[60] Moreover, his

30. The Tramways Centre around 1910. In the foreground, Blue Taxis and hansom cabs await custom.

rise to national prominence, through his leadership of Imperial Tramways and, even more significantly, London United Tramways, led many
to doubt his commitment to Bristol's interests. He thus lay open to the
charge that he was little better motivated than any other money-grubbing
'London capitalist'. Those who knew of his dealings with the Western
Wagon Co., which financed the development of the Filton 'Garden
Suburb' after the arrival of the tramway in 1907, might well have supported this view. (White also established the British & Colonial Aeroplane
Co. at Filton on land bought from Western Wagon and with funds
borrowed from the same company).[61]

Tension between the city council and White and the Tramways Co.
was manifested in a long series of disputes. The first of these blew up in
1896 when the company sought permission to electrify the entire Bristol
tramway network. Bristol was one of the first municipalities to undertake
electricity supply, and the council decided to approve the scheme only
if it was contracted to provide the necessary power.[62] This was totally
unacceptable to the Tramways Co., which threatened to abandon the
project, stating that:

> The production of the motive power was one of the most vital parts of the
> Company's working, for which the Directors were responsible to the public,
> and they would not undertake that responsibility unless they had full control
> of the management of their own undertaking.[63]

The council responded in January 1897 by setting up a Tramways
Purchase Committee to consider whether it should buy the entire system.
This had become an attractive proposition because of recent legal judgements. Under section 43 of the 1870 Tramways Act, municipalities were
empowered to purchase privately owned undertakings after 21 years, or
subsequently at seven year intervals, and in 1893 the House of Lords
ruled that the purchase price should be based upon cost of construction
less depreciation; no payment was to be made in respect of goodwill or
current or future profitability. In 1896, parliament introduced new regulations empowering local authorities to operate tramways as well as owning
them.[64] By the following year, Blackpool, Glasgow, Huddersfield, Leeds
and Sheffield had municipally owned systems, and the results were
encouraging enough to bring about a spate of takeovers. By 1905, 174
tramway undertakings in Britain were owned by municipal authorities,
with 146 remaining in private hands.[65]

In Bristol, however, George White was much better placed to resist
pressure from the local authority. Under agreements reached in previous
years the council would not have the right to purchase the tramways until
1913 – 21 years from the date of the most recent extension instead of
from the date of the company's formation. This put the Bristol Tramways

& Carriage Co. in a much less vulnerable position than other private undertakings. White informed the Tramways Purchase Committee that the company was not interested in a negotiated sale, and although the dispute continued into 1898 the council eventually gave way under public pressure for a better service. The tramways remained in private ownership, and electric power was supplied by a central power station which the company built near Temple Meads railway station.[66]

The question of municipalisation was again raised in 1913. By then, Bristol, Dublin, Edinburgh and Norwich were the only major cities with privately owned tramway systems, and the council commissioned a report to determine whether other local authorities had found it beneficial to acquire tramways. The consultants' brief was very broad; *inter alia*, they were to report on the value of the Bristol tramways, the supply of electricity to the system, and the probable income which the council could expect after municipalisation. They were also instructed to compare the Bristol system with municipally controlled tramways throughout the British Isles, and to examine the relative merits of trams, trolley buses and motor buses. The report, which was submitted in July 1913, was firmly in favour of council ownership. It set the value of the system at about £600,000, and estimated an annual profit, after all working charges, capital costs and depeciation, of about £37,000 a year. Although the increasing use of motor and trolley buses was noted, it was stated that "there is no possibility of any of the other forms of traction which are at present known being able to provide the travelling facilities required by the citizens of Bristol as effectively and economically as tramways".[67]

The council accepted the report's findings but George White remained very hostile to municipalisation. He refused to allow the council's consultants to examine the company's records, and tried to block the passage of the council's Bill through parliament.[68] He also ensured that, whilst the council was legally entitled to acquire the tramways within the pre-1904 city boundaries at cost less depreciation, the outlying parts of the system "must also be purchased with due allowance for the computed profits".[69] When the council conducted a poll to see whether Bristolians were in favour of municipalisation, White responded with a series of advertisements and articles in the *Bristol Guardian*, in which the company's case was forcefully argued. He claimed that the company was providing a good service for Bristol, and there was no need to rush into the purchase. Citizens were warned that "If you vote for buying, your rates will go up 5d. in the £".[70]

It appeared that White was fighting a losing battle. The council's Act received the Royal Assent in August 1914, and the poll produced a majority for municipalisation.[71] But White, though declaring himself ready to negotiate the sale, was not yet beaten. When the council offered

£670,000 for the system, White retorted that the company's price was £2 million.[72] At this stage the council's enthusiasm for municipalisation began to wane, and it began to press for concessions from the company instead of insisting on outright purchase. The Tramways Option Committee was instructed to discover what payments and concessions the company would be prepared to make if the council refrained from exercising its option to purchase for 7, 14 or 21 years. The company did offer some concessions; workmen's return tickets were to be valid all day instead of at rush hours only, and a reduced scale of fares was proposed; but White was unable to agree to all the council's demands, and an intriguing exchange of letters reveals his increasing exasperation with the municipal authorities.[73] Not surprisingly, the long drawn out negotiations came to nothing, and although the question of tramway municipalisation was raised yet again in 1922, 1929 and 1936 the system remained in private hands until 1938.

All credit must be given to the astuteness and negotiating skills of George White in preventing the council from gaining control of the tramways at a time when the law and public opinion strongly favoured municipalisation. However, it does not follow that this was necessarily a good thing for Bristol. The publication in 1907 of the remarkable National Civic Federation three-volume report on Municipal and Private Operation of Utilities lent credence to those who argued that the Bristol tramway system was a mismanaged monopoly which operated against the public interest. The American team which visited Britain in 1906 compared four publicly owned systems – Glasgow, Manchester, Liverpool and London – with four private undertakings in Dublin, Norwich, Surrey/Middlesex (London United Tramways) and Bristol. A mass of evidence was collected showing the privately operated systems in a very poor light. Cities taking over networks were said to have:

> Greatly extended and improved the service, scrapped the old horse cars, put on good, clean, handsome, well lighted, well ventilated trolley cars, ran the cars much more frequently, raised wages, adopted a 54-hour or 60-hour week, in place of 77 to 105 hours a week, gave men free uniforms and vacations with pay, reduced the fares much more than they had asked the companies to do, and made, not the deficits the companies had predicted, but considerable profits for the public.[74]

Bristol, though not the worst of the private undertakings, was said to be grossly overcapitalised (its assets having a book value of £1.3 million against a 'real value' of £700,000) and to exploit its customers and workers alike. It was reported that staff worked 70 hours a week for £1 5s. 6d. (£1 27½p.) compared to averages of 57 hours and £1 12s. 8d. (£1 63p.) for the four municipal tramways. Fares were claimed to be 66 per cent higher than the municipal average.[75]

Though the conclusions of the National Civic Federation's report cannot be dismissed out of hand, they should not be regarded as in any way definitive. An outstanding weakness of the research is that no real attempt was made to compare like with like. The four municipal systems examined were not typical of all British public operations. Each served a large, densely populated city and unit costs were predictably low, making comparison with cities like Bristol or Norwich somewhat invidious. The statistical basis of the work is likewise flawed. No account is taken when calculating profit rates of the fact that municipal ventures often took over private systems on extremely favourable terms. This is why Bristol Tramways was judged to be chronically overcapitalised when, in fact, the market capitalisation of the firm was much higher than its nominal capitalisation. Investors evidently had a high regard for the company even if the American investigators did not. Furthermore, since White refused to supply the Americans with any detailed information of costs, fares, hours of work or wages, the accuracy of many of the comparative statements in the report must be seriously questioned.

The National Civic Federation assessment of Bristol Tramways and its management certainly does not square with the evidence presented in this chapter. George White was with the company for 42 years until his death on 22 November 1916. Over the years his efforts caused the company to make the most of available technology. Bristol's horse-drawn tramways were more extensive and better integrated than those in most other cities of similar size. The company searched hard for an alternative to horse power and was a pioneer of electric traction and motor vehicles in the United Kingdom. All the signs are that the firm was technically efficient and well managed throughout the period. Equally impressive is the firm's financial record (see Appendix). Respectable dividends were regularly paid, but White never succumbed to the temptation to distribute an excessive proportion of the profits. Substantial reserves were built up, amounting to £252,000 by 1914, ensuring that adequate funds were available for the maintenance of the city's urban transport system – hardly a sign of financial mismanagement. White certainly set the interests of the shareholders very high, but there is no indication that customers suffered unduly in consequence. Fares were never such as to lead to vast monopoly profits and the quality of service improved steadily over the years. If any group suffered under the White regime it was the workers; although a non-contributory pension scheme was set up in 1898, their pay and hours of work did not match those of transport employees elsewhere, and White resisted all attempts at union infiltration in Bristol.[76] He also kept his own affairs carefully separate from those of the Tramways Co. He did not own a substantial interest in the company, nor did he speculate in its shares. This was in marked contrast to his other business activities, which reveal him as a shrewd and successful financial operator.[77] The reason for this contrast was White's close attachment to the city of Bristol, which had provided him with the opportunity to prosper. Towards the end of his life he became a major benefactor of the Bristol Royal Infirmary, the Red Cross and other charities, and was made a baronet for his public service in 1904.[78] However, the Bristol Tramways & Carriage Co. was his most long lasting commitment to the city. He devoted much of his time to the company, even though the opportunity cost to himself was considerable. His conservatism was a factor in his firm dealings with the council and his vigorous opponent of municipalisation, but he genuinely believed that he could provide a better transport system than the local authorities. Many Bristolians agreed with him. Certainly, the council did not possess anyone with his business acumen, and its indecisiveness over the tramways purchase issue did not inspire confidence. His personal ambition and readiness to experiment with new technology were ideally balanced by hard-headed realism and sound judgement. It is these qualities that mark him out as one of Bristol's most distinguished businessmen of modern times.

NOTES

1. The authors are grateful to Sir George White, 4th Bt., Professor Theo Barker, Dr Penelope Corfield, Dr Richard Roberts, Dr John Turner, Mr John Williams and Mrs Sheila Lang for their assistance in the preparation of this chapter.

2. H.J. Dyos and D.H. Aldcroft, *British Transport: an Economic Survey from the Seventeenth Century to the Twentieth* (Leicester, 1969), pp.215–20. T.C. Barker and M. Robbins, *A History of London Transport: Passenger Transport and the Development of the Metropolis*, vol.I (1963), pp.25–40, 59–68. J.P. McKay, *Tramways and Trolleys: the Rise of Urban Mass Transport in Europe* (Princeton, 1976), pp.12–3. A.D. Ochojna, 'The Influence of Local and National Politics on the Development of Urban Passenger Transport in Britain, 1850–1900', *Journal of Transport History*, new ser. IV (1978), pp.125–7, 132.

3. McKay, *Tramways and Trolleys*, p.14.

4. Ibid., pp.14–6.

5. 'Death of George Francis Train', *Financial Times*, 20 Jan. 1904. C.E. Lee, 'The English Street Tramways of George Francis Train', *Journal of Transport History*, I (1953 4), pp.20–7, 97–109.

6. Ochojna, 'Development of Urban Passenger Transport', p.138. Also see S.A. Munro, 'Tramway Companies of Liverpool, 1859–1899', *Historic Society of Lancashire and Cheshire*, 119 (1967), pp.182–4. Barker and Robbins, *London Transport*, vol. I, pp. 190–2. C. Klapper, *The Golden Age of Tramways* (1961), pp.31–3. E.F. Vesey-Knox, 'The Economic Effect of the Tramways Act of 1870', *Economic Journal*, XI (1901), pp.493–4.

7. *Bristol Daily Post*, 16 July 1875.

8. *Bristol Times & Mirror*, 22 Nov. 1871. *Western Daily Press*, 12 Feb. 1873. *Bristol Daily Post*, 16 July 1875.

9. *Western Daily Press*, 10 Feb. 1873. Bristol Record Office (hereafter B.R.O.), 28787/1, Bristol Council, Tramways Committee, Minutes, 26 May 1873; 18 Nov. 1873; 11 Dec. 1873.

10. B.R.O., 28787/1, Stanley & Wasbrough to Tramways Committee, 5 Oct. 1874. Tramways Committee, Minutes, 14–22 Oct. 1874.

Appendix. *The Growth and Profitability of the Bristol Tramways & Carriage Co., 1876–1915*

	Traffic and Income		Capitalisation			Profitability		
Period	Passengers Carried '000	Revenue £	Issued Capital £	Debentures £	Total Liabilities £	Operating Profit £	Operating Profit as % of Revenue %	Dividend Paid %
1876–80	3,103	24,404	71,754	6,206	87,940	4,229	17.3	5.3
1881–85	5,614	39,543	130,500	28,050	170,743	6,417	16.2	3.9
1886–90	7,598	56,109	156,451	37,697	221,319	10,840	19.3	5.0
1891–95	12,880	86,160	198,250	58,356	287,197	16,744	19.4	5.8
1896–00	22,728	142,407	418,288	106,928	663,450	39,690	27.9	5.8
1901–05	42,581	243,741	990,000	250,000	1,465,817	83,373	34.3	6.0
1906–10	46,688	277,455	1,000,000	400,000	1,733,822	76,142	27.4	5.1
1911–15	55,459	419,264	1,000,000	592,040	2,026,889	79,010	18.8	4.0

Source: Bristol Record Office, George White Papers, Annual Reports and Accounts.
* All the figures represent averages over a five year period. The end of the financial year for the company was originally 8 February. This changed in 1888 to 31 December. In the above calculations 8 February is taken as equivalent to 31 December.

11. Public Record Office (hereafter P.R.O.), BT31 2059/9064. On Butler's career, see T.H. Butler, *The History of William Butler & Co. Bristol Ltd., 1843–1943* (Bristol, 1954).

12. B.R.O., George White Papers, 35810/23, Bristol Tramways Co., Report and Accounts, March 1876; March 1879.

13. Ibid., March 1897.

14. Vesey-Knox, 'Tramways Act', pp.492–510. Klapper, *Golden Age of Tramways*, pp.31–3. B.R.O., 35810/18, J. Clifton Robinson, 'Autobiographical Notes', 1902.

15. See C.E. Harvey and J. Press, 'Sir George White, 1854–1916: a Career in Transport', *Journal of Transport History* (forthcoming, Sept. 1988).

16. *Western Daily Press*, 25 Feb. 1879. *Bristol Times & Mirror*, 5 March 1879. Bristol Tramways Co., Report and Accounts, March 1879.

17. *Bristol Times & Mirror*, 25 Feb. 1879.

18. B.R.O., 28787/1, Tramways Committee, Minutes, 25 Nov. 1875; George White to Tramways Committee, 1 Dec. 1875.

19. J. Latimer, *Annals of Bristol in the Nineteenth Century* (Bristol, 1897), pp.464–7.

20. *Bristol Daily Post*, 17 Oct. 1878. *Western Daily Press*, 17 Oct. 1878; 24 Oct. 1878.

21. See, for example, G. Wilson, *London United Tramways: a History, 1894–1933* (1971), pp.39–41. M. Jahn, 'Suburban Development in Outer West London, 1850–1900', in F.M.L. Thompson, ed. *The Rise of Suburbia* (Leicester, 1982), p.135.

22. *Western Daily Press*, 3 Oct. 1878.

23. *Bristol Mercury*, 17 Oct. 1878.

24. B.R.O., 28787/1, George White to Tramways Committee, 15 Nov. 1880.

25. Ibid., Tramways Committee, Minutes, 23 Dec. 1880.

26. Ibid., 29 Sept 1881; 17 Nov. 1881. Also see J.B. Appleby, *Bristol's Trams Remembered* (Westbury-on-Trym, 1969), p.6.

27. Bristol Tramways Co., Report and Accounts, August 1881. For the Bristol Cab Co., see P.R.O., BT31 3674/22794.

28. P.R.O., BT31 9071/17512; 3774/23562. Also see *Bristol Evening News*, 5 Sept. 1878.

29. B.R.O., 35810/23, Bristol Tramways & Carriage Co., Memorandum and Articles of Association, 1 Oct. 1887.

30. Bristol Tramways & Carriage Co., Reports and Accounts, 1886–91.

31. See, for example, 'Lesser Columbus' [Laurence Cowen], *Greater Bristol* (1893), pp.54–7. On operating costs, see *Report of the Select Committee on Tramways (Use of Mechanical Power)* (P.P. 1878, XVIII), QQ.635, 1851.

32. B.R.O., 35810/24, typescript of interview with J.C. Robinson, 1898.

33. *Bristol Times & Mirror*, 4 Dec. 1878. Bristol Tramways Co., Report and Accounts, Sept. 1880.

34. P.W. Gentry, *The Tramways of the West of England* (1952), p.26. Appleby, *Bristol Trams*, pp.7–9.

35. Klapper, *Golden Age of Tramways*, pp.47–9.

36. 'Mr. J. Clifton Robinson', *Railway News*, 27 Dec. 1902.

37. Bristol Tramways & Carriage Co., Report and Accounts, Sept. 1884.

38. J.C. Robinson, 'Tramways of the World' (Address to the Tramways and Light Railways Association at the Franco-British Exhibition, 1908), pp.4–5.

39. G.W. Hilton, 'Transport Technology and the Urban Pattern', *Journal of Contemporary History*, 4 (1969), p.126, quoted in McKay, *Tramways and Trolleys*, p.51.

40. Barker and Robbins, *London Transport*, vol.II, pp. 16–19. I.C.R. Byatt, 'Electrical Products', in D.H. Aldcroft, ed. *The Development of British Industry and Foreign Competition, 1875–1914* (1968), pp.239–45, 250–6. McKay, *Tramways and Trolleys*, pp.35–67.

41. B.R.O., 35810/24, Imperial Tramways Co., Report of Proceedings at the Ordinary General Meeting, 25 Feb. 1892. 35810/5, Imperial Tramways Co., Report and Accounts, 1892–4.

42. On Robinson's career, see B.R.O., 35810/18, J.C. Robinson, 'Autobiographical Notes', 1902. Wilson, *London United Tramways*, pp.27–34.

43. Bristol Tramways & Carriage Co., Report and Accounts, Aug. 1893.

44. J.C. Robinson, *Bristol Tramways: Report on Proposed Introduction of Electric Traction on the St. George Line, and the Proposed Extension to Kingswood* (Bristol, 1893), p.8.

45. Bristol Tramways & Carriage Co., Report and Accounts, Feb. 1894.

46. Ibid. Also see B.R.O., 35810/23, Bristol Tramways & Carriage Co., Reconstruction and Electrification Expenses, 1895. 'The Bristol Electric Tramway', *Electrical Review*, 37 (1895), pp.442–53.

47. Barker and Robbins, *London Transport*, vol.II, p.21. On the boom, see W.W. Duncan, *Manual of British and Foreign Tramway Companies* (printed annually, 1875–1905). P. Jones, 'The Spread and Diffusion of Urban Tramway Services in the British Isles' (unpublished Ph.D. thesis, University of Aberdeen, 1977), pp.128–34.

48. Bristol Tramways & Carriage Co., Report and Accounts, Feb. 1895.

49. Ibid., Feb. 1900.

50. Barker and Robbins, *London Transport*, vol.II, pp.118–36. Dyos and Aldcroft, *British Transport*, pp.336–7.

51. Bristol Tramways & Carriage Co., Report and Accounts, 1905–14. M. Curtis, *Bristol: a Century on the Road* (Falmouth, 1977), p.9. Bristol Omnibus Co., *The People's Carriage, 1874–1974* (Bristol, 1974), pp.31–2.

52. Bristol Tramways & Carriage Co., Report and Accounts, 1909–10.

53. Ibid., Feb. 1912.

54. Ibid., Feb. 1913.

55. Ibid., Feb. 1914.

56. B.R.O., 35810/23, Bristol Council, Reports, Correspondence and Negotiations on Electric Traction, 1894–8, p.27.

57. Bristol Tramways & Carriage Co., Report and Accounts, Feb. 1914.

58. Ibid., Sept. 1879. Also see *Western Daily Press*, 24 Oct. 1878.

59. The process requires further study along the lines pioneered by Sam Bass Warner in his *Streetcar Suburbs: the Process of Growth in Boston, 1870–1900* (Cambridge, Mass., 1962).

60. Bristol Omnibus Co., *People's Carriage*, p.63. Also see B.R.O., 28787/1, Tramways Committee, Minutes, 25 Nov. 1875. 35810/23, Bristol Council, Reports, Correspondence and Negotiations on Electric Traction, 1894–8, pp.24–30. Latimer, *Annals*, pp.55–6.

61. C.E. Harvey and J. Press, 'The George White Papers at Bristol Record Office', *Business Archives*, 54 (1987), p.23.

62. L. Hannah, *Electricity before Nationalisation: a Study of the Development of the Electrical Supply Industry in Britain* (1979), p.8. B.R.O., 28787/2, Bristol Council, Electrical Committee Report, 14 Feb. 1896. D.G. Tucker, 'The Beginnings of Electricity Supply in Bristol, 1889–1902', *Journal of the Bristol Industrial Archaeological Society*, 5 (1972), pp.17–8. P.G. Lamb, *Electricity in Bristol, 1863–1948* (Bristol, 1981), pp.2–15.

63. Bristol Tramways & Carriage Co., Report and Accounts, Aug. 1896. Also see ibid., Feb. 1897. *Western Daily Press*, 22 Feb. 1897.

64. M. Falkus, 'The Development of Municipal Trading in the Nineteenth Century', *Business History*, XIX (1977), pp.153–4.

65. Jones, 'Spread and Diffusion', p.128. Fabian Society, The *Municipalisation of Tramways* (1897), pp.1–15. B.T. Leech, 'Tramways and their Municipalisation', *Transactions of the Manchester Statistical Society*, (1897–8), pp.127–52. J. Sleeman, 'The Rise and Decline of Municipal Transport, *Scottish Journal of Political Economy*, 9 (1962), pp.46–64. B. Aspinwall, 'Glasgow Trams and American Politics, 1894–1914', *Scottish Historical Review*, 56 (1977), pp.64–5. McKay, *Tramways and Trolleys*, pp.163–191.

66. Bristol Tramways & Carriage Co., Report and Accounts, Aug. 1894. B.R.O., 28787/2, Bristol Tramways & Carriage Co. to Tramways Purchase Committee, 12 Dec. 1897; Tramways Purchase Committee, Minutes, 21 Dec. 1897.

67. B.R.O., 35810/23, J.B. Hamilton and J.F.C Snell, *Joint Report on the Bristol Tramways* (July, 1913), pp.38–9, 63.

68. B.R.O., 28787/4, Tramways Option Committee, Minutes, 20 May 1913; 21 July 1914.

69. Bristol Tramways & Carriage Co., Report and Accounts, Feb. 1915.

70. *Bristol Guardian*, 13 June 1914.

71. B.R.O., 28787/4, Tramways Option Committee, Minutes, 21 July 1914; 22 Sept. 1914.

72. *Bristol Times & Mirror*, 23 Feb. 1915. *Western Daily Press*, 23 Feb. 1915. B.R.O., 28787/4, George White to Tramways Option Committee, 11 March 1915.

73. B.R.O., 28787/4, George White to Tramways Option Committee, 11 March 1915; 29 March 1915; 14 July 1915.

74. National Civic Federation, *Municipal and Private Operation of Public Utilities* (New York, 1907), vol.I, p.263.

75. Ibid, pp.272–302.

76. B.R.O., 35810/23-4, Bristol Tramways & Carriage Co., *Notice to Staff*, 29 July 1901; *To the Citizens of Bristol*, 31 July 1901; *Complete Refutation of the Mis-Statements of Agitators*, 31 July 1901; *Annual Report and Accounts*, 1902.

77. Harvey and Press, 'Sir George White', passim.

78. *Bristol Times & Mirror*, 23 Nov. 1916, p.8. *Who was Who*, 1916–1928 (4th edn. 1967), p.1116. G.M. Smith, *A History of the Bristol Royal Infirmary* (Bristol, 1917), pp.416–8. C.B. Perry, *The Bristol Royal Infirmary, 1904–1974* (Bristol, 1981), pp.20–4.

Georges and Brewing in Bristol

GEOFFREY CHANNON

Beer has been produced in the vicinity of Bristol Bridge for more than 250 years. The original beer-house appears to have been built in or about 1730 by a consortium of Bristol merchants, including Isaac Hobhouse, a wealthy slave trader. Hobhouse left his interest in the beer-house to his two nephews, John and Henry Hobhouse, who subsequently built the Old Porter Brewery. This went through several hands before passing in 1787 to a new partnership managed by Philip George, which soon purchased the freehold of the Bath Street brewery and adjoining property. Eighteenth-century partnerships typically went through various transformations as partners died or retired and new men joined. Georges was no exception. In 1888, however, a hundred years after the formation of the first partnership, Georges and Co. became a public company, and thus the brewery was freed from the effects of lickle mortality. In the years following, through a process of internal growth, and more especially the acquisition of brewery concerns in Bristol and in the surrounding area, Georges became the largest brewery in the West Country. The firm's biggest rival, Bristol United, was absorbed in 1956 and its brewery closed down. But in 1961 Georges itself was caught up in the wave of horizontal mergers then sweeping through the industry, which resulted in a rapid increase in the level of concentration in U.K. brewing. The brewery was absorbed by Courage Barclay & Simonds Ltd. Courages was acquired in 1972 by the conglomerate Imperial Tobacco Group, which moved into brewing from a large and recently-acquired base in the food industry.[1] The main concern of the present survey, however, is not the dramatic developments of the post-war years, but the earlier history of the firm from 1788 to 1939. Because sources are somewhat fragmentary for the period before 1888, greater emphasis is given to the firm's history after its conversion to a limited liability company. In a survey of this length there are inevitably many untouched aspects of the firm's development. It is intended to highlight the main contours and so to provide a case study of a firm which was important not only to Bristol but also to the brewing industry as a whole, and within which it was justifiably regarded as an exemplar of good practice.[2]

Brewers commonly came from families with an existing interest in the drink trade that could offer their sons training and finance without any loss of social status.[3] Philip George, who dominated the affairs of the brewery in the early years, and whose family was involved with the firm thereafter, was the elder son of a wine merchant and distiller in Baldwin Street, Bristol. William George became a Freeman of the City in 1739 and was a full participant in Bristol's merchant patriciate. Philip had spent some years working in the distillery, but by the time the brewery partnership was formed he was a substantial businessman in his own right. He was 38 years old. Like many Bristol entrepreneurs of this period, including the six other members of the partnership, he moved easily between different business ventures. He dealt in hops and malt and engaged in a world-wide trade in wines and spirits – a natural extension to his interest in brewing. But he was also connected with the metal trades. In 1790 he formed the Patent Shot Co. to promote the production of perfectly round shot using the technique developed by William Watts in Bristol and patented in 1782. It gave Bristol a near monopoly of lead shot production in Britain. As an adjunct to this business Philip acquired shares in Cornish lead mines. He followed his father into Bristol's public life and was elected sheriff in 1808, 1813 and 1815. He died in 1828 aged 78 at his home in Berkeley Square.[4] His fellow partners were just as eminent in Bristol's commercial and political life; indeed, together their lifetime activities reflected the importance of Bristol as one of the country's leading manufacturing and commercial centres of the eighteenth century. The glass, sugar refining, distilling, brewing, confectionery and tobacco industries were represented, as well as banking, and trade with the West Indies.[5] Differences over the great moral issue of the day – the slave trade – did not inhibit business collaboration: two of Georges' partners, Peter Lunnell and Samuel Span, were on opposite sides, and were prominent figures in the public debate.

Georges were 'common brewers'; that is, they sold beer to publicans. The main theme in the history of the brewing industry after 1750 is the process by which common brewers captured the production roles of the 'home' and 'publican' brewers. There is some uncertainty about how much beer was brewed at home in country houses and institutions but it was probably a declining proportion of the total.[6] Beer was sold in alehouses throughout the country and was in many cases brewed on the premises. High transport costs protected many from outside competition. Such publican brewers were commonplace around 1800 in the Midlands, Wales, Lancashire, and the south west, including the Bristol area, whereas, roughly speaking, the common brewers were already ascendant in the East and South.[7] London, with its mass market, had led the way, as the common brewers were able to capture the technical and economic advantages arising from volume production. The business, as practised by the leading London porter brewers in the eighteenth century, was exceptionally capital intensive. As brewing was essentially a chemical rather than mechanical process, in which handling was minimised by using the force of gravity, the industry required relatively little labour.[8] The tendency toward increased capital intensity in production was followed in other British towns and cities in the nineteenth century. Bristol, for example, had a large and growing market – the fourth largest outside London in the early nineteenth century – and access to the city's major trading areas in Ireland, the West Indies and north west Europe. It was already an important centre for the export of beer and for many years Georges combined an extensive overseas trade with the supply of beer to the city's publicans.

The Bristol Porter Brewery occupied a prime city-centre site by the River Avon with a supply of good water (thought to give its beers their special flavour) and close to the docks through which raw materials and beer could be transported. However, despite these advantages, Georges faced very difficult market conditions for some years after 1788, and the firm was unable to return a trading profit until 1797.[9] The business only kept going because Philip George was prepared to put in some of the profits from his other businesses. All brewers had to face unprecedented increases in the malt tax and beer duties and rapidly rising raw material prices during the French Wars (1793–1815). There were years of severe dearth and distress, such as 1794–5, 1799–1800, and 1812. Beer consumption was, at the very least, checked.[10] Furthermore, Georges found that the business was too dependent on one product – porter, which was a strong, dark beer, brewed from malt which had been partly charred or browned by drying at high temperatures. It was favoured by the poorer sections of the community. Porter was relatively easy to ship and within a year of opening the business, Georges had made sales in Liverpool and Ireland. Not satisfied with the size of the Irish trade, in January 1792 Philip George sent a traveller, John Bradley, to Ireland to develop it further. He discovered a strong preference for London-brewed porter. Moreover, large-scale Irish breweries, such as Beamish & Crawford in Cork and Guinness in Dublin, were making inroads into the market. Imports into Ireland reached a peak in 1793 but fell away sharply after, so that by 1804 Ireland exported more beer than it imported.[11] The partners responded in two ways. First, they extended their product range to include pale ale. This was more expensive to produce than porter but was favoured by the better-off. A new, large pale ale brewery was built alongside the original Porter Brewery near Bristol Bridge and opened in 1796. Second, over the years new overseas markets were developed. A letter book covering the period 1818–45 provides us with a vivid insight into how these markets, which stretched across the globe from Lisbon to New York, Quebec, Kingston and Rio in the Americas, to India, were developed. Bills of exchange supplied the life-blood of the trade. The framework for local distribution was provided by agents who were first sent samples to see if there was any enthusiasm for Georges' beers. Two groups of English brewers set the standard: the large London brewers, who had a reputation for producing a top quality product, and the Burton brewers whose best brew was high-quality pale ale. In 1818 Georges sent 500 dozen bottles of Bristol porter to their agents in Boston and commented:

> We are aware that from prejudice the London Porter is thought superior to that of Bristol and any other place but by continuing to send you a good article and enabling you to supply your friends at 1/4 to 1/2 dollar per dozen under the price of the former, we hope that by perseverance to establish ourselves in your market.[12]

Here, price competition was used to open up the market. Correspondence with a Calcutta agent makes it clear that in 1828 Georges were trying hard to emulate the ale produced by Allsopps, one of the leading Burton brewers:

> On this occasion we made a slight alteration in the Ale, by brewing it rather a pale colour ... to make it as similar as possible to a sample of Allsopps' ale which has recently been presented to us.[13]

There was a great deal of trial and error in all this as Georges grappled not only with the demands of the market but also with technical problems posed by climatic variations. If an agent alleged that some beer was below standard, a lively correspondence usually ensued in which the agent would point to a bad brew and Georges would respond by suggesting that advice given on storage had been ignored.

Georges experienced a steady if unspectacular growth from 1815 to 1830, seeking, through a strategy of market diversification, especially overseas, to offset the effects on profits of postwar deflation. Beer and malt taxes continued at high levels even after the French wars, and despite the fall in raw material prices, brewers could not lower prices enough to sustain consumption at home.[14] Market conditions improved after the mid-1830s. On the demand side there was the continued rise of the urban population – Bristol's increased from 104,000 in 1831 to 183,000 40 years later – coupled after 1843 with rising working class incomes. Two measures in 1830 helped to lower prices and to stimulate demand: the removal of beer duties in the budget and the 'freeing' of the trade through legislation. The Beer Act of 1830 was intended to create a new type of drinking establishment – the beer-house – outside of the control of common brewers and the magistrates.[15] The intention was to lower prices through increased competition. Within a decade, 40,000 beer-houses had been licensed and during the lifetime of the Act (1830-69) the number of beer-houses rose to 46,135 (the average for 1865–69). The number of licensed public houses rose from an average of 52,900 (1830-34) to 68,300 (1865–69).[16] This extraordinary expansion of retail outlets provided an excellent opportunity for the larger provincial common brewers, like Georges, which were able to increase their sales significantly without the protection that was later afforded by the 'tied' system. Nationally, the proportion of beer brewed by publicans fell from 40 per cent in 1841–5 to 10 per cent in 1886–90, and the trade became concentrated in the hands of the common brewers. In Bristol, they produced 58 per cent of output in 1861, rising to 88 per cent in 1880. There were also fewer of them: 32 in 1860 and 21 in 1880.[17] The interaction of these factors led to a substantial rise in beer output and per capita consumption, greatly improving the fortunes of the industry. Georges increasingly specialised in supplying beer to publicans in Bristol, giving less attention to overseas markets.

The partnership went through a number of tranformations. By 1816 only two of the original partners, Jacob Wilcox Ricketts and Philip George, remained. They decided to retire in favour of their sons and a new partnership was formed which consisted of three Georges and four Rickettses. It was styled Georges, Ricketts & Co. The Rickettses were manufacturers of glass bottles, which were supplied for Hotwell water, and they may have bottled beer for Georges. These two families seem to have dominated the partnership until 1827, when Richard Vaughan became a partner. The Vaughans were prominent merchants and bankers in Bristol and they eventually replaced the Rickettses. In 1860 the last of the Ricketts family to be a partner died, and his capital of £10,000 was paid out to his executors. The partners were then Alfred George, Richard Vaughan and John William Cornish. Cornish died in the following year and the partnership became Georges & Co. The interest of the George family was still strong, and when the firm was incorporated in 1888, Charles George became managing director. The first chairman was Philip Henry Vaughan. He was soon succeeded in 1890 by Charles George. Thereafter the chairmanship was always held by a member of the George family.

At the very point at which Georges adopted limited company status in 1888, the retailing end of the industry was in the throes of a fundamental transformation. Brewers everywhere were scrambling to acquire public houses. Having already displaced the publican-brewers, common brewers next turned to securing the ownership and lease of retail outlets – a development foreshadowed much earlier in London. The effect was to transform their asset structures, and, in a more limited way, their

operations. Declining per capita consumption of beer from 1878, and the
end of the free trade in licenses with the restrictive legislation of 1869–72,
meant that market control depended increasingly on the ownership of
public houses. Once the process had started no firm was untouched by
it. The movement started in London and the Home Counties and by the
1860s had reached the West Country. By 1888 Georges already had 70
public houses, most of them recently acquired. The brewery was capable
of producing about 70,000 barrels a year, six times as much as 50 years
earlier.[18]

The costly process of purchasing public houses was invariably motivated
by the ambition to acquire control of the rapidly diminishing number of
outlets that remained 'free'. By 1896 about 90 per cent of Bristol's
on-licenses were tied.[19] Without access to the resources of the capital
market, the large-scale expansion of the late nineteenth century would
not have been possible. Brewers were in a good position to attract the
attention of investors because a growing proportion of their assets was
invested in property and therefore looked reasonably secure. Many,
including Georges, had a good local reputation and profit record. Leading
the way, however, was the remarkable public conversion of Guinness in
1886, a firm which did not engage in the scramble for retail outlets, but
rather relied on the qualities of its product to sustain its market position.
Guinness was floated during a general upswing in the trade and its
enormously successful launch offered a foretaste of a great deal of
speculative interest in the brewing industry. Other leading partnerships
such as Ind Coope, Samuel Allsopp, Whitbread, Courage, and Bass soon
followed. Large numbers of provincial companies were also floated, and
often these were based on the amalgamation of several firms. In the
Bristol area, for example, the Bath Brewery and Bristol United (two
firms which much later were absorbed by Georges) were launched in
1889. The Bath Brewery Ltd. was established to acquire six breweries in
the Bath area, while Bristol United, which consisted of four previously
independent firms, was formed as a defence against Georges which had
gone public the year before.

In Georges' case the decision to go to the market at this time was
prompted by a number of internal and external considerations. The
retirement of the senior partner, Richard Vaughan, in 1886, and the
death a year later of one of the managing partners, Philip Herbert George,
presented an opportunity for the surviving partners to reappraise the
firm's strategy. The conviction grew that future prosperity would depend
on buying more public houses, and that this could only be achieved if
the firm had more money. The partners also realised that in a rising
market, which put a high value on the firm's assets, they stood to make
sustantial personal gains from the flotation and would be free to redeploy

their resources should they wish. (The four partners received £232,000 in cash from the sale of the business.) However, the George and Vaughan families had no intention of losing control of the firm, and while their stakes were significantly less in the public company than in the partnership, and were insufficient to command a majority of votes among holders of ordinary shares, they retained enough shares to wield control.[20]

The prospectus for the company advertised a share capital with a nominal value of £300,000, divided equally between ordinary and preference shares of £10 each. Debenture applications to the value of £100,000 were also sought. The public's response was remarkable: in five hours of trading, the lists were over-subscribed nearly sixteen times.[21] Although interest was evenly divided between London and Bristol, the directors, who were all prominent Bristolians, were keen to maximise local support, not just from the 'trade' but also from important business and political interests, and they went through the lists with that in mind. A wide variety of occupations was revealed, ranging from beer-house and hotel keepers to bankers, merchants and the usual sprinkling of 'gentlemen'. The size and range of interest shown by Bristolians in the issue points to the maturity of the local capital market, the diversity of the local economy and the reputation enjoyed by Georges.

For some time business historians have been interested in the relationship between a firm's growth and changes in its organisational structure.[22] It has been observed that, in many cases, corporate growth forced changes in the way a business was organised and managed. The brewing industry is perhaps something of an exceptional case, in this period at least, since many medium-sized provincial firms like Georges were able to promote and absorb substantial growth without marked changes in structure or management. Essentially, the firm had a departmental form of organisation which reflected the main functional areas of activity: brewing and bottling; deliveries; and estate. There were also departments that looked after accounts, share registrations and general administration. A new and rapidly expanding aspect of management after 1888 was, of course, the acquisition and management of the public house estate. How was the relationship between the company – the landlord – and the growing number of tenants managed? The tied system was attractive because it offered an opportunity for brewers to exert more control over the conditions in which their beer was sold. To achieve this Georges took care to select good tenants and devise sound, legally binding agreements, which, among other things, insisted on the sale of its beers. Georges provided most of the capital (principally the cost of the building), while tenants paid for their fixtures, fittings and stock. The tenant was charged a low fixed rent (the 'dry' rent) and a surcharge on beer sold (the 'wet' rent). This form of 'co-partnership' was much preferred by Georges to the employment of managers, as it was in the industry as a whole. Travellers acted as watchdogs; they collected cash, took orders and generally supervised standards. This was an important and well rewarded function. In 1907, for instance, the six travellers responsible for the tied trade earned between £240 and £260 a year, excluding commission, which compared well with the £270 earned by the chief brewer, Philip George.[23]. The brewing department, of which George was head, was the largest in the firm, employing about 64 men; deliveries had 30; bottling employed a further 17; and the office had a staff of 30. Altogether the firm employed around 164 people, which was a small number in relation to the substantial and growing capital investment in the brewery and the public houses.[24] The workforce was not unionised and labour relations were managed in a traditional 'paternalistic' way; the directors took pride in what they regarded as the co-operative spirit which pervaded the firm. From 1891 the company paid a Christmas bonus which depended on the profits of the preceding year. Welfare benefits, including pensions, were dispensed at the discretion of the board, a practice which continued even after the decision was taken in 1924 to introduce a Pensions and Benevolent Fund financed from revenue and invested in the stock market. In 1931 the company bought a six acre field in West Town Lane, Brislington, for development as a sports ground.

After the flotation, as in most breweries, ownership and management continued to overlap. The sharpening of the distinction between the fee-paid director and the salaried manager, which became increasingly common in large concerns in other sectors, did not occur. In part this was because the brewing industry did not experience technological change on a scale which might have undermined existing arrangements. The firm's labour force, as we have seen, remained small and could be managed in a traditional, personal way. And lastly, an active involvement in brewing did not compromise social position or aspirations. A number of the directors at one time or another became involved in the day-to-day management of the firm and were usually given reponsibility for a particular aspect of the business, according to their talents, experience and contacts. The first chairman, Philip Henry Vaughan, looked after the brewing side, while Charles George concerned himself with financial questions. Other directors, for example Francis Tothill, the father-in-law of Charles George and a barrister, who was on the board from 1888 to 1901, were less involved in regular management but were valued for the public and professional position they held. For a firm in an industry that was often in the public limelight, and which had to keep on the good side of the licensing authorities, such people were very valuable. One of the advantages of the management system used by Georges was that it was flexible enough to bring talented managers into the boardroom.

Thus Wilfred Bisdee, who, as we shall see, master-minded the firm's growth strategy after 1910, was elected to the board in 1891 and carried on as manager of the estate office. He also had overall responsibility for financial matters. When he became a joint managing director in 1907, his fellow managing director, Arthur Terry, continued as head brewer, so that together they directly managed all the main activities of the firm. When Terry resigned in June 1913, Bisdee became the sole managing director, retaining that position until his retirement in September 1929.[25] The chairmanship was another matter. From 1891, after Philip Henry Vaughan's brief period in office, it was always occupied by a member of the George family.[26] Care was taken to prepare the successor by giving him a thorough grounding in the industry. For instance, before his recruitment to the board in 1911 W.E. George's son Christopher had worked for Whitbreads for seven years, and before that had been a principal of Messrs Ridgen & Co. of Faversham. Christopher, who was a strong supporter of Bisdee's expansion plans, succeeded his father in 1919.

With this rather traditional but flexible pattern of organisation and management, Georges grew into the largest brewery company in the West Country and was for a time one of the largest in the country. Expansion was very rapid in the early years, and was based upon the acquisition of public houses in Bristol. By 1892, it had around 350, which put it in fourth place nationally behind Peter Walker & Sons Ltd. (410), Steward & Co. (479) and Greenhill Whitely & Co. (681).[27] Georges and Bristol United, which ran neck and neck until the First World War, when Georges drew ahead, were throughout the dominant firms in Bristol. Both made excellent profits, which offers an important counter to some of the critical generalisations that have been made about entrepreneurship and profitability in the brewing industry in the period before the First World War.[28] Before 1910, when the firm's business strategy changed, public houses were acquired in two main ways. The first was the addition in 1889 at a cost of £215,000 of the business of James & Pierce, owner of the Bedminster Bridge Brewery. The other was less dramatic: the purchase of individual, formerly 'free' houses. The effects could be quite different. The acquisition of the brewery brought new business because the public houses that came with the deal had been tied; the free houses, because they had often been supplied by Georges, brought old but now more secure business and therefore had less immediate effect on turnover. What principles guided the general strategy? First, new houses had to be within a radius of about 5 miles from the Bath Street Brewery. The level of freight costs, fears about the deterioration of cask beer if it were transported too far, and case of management, were important factors.[29] Second, because the firm wanted a stable and tightly

31. Drays at Georges' Brewery, drawn by French Percheron shire horses.

controlled estate, it sought freehold rather than leasehold properties. Very few of the houses were leasehold. This, of course, had a dramatic effect on its asset structure: already by 1894 its houses were valued at just over £500,000, representing a more than fivefold increase since 1889.[30] Third, before making a purchase there was always a very careful assessment of actual and potential turnover as well as the condition of the building. In the first few years this was the particular province of Charles George, and, in later years, of Wilfred Bisdee. Finally (and this happened throughout the firm's history, as it often did in the industry as a whole), when a brewery company was taken over, brewing was discontinued, the premises were sold for other purposes and production concentrated at Bath Street. If the brewery was large or its owners were in a strong position to demand favourable terms, Georges offered the directors a place on the board – as, for instance, in the case of the owners of the Bedminster Bridge Brewery, S.G. James and R.B. Pierce. The financial aspects of this deal were criticised by shareholders led by Sir George White, who argued that the board was being too generous in letting James and Pierce collect substantial premiums from the shares and debentures paid to them by Georges.[31] The Bedminster Bridge Brewery had to be kept going for a couple of years while preparations were made for increased production at Bath Street. Adjoining freehold properties were bought and converted for the brewery's use. In the flat market conditions of the early 1890s it took some time before Georges felt the benefit of the new arangements. However, once all the adjustments had been made, savings were reported from running one brewery rather than two. In particular, labour charges, taxes and rates were reduced.[32] By 1896 the firm had returned to the high levels of profitability achieved during the years immediately after incorporation. Dividends on ordinary shares varied from $17\frac{1}{2}$ per cent to $18\frac{1}{2}$ per cent until 1904 and the net rate of return on capital varied between 12.3 per cent and 13.2 per cent during the same period, as can be seen from Table 1.

Even by the standards of the brewing industry – which were by no means low – George's record of profitability was indeed very impressive. Taking the entire period between 1888 and 1910 the net rate of return on capital was always 9 per cent or more and dividends on ordinary shares never fell below 10 per cent. The firm's financial strategy, described below, undoubtedly served to protect it against the worst effects of market fluctuations, in particular after 1903, when many firms (the 'bloated dinosaurs' as Gourvish and Wilson call them) were facing grave problems because of earlier financial miscalculations.[33] The race to acquire public houses, which became almost frantic between 1894 and 1901, had expensive after-effects. Those brewers which had paid high prices and had financed their acquisitions through large increases in debenture stock and preference shares were dangerously over-geared and were only able to survive through capital restructuring. A number of famous London and Burton brewers were in this position. Moreover, the beer market was hardly promising in the early twentieth century. Real wages were stagnant or falling, and ale consumption was also hit by changes in working-class spending and leisure patterns. The Liberal governments after 1906, pressurised by the temperance lobby, seemed to the brewers to be determined to introduce restrictive legislation. But before then the brewers' party, the Conservatives, had devised a compensation fund in the Licensing Act of 1904 which established the principle that public houses in areas where they were not needed would be closed. A levy was imposed on all licensed properties by the compensation committee of the quarter sessions. While brewers, including Georges, chose in public to indict the Act as yet another restriction on their commercial freedom – "the immoral principle of compensation" as Georges' chairman declared in 1908 – it did in fact offer an opportunity for rationalisation.[34] In bad trading years Georges was quite happy to get rid of its least profitable houses. The firm paid between £3,000-4,000 a year in levies. By 1910 it had paid a total of £21,936 into the fund and had received back £18,528 as compensation for houses closed by the authorities. The licensing

Table 1. *Georges & Co: Ordinary Dividend and Net Rate of Return on Capital, 1888–1914*

Year	Dividend %	Rate of return %
1888	15	10.5
1889	18	11.5
1890	19	12.1
1891	16	11.5
1892	16	11.4
1893	15	11.1
1894	15	11.0
1895	16	-
1896	$17\frac{1}{2}$	12.5
1897	19	13.0
1898	$18\frac{1}{2}$	13.0
1899	$18\frac{1}{2}$	13.1
1900	$18\frac{1}{2}$	13.2
1901	$18\frac{1}{2}$	12.5
1902	$18\frac{1}{2}$	12.9
1903	$18\frac{1}{2}$	12.3
1904	17	11.5
1905	15	10.9
1906	15	11.0
1907	15	10.8
1908	12	10.8
1909	12	10.3
1910	10	9.0
1911	10	10.2
1912	10	9.8
1913	11	11.0
1914	11	12.3

Source: T.R. Gourvish and R.G. Wilson, 'Profitability in the Brewing Industry', *Business History*, XXVII (1985), p. 164.

authorities were prepared to interpret the Act flexibly, so that when in 1910 trading conditions were less favourable than at any time since Georges' flotation, the Bristol magistrates agreed that there should be no levy during the year.[35] Keeping the goodwill of the magistrates and offering up unprofitable houses for sacrifice was sound business practice in the circumstances. For the industry as whole, the elimination of uneconomic retail outlets through legislative intervention satisfied the need to adjust to a lower level of demand. By the outbreak of the First

World War very few of Georges' 600 houses were unremunerative. It was the temperance movement, not the brewers, which had reason to be dissatisfied, for the Act acknowledged the 'legitimate' right of the industry to conduct its business and implied that for the most part this was compatible with social order. Georges' directors also complained publicly, and privately too, about the imposition of higher duties on retail licenses. The backdrop was the constitutional crisis of 1908 and 1909. The budget proposals of 1909 contained an assault on the brewers' tied houses. The rejection of the budget in the Lords led to a general election. A new budget followed in 1910 which included a sharp increase in the license duty on public houses. However, Georges, like brewers elsewhere, was able to moderate the effect of the rise by successfully contesting the rateable valuation of its houses on the grounds that the annual values had, as a consequence, declined significantly.[36]

The incidence of recession in the early twentieth century varied greatly within the brewing industry. In Bristol, Georges managed to preserve its leadership of the industry. Profitability dipped slightly between 1908 and 1910, but from 1911, the year which marks the beginning of renewed growth, there was a strong recovery. A year later prosperity was evident throughout the industry.[37] Georges' success was due in part to the firm's response to new market trends. Its reputation had been built up on the sale of heavy beers, but in their heyday, between the 1840s and 1880s, the Burton brewers had stimulated a national demand for pale bitter beers. During the early 1890s, when there was a small decline in the brewery's trade, the chairman, Charles George, decided to commit the firm to the development of fresh bitter and mild beers, and to bottled beers.[38] By this time it was technically possible for medium-sized brewers like Georges to brew and bottle a consistent, 'Burton' type of beer, and to seek a local niche in a market which had been so brilliantly developed on a national scale by the Burton brewers in the mid-nineteenth century. The problems of improving the keeping qualities of bottled beer were also being overcome. The 1880s and 1890s saw the mass production of glass beer bottles and crown corks, and the application of the processes of pasteurisation and chilling.[39] In Georges' case, the capital needed for the new plant came from the proceeds (£9,500) of the sale of the Bedminster Brewery and from current profits. In the years which followed there was a substantial increase in bottling capacity.

In 1910, the important decision was taken to accelerate the growth of the business through the acquisition of other brewery companies. Between 1911 and 1923 Georges acquired five firms and 305 licensed properties, making a total of 850 pubs (See Table 2). The architect of expansion was Wilfred Bisdee. He understood that the adoption of motor transport meant that the firm's distribution area could be extended up to a radius

Table 2. *Breweries acquired by Georges, 1911–23*

Name	Date	Location	Licenses	Price
R.W. Miller	1911	Stokes Croft, Bristol	48	£86,000
Hall & Sons	1912	Lodway (Pill), Somerset	39	£77,957
J. Arnold & Sons	1918	Wickwar, Gloucs.	40	£35,000
Welton Breweries	1918	Welton, Somerset	100	£135,000
Bath Brewery	1923	Bath, Somerset	105	£160,750
				£494,707

Source: Bristol Brewery, Georges & Co. Ltd., Annual Report and Accounts.

of around twenty miles, offering some release from the tight conditions of trading that existed in the centre of Bristol where the market was effectively divided between Georges and United. Smaller, less viable breweries in Gloucestershire and Somerset, weakened by the tight trading

32. Steam lorries at Georges. Motor transport permitted the company to expand its sphere of operations.

conditions of the previous decade, offered attractive pickings. Georges was interested in their licensed properties and sold off the breweries as soon as possible. The acquisitions are listed in Table 2.

What is striking about the management of the expansion strategy was the reliance upon internally generated funds. From the formation of the company the directors pursued a conservative financial policy. Perhaps the most risky phase was at the very beginning when the Bedminster Brewery was acquired and financed through a substantial increase in share capital. But generally the firm was able to build up a substantial reserve from share premiums and profits. It could therefore weather poor trading conditions, write off revaluations as licensed properties depreciated, and finance expansion. Between 1911 and 1918, when £333,957 was spent on buying small breweries, the share capital was increased by only £44,000.[40] Profits and short-term loans supplied most of the finance for additions and changes to plant, and the acquisition of property. A good example was the acquisition in 1911 of the properties of R.W. Miller & Co., a firm in the hands of the receivers following the death of the principal director. Georges paid £86,000 for Millers' 48 licensed properties, acquiring a trade of about 8,000 barrels of beer a year. A loan of £45,000 at 4 per cent was obtained from Georges' bankers, National Provincial, repayable over four years without special security. It was described as "a perfectly safe advance and seeing they keep a large credit balance it is recommended".[41] By the end of 1912 all but £5,000 had been repaid. By keeping down the growth of total capital, maintaining a low gearing ratio compared with many brewery companies, and nourishing a healthy reserve, Georges managed to combine a low-risk policy of expansion with the distribution of attractive dividends. The stock market accordingly gave the firm a high valuation. For instance, in 1904/5, when its paid-up capital was £744,000, its market value was more than twice that figure – £1.7 million.[42] One final indication of the firm's cautious financial management is to be found in the early creation of a dividend reserve fund. The fund was invested in railway and local government stocks, and, during the First World War, in war loans. Its purpose was to offer a hedge against a drop in net income so that dividends would be protected. For a long while it was thought that the fund would have to be raided if the dividend was in danger of slipping below 15 per cent. In fact it was used only once before the First World War: in 1910, when £5,000 was taken to pay a dividend for the year of 10 per cent.[43]

For the industry as a whole, the First World War reinforced the trend of declining output and consumption. Beer output in the United Kingdom averaged 34.1 million standard barrels between 1910 and 1914 and fell to an average of 22.7 between 1915 and 1919. Consumption per capita fell from an average of 26.9 gallons in the first period to 16.5 in the second.[44] During the conflict the duty on beer was increased substantially, which pushed up retail prices, opening hours were drastically reduced, and there were restrictions on barley and sugar supplies. Brewers were asked to reduce the gravities and volumes of their beers to make them weaker. As men joined up – over 100 from Georges – brewers had to find replacements. Three of the assistant brewers at Georges were commissioned, placing a great deal of additional pressure on the head brewer, Hadley. One of the directors, Joseph Hall, was brought out of semi-retirement to assist him. Women were employed for the first time in the brewery itself, and by the early part of 1916 there were sixty females on the firm's books.[45] Despite the rapid rise in the price of labour and brewing materials after 1916, brewers were able to pass on higher costs to consumers, who, in effect, paid more for an inferior, weaker, product. Even after Income Tax and Excess Profit Duty were provided for, breweries made very good profits during the war. Georges was no exception. The firm had so much liquidity in 1917 and 1918 that it bought two breweries from its own resources – J. Arnold & Sons and Welton Breweries Ltd. – and thereby added 140 public houses to its estate. If it had been necessary to raise capital on the market, Treasury approval would almost certainly have been withheld. A year later a part of the general reserve (£81,000) was capitalised as a bonus for ordinary shareholders. No less than £50,000 had been added to the reserve in the previous two years, so, as the chairman put it, "the shareholders are entitled to a share".[46] It did something to correct the imbalance between the value of the company's assets and its capital.

From a national perspective the interwar period presents a dismal picture for brewing, as aggregate and per capita consumption of beer continued to fall. Yet Georges managed to achieve impressive financial results. The agricultural depression had some impact in the early 1920s on returns from the recently acquired rural public houses, but by the middle of the decade the firm's trading profits and dividends were extremely healthy. Dividends climbed from 16 per cent in 1919–23 to 20 per cent in 1925 and 1926, fell slightly to 18 per cent in 1927 and 1929 but then, remarkably, held at 20 per cent for the next four years – the period of the cyclical downturn in the economy and trough of 1929–33.[47] Apart from 1932, when the dividend was maintained by a reduction in the sum set aside for reserves, these results were based on increased trading profits. At first sight the position in 1932 was rather worrying for the board. The year before, the Ashton Gate Brewery in Bristol, with 200 public houses, had been acquired, yet total output had actually fallen, bringing a decline in disposable income.[48] The difficulty was attributed to depressed working-class incomes and to the imposition of a higher level of duty in the emergency budget of September 1931 which increased retail prices by at least 1d. a pint. The sum needed to protect the existing dividend rate was larger than before because, contrary to the firm's traditional financial strategy, the Ashton Gate Brewery had been purchased through an enlargement in the ordinary share capital of £174,046. In the event, the 1932 results proved to be exceptional. However, a review was made of the economics of the brewery itself which led to the decision to close the bottling and transport departments on Saturdays until trade picked up, which it did within a few months, and to undertake bottling for Guinness and Bass.[49] The budget of 1933 assisted trade because the concept of a barrel of standard gravity of 1055 was abolished, and the duty was in future levied on the actual gravity of the beer. As a consequence, Georges' beer was reduced by a minimum of 1d. a pint. The remaining few years of peace were profitable for most brewers, especially those, like Georges, in the more prosperous parts of the country. Indeed, by the end of 1934 the board was in a position to recommend the creation of new shares to the value of £302,000 which stood to the credit of the general reserve and to allocate them on the basis of one share for every two already held.[50] By 1937 production nationally had recovered to its pre-depression levels, although in per capita terms it was only half pre-1914 levels.[51] Georges was able to maintain its outstanding performance.

Georges' apparent insulation from the ravages of the depression was in part due to the firm's location in a part of the country which had a diversified economic structure with a number of expanding industries, such as chemicals, aeroplanes, and zinc. Retailing and building also saw growth. The vast new municipal housing estates on the outskirts of Bristol, in Bedminster, Knowle, Fishponds, Sea Mills, Southmead, Speedwell, Horfield,and Shirehampton, which the City Council sought to preserve as dry areas, offered some limited opportunities for expansion in the 1930's, although more was to come after the Second World War. The firm's territory outside Bristol also represented a diversity of economic settings and nowhere, save the Somerset coalfield, did unemployment match the severity found in the old industrial areas of the north.

Yet Georges could not afford to be complacent. After the First World War, the switch in leisure preferences accelerated, especially among the young who were more often to be found in the cinema than in the public house. Moreover changes in drinking tastes towards lighter and bottled beers, also in evidence earlier, became more pronounced. The managing director, Wilfred Bisdee, showed an acute awareness of these trends. He realised that the firm had not only to extend its retail outlets as a means of maintaining and developing production, but it needed also to attract new customers and to respond to changes in public taste. This was to be achieved in three principal ways. First, more of the firm's production would be given over to lighter and bottled beers. The new bottling plant, which came into use in 1915, was capable of washing, bottling, corking and labelling 100,000 bottles a day.[52] By the mid-1930s, roughly one-third of production was devoted to bottled beers and this was the most profitable part of the business, as it was nationally.[53] The second response was to make public houses more attractive, accessible and flexible in the range of services that they were able to offer. Tenants were offered prizes as an incentive to liberate their premises from the traditional image of dark places frequented by working men simply for the purpose of drinking beer. Encouraged by record sales and buoyant profits in the mid-1920s, the firm increased its expenditure on upgrading public houses. Lounges, brighter decorations and skittle alleys were introduced, and tenants were encouraged to supply food. Finally there was a tendency, largely developed after Bisdee's death, to offer a wider range of drinks, especially wines. In 1931 the wine and spirit business of the Ashton Gate Brewery was acquired, along with the brewery, and this prompted the board, when the opportunity arose during the following year, to purchase a controlling interest, at a cost of £25,000, in Messrs Wyld & Co. Ltd. This was an old-established firm, founded in 1803 in Redcliff Street, which supplied quality wines. It proved to be a good investment.[54]

A vital condition for the continued growth of Georges after 1910 was the availability of land adjacent to the Bath Street brewery to accommodate enlargements to the plant. As brewery companies were acquired, their capacity was closed down and orders transferred to Bath Street, where modern equipment was installed. With the rapid expansion after 1911 there was increasing pressure on existing facilities. The purchase of the extensive Talbot Hotel premises on the corner of Victoria Street and Bath Street in 1919 led to the relocation of the stables and offices and provided an opportunity for the enlargement of the brewery itself. However, the real breakthrough came in 1924 when Georges acquired a $\frac{2}{3}$-acre site between the Counterslip and the river, adjoining its brewery on the east side, with an entrance on the Counterslip. Here an up-to-date building was erected on the river bank. Below the level of the river a vast cellar was created with a garage above for the firm's fleet of vehicles. Above this, with access through a huge automatic lift, an automatic washing plant was installed. Each cask was washed out, sterilised by superheated steam, revolved and scrubbed inside. Then, further up, there was the cooperage. Modern fermenting vessels and yeast backs were installed. The bottling stores were extended into premises in Tucker Street which helped Georges to deal with the most rapidly expanding part of the business, the trade in bottled beer. Rising profit levels based upon increased trade provided the means to finance this programme of enlargement and modernisation. It took until 1933 to complete. The

33. Bottling beer at Georges in the 1930s.

brewery then occupied a site of almost 3 acres, with a frontage on the river which stretched from close to Bristol Bridge to a point near St. Philip's Bridge.[55] The sales report for the year ending 31 September 1936 offers a clear picture of what the brewery was producing and where the output was distributed. In terms of sales, cask goods accounted for 168,290 barrels and bottled goods for 57,853 barrels which meant that the brewery was operating at a creditable 90 per cent of capacity. It also bottled 6,195 barrels of Guinness. Georges owned 922 houses at this time, made up of 415 full licenses, 338 beer-houses and 169 off-licenses. It leased or had on mortgage a further 40. The free trade, which a century before had been the mainstay of the firm's business, was very small, accounting for a little over 10 per cent of sales.[56]

This brief history of Georges over its first fifty years as a public company illustrates in a small way how a traditional management was able to adapt its marketing strategy to changed circumstances and produce an excellent return for its shareholders. It was no less or more innovative in technical terms than most other brewery companies. As a glance at the managing director's notes on "monthly averages" reveals, there was an extraordinary attention to detail. Knowing and anticipating market prices for hops, malt and fodder, and other inputs, was an essential factor in good management.[57] Overlaying everything, however, was a cautious but highly successful financial policy: "good finance and good beer ... produced a good balance sheet", declared the chairman in 1914.[58]

NOTES

1. K.H. Hawkins and C.L. Pass, *The Brewing Industry: a Study of Industrial Organisation and Public Policy* (1979), pp.60-79.

2. The historiography of the English brewing industry is variable in quality. For the period before 1830 there is the excellent study by P. Mathias, *The Brewing Industry in England, 1700-1830* (Cambridge, 1959). T. Corran is writing a second volume to cover the period 1830 to 1969. For surveys of the nineteenth and twentieth centuries see Hawkins and Pass, *Organisation and Public Policy*, and J.E. Vaizey, *The Brewing Industry, 1886–1951* (1960). By far the best company history is R.G. Wilson, *Greene King: a Business and Family History* (1983).

3. Brewers along with bankers were able to remain active in their business avocations without much loss of status in county society. See L. Stone and J.C. Fawtler Stone, *An Open Elite? England, 1540-1880* (Oxford,1984), p.290.

4. J. Latimer, *Annals of Bristol in the Eighteenth Century* (Bristol, 1893), pp.453-54. L. Wiltshire, *History of the Bristol Brewery Georges & Co. Ltd. 1788–1961* (bound typescript by the Public Relations Officer, Courage Western Ltd., n.d.), p.2.

5. The original partners, who had equal shares of £2,000 each were: Philip George, William Fry, Peter Lunell, John Maxse, Jacob Wilcox Ricketts, Samuel Span and Samuel Worrall. For further information on how their business careers interacted see B.W.E. Alford, *W.D. & H.O. Wills and the development of the U.K. tobacco industry, 1786–1965* (1973), pp.65, 67.

6. Wilson, *Greene King*, p.13.

7. Ibid., p.13.

8. S. Pollard, *The Genesis of Modern Management* (1968 edn.), p.119. For an excellent description of scientific and technical changes see Wilson, *Greene King*, pp.65–70.

9. Wiltshire, *Bristol Brewery*, p.4.

10. See figures for beer charged with duty in B.R. Mitchell and P. Deane, *Abstract of British Historical Statistics* (Cambridge, 1962), pp.251–2.

11. H.S. Corran, *A History of Brewing* (1975), pp.150-1.

12. Bristol Record Office (hereafter B.R.O.), George Ricketts and Co., 35740/GR/5, Foreign Letter Book, 20 Oct. 1818.

13. Ibid., 22 Dec. 1828.

14. B. Harrison, *Drink and the Victorians* (1971), p.72.

15. Ibid., pp.64–86.

16. Hawkins and Pass, *Organisation and Public Policy*, p.18.

17. Ibid., pp.22–3.

18. B.R.O., Bristol Brewery Georges and Co. Ltd., 35740/B6/81, Directors' Minute Book no.1, 5 Feb. 1889. Anon, *History of the Bristol Brewery, Georges & Co. Ltd.* (Bristol, 1921), p.16.

19. Hawkins and Pass, *Organisation and Public Policy*, p.30, from the Royal Commission on Licensing (1896–9).

20. At the time of the initial allotment in 1888, the seven directors together held about one-third of the ordinary shares. Vaughan and the two Georges held almost 25 per cent between them. The directors were: P.H. Vaughan (esquire), R.W.Butterworth (iron merchant), W.E. George, C.E.A. George, C.Bowles Hare (merchant and manufacturer), W.H. Harford (banker) and Francis Tothill (barrister). B.R.O., 35740/136/1(b), Memorandum and

Articles of Association of the Bristol Brewery Georges & Co. Ltd. Ordinary Share Ledger, vol.1, 1888–93.

21. B.R.O., Bristol Brewery Georges & Co. Ltd., 35740/B6/81, Directors' Minute Book no.1, 23 Feb. 1888.

22. The seminal work is A.D. Chandler's, *Strategy and Structure: Chapters in the History of American Industrial Enterprise* (Cambridge, Mass. 1962).

23. B.R.O., Bristol Brewery Georges & Co. Ltd., 35740/B6/24, Salaries, 1907.

24. Ibid. For comparison, in 1888 there were about 70 employees.

25. He continued as a director until his death by suicide on 6 April 1932 on the railway line near his home at Hambrook.

26. Charles Edward Alfred George, 1891–1907 (died); Wilfred Edward George, 1907–1919 (retired); Christopher George, 1919–1951 (retired).

27. Hawkins and Pass, *Organisation and Public Policy*, p.30n.

28. For a valuable review of the literature and a convincing corrective, see T.R. Gourvish and R.G. Wilson 'Profitability in the Brewing Industry, 1885–1914', *Business History*, XXVII (1985), p.2.

29. Report in the *Bristol Times and Mirror* of the Annual General Meeting held on 15 Feb. 1897.

30. The firm's freehold houses were valued at £90,000 in 1889 and £511,000 in 1894.

31. Report in the *Bristol Times and Mirror* of the Extraordinary General Meeting held on 10 April 1889.

32. Report in the *Bristol Times and Mirror* of the Annual General Meeting held on 15 Feb. 1893.

33. Gourvish and Wilson, 'Profitability', p.159.

34. Report in the *Bristol Times and Mirror* of the Annual General Meeting held on 15 Feb. 1908.

35. Ibid., 10 Feb. 1911.

36. Wilson, *Greene King*, p.144.

37. Ibid., p.135.

38. Report in the *Bristol Times and Mirror* of the Annual General Meeting held on 15 Feb. 1893.

39. Wilson, *Greene King*, p.153.

40. Calculated from the firm's annual accounts.

41. Dr P. Ollerenshaw kindly provided this reference.

42. I am indebted to Dr P. Wardley for this information which is from his large scale study of British big business.

43. Report in *The Bristol Times and Mirror* of the Annual General Meeting held on 10 Feb. 1911.

44. B.R. Mitchell and P. Deane, *British Historical Statistics*, p.253.

45. Report in the *Bristol Times and Mirror* of the Annual General Meeting held on 11 Feb. 1916.

46. Ibid., 14 Feb. 1919.

47. From the firm's published accounts.

48. Inman H. Harvey, an Ashton Gate director, was appointed to Georges' board. B.R.O., 35740/B6/90, Directors' Minute Book no.9, 8 Oct. 1931 – 26 May 1932. The Ashton Gate Brewery was profitable and in its last year of independent operation (to 30 Sept. 1931) paid an ordinary dividend of 13 per cent.

49. B.R.O., 35740/B6/91, Directors' Minute Book no.10, 5/19 Jan. 1933; 25 July 1933.

50. Ibid., 15 Nov. 1934.

51. Wilson, *Greene King*, p.190.

52. Anon, *Georges & Co.* (Bristol, 1921), p.17.

53. B.R.O., 35740/B6/25, Sales Report for 12 months ending 30 Sept. 1936.

54. B.R.O., 35740/B6/90, Directors' Minute Book no.9, 4 Jan. 1932; 12 May 1932.

55. For a detailed description see Anon, *Georges and Co. Ltd.* 1788–1932: 144 *years of Brewing* (Bristol, c.1933), pp. 6–7.

56. B.R.O., 35740/B6/25, Sales Report for 12 months ending 30 Sept. 1936. 51 per cent of the free trade was in bottled goods.

57. B.R.O., 35740/B6/25, Monthly Averages, 1904–1925.

58. Note the similarities between Georges and the East Anglian brewer, Greene King; see Wilson, *Greene King*, passim.

Rearmament, War and the Performance of the Bristol Aeroplane Company, 1935–45[1]

GLYN STONE

The tremendous growth of aircraft manufacturing in the twentieth century was not an inevitable consequence of the revolutionary nature of air travel. Nor did it grow at an even pace. Without the pressure and experience of two world wars, in particular the Second World War and the period of rearmament which preceded it, it is likely that the development of the aircraft industry everywhere would have been severely retarded. As late as 1935 the number of employees engaged either directly or indirectly in the production of aircraft in Great Britain was no greater than 50,000. Yet by 1940, almost a million people were so engaged, and in 1943 total employment in the industry reached an all time high of 1.8 million. An investment of £350 million was made between 1935 and 1945 of which £150 million was laid out on new buildings and £200 million on plant. Wartime production totalled 131,549 aircraft.[2]

The Bristol Aeroplane Co. developed according to the pattern of the British aircraft industry as a whole, showing quite spectacular growth during World War One, severe retrenchment during the period 1920–1934, and then accelerated production on a very large scale following the adoption of the government's rearmament programme with its increasing emphasis on air power; initially, bomber offensive as deterrent and then a combination of that and fighter defence.[3] This chapter concentrates upon the last period – including the Second World War – by describing the growth of the company; by comparing its development to that of the overall performance of the British aircraft industry; and by stressing the great importance of the company's relations with the Air Ministry; but, first of all, it is necessary to provide a context by giving a short history of the company's development up to 1935.

The Bristol Aeroplane Co. was founded in 1910 as the British & Colonial Aeroplane Co. by Sir George White, chairman of the Bristol Tramways & Carriage Co. British & Colonial was financed entirely by the White family, and in its first year employed 80 people. Between 1910 and 1914 the company produced barely more than 200 aircraft. At the outbreak of the First World War its personnel numbered 400; by the end of the

war there were over 3,000 on the payroll. The rapid expansion of the
company had been based largely on the remarkable success of the Bristol
Fighter.[4] Within fourteen months of the Armistice the company's name
was changed to that of the Bristol Aeroplane Co. in order to avoid the
punitive effects of the Excess Profits Duty because existing businesses
which were discontinued and their assets transferred to a new trading
company paid less. In this way much of the wartime profit was retained
and the company's future secured. The authorised share capital of the
new company amounted to £1 million of which £553,000 was fully secured
by the assets of the British & Colonial Aeroplane Co. At the same time,
encouraged by the Air Ministry, the new company took over the Cosmos
Engineering Co. in Fishponds, Bristol, together with its chief engineer,
Roy Fedden, whose team of designers was to provide the nucleus of the
aero engine department. The takeover proved highly significant, since
it made the Bristol Aeroplane Co. the leading airframe *and* aero engine
manufacturer in the United Kingdom.[5]

In view of the future significance of the engine department it is ironic
that the company intended in 1921 to close it down because sales had not
matched investment. The department was saved only through the success

34. Bristol Boxkites under construction at Filton, around 1912. Surprisingly
robust, they were very successful as training aircraft, although soon superseded
by more advanced designs.

of its Jupiter air-cooled radial engine in attracting the attention of the French Gnôme Rhône Co., which, after an exhibition in Paris, decided to acquire a Bristol engine licence.[6] Subsequently, the company won its first production order for 42 engines from the British government and this was followed by further orders. Indeed, during the 1920s the company was one of four manufacturers within an Air Ministry protection ring which received all official orders; the other three were Rolls-Royce, Armstrong Siddeley, and Napier.[7] During the early part of the decade the Bristol company's position was inferior to that of Armstrong Siddeley, at that time the dominant British manufacturer of air-cooled engines. However, by the late 1920s the Bristol Aeroplane Co. emerged as the dominant producer of air-cooled engines to complement the water-cooled engines produced by Rolls-Royce. Indeed, between 1920 and 1930 Bristol air-cooled radial engines were installed in 262 different prototype aircraft throughout the world, over 70 of which went into production. Unlike Armstrong Siddeley, the company had been prepared to invest heavily on the development side, largely owing to the persuasive powers of Fedden who "stimulated the engineers of the company to give their best efforts, persuaded the management of the company to approve courses of action he believed technically advisable, and obtained from the government the funds needed to support the work".[8] Armstrong Siddeley's relative indifference is surprising in view of the fact that the government was willing to pay the development costs. The total official payments to Bristol Acroplane for the development of the whole series of Jupiter engines between 1920 and 1931 amounted to £348,000 and when, in 1931, the company still claimed that it had lost £124,000 on development costs the government agreed to amortize the deficit by authorising the addition of a sum of £50 to the selling price of future engines. The success of the engine department during this period can be inferred from the growth in employment from about 50 staff in 1920 to almost 2,000 in 1930.[9]

On the airframe side, the years before 1934 were lean ones for the company as government orders were extremely limited, with the exception of the Bristol Bulldog, of which nearly 450 were produced for the Royal Air Force and eight other national air forces.[10] The British aircraft industry, including Bristol Aeroplane, failed to respond to the scarcity in orders for military aircraft by developing a successful civil airline sector; this compared badly with the Americans, whose advanced developments such as the Boeing 247 and the Douglas DC1 came into production in 1933.[11] During the 1920s and early 1930s aircraft firms responded to the dearth of orders by resorting to other kinds of work in the hope of better times ahead. In the south west, Gloster produced car bodies, milk churns, all-metal shop fronts and fish friers. Pigs were kept in the hangars which were also used for cultivating mushrooms. Westland in Yeovil

35. The Jupiter engine shop in the late 1920s. A.H.R. Fedden instituted an almost fanatical programme of trials and development to improve the power and reliability of the Bristol company's engines. Engines which caused problems were stripped down and examined in workshops like this.

produced milk churns, pianos, and light engineering assemblies while the Bristol company manufactured coach bodies for the Bristol Tramways & Carriage Co.[12] However, these firms did enjoy the advantage of being members of the government's airframe protection ring, whereby only they received the aircraft specifications which were issued for information when the Air Ministry wanted a new civil or military aircraft.[13]

When the government began its massive military expansion programme after 1934 the Bristol Aeroplane Co. was better placed than most other firms in the industry. It was an established producer of both aero engines and airframes, and it was located in a government-designated 'safe zone' containing reserves of skilled engineers capable of adapting to aero engine production and female labour which was to become more important as the Second World War progressed. In addition the firm employed two of the country's most respected engine and airframe designers, Roy Fedden and Captain Frank Barnwell.[14] To meet the challenge of rearmament, the company was reorganised on 15 June 1935 as a public limited liability company with an issued capital of £1,200,000.[15] Despite the change the board of directors continued to be dominated by the White family. Sir George White's son, Sir G. Stanley White, continued as managing director, while his nephews, William G. Verdon Smith and Herbert J. Thomas, continued as chairman and assistant managing director respectively. Sir G. Stanley White's son, George White, and Verdon Smith's son, William R. Verdon Smith, also occupied seats on the board.

Unquestionably, the Bristol Aeroplane Co.'s fortunes improved dramatically after 1934 as it sought to satisfy the insatiable appetite of the Royal Air Force. At the beginning of 1935 the company employed fewer than 4,300 people, of whom 60 per cent were engaged in engine production. Within a year its employees numbered more than 8,000 rising to over 14,000 by the end of 1938, and thereafter rising even faster to a peak of 52,000, including those working at its agency factories at Weston-super-Mare and Accrington in Lancashire.[16] The balance sheets of the company confirm the significant advances made between 1935 and 1945 (see Table 1). In 1935 the total capital employed was £1,977,000; by the end of 1937 it had reached £5,016,000 and by the end of 1939 it had more than doubled to £10,534,000. A peak figure of £15,177,000 was reached in 1943. It is significant that fixed assets increased far less than current assets. The former amounted to £1,018,000 in 1935, reaching a peak of

Table 1. *Financial Profile of the Bristol Aeroplane Co., 1935-44*

	Total Capital Employed £000	Issued Share Capital £000	Net Profit* £000	Dividend on Ordinary Shares %
1935	1,977	1,200	237	22.5
1936	3,858	1,800	295	22.5
1937	5,016	1,800	345	25
1938	6,940	3,900	378	15
1939	10,534	3,900	320	10
1940	12,979	3,900	296	10
1941	13,632	3,900	285	10
1942	14,157	3,900	282	10
1943	15,177	3,900	309	10
1944	14,818	3,900	314	10

Source: Filton, Bristol Aeroplane Co., Annual Report and Accounts, 1935-44.
* Net profit after tax.

£2,357,000 in 1940. Current assets stood at only £958,000 in 1935 but had soared to £7,830,000 in 1939, and to a peak of £12,887,000 in 1943. Clearly, the company's fortunes, and those of its employees, depended heavily upon a continuing high level of official orders.

At the beginning of the rearmament period the company's ordinary shareholders enjoyed very high dividends. They were paid dividends before tax of 22.5 per cent in 1935 and 1936, and 25 per cent in 1937. However, from 1938 onwards, and despite the increased turnover, dividend payments fell to an annual level of about 10 per cent.[17] This reduction was largely a consequence of the government's insistence upon the payment of higher National Defence Contributions by the armaments companies following critical comments on their profit levels by the House of Commons.[18] The highest net profit achieved by the Bristol Aeroplane Co. during the period under review was £378,000 in 1938. After 1940, however, net profits began to fall, dipping below £300,000 for the first time since 1936. Two causes may be cited: the Finance Act of 1940; and the more strongly urged insistence of the Ministry of Aircraft Production that pre-tax profits on production should be reduced. Even at the height of the company's productive activity in 1943 net profit rose only slightly above £300,000.[19]

Dependent as the company was on government orders for its development, the directors had no alternative but to accept the limitations placed upon profit levels with a good grace. As Verdon Smith told the shareholders in October 1941:

> In this matter your Company, as is the case with many others, is called upon to make heavy contributions to the current cost of the war in accordance with the financial policy of His Majesty's Government. For these reasons the amount of profit available for distribution to shareholders bears no relation to the vast scope of the Company's business and activities in connection with the War. At the same time, under present conditions shareholders will no doubt willingly accept this position and indeed be glad to feel that in the time of the nation's need the Company has been able to place resources on so great a scale at the service of the Empire.[20]

Unfortunately, the willingness of aircraft companies - including the Bristol Aeroplane Co. - to accept restrictions on profit levels did not exonerate them from contemporary charges of inefficiency, sometimes gross, in their production operations.[21] Historians have been no less critical. As early as 1952, Professor Postan, the normally sympathetic official historian of British wartime production, was moved to make a number of critical observations of an aircraft industry freed from Treasury restraint after 1938.[22] More recently, a number of historians (notably Peter Fearon and Corelli Barnett), while recognising the improvised nature of the rapidly expanding aircraft industry, have written critically of the performance of British aircraft firms during the period 1934–1945. Even Alexander Robertson, who has generally adopted a more optimistic view of the performance of the industry, has emphasised the limits of growth before 1939 and "the inflexibility of approach and lack of enterprise on the part not only of the state but also of the aircraft industry itself, which with apparent equanimity went on making useless and obsolete aircraft – many of which never left storage – long after better alternatives became available".[23]

Fearon does not deny that the aircraft firms shared responsibility for production deficiencies, such as the very high time lags between the preparation of a specification and the placement of production orders; however, he tends to be more critical of the state's role, in particular its failure before 1934 to rationalise the industry by forcing out a number of weaker firms.[24] Also, the Air Ministry failed to promote with any vigour the development of the all metal monoplane in Britain, and, unlike the United States, it failed to concentrate on the development, for the civil market, of large landplanes embodying the latest technology. All this resulted in a weaker industrial base upon which to develop the rapid aircraft expansion after 1934.[25]

Critical as Fearon is, his comments seem quite mild in comparison to Barnett, who is absolutely scathing about the performance of the British aircraft industry between 1935 and 1945. He asserts that on the eve of major rearmament in 1936 "the British aircraft industry remained a cottage industry with obsolescent products; sleepy firms with factories little more than experimental aircraft shops employing hand-work methods and centred on their design departments". As an industrial operation, the industry displayed the same weaknesses in management, organisation and productivity and labour relations that had so long beset old-established British industries. There was also a critical shortage of appropriate training and experience from senior and middle management down to routine staff, draughtsmen and skilled labour. Another weakness was that from the beginning of rearmament Britain was compelled to purchase key items of aircraft equipment from abroad, including machine tools, armaments and instrumentation. The overall effect was that the industry failed to deliver both in terms of quantity and delivery dates before 1939. Barnett goes so far as to argue that this failure was responsible for the critical weakness of the Royal Air Force during the Czechoslovakian crisis, "a weakness which because of the prevailing fear of the German bomber, provided in turn a major factor in Chamberlain's policy of yielding to Hitler rather than risk war".[26]

The impressive output of Britain's aircraft industry during the Second World War merely reinforces Barnett's critical judgement, because for him it was only Britain's access to America's "colossal productive and technological resources" which enabled her to expand her war factories, and especially aircraft factories, far beyond the limits of British industry's own ability to equip them. The rise in British aircraft production from 1939 to the end of 1942 was not a miracle of productivity but rather the consequence of deploying 111,500 extra machine tools and over one million extra workers. The aircraft industry was in Ernest Bevin's words "the one industry which had failed to improve its output in proportion to the amount of labour supplied", and as Minister of Labour and National Service he was well placed to know. Certainly, British productivity compared unfavourably with that of Germany and the United States. The highest British monthly production of aircraft in terms of structure weight, in March 1944, amounted to only 1.28 lb. per man day compared to a German monthly peak of 1.93 lb. and an American peak, in May 1944, of more than 3 lb.

The relatively poor output of the industry was, Barnett argues, partly a consequence of the retarding force of union restrictive practices and of the absence of skilled management. British managers and engineers tended to be involved in day-to-day crisis management, unlike their American counterparts, who concentrated their efforts in preparatory planning before the assembly lines began to roll. For Barnett, the evidence for Britain's relative inferiority is conclusive; in particular, the observations of various war-time British missions to the United States – including those led by Sir Alexander Dunbar, Controller General of the Ministry for Aircraft Production, in September and October 1942, and by Sir Roy Fedden, late of the Bristol Aeroplane Co., in April 1943 – attested to the great superiority of the American system of production. This inferiority was confirmed again during the period immediately following the end of the Second World War when a number of missions – led respectively by Fedden, Sir Roy Farren, Director-General of the Royal Aeronautical Establishment at Farnborough, and L.R.M. Clarkson of de Havilland – confirmed the superior development of the German aircraft industry. It was recognised that the German system, like the American, was based on a level of technical education far in advance of that which existed in the United Kingdom.[27]

It is clear, in the light of these criticisms, that the expansion of the British aircraft industry during the period 1935–45 was far from smooth and that it was beset by considerable problems, not least of which was the absence of a strong civil and commercial base.[28] The Air Ministry maintained practically no design staff of its own and had kept out of manufacturing since the First World War. Consequently, it did not perform a competitive role as did the War Office through the Royal

Ordnance Factories, but it nonethless acted as a senior partner in its relations with the aircraft firms, contributing "handsomely" to their research and development expenses.[29] Before 1934, production of aircraft was under the authority of the Air Member [of the Air Council] for Supply and Research. With the beginning of expansion the functions of design and development were separated and allocated to the Air Member for Research and Development. In 1938 Research and Development was combined with Production under the newly created office of the Air Member for Development and Production, with Air Marshal Sir Wilfred Freeman in charge. The new office became effectively a fully self-contained production department and provided the foundation for the wartime Ministry of Aircraft Production. Freeman was supported in his work until 1940 by Sir Ernest Lemon (a leading railway engineer with the London, Midland & Scottish Railway) in the post of Director General of Production, whose tasks included mediating between firms and the Ministry in technical matters and the general planning of production.[30]

In view of their dependence on government orders for their future development, the aircraft firms had to establish positive and co-operative relationships with the Air Ministry. They did not, however, accept subordinancy. The Bristol Aeroplane Co. regarded itself as an equal partner and was not backward in expressing criticism of the Ministry or in refuting its criticisms when such action was felt to be warranted. There were occasions, however, when members of the company completely failed to move the Ministry officials in the direction they wished them to go, such as the acceptance of new aircraft specifications. The relationship which existed between the Air Ministry and the company could hardly be described as harmonious. The lack of harmony was partly a consequence of differences with regard to objectives and demarcation of functions. Where production of military aircraft was concerned, the government's objective during the period after 1934 was to strengthen its negotiating position in preserving peace, while at the same time securing the defence of the United Kingdom, and in particular the protection of the civilian population against enemy bombing. Lord Swinton, the Secretary of State for Air, made this clear in April 1936 when he advised Sir Stanley White that "in a situation vitally affecting the Safety of the Country, it is the bounded duty of the Government to frame its plans in the way, which, in their considered judgement, will best ensure that Safety and maintain peace".[31] But while the company appreciated the huge responsibilities which the government bore in matters of defence, and was anxious not to appear to be unpatriotic, nevertheless it expected to profit from the expansion of the air programme. This objective was stated frankly in a memorandum addressed to the Air Ministry in March 1936:

Furthermore, having regard to the difficulties with which the Company have been confronted in the past and to the valuable experience, technique and organisation which have been built up as a result of past expenditure on research and development, the benefit of which is now being placed at the disposal of the Government, the Company consider that any further expansion of their business, necessarily involving increased effort and organisation, should be adequately rewarded and that the remuneration to be received for the work which they are to undertake should be fixed on a fair and reasonable basis.[32]

In the event, as we have seen, the degree of profit which they could reasonably and fairly expect was limited by government measures.

Before the Second World War the Ministry did not intervene directly and formally in the production process. Instead it concentrated upon determining the total requirement of engines and airframes for a number of years ahead, defined specifically in respect of the basic type, total quantity and the rates of delivery. Thereafter, the problems this set were ones for the industry to manage; Freeman's Department acting throughout as a partner, helping wherever it could but otherwise keeping out of the way.[33] While this was the Department's preference, aircraft firms, including Bristol Aeroplane, were not assisted by the lack of clear guidance and firm commitment concerning future developments. This less than satisfactory position was emphasised to Fedden by Freeman in September 1936 when he stated:

I have carefully considered your request for my advice on your future engine development policy...You must realise that when one allows for the time necessary for developing new engines from an original sketch project to the real thing in production, the rapid design technique changes in aeroplanes, with all the risks and uncertainties which we have had to face with the expansion programme, any advice which I myself or anyone else could give you is liable to be seriously upset by the march of events. So that if you come along to my successor in four or five years time, and say that I advised you wrongly, I am afraid that you will receive only scant sympathy.[34]

Unfortunately for the Bristol Aeroplane Co. and other aircraft firms, when the government chose to intervene more directly and formally in the industry during World War Two, it was not to offer unambiguous advice on future development policy, but to sort out production difficulties and to attribute blame for the failure to deliver the right quantities at the right time.

The Air Ministry's reluctance to interfere directly in the production process before 1939 was not due to complacency. Indeed, Freeman's Department was fully aware of the shortcomings of the aircraft firms and their specific weaknesses. After a promising start the Bristol Aeroplane Co. increasingly attracted official criticism. In May 1936 an Air Ministry report which focused on the production capabilities of aircraft manufacturers was very complimentary about the company's progress: "This is undoubtedly a most efficient production unit and if handled properly is capable of a very large output. Bristol are capable of producing all the medium bombers we want of them." Later, in July 1936, Lord Weir, personal adviser to Swinton, complimented Verdon Smith on the spirit shown by the Bristol company: "Fresh burdens had repeatedly been put on them and they had responded well on each occasion".[35] By the summer of 1937, however, when work was proceeding on the development of the Blenheim and Bolingbroke medium bombers, the assessment of the company's performance had changed quite dramatically. A further report by the Air Ministry was damning about the airframe side:

> Considering the wealth, size and facilities possessed by this firm their perform-ance was considered to be more disappointing than that of any other firm in the industry. It was repeatedly pointed out to Messrs Thomas and Fedden and Verdon Smith the necessity of strengthening their organisation by the addition of a first class manufacturing man. The Board of the Company, however, refused to take action. Their manufacturing efforts were excellent for amateurs but could be very greatly improved by experienced men. It was considered that the time taken....to design the long nose of the Blenheim and also the Bolingbroke to be absolutely inexcusable. Neither had yet flown. It was anticipated that the Rootes Shadow Factory [at Speke] would turn out Blenheims at a very much less cost and therefore more efficiently than Bristol.[36]

The critical thrust of this report was confirmed in September 1937 when the Director of Aeronautical Production, Lieutenant-Colonel Henry Disney, informed Lord Weir that "there was no doubt about it that the aircraft side, as against the engine side, is in a muddle and is being run very extravagantly". Disney thought that the company needed "two big men, one as General Manager on the Aircraft Side and another in charge of the factory". Shortly afterwards he told Lord Weir, in somewhat sarcastic terms, that there was a lack of co-operation between the chief designer, Barnwell, and the factory side, and that the chief designer "is not adapting himself to the new state of affairs whereby aircraft are made in 500 lots instead of lots of 5". Weir took up Disney's criticisms with the chairman, Verdon Smith, complaining of "deplorable" delays and stating that until it was felt that these weaknesses had been remedied "the Air Council would continue to have a measure of lack of confidence which was a great matter both nationally and from the point of view of the firm". Verdon Smith was left in no doubt that he should take up the matter seriously with his staff and initiate steps to remedy the weakness. This he promised to do at once "as a matter of real urgency and import".[37]

The Bristol Aeroplane Co. was not alone in attracting the wrath of the Air Ministry though the latter's perception of the company had somewhat improved by the time of the Czechoslovakian crisis in the summer of 1938. Swinton's successor as secretary of state, Kingsley Wood, had expressed his disappointment at the slow delivery of aircraft and had asked Freeman whether anything could be done to speed up delivery and increase production. The Air Marshal thought that, if there was any possibility of war breaking out in the autumn, the Speke factory, in Liverpool, which produced Blenheims and later Beaufighters under contract, should be taken out of Rootes' management, about which he was quite contemptuous, and handed over to Bristol or A.V. Roe, or a combination of both. Freeman also contemplated, if the immediate risk of war was grave, to increase production of Blenheims, instructing the Bristol company to attain maximum output without consideration of cost.[38] In the event, of course, war was averted at the Munich Conference of 30 September and the vote of confidence of August evaporated, with the Air Ministry rejecting Bristol Aeroplane's proposals to design and construct a new bomber - specification 1/39, which was revived in 1942 as the Buckingham medium bomber.

The early confidence reposed in the Bristol Aeroplane Co. was based partly at least on its success in 1935 in producing a private airliner, *Britain First*, for Lord Rothermere, the press baron, which was a full 50 m.p.h. faster with a full load than the latest Royal Air Force fighter. The aircraft was later converted into a medium bomber, the Blenheim, which became the main production aircraft for the company until 1939, when production was begun on the Beaufort and the Beaufighter.[39] Air Ministry confidence in the engine capabilities of the company was also confirmed early in the rearmament programme when more than half of the government's engine requirements were allocated to it.[40] As time went by, however, the demands of the air programme increased; greater pressures resulted and greater strain was imposed on the company's relations with the Air Ministry, which became increasingly critical of the failure to meet production targets and delivery dates, while the company was increasingly frustrated by the lack of official appreciation, as they saw it, of their efforts and by the unrealistic expectations of the Air Staff.

During the first part of 1938, for example, Fedden was singularly unimpressed by the unrealistic expectations of the air authorities regarding engine production. He had gathered from his conversations with the Minister for Co-ordination of Defence, Sir Thomas Inskip, and the Chief of the Air Staff, Air Marshal Sir Cyril Newall, that the Government looked to the Bristol engine department for a large proportion of its aircraft engine output for the following few years from the new double row sleeve valve engines. Indeed, Fedden had been "beseeched to do anything and everything I could do to further this project, and exhorted to leave no stone unturned both in regard to my staff, and our general organisation, to accomplish this end". Unfortunately, the company was in no position to meet all of the requirements because of insufficient forward planning on the part of the Air Ministry:

> Is it appreciated that to get this output certain definite steps have got to be taken years ahead? The delivery of special machine tools, such as are required for sleeve valve manufacture, is at least 12 months. Is it realised that the Bristol Company ought to have ordered about £100,000 worth of machine tools? That they ought to have put in hand additional machines, shop bays, and office accommodation, some months ago? That they ought to have given orders for £75,000 to £100,000 worth of jigs some weeks ago? In other words, that in order to obtain a proper smooth and efficient production of our row engines in the quantities, and at the time it is understood is required by the Government, the Bristol Company ought to have made about £300,000 additional capital expenditure.[41]

To its credit the Air Ministry recognised the urgent need for new capital expenditure and in June 1938 the Air Council approved additional expenditure on buildings, plant and equipment for the Bristol Aeroplane Co. – £400,000 for the airframe works and £966,000 for the engine works.[42] The Ministry was equally responsive to a request by Bristol Aeroplane, at the height of the Czechoslovakian crisis, for a further order of 70 Blenheims. The company argued that this order was essential to tide it over the period between the completion of the Blenheim order in the late summer of 1939 and the acceleration of production of the Beaufort twin-engined torpedo-bomber; if an additional order was not forthcoming the company would have to lay off men. The Air Ministry confirmed the order, despite the apparent success of the Munich Conference and the fact that the Blenheim was already becoming obsolete.[43] When the Bristol company requested an immediate order for 62 more Blenheims in January 1939 as a stop-gap, there being an unavoidable delay in Beaufort production, it was duly sanctioned.[44]

In early August 1939, however, the air authorities refused the company's request that they provide a fresh order for 150 Blenheims.[45] They were also less than forthcoming in agreeing to proposals from Bristol for new specifications which, it was admitted, would have radically revised the programme envisaged for the company. At a meeting held at the Air Ministry during October 1938 which was attended by members of the Bristol management including Verdon Smith, George White (son of Sir Stanley), Leslie Frise and Harold Pollard (the company's production manager), the Bristol chairman argued that the Beaufort could easily be converted into a fighter aircraft and he suggested that the company should undertake the manufacture of such an aircraft instead of the

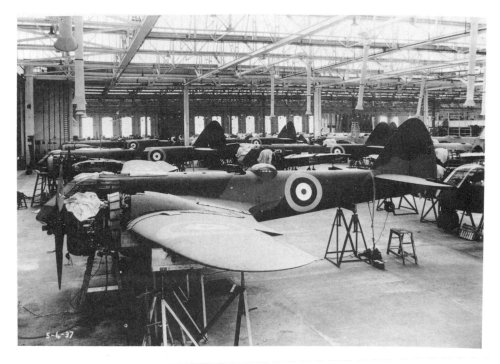

36. Blenheims under construction in April 1937.

Beaufort. He further proposed that Bristol should cease to be involved in the production of the B12/36 (Stirling) bomber in order to undertake the manufacture of a bomber which would utilise a tricycle undercarriage and be designed entirely at Filton. Frise, Barnwell's successor as chief airframe designer, assured the Air Ministry officials that acceptance of the company's design would entail a delay of only three or four months, as compared with the production schedule for the B12/36.

Unfortunately, the officials remained distinctly unimpressed by this proposal, raising several objections: that past experience showed that it was highly improbable that the company's estimates would be achieved and their forecast would probably be upset by the need for modifications to the design; that the tricycle undercarriage was an untried proposition; that repair and maintenance questions would arise in the case of a new type; and that acceptance of the proposal would mean a departure from the Ministry's policy of increased standardisation and the regional concentration on types which they had in mind.[46] Eventually, the Air Staff agreed that the company could go ahead with the proposal for a converted Beaufort fighter – the Beaufighter – but they rejected the second proposal for a new and specifically Bristol bomber. The rejection of their proposal, despite the reasoned nature of the Ministry's objections, struck a raw nerve at Filton. Sir Stanley White used the occasion to deliver a stinging rebuke which revealed the company's pent-up frustrations concerning official criticism:

> We have always considered, and still consider, that we have suffered from criticism on the part of the Ministry ... without full regard being given to the many types of aircraft which we had to produce within a short period and to the consequent variations in the order of priority which had to be given to each one of them. In spite, however, of the magnitude of our task the outstanding fact is that since July 1935 we have brought to the production stage from the drawing board two types of medium sized aircraft, the Blenheim and the Beaufort, and also completely redesigned for production by Short and Harland the Transport Bomber, the Bombay, all in addition to other prototype aircraft including the Bolingbroke, which had necessarily to take their proper place in a heavy programme of design and experimental work. I would submit that the Company's record in this respect compares favourably with that of any other Construction.[47]

The engine department of the company also resented official criticism, particularly when it appeared to be unjustified. Shortly before the outbreak of the Second World War, Fedden complained bitterly to Freeman about the Air Ministry's exclusion of Bristol engines from the new type of fighter aircraft, notably the Spitfire and Hurricane which were powered by Rolls-Royce Merlin engines.[48] He was even more incensed when the Air Member replied on 1 September 1939, casting doubts on the performance potential of a number of Bristol engines. Indeed, Freeman had stated that the Mercury and Pegasus – both of them poppet valve engines – were the only Bristol types fit to go into quantity production. If such a judgement was to be sustained, four engine types – Hercules, Centaurus, Taurus and Perseus – would have to be scrapped. Fedden refuted criticism of these engines which were part of "a first class family of sleeve valve engines":

> In spite of the fact that Bristol have carried through successfully an operation bigger than any other aero engine firm has had to tackle in any Country, namely: putting three entirely new types of engines into practically simultaneous production, employing an entirely new principle, I think we have had no more troubles than any other manufacturer, and the way the Perseus, Taurus, and Hercules have, to date, gone into production is a great credit to our organisation as a whole.[49]

Later, in an article in *Flight Magazine*, published in December 1939, Fedden claimed that these engines, which had been developed over a period of ten years by his company, were more attractive for wartime quantity production than any known and developed type of engine: the geometry was such that stressing was simple, the design compact and the material obtainable in large quantities; special machine tools were not essential for manufacture; the layout was such that assemblies could easily be isolated for efficient production by sub-contractors under shadow production; once produced no servicing was required except for routine plug inspection and rather than suffering gradual deterioration over time, as in the case of the poppet valve engines, there was usually improvement. Fedden also claimed that the sleeve valve engine avoided hot spots in the combustion chamber which was advantageous when the utmost performance was to be obtained by boosting and the control of turbulence which it afforded was an important asset for petrol injection. However, Fedden's refutation was hardly necessary in view of the out-break of war in September 1939 when there was no question of abandon-ing an established engine programme. Consequently, the Bristol engine department continued to control a large part of the nation's output of aero engines during World War Two. Between June 1939 and December 1945, Bristol Aeroplane delivered 100,932 aero engines (compared to 112,183 delivered by Rolls-Royce), representing 38.5 per cent of the country's total output excluding jet engines.[50]

While the Bristol Aeroplane Co. was ready to defend its corner in its relations with the Air Ministry, it never adopted a wholly unco-operative or intransigent attitude, not even with regard to what was probably the most sensitive issue of all – the shadow factory scheme, which was intended to reinforce the existing industry in the pursuit of an accelerating expansion programme but which necessarily created potential rivals to the established firms. The company's co-operation in the shadow factory scheme was first requested by Lord Swinton at a meeting held on 13 March 1936 between Air Ministry representatives and members of the company's management led by Sir Stanley White. Swinton was adamant that the scheme was the only practical way of rectifying the very difficult and dangerous situation prevailing in defence and that the shadow factories must be brought into production quickly, to supplement the deficiencies under the present emergency and to acquire experience for wartime production. The Secretary of State, speaking with the full authority of the government, wished the company to appreciate that "in regard to the Shadow Industry he was not asking them to undertake a commercial proposition but a piece of national service" and he asked for "their frank and wholehearted co-operation in accomplishing the heavy task of providing for Air Force requirements in the present emergency".[51]

The management agreed to participate in the shadow scheme but also desired that the company's interests be protected. They viewed with concern the proposal that aircraft designs, which embodied years of patient study, research and cost, should be passed over to another com-pany, or companies, which were potential competitors. In addition, they were conscious of the effort which would be required in the education of as many as five separate firms in the construction of complete engines. Accordingly, Bristol insisted that the value of the knowledge, experience and technique in the manufacture of aircraft and engines must be acknowledged and that no firm should be selected for the manufacture of the company's designs which was already manufacturing or contemplating the manufacture of aircraft, engines, or both. Mindful of potential competition, the company emphasised that much better and cheaper production could be obtained by dispersing specialised functions rather than having each shadow firm construct complete engines.[52]

After conferring with the seven car companies which would form the shadow group for the production of engines – Austin, Rootes, Rover, Singer, Standard, Daimler and Wolseley – Swinton was able to assure Verdon Smith and Stanley White that he was not offering the shadow firms a commercial proposition, nor was he inviting them to enter the aero engine industry. At the close of the rearmament period there would be no government orders of this nature for the shadow firms, unless, of course, the international situation demanded the same high rate of output. The Secretary of State also stressed that owing to the noncommercial nature of the shadow scheme and its definite termination "there would not be strong motives as might otherwise be the case for an automobile firm to attempt to set itself up in competition".[53] The company was also reassured by the decision of the shadow firms, taken against the advice of the Air Ministry, to disperse their production so that each firm would specialise in a group of components which would then be assembled and tested in two factories, which turned out to be those of Austin and Bristol.[54] Further reassurance came in June 1936 with Swinton's decision to allow the amount of remuneration for Bristol designs used in shadow manufacture to be determined by arbitration rather than insisting on the Treasury's right to fix royalties.[55]

In taking an active role in shadow production the company had, of course, to risk facilitating the entry into the field of a potential rival. The Air Ministry recognised that because of this risk they were asking a great deal of the Bristol Aeroplane Co., and no more so than in July 1936, when they informed Verdon Smith and Stanley White that they intended to award an order to produce Bristol engines to the Alvis Co., despite its potential to become a competitor, because from the national point of view that fact alone could not be allowed to stand in the way of urgent supply needs. Bristol Aeroplane accepted the argument and raised no objection to Alvis's joining the shadow scheme provided it agreed not to develop engines exceeding 12 litres' capacity.[56] The company was not so accommodating later in the year over proposals for the erection and equipment of an assembly and testing factory for the construction of Bristol engines as part of the shadow industry. The factory was to be sited on land in the company's ownership at Filton, the freehold of which was to be acquired by the Air Ministry. However, Bristol Aeroplane insisted on the right of first refusal, should the Ministry decide to dispose of the land. If the factory were disposed of to a third party, the purchaser should be prevented from utilising the property for any business connected with the aircraft industry. The Air Ministry was not at all opposed to the first condition, but objected to the second. Bristol Aeroplane continued to insist on the inclusion of the stipulation in the contract, informing Disney "with the greatest courtesy but also with absolute firmness" that "they were not going to give way on this point". As it happened, the company did give way, and accepted a revised Treasury stipulation involving arbitration in the event of disagreement.[57]

While Bristol Aeroplane had made a number of concessions in regard to the shadow factory engine scheme, it was not, before 1939, confronted with the threat either that priority of orders would be shared with the shadow firms, or that one of these firms would be placed on the Air Ministry list of contractors. However, both of these possibilities threatened to materialise with the extension of the shadow scheme during the spring and summer of 1939, when a second shadow group of four firms was formed - Rootes, Daimler, Rover and Standard. At the time when the original shadow factories were created it had been anticipated that they could be 'laid up in vaseline' when the immediate need for expansion was over. In the new circumstances which followed Hitler's annexation of Czechoslovakia and the British guarantee to Poland, the Air Staff foresaw that, even if expansion and the corresponding flow of orders could be slowed down at some future date, it would still be necessary to keep the shadow factories ready to work up at any time to full capacity within six months of war breaking out. Maintaining such a degree of readiness meant allocating a substantial flow of work to the shadow factories during the first three year period of the new scheme, which naturally had implications for the parent company. This proposition was put by Freeman to Verdon Smith, Stanley Daniel, the company's commercial manager, and Norman Rowbotham, its general works manager, on 15 May 1939. At the same meeting, Freeman, together with Sir Henry Self, Deputy Under Secretary of State at the Air Ministry, asked how the company would react if one of the shadow firms applied for inclusion in the list of Air Ministry contractors. It was suggested that the Air Ministry ought not to be substantially dependent on two firms only – Bristol Aeroplane and Rolls-Royce – and that competition was no bad thing. Verdon Smith pointed out that his company always faced competition from abroad, because it was bound to keep up with the technical progress of foreign firms, and he argued that as Bristol Aeroplane had taught the shadow firms their business it would be inequitable if one of them achieved its inclusion on the Air Ministry list.[58]

For a number of weeks afterwards the management of the Bristol Aeroplane Co. continued to maintain that the proposition was contrary to the spirit of their original agreement with Lord Swinton but, eventually, they suggested a compromise which proved acceptable to the Air Ministry: the company should be safeguarded during the proposed three year period against a reduction of the employment of their works below 90 per cent of single shift, even if this meant that the shadow firms were reduced below the minimum war readiness level. The Air Ministry felt that this was a safe undertaking to give because 90 per cent of single shift working at Filton was probably the minimum at which Bristol Aeroplane as a design firm could safely be kept if it was to be ready for war.[59]

The outbreak of war in September 1939 resulted, of course, in full employment for both the Bristol parent company and the two shadow factory groups. These groups were brought under a joint management committee in May 1940, and in 1942 there was a general merger of capacity and operation with a joint output target of 1,500 engines a month. The effect of this large scale planning was to reduce substantially the need for further expansion under Bristol control, particularly as an agency factory under Bristol management had been established previously at Altham, near Accrington, Lancashire. It was planned that this factory, which was equipped with the latest types of machine tools from the United States, would produce 260 and then 400 engines a month, a target it eventually achieved in 1944.[60] Finally, during 1942 an underground factory was set up at Corsham near Chippenham in Wiltshire. It was equipped with £3 million worth of machine tools and produced Bristol Centaurus engines. Shortage of skilled labour, which bedevilled the production of aircraft in the south-west during the war, meant that this factory was under-utilised with a peak output of only 42 engines per month. By 1943 the underground factory, Accrington and the parent factory employed between them over 31,000 people producing Bristol engines.[61] Of the 101,000 engines produced by Bristol Aeroplane and the shadow factories, only 33,000 were produced by the parent company. The following table demonstrates the lower output of the company in relation to its agency factory at Accrington and the shadow groups:

Table 2. *New Engine Deliveries: Monthly Averages, 1939–44*[*]

	1939	1940	1941	1942	1943	1944
Bristol parent factory	233	272	270	300	288	213
Bristol agency factory	–	–	33	265	342	405
Shadow groups	348	593	992	1148	1133	1511

Source: W.S. Hornby, *History of the Second World War: Factories and Plant* (1958), p.256.

[*] Based upon second quarter figures except 1939 (June) and 1944 (first quarter).

The impressive shadow production was achieved by a labour force which reached a peak of over 41,000 in 1943. In contrast, after the end of 1941, output of engines from the Bristol parent factory remained virtually unchanged although the labour force continued to expand until November 1943. The greater efficiency of the shadow factories and the agency factory is partly accounted for by the modern structure and layout of their buildings and the newly installed plant including the latest machine tools. At the same time, the Bristol parent factory was required to continue development and experimental work which was of vital importance in enhancing quality but disruptive of the production process.[62]

While there are sound reasons for the company's poor productivity record, the Bristol engine department by no means satisfied official scrutiny. Early in 1943, a joint investigating panel, composed of Ministry of Aircraft Production and Ministry of Labour representatives, visited the aero engine factory at Bristol and reported that it was badly organised, with no proper layout of production lines. The result was that "machine parts perambulated the shops on a vast scale", while "elaborate machine tools were either misused on simple operations or allowed to stand idle". Moreover, "the atmosphere was one of lassitude, and female labour was discouraged and cold-shouldered". In its response the company insisted that these charges rested on "pure unproved assertion" and that the inspectors did not appear to have understood the basic purpose of the parent factory which was development and pre-production. Necessarily, these functions precluded a neat symmetrical flow of components and no allowance had been made for the fact that Bristol Aeroplane was continually engaged on introducing new types for which proper jigs and tools were not yet available.[63]

The airframe side of the company's wartime activity also attracted the attention of the Ministry of Aircraft Production. Early in 1941, technical costs staff of the Ministry began an investigation, which lasted several weeks, into the reasons for the disappointingly small output of the company. The investigation concluded:

> The main fault at the Bristol Aeroplane Company which is retarding production is that the firm are focussing their attention at the wrong end of their production line. All the managerial effort is concentrated on clearing priority shortages in the erecting hall and flight sheds and insufficient attention is paid to the building up of a flow of production parts. It is essential that very considerable improvement is made in the organisation of the Planning Department, the Progress Department and the Sub-contracts Department. The Management at B.A.C. are endeavouring to improve these departments by shuffling the existing staff, but ... new blood must be infused before satisfactory results are obtained.[64]

Stanley White did his best to deflect the criticism, pointing out that "certain weaknesses are accentuated by the way in which we released our best men for Weston and the loss was particularly felt at a time when we were making every effort to turn out the Beaufighter for urgent operational requirements before it was a straightforward production proposition". The Ministry, aware that the company's management weaknesses were quite longstanding, remained unimpressed.[65] Although the management at Filton was less than forthcoming in drawing attention to these weaknesses they were not so reticent when it came to criticising the shop floor. In October 1942, Verdon Smith drew the attention of shareholders to the problems of lateness, absenteeism and idleness amongst the workforce as contributing to the inefficiency in aircraft factories, though he admitted that only a minority of the staff were offenders.[66]

While managerial inadequacy was a common feature of the aircraft industry during the Second World War, Bristol's management, along with colleagues in other firms, could claim with some justice that "the constant pressure for improvement of current types, for additional numbers of later types and for the substitution of new types for old" seriously retarded output. So too did the shortage of skilled labour, which was a chronic problem for Bristol factories.[67] Moreover, the company had proved willing to circumvent established practices to meet the Air Ministry's requirements. One such case was the production of the Beaufighter straight from the drawing board, without building and testing a batch of prototypes. It proved to be the most successful Bristol aircraft of World War Two.[68] Occasionally, the Ministry of Aircraft Production acknowledged that in the pursuit of quality it was not always possible to achieve the desired output; the Director General of Research and Development, Roderic Hill, admitted this in February 1941 when he sought to defend the Bristol company against its critics:

> While a number of subsidiary causes of delay undoubtedly existed, though it would be hard to disentangle them, the real point is that Bristols concentrated first and foremost on putting the Beaufighter itself right [for night fighting]. It had to be altered again and again before becoming the successful aircraft we now know. If a job is so important, as the Beaufighter for night fighting undoubtedly was, that it pays to concentrate all your best strength on it, you must be prepared to accept the consequences, namely some delay in other jobs involving the same materials and the same people.[69]

The Bristol management had no excuse, however, for failing to work with other firms in the solution of design problems, most notably in the case of the Centaurus engine and the Buckingham aircraft (type 1/39 proposed originally in 1939). The production of this particular aircraft was held up by problems connected with the engine supercharger, yet Rolls-Royce, which had made greater progress in solving these problems,

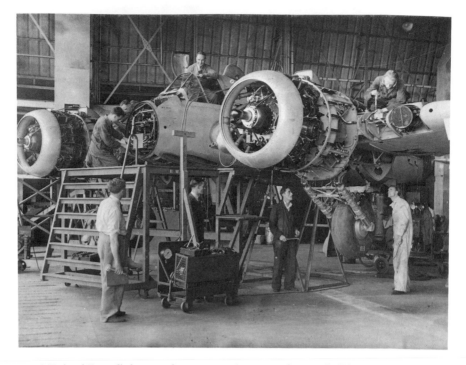

37. A Bristol Beaufighter at the company's agency factory in Weston-super-Mare, August 1943.

was not called in by the Bristol Aeroplane Co. until much valuable time had been lost. By the time the Buckingham medium bomber made its appearance at the end of 1943 it was more than 12 months late and already becoming obsolete in comparison to the excellent and more versatile Mosquito.[70]

On the whole, the company was well served by its design staff during the period under review, in particular Barnwell, Frise and Fedden. Though less well known than his predecessor Barnwell, Frise was highly regarded by the Air Ministry, not least because he settled the anxieties of the Air Staff in 1938 by procuring a cannon-firing fighter in the form of the Beaufighter. Fedden, in addition to his pioneering work during the 1920s and early 1930s, may be given credit for developing a whole series of air-cooled engines during the rearmament period and for persuading the Bristol board to participate in a successful joint venture with Rolls-Royce – Rotol – for the production of propellers. Indeed, during the interwar years he acquired an international reputation as an air-cooled engine designer of impressive stature. When he left the Bristol Aeroplane Co. at the end of 1942 for personal reasons he became an advisor to the Ministry of Aircraft Production, leaving the engine department at Filton to be, in Lord Brabazon's words, "Hamlet Ltd., without the Prince of Denmark".[71]

Yet, despite the size of its organisation and the undoubted quality and commitment of certain personnel, the Bristol Aeroplane Co. produced aircraft and engines during the Second World War which were, with the possible exception of the Beaufighter, largely second rate. By common consent, the five most successful British aircraft of the war were the Spitfire, the Hurricane, the Mosquito, the Lancaster and the Wellington. Apart from the provision of engines for the Wellington, Bristol Aeroplane had no hand in the production of these aircraft.[72] Accordingly, when reductions were made in the overall labour force of the industry at the end of 1943, the company was unable to claim preferential treatment, unlike de Havilland, Vickers and A.V. Roe.[73] The engine department also failed to participate in the development of the jet engine during the war despite the urgings of Frank Whittle. This less than impressive record was not improved by the failure of the company – admittedly for reasons beyond its control – to bring the Brabazon airliner into revenue-earning service after 1945.

These setbacks notwithstanding, the Bristol Aeroplane Co. played a significant role in the postwar British aircraft industry which, although smaller than it had been during the war, was far larger than it had been before 1935. In June 1960, 50 years after its formation, the aircraft side of the company amalgamated with Vickers and English Electric to form the British Aircraft Corporation. In 1966 the engine department, having previously joined with Armstrong Siddeley to form Bristol Siddeley Engines, was absorbed by Rolls-Royce. These developments ensured the continuation of aircraft and engine production at Filton, which remains the largest industrial employer in the south-west of England.[74]

NOTES

1. The author would like to thank Mr Michael Fish, British Aerospace PLC and the Public Record Office for their assistance in the preparation of this chapter.

2. W.S. Hornby, *History of the Second World War: Factories and Plant* (1958), p.251. R.J. Overy, *The Air War, 1939–1945* (New York, 1982), p.171. C. Barnett, *The Audit of War: the Illusion and Reality of Britain as a Great Nation* (1986), pp.126, 145–6.

3. M. Smith, *British Air Strategy Between the Wars* (Oxford, 1984), pp.140–226.

4. C.H. Barnes, *Bristol Aircraft since 1910* (1964), pp.13–28. B. Little, *The City and County of Bristol* (2nd edn. Wakefield, 1967), p.295. P. Fearon, 'The Formative Years of the British Aircraft Industry, 1913–1924', *Business History Review*, XLIII (1969), p.487.

5. Barnes, *Bristol Aircraft*, pp.28–31. R. Schlaiffer and S.D. Heron, *Development of Aircraft Engines and Aviation Fuels: Two Studies of Relations between Government and Business* (New York, 1970), pp.137–8. R. Fedden, 'The First 25 Years of the Bristol Engine Department', *Journal of the Royal Aeronautical Society*, LXV (1961), pp.335.

6. P. Fearon, 'Aircraft Manufacturing', in N. Buxton and D.H. Aldcroft, eds. *British Industry between the Wars: Instability and Industrial Development, 1919–1939* (1979), p.218.

7. Ibid., p.226.

8. Schlaiffer and Heron, *Aircraft Engines and Aviation Fuels*, pp.143–52. H. Penrose, *British Aviation: Widening Horizons, 1930–1934* (1979), pp.172–3. M.M. Postan, D. Hay and J.D. Scott, *History of the Second World War. Design and Development of Weapons: Studies in Government and Industrial Organisation* (1964), p.106.

9. Schlaiffer and Heron, *Aircraft Engines and Aviation Fuels*, pp.153–5.

10. Barnes, *Bristol Aircraft*, p.34. P. Fearon, 'The British Airframe Industry and the State, 1918–35', *Economic History Review*, 2nd ser. XXVII (1974), p.243.

11. For details see P. Fearon, 'The Growth of Aviation in Britain', *Journal of Contemporary History*, XX (1985), pp.21–40.

12. Fearon, 'Aircraft Manufacturing', pp.222–3. Barnes, *Bristol Aircraft*, p.33.

13. Fearon, 'Aircraft Manufacturing', p.222. There were 16 firms in the ring.

14. J. Lovering, 'Defence Expenditure and the Regions: the Case of Bristol', *Built Environment*, XI (1985), pp.196–7.

15. H. Penrose, *British Aviation: the Ominous Skies, 1935–1939* (1980), pp.90–1.

16. M. Boddy, J. Lovering and K. Bassett, *Sunbelt City? A Study of Economic Change in Britain's M4 Corridor Growth* (Oxford, 1986), p.9. W.J. Reader, *Architect of Air Power: the Life of the First Viscount Weir of Eastwood* (1968), p.210. Barnes, *Bristol Aircraft*, pp.35, 43. Hornby, *Factories and Plant*, pp.262–3. At the height of the war almost 72,000 people were employed in manufacturing Bristol engines including the shadow factories. Fedden, 'The First 25 Years', p.350.

17. British Aerospace Archives, Filton (hereafter Filton), Bristol Aeroplane Co., Balance Sheets, 1935–1944.

18. *Hansard* (Commons), 5th ser. CCCXXXIII, cols.252–3, 272–3, 316–7, 335–6. Robin Higham contends that the fear of Parliamentary investigations, contract renegotiation or actual nationalisation in response to excess profit levels was sufficient to deter investment in the industry. 'Quality versus Quantity: The Impact of Changing Demand on the British Aircraft Industry, 1900–1960', *Business History Review*, XLII (1968), p.451. On the Excess Profits Tax and government attempts to regulate pretax profits, see W. Ashworth, *History of the Second World War: Contracts and Finance* (1953), pp.84–6, 117–22.

19. Filton, Bristol Aeroplane Co., Balance Sheets, 1935–1944.

20. Filton, Bristol Aeroplane Co., Chairman's Statement, 21 October 1941.

21. For the Air Ministry view, see Fearon, 'Aircraft Manufacturing', pp.234–6.

22. M.M. Postan, *History of the Second World War: British War Production* (1952), p.18.

23. A.J. Robertson, 'The British Airframe Industry and the State in the Interwar Period: a Comment', *Economic History Review*, 2nd ser. XXVIII (1975), p.653. *Idem*, 'British Rearmament and Industrial Growth', *Research in Economic History*, VIII (1983), pp.288–9. See also M. Smith, 'Planning and Building the British Bomber Force, 1934–1939', *Business History Review*, LIV (1980), pp.47–53.

24. Fearon, 'The Growth of Aviation in Britain', p.35. See also P. Fearon, 'The British Airframe Industry and the State in the Interwar Period: a Reply', *Economic History Review*, 2nd ser. XXVIII (1975), pp.661–2. During the early 1930s, the Air Ministry expected between five and a half and eight years to elapse between the preparation of a specification and the placement of production orders. Postan, Hay and Scott, *Design and Development of Weapons*, p.504.

25. Fearon, 'The British Airframe Industry: a Reply', pp.661–2.

26. Barnett, *The Audit of War*, pp.126–39. Postan, *British War Production*, pp.15–23.

27. Barnett, *The Audit of War*, pp.143–58.

28. Ibid., pp.126–7.

29. Reader, *Architect of Air Power*, pp.212–3.

30. Postan, *British War Production*, pp.20–1. Robertson, 'British Rearmament and Industrial Growth', p.289.

31. Public Record Office (hereafter P.R.O.), AIR6/44, Swinton to White, 2 April 1936.

32. Ibid., White to Swinton, 31 March 1936.

33. P.R.O., AVIA10/5, Minute by Major Bulman, AD/RDE, May 1939, in response to a memorandum from Fedden of 3 May 1939. A.J. Robertson, 'Lord Beaverbrook and the Supply of Aircraft, 1940–1941' in A. Slaven and D.H. Aldcroft, eds. *Business, Banking and Urban History: Essays in Honour of S.G. Checkland* (Edinburgh, 1982), p.83.

34. Ibid., Freeman to Fedden, 3 Sept. 1939.

35. P.R.O., AIR2/1790, Air Ministry Report, 11 May 1936. AIR6/46, Secretary of State's Progress Meetings: Meeting with Bristol Aeroplane Company Ltd., 17 July 1936.

36. P.R.O., AIR/1790, Air Ministry Report, 27 Aug. 1937.

37. Reader, *Architect of Air Power*, pp.260–1.

38. P.R.O., AVIA10/14, Freeman to Kingsley Wood, 13 Aug. 1938.

39. For details see Barnes, *Bristol Aircraft*, pp.257–61.

40. The Air Ministry placed orders for engines as follows in May 1936: Rolls-Royce, 4,146; Bristol, 6,671; Armstrong Siddeley, 1,200; Napier, 264; de Havilland, 300. P.R.O., AIR6/45, First Progress Report by the Air Ministry, 1 May 1936.

41. P.R.O., AVIA10/5, Fedden to Freeman, 26 April 1938.

42. P.R.O., AVIA10/5, Minute, Freeman to the Chief of Air Staff, 29 April 1938. AIR2/3291, Secretary of State's Progress Meetings confirming decisions of Air Council Committee on Supply reached at meetings on 23–4 June 1938.

43. P.R.O., AVIA10/5, Verdon Smith to Freeman, 27 Sept. 1938. AIR2/3291, Air Council Committee on Supply, Informal Meeting, 30 Sept. 1938.

44. P.R.O., AIR2/3291, Air Council Committee on Supply, Bristol Aeroplane Co. Aircraft and Engine Programmes, 6 Feb. 1939. Air Council Committee on Supply, Notes of an Informal Meeting of 21 Jan. 1939. On the stop-gap orders for Blenheims see Postan, Hay and Scott, *Design and Development of Weapons*, pp.494–8.

45. P.R.O., AVIA10/6, White to Freeman, 25 July 1939. Freeman to White, 2 Aug. 1939.

46. P.R.O., AVIA10/5, Notes of a meeting of 13 Oct. 1938 to discuss proposals by the Bristol Aeroplane Co. regarding its future aircraft programme.

47. P.R.O., AVIA10/6, White to Freeman, 13 Feb. 1939.

48. P.R.O., AVIA10/5, Memorandum from Fedden to Freeman, Urgent matters affecting the Bristol Engine Department, 9 Sept. 1937. Fedden believed that the omission of Bristol engines from the new prototype was largely due to Rolls-Royce's success with racing aircraft such as the Schneider Trophy winners. Fedden, 'The First 25 Years', pp.347–8. On the Merlin engine, see I. Lloyd, *Rolls-Royce: the Merlin at War* (1978).

49. P.R.O., AVIA10/6, Fedden to Freeman, 6 Sept. 1939.

50. Hornby, *Factories and Plant*, p.254.

51. P.R.O., AIR6/44, 32nd Progress Meeting, Interview with the Bristol Company, 13 March 1936.

52. Ibid., White to Swinton, 31 March 1936.

53. P.R.O., AIR6/45, Secretary of State's Progress Meetings: Note on Second Meeting with the Bristol Company, 9 April 1936.

54. Reader, *Architect of Air Power*, pp.263–4. Subsequent to this decision both Singer and Wolseley pulled out. Lord Nuffield withdrew Wolseley because he disagreed with Bristol's dispersion plan, wishing his firm to produce complete engines. *Note on the Policy of His Majesty's Government in relation to the Production of Aero-Engines* (P.P. 1936, XVI). Reader, *Architect of Air Power*, pp.264–9. P.W.S. Andrews and E. Brunner, *The Life of Lord Nuffield*:

a *Study in Enterprise and Benevolence* (Oxford, 1959), pp.219–22. R.J. Overy, *William Morris, Viscount Nuffield* (1976), pp.118–9.

55. P.R.O., AVIA8/170, Meeting between Lord Swinton, Verdon Smith and Sir Stanley White, 19 June 1936.

56. P.R.O., AIR6/46, Secretary of State's Progress Meetings: Meeting with the Bristol Aeroplane Co. Ltd., 17 July 1936. Postan, Hay and Scott, *Design and Development of Weapons*, p.100.

57. P.R.O., AIR2/2366, White to Disney, 29 Oct. 1936. Disney to Bristol Aeroplane Co., 16 Nov. 1936. Bristol Aeroplane Co. to Secretary, Air Ministry, 17 Nov. 1936. AIR6/47, 54th Progress Meeting and Further Meeting with Bristol Aeroplane Co., 11 Dec. 1936. AIR2/2384, Air Ministry Minutes 15 Jan. 1937; 26 Jan. 1937; 19 March 1937. Air Ministry to Treasury Solicitor, 23 March 1937; 20 April 1937.

58. P.R.O., AVIA10/6, Note of Meeting on 15 May 1939; Air Ministry Memorandum, Hercules Shadow Group, 9 June 1939.

59. Ibid., Verdon Smith to Freeman, 19 May 1939. Daniel to W.L.Scott, Air Ministry, 6 June 1939. Air Ministry Memorandum, Hercules Shadow Group, 9 June 1939.

60. P.R.O., AIR2/3683; AVIA10/6.

61. Hornby, *Factories and Plant*, pp.207, 255–6, 262.

62. Ibid., pp.262–3.

63. P.R.O., CAB102/51, Reciprocating Aero Engines and Engine Accessories Production and Programmes, 1935–1945. See also Barnett, *The Audit of War*, p.154.

64. P.R.O., AVIA10/95, Summary of Investigation at the Bristol Aeroplane Co., 20 May 1941.

65. Ibid., Westbrook, Ministry of Aircraft Production, to White, 27 April 1941; 9 May 1941. White to Westbrook, 5 May 1941. Sholto Douglas to Westbrook, 22 May 1941. Westbrook reminded White that "such weaknesses have been inherent for some long time and I am sure you will realise that I would be lacking in my duty to the Secretary of State were I not to be continually reminding you of them", while Sholto Douglas agreed that on the production side "Bristols are not a very strong team" and he hoped Westbrook would "keep kicking them in the pants".

66. Filton, Bristol Aeroplane Co., Directors' Report and Statement of Accounts, year ended 31 Dec. 1941. See also *The Times*, 27 Oct. 1942.

67. P.R.O., CAB102/51. Barnett, *The Audit of War*, pp.153–6. Postan, *British War Production*, pp.314–5, 322. Hornby, *Factories and Plant*, pp.261–2.

68. Postan, Hay and Scott, *Design and Development of Weapons*, p.39. Smith, 'Planning and Building the British Bomber Force', p.47. Postan, *British War Production*, p.334.

69. P.R.O., AVIA10/95, Minute, 19 Feb. 1941.

70. Postan, Hay and Scott, *Design and Development of Weapons*, pp.131, 441. Postan, *British War Production*, pp.331–2.

71. Postan, Hay and Scott, *Design and Development of Weapons*, pp.150–1. P.R.O., AVIA10/5.

72. Fedden, 'The First 25 Years', p.348.

73. Postan, *British War Production*, pp.309, 341.

74. On the formation of the British Aircraft Corporation see C. Gardner, *British Aircraft Corporation: a History* (1981).

G.B. Britton and Footwear Manufacturing in Bristol and Kingswood, 1870–1973[1]

JON PRESS

During the nineteenth century, the footwear industry in Britain was gradually transformed from a handicraft trade to a factory-based industry. The population of Britain grew steadily, from 16 million in 1801 to 27 million in 1851 and 42 million in 1901,[2] and, although the better off continued to buy made-to-measure footwear, a large market developed for cheap mass-produced boots and shoes. By the 1850s factory production was well established, and had become concentrated in a few major centres – notably Northampton, Stafford, Leeds and Leicester.[3] The early 'wholesale' manufacturers, however, continued to use traditional handicraft methods; leather uppers were hand cut by 'clickers', stitched by 'closers' and attached to the sole by 'makers'. 'Finishers' tidied up the boot or shoe and readied it for sale. Factories operated on a small scale. The biggest firms had several hundred employees, but the great majority of these were outworkers; almost invariably, making and finishing were done in cottage workshops.

In the third quarter of the century, there was a marked acceleration in the rate of technological innovation in the footwear industry. Industrial sewing machines were first used in the 1850s to stitch uppers, the Blake sole sewer followed in 1858–9, and in the 1870s the Goodyear chain-stitching machine permitted for the first time the replication of the hand-stitched (welted) boot. Early Goodyear machines were more than 50 times as fast as hand stitching. Riveting, a cheap method of attaching soles to heavy boots, was also mechanised by the 1870s.[4] Progress, however, was erratic. The production of a pair of boots or shoes was (and is) a highly complex series of operations, and some processes proved more difficult to mechanise than others. In the 1880s clicking, lasting and most finishing operations remained unmechanised. A machine laster came into use after 1882, but the first clicking presses did not appear until the turn of the century. Furthermore, some firms and some centres of production were slower to mechanise than others, and for several decades footwear manufacturing embraced both hand and machine processes.[5] But by about 1900 it was possible to perform all operations by machine, and to produce boots or shoes which could match all but the best hand-made examples.

Changes in manufacturing methods led to important developments in footwear distribution. Bespoke shoemakers survived, albeit in declining numbers, but in the ready-made footwear market specialist wholesale and retail enterprises were beginning to take over from drapers and general clothing shops. Independent firms predominated in terms of numbers, but multiple retailers began to appear as early as the 1860s and 1870s. Well known companies like George Oliver, Stead & Simpson and Freeman, Hardy & Willis were well established by the beginning of the twentieth century, and by 1913 multiples accounted for about a third of retail sales in Britain.[6] These developments in turn had important effects on footwear manufacturing; above all, the creation of national rather than local or regional markets enabled manufacturers to specialise in a particular sector of the industry, producing a limited range of boots or shoes in volume rather than a 'mixed bag' in small quantities.

In the south west, two main centres of footwear production emerged, which responded in different ways to the new opportunities of the late nineteenth century. At Street, in Somerset, the firm of C. & J. Clark was already well established, and led the way in adopting new techniques and machinery. William Clark invented the first simple machinery for build-ing and attaching heels in the early 1850s, and American treadle machines for cutting leather were introduced at Street around 1859.[7] The firm concentrated upon better class women's and children's shoes, and by the 1880s it was offering multiple width fittings, stressing the comfort and "anatomical correctness" of its products.[8] In Bristol, however, cheap, heavy working boots were the staple product. The industry originated in Kingswood and the other villages to the east of the city; cobbling was a suitable trade for retired miners from the Bristol and Gloucestershire Coalfield, and many cottages had a room or workshop set aside for bootmaking.[9] In the 1860s and 1870s, wholesale manufacturers began to set up factories in the region, and soon the Bristol and Kingswood district was challenging older centres like Leeds for the heavy boot trade. This sector was very attractive to newer firms because the technical skill required was much less than for other types of footwear; durability rather than fine workmanship or comfort was of prime importance. Moreover, a limited range of styles could be made and sold in very large quantities. The main sources of demand were agricultural workers and miners, but very similar styles – high lace-up fronts, and thick leather soles attached by rivets or screws – were also manufactured for women and children. Table 1 gives some indication of the growth of wholesale manufacturing in the region. The labour force had risen to something like 10,000 men, women and children by the early twentieth century, and, in terms of

Table 1. *Number of Wholesale Footwear Manufacturers listed in Trade Directories: Bristol and Eastern Suburbs, 1871–1970*[*]

Year	Central Bristol	Kingswood	St. George	Staple Hill and Soundwell	Hanham	Warmley	Total
1871	18	1	—	—	—	1	20
1881	35	8	5	1	1	3	53
1891	49	44	15	6	7	5	126
1901	45	43	15	4	11	1	119
1911	28	40	16	6	6	1	97
1921	20	50	11	8	3	2	94
1931	14	39	8	7	2	1	71
1940	12	27	5	7	3	1	55
1950	7	5	2	3		—	17
1960	8	2	—	1	—	—	11
1970	2	1	—	—	—	—	3

Sources: Mathews' *Bristol and Clifton Directory* (1871). Wright's *Bristol and Clifton Directory* (1881–1911). Kelly's *Bristol Directory* (1921–70).
* Excludes all references to "boot and shoe makers".

numbers employed, footwear ranked as one of the most important industries in Bristol.[10]

Most of the early factories were set up in the parishes of St. Pauls and St. James, within the city of Bristol. In Portland Square, once a prestigious residential area, 18 of the 34 houses were converted to boot manufactories in the early 1870s.[11] Cheap premises were available in this part of the city, and these were workshop enterprises rather than factories in the modern sense of the word. As in other centres of footwear manufacturing, the 'putting out' system was utilised, and capital requirements were consequently low. Moreover, these concerns lacked the expertise and managerial strength to organise the marketing of their products. In the main, they dealt with substantial wholesalers or agents, who served retailers in the Bristol and Somerset coalfields, in the rapidly growing industrial areas of south Wales, and in Ireland. Nevertheless, some of the footwear firms in the region were substantial concerns. The largest was Derham Brothers of Barton Street, St. James. Originally established at Wrington in Somerset in 1839, the firm moved to Bristol in the 1850s, and grew rapidly. For a time, it was one of the biggest employers in the city; in 1883, between 1,200 and 1,500 workers were regularly employed, and at times of peak demand the labour force exceeded 2,000. The other leading boot and shoe manufacturers in the city were considerably smaller; Brightman Brothers employed 400 in 1873, when it moved to a new factory in Lewins Mead, and Coe, Church & MacPherson of King Square had about 450 workers.[12] Many of these city manufacturers produced lighter footwear to fill in the gaps in the very seasonal heavy trade. In the 1880s and 1890s, factories were also set up in Kingswood, St. George and nearby districts. Though these were still independent communities, they were gradually absorbed into Bristol as the city spread eastwards. Before the 1890s, Kingswood firms were generally smaller than those within the city of Bristol. A. Fussell & Sons and D. Flook & Co. were among the biggest in 1883, with 3–400 workers, but many of the new concerns which appeared in the area in the 1880s employed only a handful of workers. The firm of G.B. Britton & Sons, which later attained national prominence, also traces its origins back to 1880, when George Bryant Britton and George Jefferies set up in partnership and opened a factory in Waters Road. The partnership employed about 50 people in its early years.[13]

Machinery began to appear in the larger Bristol factories in the 1870s. Derham Brothers, and Coe, Church & MacPherson, adopted the Blake sole stitching machine, and used machines for heeling and eyeletting. Sewing machines from Singer and other leading manufacturers were widely used for closing uppers.[14] In Kingswood, Daniel Flook and Abraham Fussell introduced riveting machinery into their factories in the 1880s.[15] But, compared to their rivals in Leeds and other centres of heavy boot manufacturing, the Bristol and Kingswood manufacturers were relatively slow to organise their businesses along the latest lines; even in the 1890s, when most companies claimed to have adopted up-to-date techniques, processes like lasting and finishing had not been mechanised. Hand work remained important, and outwork common, in the region until the First World War.[16] Britton & Jefferies' factory was fairly typical of the Kingswood industry. In the 1880s, it housed 15–20 sewing machines and three crude presses for cutting out soles and insoles; the machines were treadle-operated until the following decade, when gas engines were installed. Uppers were cut out by hand in the factory, which housed store rooms, packing and dispatch departments, and offices, but making and finishing was almost entirely undertaken by outdoor workers. In 1899, Jefferies retired, and G.B. Britton built a new factory in Lodge Road, Kingswood, but even then production methods were slow to change. Although finishing was mechanised in 1904, the number of outworkers continued to grow, reaching about 150 just after the outbreak of World War One.[17] It is evident that traditional hand methods offered some advantages. For one thing, they required little in the way of capital investment, and thus facilitated entry into the industry. Britton & Jefferies began operations with a total capital of £2,200, and was able to expand their business through a gradual ploughing back of profits.[18] Moreover,

38. An early machine for cutting out soles from thick leather. Invented by James Miles in 1862, it was sold to several of the larger footwear manufacturers in Bristol and Kingswood. The press knives used to cut out the required shape can be seen at bottom left.

wages were generally lower than in other centres of the industry, and the availability of cheap labour meant that there was little incentive to adopt more capital intensive methods.[19]

The footwear manufacturers of Bristol and Kingswood, though somewhat isolated from the other centres of production, were not immune to the changes which were taking place within the industry. One consequence of the transition to wholesale production was the growth of trade unionism; the National Union of Boot and Shoe Operatives (N.U.B.S.O.) was established in 1874,[20] and during the 1880s and early 1890s membership of the Bristol branch grew steadily. This was in line with the national trend. Many operatives feared technological change, and, in addition, "the excitements of the New Unionism and of socialist doctrines and socialist organisations were inspiring a minority to a new militancy of sentiment and action".[21] In Bristol, as elsewhere, strikes became more frequent as the union grew in strength and confidence. There were interminable disputes over reductions in wage rates as employers began to bring in machines to replace hand work, and some of the more progressive firms like Cridland & Rose and Hutchins & May earned a reputation for intransigence in union circles.[22] Traditionally, boot and shoe makers had been paid on piece work rather than day rates, but the advent of new machines and processes rendered existing agreements unworkable. The union was not opposed to machines as such, but it wanted the workers to benefit from increased productivity, and fiercely resisted reductions in piece rates. When the manufacturers turned to day rates, the union tried to restrict output. Other strikes occurred when manufacturers refused to recognise the union. In 1883, for example, Brightman Brothers ordered its workforce to sign the following declaration:

> I hereby declare that I am not a member of any Trades Union or Society having for its object interference between employers and employed, and undertake, in the event of my joining any such Society while I am employed by Brightman Bros., to give them immediate notice of my having done so, with the understanding that it will subject me to immediate dismissal.[23]

In this instance, a strike failed to break Brightmans' resolve, but gradually employers had to come to terms with trade unionism. In footwear, as in many other industries, the manufacturers responded to the growth of union militancy by closing ranks; employers' associations were set up to present a united front to union demands. One of the earliest was the Bristol, West of England and South Wales Boot Manufacturers' Association, founded by 17 firms in 1886. A separate association, the Kingswood and District Boot Manufacturers' Association, was formed six years later, with G.B. Britton as its first chairman. Both bodies were affiliated to the Federated Associations of Boot Manufacturers of Great Britain, which sought to unite all the important footwear centres.[24]

Labour militancy in central Bristol favoured expansion in Kingswood; many employers moved out to take advantage of union weakness and lower wages. As late as 1887, the union branch at Kingswood had only 28 members, although it had grown to over 1,000 by the mid 1890s.[25] By 1893, nearly all the large Bristol boot manufacturers, including Derham Brothers, Coe, Church & MacPherson, Hutchins & May and R.W. Ashley & Sons had established branch factories in Kingswood, St. George, Hanham and Warmley. These eastern districts were for similar reasons the preferred location for new companies like J. Bevan & Sons, whose Hanham factory opened around 1890 and regularly employed about 400 workers.[26]

Tension between manufacturers and the union reached a peak in the early 1890s, with a succession of bitter disputes over the introduction of the 'team' system. This was developed by the devotees of Taylorism, and involved the reorganisation of the workforce – whether hand or machine workers – into small teams. Where possible, complex and skilled processes were divided into several simpler tasks, and the number of workers was adjusted to minimise production bottlenecks. For the manufacturers, the team system offered substantial increases in labour productivity, but the union saw the subdivision of labour as very harmful to the status and prospects of its members. It also insisted that any productivity gains be shared amongst the team members – a demand which seemed quite unreasonable to the manufacturers. In Bristol, the adoption of hand work team methods in 1893 led immediately to an official strike. In the subsequent negotiations, the union fought so fiercely that the Federation was obliged to back down.[27] However, employers were becoming increasingly concerned about the growing inroads of American footwear manufacturers into their traditional markets, and wanted a free hand to run their businesses without 'union interference'.[28] *The Shoe and Leather Record*, which strongly supported the manufacturers, stated that "The Unions are engaged in a gigantic conspiracy to hinder and retard the development of labour-saving appliances in this country".[29]

Strikes in Bristol and St. Albans in 1893–4 caused the manufacturers' Federation to issue a series of demands, which became known as the 'Seven Commandments'. Essentially, the employers wanted a free hand to reorganise their factories: to set conditions of employment, to choose between piece and day rates, and to introduce machinery at any time.[30] These demands were rejected by the union in January 1895, making it certain that strike action would be followed by a general lockout. The lockout began on 13 March 1895, and involved about 46,000 workers throughout the United Kingdom.[31] As chairman of the Kingswood and District Boot Manufacturers' Association, G.B. Britton played a prominent part in the dispute. Although widely regarded as a generous and benevolent employer, he took a firm stand, defending the lockout on the grounds that non-union men would be terrorised by pickets if they were kept on at work.[32] He attempted to form a 'free labour union' to be known as the Industrial Benefit Society for Employers and Employees, and non-union men were asked to sign a declaration that they would not join the union or contribute to its funds during the dispute. Britton also made repeated efforts to persuade the non-federated manufacturers in the Bristol region to lock out their union men.[33] The strike was relatively weak in Kingswood because of the availability of non-union labour, but this contributed to the bitterness of the dispute – many cases of intimidation were reported in the local press.[34]

The strike ended in defeat for organised labour. Despite contributions from other unions, N.U.B.S.O.'s funds were exhausted after six weeks, and it was forced to give way to the employers' demands. Total union membership fell by almost half in the next ten years. Many branches, including Kingswood and Bristol, had a long struggle rebuilding their benefit funds.[35] With hindsight, it may be argued that the experiences of 1895 marked the beginning in footwear of "a notable record of industrial peace"; the terms of settlement still provide the basis for industrial relations in the industry.[36] At the time, however, the employers were clearly in the ascendancy. Henceforth, manufacturers in Britain were able to reorganise their factories, adopt new processes and machinery, and choose between piece work and day work without hindrance. They agreed that as far as possible all workers should be reinstated, but a blacklist of "objectionable men" was drawn up in both Bristol and Kingswood.[37]

Industrial peace helped to make the early 1900s a prosperous time for footwear producers. Increased mechanisation, improvements in factory organisation, and greater attention to quality, fit and appearance enabled British manufacturers to fight off the American challenge.[38] However, not all manufacturers shared in these developments. A typical small firm was Thomas Miles & Co., whose factory was next door to Brittons' in Lodge Road. In the decade before World War One, this firm produced about 1,500–2,000 pairs of boots a week, and had an annual turnover of about £10,000. This, however, was barely sufficient to cover overheads, and profits of a few hundred pounds alternated with small losses.[39] But most of the more substantial Bristol and Kingswood firms were expanding output and recording higher profits, especially after 1907, when there was a marked improvement in trading conditions. George Bryant Britton, for example, took his two sons, George Ewart and Samuel Wesley, into partnership in 1904, and the capital employed by the firm – now styled G.B. Britton & Sons – rose from £11,818 in 1904 to £23,535 in 1914. Factory extensions were built in 1908 and 1914, and output had risen to about 5,750 pairs a week at the outbreak of the First World War. Pre-tax net profits rose from £1,309 in 1904 to a prewar peak of £5,212 in 1912, which represented about 6 per cent of turnover, or a return of 27 per cent on capital employed.[40]

Another successful company was F. Wilshire & Co. It was founded by Alfred Wilshire in 1904, and began operations in premises in Church Road, Kingswood, producing heavy boots for the south Wales market. Like many of the other manufacturers in the area, Wilshires was heavily dependent upon the putting out system; only clicking, eyeletting and finishing was done in the factory. Alfred Wilshire, however, was young and ambitious, and by 1913 he was confident enough to commission a new factory at a cost of £1,000. This proved to be something of a revolution in footwear manufacturing in Kingswood, because the entire labour force was brought under one roof. Hand work was dispensed with, and a complete heavy boot manufacturing plant was installed by the American-owned British United Shoe Machinery Co. By the early twentieth century, British United had become the dominant force in the shoe machinery industry, through its policy of leasing well balanced 'teams' of machines.[41] But the company had made little impact in Bristol and Kingswood, where most manufacturers used a few machines along with more traditional practices. British United therefore offered very attractive terms to Alfred Wilshire, to the benefit of both companies. Other producers were obliged to follow Wilshire's lead – Brittons began the switch to machine lasting in 1917 – and British United took firm root in the region.[42] This development had its drawbacks. Most importantly, 'tied leases' meant that manufacturers were not allowed to use the machines of British United's competitors, and there was an inevitable tendency for rentals to rise once the firm had achieved a near monopoly. But in the early twentieth century the benefits for manufacturers generally outweighed the costs. The availability of a full range of up-to-date machines with well balanced outputs on a royalty basis kept capital costs to a minimum, and ensured that the many small or medium sized firms which were typical of the footwear industry could be run efficiently. Moreover, British United was able to provide efficient research and development services and maintenance facilities which could not otherwise have been afforded.[43] Wilshires immediately began to benefit from its initiative, and was able to undertake large government contracts during the First World War; on average, 2,000 pairs of service boots were produced a week, which represented half the factory's output.[44]

The demands of war brought fresh challenges and opportunities to Bristol firms. Raw materials were often in short supply, especially at the height of the U-boat offensive in 1917. Government attempts to harmonise industrial production were not always successful. The manufacture of boots and shoes to standard specifications, for example, was resisted by consumers, and large quantities remained unsold. Labour shortages also created persistent problems. Employers were obliged to pay above nationally-agreed rates to keep skilled men, and there was some poaching from rival firms. There was in fact an agreement that workmen should not be recruited from other federated firms at higher rates than they had previously been earning, but not all firms complied.[45] Loss of skilled workers also meant an increased use of female labour. Women had traditionally been employed to close uppers, but their introduction into previously all-male departments like clicking, lasting and finishing was commonly viewed with suspicion. In 1915, Lloyd George, the Minister of

Munitions, made an agreement with the employers and the union that females could be brought in to fill vacancies if the local N.U.B.S.O. branch was unable to supply men. It nonetheless remained a contentious issue.[46] The government was critical of the small number of women brought in to replace local men eligible for military service. The Manufacturers' Association, however, commented that opportunities were limited; despite the introduction of machinery, shoemaking remained a skilled trade. The local labour force was also strongly opposed to the employment of women. In 1916 G.B. Britton attempted to use women to cut sole leather in the press room, but a strike forced the company to back down.[47]

Yet, whatever the production difficulties, the First World War provided good trading opportunities for boot manufacturers. Service boots were required in vast quantities for Britain and her allies, and firms in the Bristol region were able, through their expertise in heavy footwear, to win substantial contracts. Output and profits soared, and towards the end of the war most companies were paying substantial sums in excess profits tax. At G.B. Britton, sales rose from £88,740 to £215,304 between 1913 and 1918, and net profits tripled, to £17,433. Thomas Miles & Co. expanded even faster in this period. Turnover rose more than four times from £11,043 to £50,814, and net profit grew from a paltry £332 to £5,713.[48]

The ending of the war, however, brought leaner times for the footwear manufacturers of the Bristol region. Most of them had been working at full capacity, and had little time to adjust to postwar conditions. For a while, civilian demand kept sales at a high level, but as 1921 wore on the full force of the economic recession was felt. Service contracts dried up, and chronic high unemployment in mining and agriculture depressed traditional markets. Like other industrialists, footwear manufacturers experienced something of a recovery in the later 1920s, only to suffer a further setback with the onset of the Great Depression. The weaker firms in the industry disappeared as the market shrank and production was concentrated in fewer hands. The number of firms operating in the Bristol region was almost halved, from 94 in 1921 to 55 in 1940. (Table 1.) Many of the survivors barely kept going; Thomas Miles, for example, made losses from 1921 to 1924, and despite good results in 1927 and 1928 only just broke even betwen 1929 and 1934. Brittons too found that profits dropped alarmingly, from an annual average of £7,200 in 1920–4 to £4,000 in 1925–9 and £1,900 in 1930–4. Weekly output between 1930 and 1934 was 2,500 pairs, less than half the prewar rate.[49] Short time working was the rule in most factories, and unemployment was high. Between the wars "the boot and shoe industry was suffering from something more than its share in the general depression of British industry".[50] In most years, unemployment in the industry was worse than the national average – which was heavily weighted by a few chronically depressed industries like coal, cotton, shipbuilding and heavy engineering. In Bristol and Kingswood, unemployment fluctuated between 10 and 20 per cent of the workforce, and this was above that of other industries in the region.[51]

The problems facing the Bristol and Kingswood manufacturers were compounded by their dependence on sales of heavy boots at a time when consumer tastes were changing. Urban lifestyles meant that the majority of the British public was beginning to demand lighter, more fashionable footwear. Even in rural areas better roads, the spread of tractors, and the development by the Dunlop Co. of cheaper and more waterproof rubber wellingtons reduced demand for the traditional leather boot. As the heavy boot market contracted Bristol's share of national output fell.[52] Furthermore, the spread of protectionism was affecting overseas sales. For example, Ireland was an important market for agricultural boots, and in 1925 nearly 90 per cent of the footwear sold in the Free State was made in British factories.[53] But the Irish government imposed a 15 per cent duty on imported footwear in 1924, and in 1932 Eamon de Valera's Fianna Fail party came to power pledged to bring about economic self-sufficiency in the Free State. Prohibitive duties and quota restrictions meant that imports of heavy boots virtually ceased within two or three years. Between 1931 and 1934 G.B. Britton lost Irish sales worth over £25,000 – a quarter of total turnover.[54]

The responses of firms to declining sales varied. Most of the Kingswood manufacturers soldiered on making heavy boots, and as a result few did well. Even so, F. Wilshire & Co. demonstrated that it was still possible to sell heavy boots profitably. Despite operating in the fiercely competitive medium grade market, Wilshires was the most successful of the Kingswood boot manufacturers in the interwar years. Its highly mechanised factory gave it a valuable advantage over rival establishments; even in the late 1920s outworkers were still employed by some Kingswood companies, and an attachment to hidebound methods was common in the industry. Wilshires did most of its business with a few large wholesalers. This was important because, in the footwear industry, economies of specialisation were much more important than economies of scale. Size alone did not confer significant advantages on a footwear producer; this was partly due to the leasing policies of the British United Shoe Machinery Co., which did not offer preferential terms to large companies.[55] Specialisation and long production runs, however, were the keys to efficiency, and Wilshires was able to produce a limited range in large quantities. Another factor behind the company's success was the personal involvement of Alfred Wilshire. He retained control of production processes, and also dealt directly with his major customers.

Other heavy boot manufacturers responded to changing circumstances by setting up branch factories in protectionist nations like the Irish Free State. J.H. Woodington & Son, which had factories in Bristol and Clevedon, began operations in Drogheda in 1932. S.A. Wiltshire & Co. of Kingswood (not to be confused with F. Wilshire & Co.) opened a Dublin factory at about the same time. Although the activities of foreign companies in Ireland were closely regulated by the Control of Manufactures Acts of 1932 and 1934, setting up behind the tariff barrier was attractive to many heavy boot manufacturers, and in a number of cases – including the examples mentioned – the Irish subsidiaries outlived their parent companies.[56]

What was really needed, however, was greater responsiveness to changes in the footwear market. As early as 1923, the *Shoe & Leather Record* called on Kingswood manufacturers to prepare themselves for a switch to lighter footwear, and in the next decade some firms responded by producing lighter and more comfortable boots to replace the traditional nailed heavy boot.[57] More adventurous was Brittons' decision in 1930 to install the latest Goodyear machines for the production of men's welted shoes.[58] This initiative came from George Bryant Britton's youngest son, Jack Britton, who had become a partner in 1927. He took control two years later when his father died at the age of 72, and when G.E. Britton retired in 1934 he became managing director of a new limited company, G.B. Britton & Sons Ltd. He was to be a leading figure in the industry until his retirement 30 years later. His decision to begin making good quality light shoes was not, however, a recipe for instant success. It was difficult for a company specialising in heavy boots to establish itself in a different sector of the market, especially at a time when trade was generally depressed. It meant challenging Northampton manufacturers, who had considerable expertise in this type of footwear. Customers – who tended to identify a manufacturer with a certain type of footwear and a certain price bracket – had to be persuaded to buy the new lines. In the long term the company benefited from the experience gained, but in the 1930s its shoes were never entirely satisfactory in terms of quality or unit cost and did not do much to help G.B. Britton to recover from the depression.

Those manufacturers who continued to concentrate upon the traditional product in the hope that market conditions would improve were vindicated, in the short term at least, by rearmament and the advent of the Second World War. The output of civilian footwear was cut, but substantial orders for army boots were placed with Kingswood companies. There were of course new problems for manufacturers to overcome. Materials were often in short supply, and the industry suffered from severe labour shortages. An Essential Work Order was eventually applied to the industry in February 1943, but the labour force continued to fall and, as in the First World War, women had to be trained to replace male operatives.[59] In March 1941 the government annnounced its Concentration of Industry Scheme, which was intended to group manufacturers together to release factory space and labour for vital war work. Britton's Lodge Road factory was requisitioned by the Ministry of Aircraft Production for aircraft repair work, and the company had to find room for its machinery at the factories of two of its erstwhile competitors, F. Wilshire and E.J. Bees Ltd. Although inconvenient and disruptive it had important consequences, because in December 1941 Wilshires became a fully owned subsidiary of G.B. Britton & Sons Ltd. The company had done relatively well in the difficult interwar years, but Alfred Wilshire was getting old, and wished to hand over to a younger man. The results of the takeover were very satisfactory. Despite all the problems of wartime production, output averaged 3,300 pairs per week between 1941 and 1945, including about 1,000 pairs of service boots.[60] Profits averaged £22,250 per year, which was more than double the figures achieved by the two companies during the 1930s.[61]

The end of war in 1945 was marked by fears that the end of government contracts would bring a return to depressed trading conditions. In civilian markets, the prewar trend towards lighter and more stylish footwear returned with renewed force once derationing in 1948 brought an end to 'utility' boots and shoes. Moreover, the rate of technological change in the footwear industry was beginning to accelerate. Traditional techniques were generally labour intensive; mechanisation had not resulted in the demise of the skilled worker, and wages made up more than a quarter of manufacturing costs. The rapid advance of manufacturing wages in the first postwar decade led to a search for new methods which offered lower unit costs. Factories were reorganised to minimise production bottlenecks, and work study methods began to appear. An important development was the adoption of the cemented or 'stuck on' rubber sole, which had originated in the interwar years with the development of cellulose cements. Rubber was lighter and more durable than leather as a soling material, and the process offered substantial savings over conventional machine sewn constructions. The stuck on sole led in turn to a revolutionary new process, which resulted in the emergence of Brittons as the dominant force in the Bristol/Kingswood footwear industry – and, indeed, as the U.K. market leader in men's boots and shoes.

In 1949 C. & J. Clark Ltd. acquired the world rights to what became known as the CEMA or direct moulding process. (CEMA was a acronym for Construidores Espagnoles Maquinas Automaticas [Spanish Automatic Machinery Constructors].) The CEMA machine was invented by a Barcelona businessman, Gonzalo Mediano, and it represented a significant advance on existing methods. In one operation, a pair of rubber soles and heels were moulded, vulcanised and bonded to leather uppers. Combining several operations into one offered the prospect of substantial reductions in manufacturing costs. Direct moulded footwear was also superior to machine sewn or stuck on types; it was lighter, more flexible and more waterproof, and lasted much longer. Clarks spent five years developing the original rather crude design into a complex yet reliable machine, and in 1954 began to produce direct vulcanised children's shoes.[62] One of the obvious attractions of the process was its suitability for a wide range of footwear. But although Clarks was strongly established in women's and children's shoes the company lacked technical expertise and management strength in the men's market. After much debate, the Clarks board decided that a subsidiary, C.I.C. Engineering Ltd., should be set up to manufacture CEMA machines for sale to other footwear manfacturers.[63]

    G. B. Britton was one of the first customers. Arnold Reed, who had become factory manager after the war, had close links with Clarks, and

39. A CEMA direct vulcanising machine, late 1950s. After the completed upper was fitted on the metal last, the two side moulds were brought together and the mould filled with the rubber mix. Temperature gauges for the mould heaters can be seen at the top of the machine.

was aware of the development work which had been undertaken. He was very enthusiastic about the process, and recognised its potential for the lighter, flexible and more comfortable boots now being demanded by his firm's civilian and military customers. In February 1955, Clarks agreed to supply him with a machine on a trial basis.[64] The adaptation of the process to boot production, however, was no easy task. Heels, for example, wore badly or came off easily. Reed eventually realised that the thick rubber in the heel was not curing fully, and a fibre filler had to be inserted. Adhesion problems were also caused by the high mould temperatures, which generated steam from the uppers and insoles. Meters and dryers had to be installed to keep moisture content below 10 per cent.[65]

Once these problems had been overcome, Reed was ready to begin quantity production, and Jack Britton was urged to buy four machines at a cost of £1,000 each. At first he was reluctant to sanction such a large investment, but was eventually persuaded that the prospects for the new technology justified the risk. Although the machines were expensive to buy, it was becoming apparent that direct moulded boots could be produced at much lower unit costs than traditional types. In December 1955, Jack Britton told the *Manchester Guardian* that "the 39 processes of screwing, stitching and shaping the conventional sole and heel to the upper have been reduced to 7 processes, and the production time has been reduced from 4 days to 1 day". Savings amounted to 11 per cent of production costs for the cheapest lines, rising to 20 per cent on army boots.[66]

The decision to adopt direct moulding sparked off a period of growth which was quite unprecedented in the footwear industry. The new lines generated enormous interest in the trade, and proved very popular with the public. Brittons also became the largest supplier of army boots and industrial safety footwear in the United Kingdom.[67] Between 1955 and 1965, weekly output rose from 10,000 to 120,000 pairs. Initially, production consisted of a limited range of boots, but direct moulded shoes were introduced in 1958, and the process was extended to lightweight men's shoes and women's casuals in the early 1960s, when PVC began to replace vulcanised rubber.[68] Pre-tax profits grew more than tenfold over the period, and for nearly a decade annual ordinary share dividends of 25 per cent or more were declared. (Table 2.) The capital employed by the firm rose sharply, although to a great extent the expansion was financed by ploughed-back profits.

The new technology made great demands of managerial and supervisory staff. A Research and Development Unit was set up under Arnold Reed. New skills had to be acquired. There was a demand for chemists and engineers, who were sometimes 'headhunted' from outside the industry. Their salaries often far exceeded those of experienced

Table 2. *G.B. Britton & Sons Ltd*: *Capital Employed, Dividends Paid and Net Profit,*
1951–73

Year	Capital Employed* £000	Net Profit† £000	Ordinary Share Dividend %
1951	162	61	10
1952	162	73	15
1953	162	68	15
1954	162	83	20
1955	207	71	15
1956	207	64	15
1957	207	98	$17\frac{1}{2}$
1958	257	148	20
1959	360	254	25
1960	429	366	$27\frac{1}{2}$
1961	429	448	30
1962	552	516	30
1963	1,142	814	$27\frac{1}{2}$
1964	1,142	1,123	30
1965	1,160	1,205	$32\frac{1}{2}$
1966	1,160	1,012	$32\frac{1}{2}$
1967	2,201	1,236	$22\frac{1}{2}$
1968	2,208	933	$17\frac{1}{2}$
1969	3,708	(-361)	-
1970	3,708	8	-
1971	3,708	303	3
1972	3,708	233	3
1973	3,708	486	5

Source: Annual Reports and Accounts, 1951–73.
* Issued share capital + debentures.
† Before tax and interest.

shoemakers, which caused tensions at times. The labour force had to be retrained and expanded. The total number employed rose from 450 in 1951 to just over 3,000 in 1968, making Brittons one of the top six footwear producers in the country.[69] Reed also proposed the introduction of shift work to maximise output from the CEMA machines. This was hitherto unknown in the industry, but after prolonged negotiations with N.U.B.S.O. a system of three eight-hour shifts was introduced.

Despite this, orders far exceeded production capacity, and the firm embarked on a succession of takeovers and expansion schemes. Two Kingswood boot manufacturers, Hoare & Douglas Ltd. and Thomas Miles & Co. Ltd., were acquired in 1956 and 1959 respectively. In 1959 Brittons also began production in south Wales with the takeover of Brynmawr Bootmakers Ltd, and commenced construction of a new factory at Ballymena in Northern Ireland to produce uppers. Brittons was able to take over skilled workers from William Clarke Ltd., a long-established Irish bootmaking concern which had recently closed. In the following year, the main Kingswood factory in Lodge Road was extended by 75,000 square feet and joined to the old Thomas Miles factory next door, enabling a complete reorganisation of production.[70]

With demand buoyant at home, the directors initially showed little interest in exporting. However, direct exports to Europe and North America eventually took off, and, with the realisation that moulded footwear appealed to foreign as well as British buyers, a major overseas expansion programme took place in the 1960s. By the end of the decade, G.B. Britton had manufacturing subsidiaries in Eire, West Germany, Holland, Australia and New Zealand. There were also wholly-owned distribution companies in Belgium, Denmark and the United States, and a joint manufacturing venture in Iran.[71]

By the mid-1960s, Brittons had become the dominant force in the men's branded market. (See Table 3.)   The industry remained, numerically at least, in the hands of small firms, but technological change had now given

Table 3. *The Market for Branded Footwear in 1966*

	Men's %	Women's %	Children's %
Top Manufacturers			
G.B. Britton	13.4	negligible	7.8
C. & J. Clark	5.5	16.4	27.9
Norvic	2.2	13.1	5.3
John White	2.0	—	0.6
Startrite	—	—	13.3
George Ward	1.1	n.a.	2.2
Hush Puppies	1.0	n.a.	n.a.
K. Shoes	6.4	17.3	n.a.
Lotus	5.1	n.a.	n.a.
Others	63.5	54.3	42.8

Source: McAlley Associates Ltd., *A Background to the U.K. Footwear Industry* (1968).

a positive advantage to larger concerns.[72] Direct moulding, for instance, required a lot of capital and increased effort on research and development. Most Kingswood firms simply did not have the cash to make this sort of commitment. Brittons, as a public company since 1951, had climbed into a different league, and could raise ample funds either through the retention of profits or the issue of new shares. Access to capital was a major factor in the firm's success. Equally important was the willingness of Jack Britton and Arnold Reed to take the risks involved in developing a revolutionary process, and their ability to handle the pressures that came with rapid growth.

The company's production and marketing strategies were remarkably successful. Efforts were concentrated on a few products; even when the moulded process was extended to lighter footwear, the range of products was still much narrower than those of more 'traditional' companies. The 'Everyday' shoe, for example, was launched in 1959 in just one pattern, in brown or black. By 1961, it was selling a million pairs a year, and was claimed to be the biggest-selling single line in the history of the industry.[73] This kind of approach made for economies in labour and raw materials costs, enabling the company's to price its products very competitively. Effective marketing was equally important; Britton's 'Tuf' and 'Gluv' brands were massively promoted at point of sale and in national press, television and cinema campaigns. The use of branding was not of course a new feature in footwear, but the industry typically spent about 0.6 per cent of turnover on brand promotion. Brittons regularly spent up to 4 per cent of turnover on national advertising, a level matched only by Clarks in the women's and children's sectors.[74] The inherent reliability of the direct moulded process enabled Brittons to offer an unconditional six month guarantee, and this was strongly featured in its advertising. Other elements in the company's strategy were summed up by Jack Britton in his address at the 1962 annual general meeting:

> Tuf is manufactured in large volume and in long runs through a highly streamlined organisation. It therefore becomes possible to offer a keenly priced shoe to the public, and a profitable deal to the retailer; for although the distribution margins we allow are less than are customary in the trade, the retailer turns over his stock of the compact Tuf range at a higher rate so that his net earnings are satisfactory though his percentage markup is low. A fixed selling price and effective national advertising are the two linch-pins that hold this structure together – a structure compounded of mass production and mass selling, which yields exceptional value to the consumer.[75]

Tuf and Gluv were sold through about 10,000 outlets in the United Kingdom. About half the total turnover was with wholesalers and independent retailers, and multiples and mail order outlets accounted for about 25 per cent each.[76]

40. The closing room at G.B. Britton's Kingswood factory, 1968.

None of the other local firms could match the achievements of G.B. Britton. The industry had not become highly concentrated – small firms still predominated in footwear manufacturing[77] – but the number of firms operating in the region had continued to decline. Some had disappeared for good as a result of the government's wartime concentration scheme. Many others failed to adjust to postwar market conditions, and closed in the late 1940s and 1950s. Demand for the region's staple product was by now falling fast; rubber wellingtons were making major inroads into the market, and the success of Brittons' moulded boot of course added greatly to the difficulties of the 'traditional' firms. A few of them, as noted earlier, were taken over by Brittons, but other long-established firms, like J. Flook & Sons and Woodingtons (Bristol & Clevedon) Ltd. went into liquidation.

By 1960, only 11 firms were still in operation in the Bristol region. The survivors were, for the most part, companies which produced lighter footwear or had found a specialist niche in the market. The most successful of them was Derham Brothers Ltd. In 1906, it had moved from the centre of Bristol to Soundwell, and four years later it was taken over by H. Steadman & Co. This was another old Bristol firm with a factory at

Castle Green, run by Percy and Clifford Steadman. In the 1930s, they decided to close their Bristol factory, and concentrate upon the production of medium-priced women's shoes at Soundwell. Such products were not very profitable in the depression and war years, but they provided a good basis for postwar expansion. The firm took great care to keep abreast of styling trends, and produced cemented footwear for sale through multiple retailers. The emphasis on styling and quality enabled the firm to benefit from the expansion of the fashion footwear market in the early 1960s. The total capital employed by the firm had reached £113,000 by 1965, second only to G.B. Britton in the Bristol region.[78] Towards the end of the decade, however, a further contraction took place in the Bristol footwear industry. Technological change was continuing apace, and placed growing demands on capital requirements and managerial skills, while keenly priced imports were beginning to make serious inroads into the U.K. footwear market. In 1968 Derham Brothers went into liquidation, and only three firms were still in operation in the region by the end of the decade – two small manufacturers in Bristol, and G.B. Britton in Kingswood.

In the late 1960s, Brittons' hectic expansion also came to an abrupt end. The first signs appeared in 1968, when profits fell sharply, and 1969 saw a large loss. (Table 2.) For the first time since the war there were redundancies and short time working at the Kingswood factory. With the advantage of hindsight, it became clear that there were several reasons for this dramatic reversal of fortunes. One explanation which has been put forward by those in the industry is that this was a classic demonstration of a 'product life cycle'. An innovative and distinctive product gave Brittons an initial advantage, which the company exploited very effectively. Gradually, however, this advantage was eroded by the growth of competition, and eventually the market became saturated. The widening of the product range served to delay, but not prevent, an eventual decline. This explanation, however, is not completely satisfactory. Why, for instance, did the company not develop replacement products? The answer was partly that Brittons was too busy meeting the enormous demand for Tuf. This placed a severe strain upon management, which was preoccupied with day to day problems rather than forward planning. As early as 1960, Arnold Reed was arguing that a period of consolidation was needed; he was not heeded, and in the following year he left the company. There is some evidence to support his belief that rapid growth got out of control after his departure. For example, overseas subsidiaries lacked effective supervision, and their performance was often unsatisfactory. The business remained a family concern, and this was beginning to work to its disadvantage. By the 1960s the industry had developed to the point where a range of specialist managerial skills were required. Jack Britton had dominated the firm since 1934, and after his retirement he admitted that he had taken too much unto himself. David Wilcox, who replaced him as managing director in 1963, was not as well regarded in the industry; he was subsequently criticised for his inability to delegate authority, and was held responsible for the poor results of the late 1960s.[79]

The popularity of Brittons' products can be seen as having led to complacency; the company became too accustomed to operating in a seller's market. Furthermore, the narrow margins on Tuf meant that wholesale and retail customers were willing to switch to rival products as they became available. The immediate cause of the company's problems, however, was the market unrest surrounding the abolition of resale price maintenance in 1968. Some customers turned quickly to rival manufacturers who were more flexible in their pricing policies, or began to sell cheap imported footwear. When it became known that Brittons had received orders from Tesco, Woolworth and other leading supermarkets there was a mass boycott of the company's products. Supermarkets and hypermarkets now play a major part in footwear retailing, but at the time there was a great deal of concern in the trade that their massive purchasing power would enable them to cut Tuf prices, despite the slender profit margins. Because of its 'mass distribution' policy, Brittons was not entitled to refuse to supply supermarkets simply because they were likely to cut prices. Although it subsequently persuaded the supermarkets to cancel the orders, the damage had already been done.[80]

Poor trading results led to a drastic shake-up in late 1960s and early 1970s. The labour force was cut and David Wilcox was replaced as managing director. In 1973, a takeover bid was mounted by Ward White Group Ltd., a Northampton company which had been formed by the merger of two long-established footwear firms, John White and George Ward. The offer price for ordinary shares was 28p., which valued Brittons at £2.47 million. Initially, the offer was rejected; Brittons' published results had already shown a marked improvement before the takover bid became public, and the directors argued that the net asset value per share was much higher, at 58p. Eventually, however, Ward White's offer was improved to 50p. per share, and the board bowed to the inevitable. G.B. Britton became a wholly-owned subsidiary of Ward White on 20 July 1973.[81] The overseas subsidiaries were disposed of, and production was concentrated upon Kingswood and Brynmawr. After further redundancies, the labour force was reduced to about 1,000 by 1985, of whom 250 were employed in south Wales. Retrenchment proved a successful policy, and the company began a steady recovery. The Tuf brand now accounts for about one third of the pairage sold. Brittons has retained its position as a major producer of safety footwear and army boots, and also has a useful made-to-order business with Marks & Spencer, British Home

Stores, Lennards and Olivers (under these companies' brand names). Despite the job losses, it remains one of the most substantial employers in east Bristol.

During the last hundred years, the footwear industry in Britain has experienced great changes. Radical developments in shoe technology and changing patterns of consumer demand created difficulties for many manufacturers, but also offered new and lucrative opportunities which could be exploited. Many Bristol and Kingswood firms failed to move with the times, and closed down as the heavy boot market on which they depended began to contract. For the first 40 years of its existence, G.B. Britton & Sons was in many ways a typical representative of the Kingswood industry, but its ability to adapt to meet the challenge of new technologies and markets was the key to its postwar success. The experience of the late 1960s, however, demonstrated how quickly complacency and a lack of forward planning could erode a favourable trading position.

NOTES

1. The author is grateful to G.B. Britton Ltd. and C. & J. Clark Ltd. for permission to consult their archives. Mr P. Birch (Ward White Group PLC), Messrs D. Smith, A. Smith and P. Cockburn (G.B. Britton & Sons Ltd.), Mr P. Keith (formerly of C.I.C. Engineering Ltd.), Miss A. Ainsworth (C. & J. Clark Ltd.), and the late Mr W.A. Reed made important contributions to the preparation of this chapter. The author would also like to thank Mr P. Holmes (Bristol Polytechnic) for allowing him to examine the records of the Kingswood and District Boot Manufacturers' Association and other trade union and business records.

2. B.R. Mitchell and P. Deane, *Abstract of British Historical Statistics* (Cambridge, 1971), pp.8–9.

3. R.A. Church, 'Labour Supply and Innovation, 1800–1860: the Boot and Shoe Industry', *Business History*, XXII (1970), pp.26–8.

4. P. Head, 'Boots and Shoes', in D.H. Aldcroft (ed.) *The Development of British Industry and Foreign Competition, 1875–1914* (1968), pp.163–4. Church, 'Labour Supply', pp.30–2. H. Bradley, *The Technical Growth of the Footwear Industry* (1930).

5. Head, 'Boots and Shoes', p.177. 'Traditional' centres of the industry like Northampton tended to mechanise slower than Leicester, Norwich or Bristol. In these areas, where footwear manufacturing had developed more recently, the labour force was weaker and less well organised to resist change. Church, 'Labour Supply', p.44.

6. J.B. Jeffreys, *Retail Trading in Britain, 1850–1950* (Cambridge, 1954), pp.356–8, 373.

7. G.B. Sutton, *A History of Shoemaking in Street, Somerset: C. & J. Clark Ltd., 1833–1903* (Street, 1979), pp.32–7, 141–6.

8. On the firm's early history, see G.B. Sutton, 'The Marketing of Ready Made Footwear in the Nineteenth Century', *Business History*, VI (1964), pp.93–112.

9. It was reported that cottages could not be let in Kingswood unless they had a bootmaking workshop. 'Lesser Columbus' [Laurence Cowen], *Greater Bristol* (1893), p.210. K. Hudson, *The Industrial Archaeology of Southern England* (2nd edn. Newton Abbot, 1968), pp.104–5.

10. The exact number employed in boot and shoe manufacturing is uncertain because of the difficulty in distinguishing between wholesale manufacturers, small makers and repairers. For contemporary estimates, see J. Fussell's speech at the first A.G.M. of the

Kingswood and District Boot Manufacturers' Association, 13 Dec. 1893, and A.J. Pugsley, 'The Economic Development of Bristol', *Bristol Times & Mirror*, 5 June 1922. According to the censuses, employment in the boot and shoe industry in Bristol and Gloucestershire rose from 5,482 in 1851 to 11,081 in 1901, and then fell to just under 9,000 by 1921. F. Walker, *The Bristol Region* (1972), pp.274–5.

11. *Matthews' Bristol and Clifton Directory* (1871–3).

12. *Bristol Times & Mirror, Work in Bristol: a Series of Sketches of the Chief Manufactories in the City* (Bristol, 1883), pp.9–10, 14. *Western Daily Press*, 19 Dec. 1873.

13. G.B. Britton & Sons Ltd., *Cobbler's Tale* (2nd edn. 1958), pp.1–3.

14. *Bristol Times & Mirror, Work in Bristol*, p.12.

15. Anon, *The Ports of the Bristol Channel: Progress, Commerce* (1893), p.212. B. Little, *The City and County of Bristol: a Study in Atlantic Civilisation* (1954), p.264.

16. See, for example, G. Rimmer, 'The Leeds Boot and Shoe Industry in the Nineteenth Century', *British Boot and Shoe Institution Journal,* XII (1965), p.420. Anon, *Ports of the Bristol Channel*, pp.196–226.

17. 'G.B. Britton & Sons Ltd.', *Illustrated Bristol News*, III (June 1961), p.40. *Western Daily Press*, 29 Sept. 1952, p.3. Britton, *Cobbler's Tale*, p.4.

18. Britton & Jefferies, Balance Sheets, 1880–4.

19. Indeed, the attractions of low wages were sufficient to tempt firms from Leeds to move to the south west. A Fox, *History of the National Union of Boot and Shoe Operatives, 1874–1957* (Oxford, 1958), p.99.

20. It was originally known as the National Union of Operative Boot and Shoe Rivetters and Finishers. For clarity, the better known name is used throughout.

21. Fox, *History*, p.164.

22. See, for example, N.U.B.S.O., *Monthly Reports*, Jan. 1885, p.4; April 1885, p.7; Sept. 1885, p.7; Nov. 1886, p.6; Jan. 1887, p.3.

23. Ibid., May 1883, p.4; June 1883, pp.3–6.

24. B.U.S.M.C., *A Historical Survey of Shoemaking* (Leicester, n.d.), pp.3–5. Kingswood and District Boot Manufacturers' Association, Minutes, 27 Oct. 1892; 27 Sept. 1893.

25. N.U.B.S.O., *Monthly Reports*, Feb. 1887, pp.42–4. N.U.B.S.O., Bristol Branch, Minutes, 10 June 1896.

26. 'Lesser Columbus', *Greater Bristol*, p.209. Anon, *Ports of the Bristol Channel*, p.197.

27. Fox, *History*, p.204.

28. R.A Church, 'The Effect of the American Export Invasion on the British Boot and Shoe Industry, 1885–1914', *Journal of Economic History*, XVIII (1968), pp.237–40.

29. *Shoe and Leather Record*, 19 Feb. 1892.

30. *Bristol Mercury*, 21 Nov. 1894; 11 March 1895. Fox, *History*, p.221.

31. N.U.B.S.O., Bristol Branch, Minutes, 30 Jan. 1895. Fox, *History*, pp.223–7.

32. Kingswood and District Boot Manufacturers' Association, Minutes, 8 March 1895.

33. Ibid., 14 March 1895.

34. Ibid., 29 March 1895.

35. N.U.B.S.O., Bristol Branch, Minutes, 10 June 1896. Union membership fell from 44,000 in 1894 to 24,000 in 1906. Fox, *History*, pp.235, 243.

36. K.G.J.C. Knowles and M. Verry, 'Earnings in the Boot and Shoe Industry', *Bulletin of the Oxford Institute of Statistics*, 16 (1954), p.32.

37. Kingswood and District Boot Manufacturers' Association, Minutes, 25 April 1895. *Western Daily Press*, 26 April 1895.

38. Head, 'Boots and Shoes', pp.183–4. Church, 'American Export Invasion', passim.

39. Thomas Miles & Co., Private Ledger, 1907–1935.

40. G.B. Britton & Sons, Private Ledgers, 1904–13. 'G.B. Britton & Sons Ltd.', *Illustrated Bristol News*, III (June 1961), p.40.

41. In 1900, more than two-thirds of total U.K. output was produced on B.U. machinery. Fox, *History*, pp.422–3. Also see Head, 'Boots and Shoes', pp.181–2. Church, 'American Export Invasion', pp.240–8.

42. Interview with W.A. Reed. Also see Britton, *Cobblers' Tale*, pp.17–8.

43. H.A Silverman, 'The Boot and Shoe Industry', in H..A. Silverman (ed.) *Studies in Industrial Organisation* (1946), pp.218–20.

44. Britton, *Cobblers' Tale*, p.18.

45. Kingswood and District Boot Manufacturers' Association, Minutes, 28 Sept. 1907; 11 May 1915; 27 July 1915.

46. N.U.B.S.O., *Monthly Reports*, June 1919, quoted in Fox, *History*, p.369.

47. Kingswood and District Boot Manufacturers' Association, Minutes, 21 Oct. 1915; 30 Nov. 1915; 5 Dec. 1916.

48. G.B. Britton & Sons, Private Ledgers, 1912–8. Thomas Miles & Co. Ltd., Private Ledgers, 1912–8.

49. Private Ledgers, 1921–34.

50. H.M.S.O., *Working Party Report: Boots and Shoes* (1946), pp.68–9.

51. Kingswood and District Boot Manufacturers' Association, A.G.M., 25 July 1922. F. Walker, *The Bristol Region* (1972), p.327.

52. M.P. Fogarty, *Prospects of the Industrial Areas of Great Britain* (1945), p.364.

53. *Irish Trade Journal*, Sept. 1935, p.99.

54. J. Press, 'Protectionism and the Irish Footwear Industry, 1932–39', *Irish Economic and Social History*, XIII (1986), pp.74–7. G.B. Britton, Private Ledgers, 1930–4. On the impact of Irish protectionism upon boot manufacturers in the Bristol region, also see Kingswood and District Boot Manufacturers' Association, Minutes, 6 May 1924; 28 July 1924; A.G.M., 21 March 1932.

55. On the optimum size of footwear firms, see H.C. Hillman, 'Size of Firms in the Boot and Shoe Industry', *Economic Journal*, XLIX (1939), pp.276–93. Silverman, 'The Boot and Shoe Industry', pp.211–7.

56. Press, 'Irish Footwear Industry', p.78. M. Daly, 'An Irish Ireland for Business? the Control of Manufactures Acts, 1932 and 1934', *Irish Historical Studies*, XXVI (1984), pp.246–72.

57. *Shoe & Leather Record*, 26 Jan. 1923, p.55. 'West of England Supplement', *Shoe & Leather News*, 16 July 1936.

58. See Britton, *Cobbler's Tale*, pp.11–2. In welted footwear, the upper and insole are stitched to a narrow strip of leather – the welt. This in turn is stitched to the sole, producing a flexible and comfortable shoe. Welted footwear could also be easily repaired; an important attribute, because traditional leather soles were not particularly durable. J.H. Thornton, *Textbook of Footwear Manufacture* (1953), pp.28–9.

59. E.L. Hargreaves and M.M. Gowing, *Civil Industry and Trade* (History of the Second World War, U.K. Civil Series, 1952), pp.496–7.

60. G.B. Britton & Sons Ltd., Private Ledgers, 1941–5.

61. Companies Registration Offices, Cardiff, 496652, G.B. Britton & Sons (Holdings) Ltd.

62. C. & J. Clark Ltd. Archives, C/Lab/35(a), C.I.C Engineering Ltd., 'High Pressure Moulding by the CEMA Process' (1955). Directors' Agendas and Papers, 30 April 1950; 15 Jan. 1953.

63. C. & J. Clark Ltd. Archives, Directors' Minutes, 28 March 1955.

64. Interview with Patrick Keith.

65. Interview with Arnold Reed. C. & J. Clark Ltd. Archives, C/Lab/35, Mediano Development Unit, Minutes, 21 Dec. 1954; 17 Feb. 1955.

66. *Manchester Guardian*, 29 Dec. 1955. C. & J. Clark Ltd. Archives, C/Lab/35, Mediano Development Unit, Minutes, 21 Dec. 1954.

67. It had been one of the first companies to develop safety footwear for industry after the Second World War, and a subsidiary, Protective Footwear Ltd., was set up in 1952. *Western Daily Press*, 29 Sept. 1952. *Illustrated Bristol News*, III (Oct. 1962), p.67.

68. G.B. Britton & Sons (Holdings) Ltd., Annual Reports and Accounts, 1955–65. *Shoe & Leather Record*, 2 Jan. 1964.

69. *Western Daily Press*, 16 July 1951. McAlley Associates Ltd., 'A Background to the U.K. Footwear Industry' (report commissioned by G.B. Britton & Sons Ltd., 1968), p.47.

70. G.B. Britton & Sons (Holdings) Ltd., Annual Reports and Accounts, 1956–60. Brynmawr Bootmakers Ltd., Minutes, 19 June 1959; 21 Sept. 1959. Britton, *Cobblers' Tale*, pp.55, 63–70.

71. G.B. Britton & Sons (Holdings) Ltd., Annual Reports and Accounts, 1956–60.

72. Fox, *History*, pp.422–3. Lazard Brothers & Co. Ltd., 'The Leather Footwear Industry' (report commissioned by G.B. Britton & Sons, 1965), pp.1–6.

73. Britton, *Cobbler's Tale*, p.85.

74. McAlley Associates Ltd., 'U.K. Footwear Industry', p.50.

75. G.B. Britton & Sons (Holdings) ltd., Annual Report and Accounts, 1962.

76. *The Statist*, 16 Dec. 1962, p.781.

77. In 1963, 70 per cent of the firms in the Census of Production employed less than 100 people. Quoted in McAlley Associates Ltd., 'U.K. Footwear Industry', pp.45–7.

78. *Illustrated Bristol News*, III (Oct. 1962), p.67. Lazard Brothers, 'Leather Footwear Industry', pp.17, 76.

79. Interview with Arnold Reed. G.B. Britton & Sons Ltd., *The End of the Tale* (Bristol, 1977), pp.109, 112.

80. McAlley Associates Ltd., 'U.K. Footwear Industry', p.65. Open letter from J.H. Britton to Rt. Hon. Edward Heath, 29 Sept. 1969, reprinted in Britton, *End of the Tale*, pp.123–30.

81. G.B. Britton & Sons (Holdings) Ltd. to shareholders, 22 June 1973. *Idem*, Annual Report and Accounts, 1973. Lazard Brothers & Co. to G.B. Britton shareholders, 20 July 1973.

Old Traditions, New Departures:
The Later History of the
Bristol & West Building Society[1]

CHARLES HARVEY

All but the most passive observers of the British economic scene are sure to have noticed that the once comfortable world of personal finance, occupied by the high street banks, life assurance companies and building societies, is becoming ever more complex and competitive. Before the early 1980s, when the banks first mounted a serious challenge in the market for personal mortgages, there had long existed a mutually respected division of function: the banks handled financial transfers and provided personal credit facilities in the form of overdrafts and personal loans; the life companies offered a tax-efficient home for long term savings; the building societies borrowed over-the-counter from the public at highly competitive rates of interest and lent the bulk of deposits to would-be home owners. In the main, this was a simple, convenient and lucrative arrangement for all concerned. Once the economic difficulties which immediately followed the Second World War had been overcome, business boomed and profits ran consistently high for more than three decades. There was, of course, some overlap in the business done by the main financial intermediaries, but on the whole this tended to strengthen rather than weaken functional divisions. The provision of bridging loans by banks or the writing of house purchase linked endowment policies by life assurance companies, for example, never threatened the dominance of the building societies in the market for housing finance.

This is not the place to engage in serious discussion of the reasons for the weakening of the old financial order and the recent heightening of competitive pressures in the personal finance sector. Precisely why the banks have come to fight the building societies for mortgages, or why the building societies increasingly wish to act as conventional bankers, is as yet not completely understood. No doubt the strategic thinking in the boardrooms of major financial institutions has been influenced by several factors, such as sheer size, the culture of growth, difficulties in expanding overseas, and the more competitive economic environment of the 1980s. It will be some years yet before the full consequences of the collective strategy of growth through diversification and challenge are fully seen.

However, one thing is sure: the legal changes introduced through the Building Societies Act of 1986 – which already have been added to quite considerably – have sanctioned the demolition of the post-war system of functional specialisation.[2] The new order will be dominated by large conglomerates offering an elaborate range of financial services. These conglomerates, whether they call themselves banks, building societies or even life assurance offices, will not act in the spirit of pure competition, but will rather look to tie the customer and meet his or her every financial need from cradle to grave. The ascendant doctrine is that of total service.

The law is not passive nor merely reactionary: it can be used by government to control, liberate or even promote change. The Act of 1986, which took effect on 1 January 1987, should be seen as embracing all these potentialities. Before it came into force, the way in which building societies were regulated had changed little since the passing of the Building Societies Act of 1874. This defined building societies as non-profit making institutions which operated solely for the benefit of members, whether investors or borrowers. The only legitimate business of a society was to raise funds through issuing shares and accepting deposits, and to employ these funds by making loans against the security of houses, land or other real property. It was recognised that societies needed to have capital reserves and hold liquid assets, but non-mortgage assets were limited to such things as bank deposits and government stock. All societies had to comply with a set of strict regulations. The law demanded that societies make a fixed-format annual return to the Chief Registrar of Friendly Societies, whose task was to impose rigorous standards of accounting and reporting. Later changes in building society law (notably in 1894, 1939 and 1962) in general strengthened the regulatory framework whilst upholding the ideal of building societies as non-profit making organisations with limited and well-defined functions. It is against this background of regulation and containment that the 1986 Act appears radical and innovatory. The Act replaced all other legislation at a stroke, and, though it protected the building societies' main function as providers of mortgage finance from personal savings, it greatly extended the range of services they could provide. Hence the sudden burst of building societies into the estate agency business in 1987–8, the flowering of new types of building society accounts and services, the offer of unsecured personal loans, overdrafts and second mortgages, the promotion of new housing schemes, and tentative moves in the direction of share dealing and investment advice. At the same time, societies are now able to raise funds on the so-called wholesale money markets, and if the corset of remaining regulations is found to be too tight, then conversion to public limited company status is always possible. Already, many societies are merging and otherwise preparing for a direct assault on the traditional core businesses of the banks and life assurance companies.

It is evident that the long-term progress of the building society movement has been shaped – and continues to be shaped - by the regulatory framework imposed upon it. However, the early development of the movement and the principles on which it was founded owed nothing at all to legislators or civil servants. The first societies were formed in the last quarter of the eighteenth century in the fast expanding but squalid industrial towns and cities of the North and Midlands. They were the creation of ambitious members of the lower strata of society – skilled workers, craftsmen, retailers, clerks and the like – who were anxious to provide decent homes for their families in the face of great difficulties. Men such as these had little spare cash, but they had sufficient continuity of employment and earning power to set aside a small amount each week. The usual arrangement was that a group of men would band together, pool their savings month by month, buy land, and, as funds permitted, build houses. When a house was completed, a ballot or auction held amongst the members decided who would occupy it. All members carried on paying into the common fund until each had taken possession of a house. The building society would then be wound up.[3]

The precarious finances of most working class families and the doubtful legal status of the early societies meant that the movement was to slow to gain popularity. It is estimated that the 250 societies formed between 1775 and 1825 built or purchased just 2,000 houses.[4] Nonetheless, the work of the pioneers was invaluable in legitimising the concept of a building society. The first societies were registered under the 1793 Friendly Societies Act, and their legality, which on occasion had been questioned, was recognised by the courts in 1812. The first legislation concerned specifically with building societies was the Regulation of Building Societies Act of 1836 which created the office of 'certifying barrister' to register societies and offer advice on drawing up rules and the proper conduct of business. Legal acceptance, moreover, was accompanied by innovation. Some societies began to accept deposits and pay interest to individuals who had no wish to secure ownership of a house; they simply wanted a secure and profitable home for their savings. The advantage to societies was that they could speed up the building programme and meet their primary object more swiftly. In doing so, they fostered the notion that building societies might have both saving and borrowing members, thus severing the direct connection between saving and the building or purchasing of houses.

Permanent building societies, organised for the general purpose of accepting savings and making loans against the security of houses or land, were the outcome of such thinking. These societies were not formed by individuals to meet their own limited objectives, but to provide a general service to savers and investors for so long as that service was required and could be sustained without loss to any member. The first of the new kind of society was founded in 1845, and the idea was so popular that there were 540 in existence by 1873, compared with 959 old-style terminating societies.[5] Moreover, the permanent societies, by virtue of their greater generality, had already grown into much larger institutions, which were collectively far more important than the terminating societies. The trend continued, and it is estimated that by 1895, when there were in all 3,642 societies in existence, the greater part of the £45 million assets held by them was in the hands of permanent societies.[6]

The Bristol & West is one of a number of surviving building societies owing their existence to mid-Victorian enthusiasm for permanency in housing finance.[7] It was founded in 1850 (under the long-winded and rather pretentious title of the Bristol, West of England and South Wales Permanent Building Society - B.W.E.S.W.P.), following a meeting at the Corn Street offices of solicitor Thomas Danger to consider "the propriety of forming a Permanent Building Society on the best principles".[8] Those who attended the meeting, their motives and the character of the organisation they created, were all very typical of the age. Unlike the terminating societies, the permanents were from the beginning a middle class affair. The first chairman of the B.W.E.S.W.P. was John Lucas (1850–81) whose name was "a household word for stability and sound judgement";[9] other directors were prosperous businessmen, professionals or local worthies. Their motives were various. Some had a strong philanthropic urge, others saw the society as a means of boosting the local economy and prestige of the City of Bristol. Few had any hope of direct gain. The payment of directors' fees was provided for in the rules of the society, but the actual amounts were quite small compared to the existing incomes of most directors. Economic motives, however, were not absent from the scene. The solicitors (Thomas Danger & Co.) and bankers (Miles, Harford & Co.) appointed by the society could expect to gain some lucrative business, and these interests were certainly influential in the formation of the B.W.E.S.W.P. It is also possible, at a more general level, that some of the promoters hoped to benefit eventually as borrowers or commission agents for the new society, though little is actually known of these matters.

The B.W.E.S.W.P. was also typical of the building society movement as a whole in the form of its original organisation and in the nature of its business. For several decades, the society was run as an adjunct to the stockbroking and insurance business of G. S. Bryant & Co. (Bryant was secretary of the B.W.E.S.W.P. 1852–77 and he was succeeded by his partner C. J. Lowe). The public was invited to subscribe for shares which could be paid for in regular instalments, on terms and conditions that

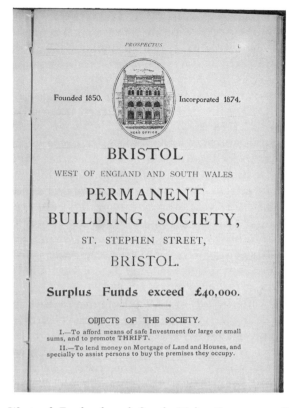

PROSPECTUS

Founded 1850.   Incorporated 1874.

BRISTOL

WEST OF ENGLAND AND SOUTH WALES

PERMANENT

BUILDING SOCIETY,

ST. STEPHEN STREET,

BRISTOL.

Surplus Funds exceed £40,000.

OBJECTS OF THE SOCIETY.

I.—To afford means of safe Investment for large or small sums, and to promote THRIFT.

II.—To lend money on Mortgage of Land and Houses, and specially to assist persons to buy the premises they occupy.

41. Bristol, West of England and South Wales Permanent Building Society prospectus, 1901. Note the straightforwardness of the Society's objectives.

were advertised from time to time in the local press. Any cash taken in was deposited with the society's bankers until being lent out on mortgage. Applications for loans were considered at monthly meetings of the board, which would have a surveyor's report before it. It was the job of the secretary to arrange surveys, make all administrative arrangements, handle all correspondence and keep the books of the society. All property deeds were kept at the bank for safety. Most loans were made to speculative builders and property developers rather than private individuals. Not until after the First World War did the permanent building societies emerge as champions of owner-occupation in Britain.

The B.W.E.S.W.P. got off to a good start. In the first nine years of operation, it advanced £21,615 to borrowers; £178,475 in the second nine years, and £380,660 in the third nine years.[10] Its example soon encouraged others to enter the field. The 1850–70 period alone saw the formation of

at least eight other Bristol societies: Bristol Equitable (1850), Bristol
Permanent Economic (1853), Union Benefit (1855), Third Bristol Benefit
(1859), Standard (1865), Bristol General Permanent (1865), Fourth Bristol
Permanent (1865), Bristol and West Gloucestershire Permanent (1869).[11]
None of these, nor any of the many other competitors formed before
1914, managed to rival the B.W.E.S.W.P. By 1878, when it moved into
new purpose-built offices in St Stephen's Street, the total assets of the
society had risen to more than £200,000.[12] A twenty-five year period
followed in which growth was negligible but reserves steadily accumulated. In 1914 total assets amounted to £291,495 and reserves £45,220.[13]
The maintenance of a healthy financial position in a 'flat' market, when
many rivals were forced into liquidation, speaks well of the management
of the B.W.E.S.W.P. The society truly was founded on "the best principles". The legendary Arthur Scratchley, building society publicist and
advocate of a thoroughly professional approach to management, served
the society as consulting actuary from its formation until his death in
1897, when the directors acknowledged the "sound advice" to which
"much of the success of the Society is attributable".[14] Scratchley insisted
that loans should only be advanced against proven first-class security,
that borrowers should have a good stake in a mortaged property, that
administration expenses be held down, that a proper balance be kept
between savers and investors, that liquid funds should never be put to
speculative ends, that adequate liquidity and reserves be maintained, and
that a properly qualified chartered accountant be employed to audit the
accounts of the society. Under this regime, the B.W.E.S.W.P. gained a
reputation for financial strength, professional management and integrity;
a reputation enhanced over the years through the recruitment to the
board of leading Bristolians such as Mark Whitwill and Sir Frank Wills.[15]

Few building societies in Britain were better placed than the
B.W.E.S.W.P. to weather the financial storm that came with the onset of
the First World War. The financial strength and reputation of the society
were such that, "despite all the adverse circumstances consequent upon
so stupendous a Campaign", the difficulties resulting "turned out to be
extremely slight".[16] Total assets and reserves changed little between 1914
and 1918, and in 1919 the consulting actuary cheerily reported that the
society had passed unscathed through "a period which was sure to be
critical for all Associations of the kind", showing that the "confidence
which the members repose in it is ... abundantly warranted". He
encouraged the board to redouble its efforts to develop the business
whilst maintaining its standards of "care and discretion, combined with
judicious economy".[17] This it certainly did; as can be seen from Table 1,
the total assets of the society rose an impressive fourteen-fold between
1918 and 1939, from £290,000 to £4.2 million.

Table 1. *Inter-War Rates of Growth and Rankings of Leading Building Societies*

Society	Total Assets (£'000)		Multiplication in Assets 1918–39	Ranking in 1939
	1918	1939		
Halifax*	7,365	129,138	18	1
Abbey Road	768	51,401	70	2
Leeds Permanent	2,181	41,773	19	3
Woolwich Equitable	1,590	40,074	25	4
National	1,226	35,696	29	5
Cheltenham & Gloucester	955	7,546	8	16
Bristol & West	290	4,163	14	34
Building Societies Movement	68,498	773,727	11	—

Sources: All the 1939 figures and rankings are drawn from the 1940 edition of the *Building Societies Year Book*, as is the movement total assets figure for 1918. The 1918 figures for individual societies are drawn from relevant annual reports and accounts.
* The Halifax Permanent merged with the Halifax Equitable in 1928 to form the Halifax Building Society. The 1918 figure given here is the sum of the assets of the two societies. The Permanent figure (£5,925,782) is from a balance sheet for 1 January 1919; the Equitable figure (£1,439,294) is from a balance sheet for 29 June 1918.

The B.W.E.S.W.P. became far more conspicuous. Growth was encouraged through the wide issue of free booklets like *Ship-Shape & Bristol Fashion* (1930), *How to Own Your Home* (1931) and *The Case for Home Ownership* (1938).[18] The target for mortgages was no longer the builder and landlord, but individuals who wanted homes of their own. They were told of the security provided by large reserves, the careful management of "experienced business men of Bristol and the West",[19] the advantages of thrift and planned saving, the simplicity and cheapness of borrowing against the security of a house, and how to go about finding a property and making application for a loan. All this was backed up with advertisements in the press and on posters which put across the message that the society had the advantage of regional and local knowledge that was applied to the positive advantage of its members. To reinforce the point, the words "South Wales Permanent" were dropped from the society's title in 1927, and in 1935 it was officially renamed the Bristol & West Building Society. Growth and prosperity were further signalled through the move in 1939 to a centrally located prestige office block, St. Stephen's House, Colston Avenue.

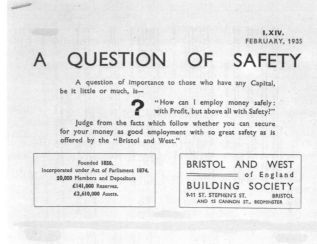

42. Bristol & West pamphlet, *A Question of Safety*, 1935, emphasising the security of investing with the Society.

The interwar expansion of the Bristol & West, though worthy by the standards of the day, was by no means exceptional. Indeed, the building society movement as a whole was kept buoyant by extremely favourable circumstances.[20] Money flowed into building societies at an unprecedented rate throughout the period, as the rising real incomes of those in work permitted many more people to accumulate savings. Building societies had a particular appeal to investors because of the comparatively high rates of interest they offered, especially in the 1930s when money was cheap. Throughout, they had an advantage in the competition for personal savings, because special arrangements with the Inland Revenue meant that income tax was paid directly to the authorities on behalf of investors at a discounted composite rate. Thus the societies could advertise healthy rates of interest free of income tax. As investors responded by placing more of their personal savings with building societies, there was a commensurate rise in the numbers seeking mortgages. Again, higher real incomes played a part, as more and more families sought the comfort of a new suburban home away from the congestion and filth of the older inner city districts. The tendency toward owner-occupation was encouraged, though not created, by the existence of rent restrictions which discouraged landlords from extending their stocks of dwellings at the pre-war rate. In this favourable climate, with both savers and borrowers clamouring to join societies, the total assets of the building society movement grew from £68.5 million in 1918 to £773.7 million in 1939 – an increase of 1,100 per cent. (See Table 1.) The level of owner-occupation in Britain rose from about 10 per cent of dwellings to 25 per cent of dwellings over the same period.[21]

However, the success enjoyed by building societies between the wars was not entirely due to favourable economic and social factors: Much credit must be given to the societies themselves. It was they which, when faced with a decline in borrowing by landlords and builders, took up and vigorously promoted the cause of owner-occupancy. They did not discourage savings, but found a new outlet for them. And by increasing their own efficiency, they narrowed the margin between the rates of interest charged to borrowers and those paid to investors, making them still more competitive and giving an additional stimulus to the movement.[22] The way was led by a group of societies – including the Halifax, Abbey Road, Leeds Permanent, Woolwich Equitable and National societies – which did more than most to encourage owner-occupancy in Britain.[23] Each built extensive branch networks to increase its business. The Halifax had risen to prominence before 1914 through the opening of branches in Yorkshire. Now, under the leadership of Enoch Hill, champion of owner-occupancy, the Halifax spread into other parts of Britain, particularly the wealthy south east.[24] Its example was followed by others. Most notable was the Abbey Road (London) whose total assets, astonishingly, multiplied by 70 between 1918 and 1939. The driving force was Harold Bellman who became secretary in 1921, general manager in 1927, managing director in 1930 and chairman in 1937.[25] He took an important local society and created out of it a national institution. He was a master of publicity, at once advertising the Abbey Road and campaigning on behalf of the building society movement in general. The Abbey Road had its own journal, and held public meetings, addressed by leading politicians and others prominent in national life, which were so popular that tickets had to be distributed by ballot. Bellman, along with other visionaries like Enoch Hill and Bruce Wycherley of the National, served the movement as a whole through leadership of the Building Societies Association, its trade association and vehicle of political influence.[26] They also played an important part in developing management skills in building societies through support for the Building Societies Institute, the professional body of the movement founded in 1934.[27]

Growth on the scale achieved by the leading societies was not without its problems. The public certainly responded positively to the campaign for owner-occupancy, but many who wished to become owners did not have the funds to make much of an initial contribution toward the purchase price of a house or flat. Before the First World War, societies had not as a rule been willing to advance more than 80 per cent of the value of a property over a maximum term of 15 years. There were, of course, many variations in practice, but normally the societies erred on the side of caution, preferring wherever possible to have ample security in the event of default. These arrangements came under increasing pressure as growth-oriented societies awash with money competed for mortgages. Ways were found of reducing loan restrictions and increasing applications. One method was to raise the maximum loan figure to 90 per cent of valuation on issue of a guarantee against loss by an insurance company; a suitable policy being issued in return for a single payment by the borrower. Another method was to have builders of new estates provide additional security for part of the money lent to purchasers. The builder usually deposited money in a 'pool', and this fund was used to compensate building societies in the event of defaults. As a borrower repaid a loan, the builder was reimbursed. He could then use the money to make fresh contributions to the 'pool'. Once a building society was associated with a particular builder and estate, then most of the mortgage business for the estate came its way. Innovations of this type contributed much toward the exceptional growth of societies like the Halifax and Abbey Road.[28]

The interwar experience of the Bristol & West, though rich and eventful, did not match that of the leading societies. The mood of management and the board was that the society should endeavour to keep abreast of the times whilst remaining true to long-established principles. They placed a high value on the reputation of the society for complete security, and did nothing whatsoever to endanger this. Like other large societies, the Bristol & West used advertising to stimulate business, relaxed mortgage restrictions to encourage the less well off into home ownership, and entered into promotional deals with builders. But, all the while, the Bristol & West was responding to the initiatives of the leading societies rather than setting the pace itself. Under the management of Hubert Bonning (1929–48), caution remained the watchword of the society. It granted mortgages to only the very soundest applicants, preferably with the personal recommendation of a solicitor or estate agent, and took "only so much money as, in the judgement of the Directors, can be employed with absolute safety to our investing members and depositors". The society liked to describe itself as "the principal West-Country Society" with "a high tradition of careful management and claims to be second to none in stability". Typical boasts at annual general meetings were that "caution has always been the guiding principle of the Society" and "a considerable amount of mortgage business has been offered and declined as unsuitable".[29] One result of this caution was that the Bristol & West remained rock-solid financially to survive the Second World War just as easily as it had done the First. A second result is less praiseworthy. Despite its location at the centre of a prosperous region, less badly hit by depression than most others, the society grew little faster than the average for all building societies. It opened just three branches (Bedminster and Gloucester Road in Bristol in 1932 and 1936 respectively, and Exeter in 1936), and progressively fell behind the leading societies in the industry. Thus, as Table 1 shows, by 1939 the Bristol & West had been eclipsed by the more aggressive societies based in the North and London, which were already organised on a national basis.

The building society movement has developed since 1945 very much along the lines laid down between the wars. Domination of the industry by the largest societies was already a fact of life before the Second World War, and this situation has been more than maintained, as Table 2 reveals.

In 1985 the Halifax was still the largest society, followed by the Abbey National, the Nationwide, the Leeds and the Woolwich. There has been remarkable stability at the top, while the leading societies have tightened their grip on the industry. Hundreds of small societies have disappeared, their engagements (assets and liabilities) having been transferred to larger societies. There have also been several important mergers between the bigger societies, starting in 1946 when the Abbey Road joined forces with the National to form the Abbey National.[30] The union in 1987 of the Nationwide and the Anglia is the most recent of a steady stream of strategic mergers aimed at forging organisations capable of competing at the highest level. The headlong rush to create comprehensive national branch networks is another trend which started before 1939. At the end of 1939, there were 890 registered societies with a total of just 625 branches. By the end of 1985, the 167 societies remaining on the register shared a total of nearly 7,000 branches.[31] The opening of so many new offices – the Halifax alone had 725 in 1985 – is usually justified by making reference to the growth in building society business since 1945. Britain's economic advance, though less vigorous than those of other European countries, has encouraged a steady rise in the numbers of people saving money as

Table 2. *Progress of the British Building Societies Movement, 1940–85*

End of Year	Indicators of Growth				Indicators of Concentration		
	Mortgage Assets (£m)	Total Assets (£m)	Real Value* of Total Assets (£m)	Index of Real Asset Growth (1985 = 100)	Number of Societies	Assets of top 5 Societies as a % of Total Assets	Assets of top 20 Societies as a % of Total Assets
1945	573	824	2,841	8.8	890	41.1	62.0
1950	1,060	1,256	3,806	11.7	819	37.4	62.5
1955	1,752	2,065	4,791	14.8	783	40.5	64.4
1960	2,658	3,180	6,477	20.0	726	45.1	71.8
1965	4,583	5,577	9,550	29.5	605	46.7	73.1
1970	8,752	10,819	14,800	45.7	481	50.3	77.7
1975	18,802	24,203	17,995	55.4	382	52.9	82.3
1980	42,708	54,317	20,598	63.6	273	54.9	83.5
1985	97,007	120,959	32,411	100.0	167	56.8	89.6

Sources: Computed from data presented in relevant volumes of the *Building Societies Year Book.*
* Total assets deflated by the retail price index (January 1974 = 100).

a regular habit. The building societies have remained a favoured home for personal savings, the real value of total assets of societies growing by more than eleven times from 1945–85. In 1985, the building societies held 53 per cent of all personal sector liquid assets, compared with figures of 33 per cent and 14 per cent for national savings and the banks respectively.[32]

Beneath the general pattern of building society expansion has lain a rich variety of individual experience. The Bristol & West has been no exception. The Second World War was not traumatic, but it did bring a sudden halt to a long period of sustained growth. Assets were redistributed away from mortgages toward less lucrative investments in government stock, and the old balance was not restored for many years after 1945. Recovery was not instant, nor was it aided by government policy. Housebuilding was strictly regulated, and, until well into the 1950s, most resources – bricks, cement, timber and other essentials – were diverted toward the construction of vast council estates. Less than thirty per cent of the new dwellings completed in the 1945–54 decade were for owner-occupation. The demand for mortgages was consequently low, though some relief came as private landlords, disgruntled by the retention of rent controls, again began to sell off stock. Inevitably, the immediate post-war performance of the Bristol & West was constrained by the general housing situation. Yet the board did not take this as an excuse to sit back and do nothing. There was a desire to get back in the groove and return to the prewar policy of safe but healthy growth. The society appointed a western area manager in 1945 with an office at Bideford and the power to appoint sub-agents.[33] A main agency was opened at Exeter in the following year on commission terms similar to those for Bideford.[34] An effort was also made to get more mortgage introductions through the payment of higher commissions to solicitors, estate agents and other intermediaries. In April 1946, the board decided to abandon a local agreement (made in 1931) which had restricted commissions paid for successful introductions to half the rates prevailing elsewhere.[35]

These initiatives were not without effect. The western area main agent, Mr Hooper, did particularly well, submitting successful mortgage applications amounting to £500,000 by November 1951.[36] The business as a whole slowly began to move forward. Total assets rose from £3.8 to £5 million between 1945 and 1950, while the proportion held in the form of mortgages recovered from 69 per cent to 81 per cent.[37] However, old attitudes and policies continued which to the critical outsider must have appeared fondly anachronistic. Caution still governed all. Builders were told that, in view of the uncertainty surrounding supplies, a maximum loan of 70 per cent of purchase price could be extended on moderately priced houses, "on terms not exceeding 18 years". Many must have looked elsewhere for more flexible terms. Similarly, large mortgages were only granted to employees of "firms of exceptional standing" provided a guarantee against default was offered by the employer.[38] Gratifying as it may have been to do only the highest class of mortgage business, such stringency began to cost the society dear. The Bristol & West stood thirty-fourth in the national league table of building societies in 1939; it had fallen to fortieth by the end of 1945, and forty-first by the end of 1950. At best the society was marking time; at worst it was passively relinquishing its leadership of the building society movement in Bristol and the west.

Traditional attitudes, policies and methods of working continued at the Bristol & West throughout the 1940s. The board, under the chairmanship of W. Danger Fripp (1945–50), who had been a director since 1918, was conservative to the core. Ambition and imagination were in short supply. It was understood that the main responsibility of the board was to keep the society on the straight and narrow, through ensuring that money was only lent against ample security. All mortgage applications went to a sub-committee of the board which met weekly. Most board meetings were devoted to routine matters such as deposits, cheques drawn, deeds held and bank balances. Policy matters, such as the terms governing mortgage offers, would on occasion demand more extensive discussion than was usual. Strategic thinking was rarely in evidence. It was thought to be enough that the society press forward gently, maintaining its local and regional contacts, high standards and sound judgement in balancing the interests of savers and borrowers. The whole approach was radically different to that adopted by leading societies like the Abbey National, which was positively committed to growth, professional management and the building of national branch networks.[39]

If there had been no change in the thinking and policies of the Bristol & West, it seems certain that the society would have entered into a long and dignified relative decline, probably ending in takeover by a more progressive competitor. This has been the fate of many other local societies in the twentieth century; but it was not to be. The powerful grip of tradition gradually weakened, and the society set out on a new course. Growth replaced stability as the central objective of policy-making, and growth relative to the growth of other societies gained acceptance as an important measure, if not the most important measure, of business success or failure. Table 3 summarises the record of the Bristol & West in the postwar era. The figures document an impressive transformation in the fortunes of the society.

The real value of total assets held by the Bristol & West doubled every five years between 1950 and 1970, hauling the society up from forty-first to fourteenth in the league table of building societies. Not unexpectedly,

Table 3. *Growth of the Bristol & West Building Society*, 1945–85

	Indicators of Growth							Indicators of Relative Size		
End of Year	Total Assets (£m)	Real Value of Total Assets (£m)†	Index of Real Asset Growth (1985 = 100)	No. of Branches	No. of Full Time Employees	No. of Investors ('000)	No. of Borrowers ('000)	Ranking by Total Assets	Total Assets as % of Assets of the Halifax*	Total Assets as % of Assets of the Chelt. & Glos.*
1945	3.81	13.14	2.2	3	n/a	13.51	8.61	40	2.81	42.40
1950	5.04	15.27	2.5	10	n/a	12.57	7.81	41	3.04	32.02
1955	13.09	30.37	5.0	7	n/a	19.81	12.32	28	4.95	48.75
1960	28.69	58.43	9.7	17	n/a	33.44	18.08	19	5.85	77.97
1965	60.21	103.10	17.1	27	n/a	55.73	25.14	18	6.49	89.97
1970	150.15	205.40	34.0	49	451	131.89	41.64	14	7.52	106.69
1975	373.87	277.35	45.9	83	564	271.44	55.34	15	8.17	106.80
1980	862.40	327.04	54.1	143	853	455.58	73.21	13	8.14	110.51
1985	2,255.68	604.42	100.0	164	918	662.55	97.80	12	9.26	67.38

Sources: Annual reports and accounts of the Society; annual returns submitted to the Registrar of Building Societies; various volumes of the *Building Societies Year Book*.

* The Halifax Building Society was the leading society throughout the period. The Cheltenham & Gloucester Building Society remains one of the second tier competitors of the Bristol & West.

† Total assets deflated by the retail price index (January 1974 = 100).

the rate of growth slackened after the initial charge, though in absolute terms the growth of real assets was maintained at a high level in the 1970s. In the 1980s, in common with other major societies, the Bristol & West has enjoyed a tremendous surge in real assets. It is a mark of high achievement that since 1950 the society has progressively gained ground on the very large societies, since these have aggressively competed for business. Of course, the societies that went national between the wars continue to dominate the industry, but the Bristol & West can boast a substantial branch network of its own, concentrated in the wealthier southern parts of the country. Its main regional competitor has been the Cheltenham & Gloucester, and comparison of the records of the two societies again reflects well on the Bristol & West. After falling further behind the Cheltenham & Gloucester in the immediate postwar years, the Bristol & West was to the fore by 1970, holding the advantage until the early 1980s; then the Cheltenham & Gloucester moved forward very quickly, once more outstripping its west-country rival.

The transformation of the Bristol & West from a traditionally-minded local society to a major financial institution, controlling funds exceeding £2.5 billion at the end of 1986, began with the retirement of Hubert Bonning as secretary and general manager in October 1948, and the appointment in his stead of Andrew Breach, then only 34 years of age. In Breach, the Bristol & West found its Enoch Hill or Harold Bellman: a person zealous in the belief that building societies are vehicles for social improvement, and who had a tremendous capacity for hard work, an ability to think strategically, and a flair for publicity. Breach was an inspired appointment. The youngest of 243 applicants for a job carrying the then healthy salary of £1,800, he was already a dedicated building society professional, having joined the Hastings Permanent immediately on leaving school in 1931. He had studied by correspondence course to become a member of the Chartered Institute of Secretaries, the professional qualification taken by many building society executives before the formation of the Building Societies Institute in 1934. With the coming of war he joined the Royal Navy. He was invalided out on contracting rheumatic fever, and spent the latter part of the war working for the Planet Building Society in the City. On his being invalided he accepted an invitation to resume his duties as commanding officer of the Sea Cadet Corps in Sussex, which he continued on a part time basis until the end of the war.[40]

It might at first sight seem strange that the conservative board of the Bristol & West should have selected someone as young and energetic as Andrew Breach as its chief executive. However, it seems that the announcement of Bonning's retirement had forced the directors to think seriously about the future, and that they recognised the need for an

43. Andrew Breach, on his appointment to the board of the Bristol & West Building Society in 1954.

injection of fresh thinking. Indeed, Bonning himself read a paper to the board in May 1947 on the post of secretary and general manager and "the trend of Building Society business".[41] But though the need for change was recognised, the direction that change should take was not clear. Hence the appeal of Andrew Breach. He appeared before the board not as a radical, but as one who shared many of their own ideas whilst understanding the direction of change in the building society movement. Breach was clean-cut, conservative in many things, sympathetic to tradition. He respected large reserves, healthy liquidity ratios and cautious lending policies. But he did not believe that these things were incompatible with a vigorous expansion of the business. Like Hill, Bellman and Wycherley before him, he felt it the duty of the soundest societies to extend their operations at the expense of the small and weak. Size and skilled management went together to safeguard the interests of members and the building society movement as a whole. Breach was not the author of this philosophy, but it was he who brought it Bristol. He redefined the role and social purpose of the Bristol & West in a way that united the virtues of the past with a more modern belief in professionalism and growth.

This is not to say that the board was immediately won over to the idea of a radical change in direction. Andrew Breach was appointed on trial as designate general manager. He seemed to have the right combination of qualities, but still had to prove himself. It was not until 1950 that he was confirmed as general manager. He had by then forged a harmonious relationship with his colleagues which owed much to his personal charm and integrity. At no point did he attempt to force the pace in a way that would have alienated the board. He was tactful and diplomatic in approach, easing, rather than forcing, the society on to its new course. There was never need of the grand strategic statement. Patience was a positive virtue, rewarded by the enthusiastic response of directors to new initiatives. Breach worked very closely with his chairman and directors, who began to play a more active role in the society than they had hitherto. He became a member of the board in 1954, and on the death of Anthony Scull in 1969 he was elected to the chair. He held office for nineteen years before announcing, at the annual general meeting in April 1988, that he would soon retire as chairman. His colleagues, however, had persuaded him to accept the honour of becoming the President of the society and to remain as a director.[42]

After his arrival in Bristol in 1948, Breach quickly realised that the immediate need was to resist the challenge of the national societies for leadership of the building society movement in the city; to persuade the local population and influential individuals that the Bristol & West was the 'natural' place to lodge their savings and apply for a mortgage. He recognised the importance of solicitors and estate agents in directing business to the society, and invested a large part of his time, inside and outside office hours, in cultivating personal relationships. His belief that "people do business with you if they like and trust you" paid off, enabling the society to disinvest in low income government securities and build its mortgage portfolio.[43] At the same time, more special agents were appointed to work for the society with a remit and terms similar to those of Hooper in Bideford. The special agency system was seen as a low cost way of extending the territory covered by the society – sod-breaking before a permanent branch could be established. Clearly the Bristol & West could never hope to catch the Halifax, but there was a determination to be "masters in our own backyard".[44] The intention was to build a strong regional network of branches and agencies as quickly as possible without undermining the stability of the society.

The first significant steps were taken in the early 1950s. Offices were opened in surrounding towns like Bridgwater, Clevedon and Weston-super-Mare, though these really operated more like agencies than fully functioning branches, and their status was recognized as such in 1955. Agencies simply collected savings and passed on requests for mortgages which were appraised at head office; they had no authority to make decisions on loans. Agents were not Bristol & West employees, but self-employed individuals working on commission. Chief agents had the authority to appoint sub-agents. Solicitors or estate agents often took on an agency or sub-agency as a means of earning more money. High street premises were thus used more fully, to the benefit of all concerned. The society had 22 major agencies at the end of 1955 and 61 just two years later. In order to recruit and motivate top class agents, a special agency agreement, embodying targets and generously rewarding performance above the norm, was drawn up by Breach and implemented in 1953.[45] Yet agencies were not regarded as an ideal or reliable means of attracting business to the Bristol & West. Much depended on the skill and personality of the individual agent, and in certain cases the arrangement just did not work out as well as had been expected. The Exeter agency is one such case. As early as October 1952, the board noted that the existing agency agreement was "not entirely satisfactory from the Society's point of view" and the general manager was asked to report on the costs of establishing a full branch office.[46] This was opened a few months later. A dedicated high-street office was seen to give a society a stronger presence in a town. Managers could form useful local contacts, devote themselves full-time to society business and look after a number of agents in their district. In other words, branches promised control, co-ordination and continuity in a way that commission agents, however special, could not. When the decision was taken in 1951 to develop the society's business in Bath, it was also decided to open a branch with its own staff rather than to appoint a special agent. Likewise, a branch was opened at Truro in 1953, because this was the "natural centre of Cornish representation",[47] from which the Bristol & West might capture a large share of the building society business done in the county.

The dual approach of developing the business through special agents and well located regional branches was very successful. The fortunes of the society improved greatly in the early 1950s. A refreshing sense of ambition permeated the organisation, and growth became a conscious object of policy. A strong effort was made to develop special mortgage arrangements with builders, by financing the purchase of parcels of land, and, at a later stage, the purchase of houses as they were completed. The society made arrangements of this kind with many developers of private estates in the 1950s and 1960s. At the same time, effort was not spared to increase the flow of funds into the society. In May 1953, for example, the board wished "to stimulate new investments during the remainder of the year in order to finance mortgage business at its present level". It was therefore decided to support the new Exeter and Truro branches with extensive advertising, which, in the case of Truro, entailed sending a circular to all "the people appearing in the Cornwall Post Office telephone directory".[48] Taking such intiatives brought the reward of more business, which encouraged still more ambition. In May 1955 the first of a series of branch development reviews was undertaken, reflecting the fact that the board was by this time accustomed to thinking much more about tactical and strategic matters than it had in the past. It agreed in December 1955, after studying a report by the sub-committee of the board on branch development, that "development during the next five years ... be confined to the S.W. area bounded by Bristol, Gloucester, Oxford and Southampton (excluding S. Wales)".[49] This the board saw as the home territory of the Bristol & West, and it was agreed that branches should be opened as soon as practicable in all major towns and cities in the region. Branches at Gloucester and Reading were already in operation, and within the next five years others were opened at High Wycombe, Salisbury, Taunton, Southampton, Farnham, Bournemouth, Plymouth, Shepton Mallet and Yeovil. By the end of 1960 the society had a network of 17 branch offices.

The rate of branch development achieved by the Bristol & West in the 1950s was not exceptional, and it might be asked why the board did not pursue its policy more vigorously. Part of the answer is that growth was never allowed to compromise the stability of the society. A high premium was placed on the maintenance of healthy reserve and liquidity ratios, and there was never any question that growth would be allowed to substantially diminish either. Old traditions still had priority over new departures. A second part of the answer is that Andrew Breach and his colleagues did not want growth at too high a price. They paid a good deal of attention at all times to quality and costs. Striving for quality meant that it was not enough to find reasonable office accommodation in a target town. Selected premises had to be in just the right location and available on favourable terms. Breach favoured freehold over lease-hold, and often the society would take on a large development and sub-let parts of the building.[50] The society has never tried to hide its interest in the ownership of top quality properties, as successive reports to sharehol-ders reveal. When inflation gathered pace in the 1960s and 1970s, this was to redound to the benefit of the Bristol & West as owner of a substantial number of choice properties. But in the short term, growth slowed because initial costs were higher, and top management spent so much time evaluating property deals. Added to this, the society recog-nised that if it proceeded too rapidly, quality of service to members would suffer through lack of a sufficiently well trained labour force. Hence it was minuted in December 1955 that "in order to maintain existing standards in regard to staff, it was thought better not to proceed too quickly".[51]

Growth through the opening of new offices, or the attraction of more business to existing offices, is known as internal growth. External growth, though the takeover of other societies, was also an option available to the Bristol & West. It is one that was exercised on a number of occasions in the 1950s, most critically in 1955–6 when the society took over the engage-ments of the British Workmen & General of Bath (total assets £1.6 million), the Provident Permanent of Exeter (total assets £3.4 million), and the Reading and High Wycombe (total assets £454,851). These were substantial acquisitions relative to the size of the Bristol & West itself, which at the end of 1954 had total assets of £9.8 million. External growth accounted, in nominal terms, for 20 per cent of the society's expansion in total assets over the five year period 1951–5, rising to 29 per cent for 1956–60.[52] The real importance of the Bath, Exeter and Reading mergers, however, was not the immediate contribution made to total assets, but the provision of useful organisations for regional development. In each case, members of the board of the dissolved society were recruited to newly formed local boards of the Bristol & West, which took on some of the work of the main board in Bristol. Local knowledge was seen as especially useful in winning mortgage business.

There has been no single reason why local societies, like the 25 that joined the Bristol & West between 1955 and 1979, have accepted loss of identity through merger with a regional or national society.[53] Many lacked proper management, having been run from the office of a local accoun-tant or solicitor, and eventually decided that the dwindling assets of the

concern could be managed better by a professional organisation. The
Chief Registrar usually encouraged a transfer of engagements in these
cases, especially if the minor society was in danger of collapse or had
failed in some way to comply with the requirements of the law. In other
cases, misdemeanour by a chief executive caused the board to stabilise
the situation through merger with a larger society. The realisation that
a small society could no longer compete effectively with multi-branch
organisations caused many more to throw in the towel. Often this realisation came when a long-serving chief executive reached retirement age,
and the question of his replacement had to be faced. The British Workmen & General of Bath underwent this experience. The society had a
secretary who had been in ill-health for three years before its takeover.
The directors felt a "moral obligation to provide him with an adequate
pension",[54] and merger ensured that this could be paid. In recommending
the Bristol & West to its membership, the board of the British Workmen
noted the "tendency of building societies of purely local character ... to
be unable to attract sufficient funds to ensure a continuous lending
policy". Furthermore, only the larger societies had the specialist staff to
cope with a business that was "becoming increasingly technical, with the
constant addition to the Statute Book of new laws relating to property
matters", and properly qualified staff were felt "essential in a business
responsible for the safe custody of substantial funds". The Bristol & West
was held up as a model of professionalism. It was described as "the
leading society in the whole of the South-West of England", whose
position would be further strengthened through merger, to the benefit
of members of both societies.[55]

Although the Bristol & West never saw merger as the key to achieving
the status of a major society, it gave every encouragement to a speedier
process of concentration. Indeed, the society often found itself competing
with others to gobble up the assets of a flagging concern. The Shepton
Mallet Building Society, for instance, was acquired in 1959 after it had
first considered an offer from the Hastings & Thanet. Geographic affinity
often proved a persuasive argument in favour of the Bristol & West.[56]
At other times, more positive inducements were offered to directors.
These included payments for loss of office, or, alternatively, membership
of a local board. The negotiating skill of Andrew Breach, who played a
key role in engineering all the important mergers, also worked to the
advantage of the Bristol & West. His enthusiasm was at times tempered
by the board, as in 1957 when merger with the Regency Building Society
was ruled out because "Brighton was at present beyond the perimeter
of the Society's planned activity",[57] but nonetheless it was he who was
behind the policy of growth though non-strategic merger. This was true
even after the appointment in 1967 of a special agent charged with

negotiating the acquisition of societies with assets between £100,000 and £5 million.[58]

After a decade of sustained, if geographically limited, progress, the board of the Bristol & West was prepared by 1960 to consider widening its horizons beyond the limits imposed in the 1950s. An office in Regent Street, central London, was opened in that year, and discussions began about a fresh round of territorial expansion. South Wales attracted particular attention, as the Severn Bridge promised an improvement in "business ties with Bristol".[59] A wide ranging review carried out in 1963 highlighted the south-west Midlands, suburban Bristol, suburban London and south eastern England as other target areas. "In-filling in the South West" was also given a high priority.[60] Lists were drawn up of the main population centres where a branch might be opened, but these were not given priority. The governing idea was that the society should respond flexibly as opportunities presented themselves, whilst actively searching for new locations within the defined territory. Eight new branches were opened between 1963 and 1965, giving the Bristol & West a presence in Wales, the Midlands and Home Counties. A further 25 were added in the next five years. By the end of the 1960s, the Bristol & West was securely established as an important regional society, with offices across southern England, south Wales and the south Midlands. It was the fourteenth largest building society in the country, and had gained an enviable reputation for innovation and enterprising management.

For this reputation, the Bristol & West owed much to the dynamism of Andrew Breach. It is true that he had the support of a chairman and directors committed to developing the organisation, but it was he who set the pace and forged the identity of the society. He wanted an organisation true to the public-service ideal of the building society movement, and that actually cared about the interests of its members. This was shown in the granting of preference to saving members over other mortgage applicants whenever funds were in short supply.[61] It was also shown in the way the society was run and staffed. Breach never acted as a penny-pincher, and did not equate minimum costs with excellence. He favoured economy, but not false economy. Mortgage applications, for instance, were examined very thoroughly, and money loaned only to those who could realistically expect to maintain the repayments. As a result, management expenses were slightly higher than those of less meticulous societies, but the rate of default on loans was, and remains, exceptionally low.[62] The Bristol & West ranked second only to the Anglia in this regard in 1985, a long way ahead of the Cheltenham & Gloucester which had the worst record in that year. In this, and in many other matters, Breach was a respector of tradition. In the 1950s and 1960s he wrote many articles on building societies and housing policy for financial journals like the

Investors' Guardian and the *Statist*. These reveal his thinking on a number of key issues, and confirm him as a man of conservative leanings, proud of the achievements of the building society movement. He rejected the concept of state-subsidised housing, and spoke out several times in favour of a "property-owning democracy".[63] The building societies' role was to further this ideal without risking the savings of investing members. Risk was minimised if societies maintained adequate liquidity and ample reserves. They should also seek to stabilise the market for housing finance by acting collectively and changing interest rates as infrequently as possible. They should not endanger stability through fierce competition at the level of interest rates or mortgage terms. In particular, he did not wish to see the day when loans approaching the full purchase price of a property were made to borrowers. The point was made very clearly in an interview given in 1970:[64]

> I feel everyone has the right to live in a house, but privileges are usually married with reponsibility. For choice, I would prefer a man who has already shown evidence of thrift and who will have a personal stake in his house as I believe that the man without anything to lose is less likely to be a responsible borrower.

Views such as these identified Breach with the mainstream of building society thinking. His writing and the advance of the Bristol & West brought him to the attention of the leading lights of the movement. He was active in the south-western branch of the Building Societies Association (B.S.A.). Membership of the national council followed in 1951. He became deputy chairman of the B.S.A. in 1961, and between 1963 and 1965 served as chairman. As chief spokesman for the movement he was active in promoting the cause of owner-occupancy, whilst resisting the plans of the Labour Government to help the lower-paid to purchase a home through 100 per cent mortgages, special interest rates and local authority finance. In the debate over Labour's plans he repeated at length his arguments against subsidies and lax finance.[65] Competition from local authorities had long proved irksome to the building societies, and the plans of the Wilson government were no doubt perceived as a threat to the long-term interests of the movement. Like most building society leaders of the postwar era, Breach wished to protect the dominant position held by the building societies in the market for housing finance. He took the view that societies should, for the sake of stability, follow a policy of maintaining common interest rates; standard rates for lenders and borrowers should be set by the B.S.A.[66] Only very recently has this cartel arrangement begun to break down.

Traditional thinking on housing finance and resistence to interest rate competition did not identify Andrew Breach with the cause of reaction.

Indeed, he was seen as a progressive, anxious to reorder the industry. His was the cause of ordered change. It was the fate of small societies to disappear, and that of the best-managed, larger societies, to expand and prosper. Advertising, quality of service and branch networking were the favoured means of competition between the majors. Innovation could occur at any level, so long as the B.S.A.'s leadership of the industry was not threatened. In this way, the movement could present a united front to the wider world, while modernising itself from within. The Bristol & West played its full part in this process. One of the most important advantages of operating on a large scale is that it allows generous amounts of money to be spent on advertising and the projection of a corporate image. The society's advertising budget rose from £15,000 in 1960 to more than £100,000 ten years later.[67] Advertising agents were commissioned in 1960 to "identify the Society with some form of attractive advertising",[68] and thereafter the old approach of extolling the virtues of thrift and home-ownership gradually gave way to more subtle methods of persuading the public to join the Bristol & West. The society appointed a firm of public relations consultants in 1965 to win business through the issue of confidence-inspiring stories to the press, radio and television.[69] The whole idea was to characterise the Bristol & West and its management as sound, innovative and on the way up. The opening in 1968 of Broad Quay House, a 16 floor prestige headquarters costing £1.2 million, provided a splendid opportunity to sing the praises of the society. So too did the launching of its Extra Growth Bonds in the following year. The Bonds were issued by the Vehicle and General Insurance Group on a ten-year term, and the premium income, which qualified for tax relief, was invested mainly with the Bristol & West. The tax-efficient nature of the scheme meant that an average gross rate of return of 10.2 per cent could be offered on the investment – a figure well above the prevailing ordinary share rate recommended by the B.S.A. The press release announcing the bonds was picked up and used by almost every national and regional newspaper in the country. The scheme was described as a "step forward in building society thinking"; a "breakthrough on the savings front"; a "clever idea to boost house-loan funds". Breach, architect of the scheme, was hailed as "innovator", "genius"; the "go-ahead general manager" with "an undeniable talent for publicity".[70]

The idea of Extra Growth Bonds was just one of many developed by Breach to keep the Bristol & West 'in the limelight'. Yet possibly the most important contribution made by him to the long-term health of the society, aside from matters of policy, was to forge, through a process of progressive refinement, an efficient system of organisation and management. Before he joined the society, it was run in much the same way as most local societies across the country. A general manager, who was also secretary to the board, ran the operation day by day with the assistance of a number of clerks of different levels of seniority. It was their job to administer and record financial transactions; calculate mortgage repayments with the assistance of printed tables; process mortgage applications; correspond with members, solicitors and the like; and keep the books of the society. A local surveyor was called in whenever a property valuation was required, and other professional advice was sought as required. The main functions of the board were to oversee the business, approve or reject mortgage applications, decide on the placement of liquid assets, and fix the terms on which the society was prepared to lend and borrow money.

Arrangements such as these worked well enough so long as the Bristol & West remained limited in size, scope and ambition. But once extensive growth had become a main objective, it was gradually realised that new business methods would be needed if projected rates of expansion were to be achieved. A particular problem of the traditional approach was that both the general manager and the board had extensive responsibilities of a routine kind, and little time to consider wider issues of policy and corporate strategy. Growth and consequent overloading at the top indicated the need for a more devolved form of organisation. The appointment of area boards in the mid-1950s represented an important step in this direction, as did, a little later, the appointment of a mortgage manager in charge of a specialist department. At a later stage, in the 1960s, a greater share of the responsibility for mortgage matters was passed still further down the line to branch managers. These had their performance assessed according to criteria devised by Breach and put to the board between 1959 and 1963 in a series of documents on cost allocation.[71] Thus, as routine decision-making became ever more dispersed, executive control was retained through the introduction of new accounting and management tools. The Bristol & West was becoming a more complex and professional organisation, and to manage this a better-qualified staff was needed. It appointed a staff solicitor as early as 1952;[72] a succession of other specialist and senior staff appointments followed. Meanwhile, junior staff were encouraged to better themselves through taking part-time professional courses subsidised by the society.[73] An organisational hierarchy, related to salary scales, was created as a spur to the young, who could see before them the route to promotion and a good career.[74]

Periodic organisational reviews and reorganisations continued after Andrew Breach became chairman in 1969. These were made necessary, for the most part, by growth and the possibilities for specialism which it created. The general thrust was to establish a stronger head office team with clear functional divisions and lines of authority. Particularly significant was the appointment in 1975 of three assistant general managers, each responsible for an particular set of functions.[75] This enlargement of the senior management team meant that Breach could be relieved of certain duties, like branch development, to concentrate more on matters of policy and general administration. The business gained fresh momentum, adding 60 new branches between 1975 and 1980. A further 20 followed in the early 1980s, before high-street saturation caused a sharp fall in numbers of new branches. By 1985 the Bristol & West was the twelfth largest building society in Britain, with 164 branches, 1,207 employees, 348 agencies, 662,500 savers, 97,800 borrowers and total assets of £2,256 million.[76]

It is a tribute to the leadership of Andrew Breach that he kept the Bristol & West moving forward at a time when competition between building societies was becoming more severe. Yet it must be recognised that his personal contribution to the society in the 1970s and 1980s was not all that counted. In earlier years, he was the spring from which nearly all the important initiatives flowed, but as the organisation grew in size and complexity many others came to play a significant part. Head office was divided into numerous departments with different functions, and the managers in charge of these were given much freedom of action. The treasury department, for instance, became responsible for managing the very large liquid assets of the society. A job once done by Breach in a fraction of his time, has grown in importance and is now the work of a whole group of money market specialists. Departmental chiefs report variously to the secretary, assistant general managers and general manager. The burden of top management has become a collective one. No one individual is ever again likely to play the free-ranging innovative role enjoyed by Breach in the 1950s and 1960s. Organisation, to some degree at least, has displaced individualism.

This has been the fate of the building society movement as a whole, not just of the Bristol & West. The trend throughout the twentieth century has been for the big to displace the small – a process of concentration that looks set to continue. To keep up with competition at the top, many more societies will submit to large-scale strategic mergers of the kind which brought together the Nationwide and the Anglia in 1987. There is nothing new in this. The board of the Bristol & West first gave serious thought to the possibility of merger with a similarly sized society in 1965/6,[77] and there have been tentative discussions with a number of societies since that time. Yet, while the Bristol & West has kept an open mind about the possibility of strategic merger, its preference has been to remain independent. The reasons for this are not difficult to find. Building societies are not all alike, and Breach and his fellow directors would never have allowed union with a society which had a radically different way of doing things. And since the Bristol & West has had a

44. Money market dealing at the Bristol & West's Treasury Department, Broad
Quay.

very distinctive approach to building society work (keeping an exceptionally high proportion of its assets liquid, for instance), the likelihood
of its finding an ideal partner has not been high.

Furthermore, the directors of the society have continued to take pride
in its origins, traditions and regional identity. Losing these has been

something that the board has found difficult to contemplate, especially with a fiercely independent man like Breach at the head of the organisation. At the height of his career, he was approached by some of the very largest societies about the possibility of his becoming their chief executive. He rejected them all. Instead, Breach found an outlet for his talents locally. The board of the Bristol & West traditionally has been recruited largely from the ranks of the local business community; men "with general business experience" being preferred to professionals other than chartered accountants.[78] Thus Breach was well connected at an early age, attracting offers to join the boards of many companies. Some of these he accepted. In 1968, for example, he became a director of the Bristol *Evening Post*; taking over as chairman in April 1974. At the *Post* he showed the independent spirit that likewise characterised his leadership of the Bristol & West. This was demonstrated in dramatic fashion in 1981 when the group narrowly staved off a takeover bid by Associated Newspapers. Much of the credit for persuading the shareholders that they should remain independent is due to Breach, who shortly after the battle remarked that he "didn't want to go down in Bristol's history as the man to sell the past".[79] He had formed a powerful attachment to his adopted city, through involvement in bodies like the Merchant Venturers and the University, as well as the *Evening Post* and the Bristol & West, and he had become convinced that there is nothing incompatible between a strong regional identity and business success.

There are many who would not agree with Breach. It is fashionable, at both ends of the political spectrum, to argue that there is an inevitability about the advance of national and international capitalism at the expense of local and regional business communities. Some believe that only giant corporations can be competitive, because of the lower costs and prices which result from economies of scale. Others, whilst predicting the triumph of bigness, resist the notion that the consumer necessarily benefits from the expansion of large scale business across an ever widening front. The critics of capitalism point to monopoly power as the consequence of business concentration, with the result that the public suffer needlessly high costs and prices.[80] On this matter, the evidence of the building society industry is mixed. Business concentration and resistance to price competition certainly went hand in hand until quite recently. Moreover, costs per unit of business handled have not shown any marked tendency to decline as building societies have grown bigger. Indeed, societies the size of the Bristol & West have generally managed to keep their costs in line with those of the giants of the industry, while the very best cost record in recent years is that of the Cheltenham & Gloucester. Building society customers have yet to benefit in narrow financial terms from concentration and rising organizational efficiency. Any gains they

Table 4. *The Spread of Owner-Occupancy in Britain, 1944–85*

End of Year	Total Stock of Dwellings (millions)	% of Dwellings Owner-Occupied	% of Dwellings Rented from Local Authorities	% of Dwellings Rented from Other Owners
1944	12.89	25.6	n/a	n/a
1951	13.90	29.5	n/a	n/a
1961	16.45	42.8	26.5	30.7
1965	17.47	46.3	27.9	25.8
1970	18.73	50.0	30.4	19.6
1975	19.87	53.4	31.1	15.5
1980	21.03	56.2	31.2	12.6
1985	21.91	61.9	27.3	10.8

Sources: The figures for 1961 and succeeding years are drawn from relevant editions of *Housing Statistics* (H.M.S.O., 1966–72) and *Housing and Construction Statistics* (H.M.S.O., 1972 onwards). Earlier figures are drawn from *Factual Background* (Bristol & West Building Society, Summer 1987 edition).

might have made have been dispersed in the form of better service, stability and more opportunities to save and invest. All this, however indirectly, has worked in the end to the good. Table 4 documents the spread of home ownership in Britain in the postwar era. It reflects most creditably upon the building society movement, which provided the greater part of the funds needed to transform the national housing situation.

For those who have devoted a large part of their careers to the promotion of owner-occupation, figures such as these must be highly gratifying. That the Bristol & West has contributed so much to the building societies movement must be doubly rewarding for Andrew Breach. He took a traditionally-minded society, lacking in inspiration but operating on sound principles, and forged over the years a modern organisation: flexible and innovative, and with a distinctive, independent identity. The Bristol & West looks well placed to respond positively to the challenges and opportunities created by the Building Societies Act of 1986. Substantial reserves, a well-trained labour force, and forward looking management, are there to be drawn upon as competitive pressures build up. A chain of estate agencies - Bristol & West Property Services – has already been formed, and this promises to grow longer as the years go by. New services are being marketed vigorously. Advanced computer systems – including a network of automatic teller machines – are already in operation, speeding transactions and reducing operating costs. The society is well in tune with current financial trends. Most large societies are proceeding along broadly similar lines, watching the moves of competitors more intently than ever before. For those which make the correct strategic decisions, the future looks extremely bright. But along the way there will surely be casualties. Those weakened by strategic error or inertia will be drawn into mergers with progressive societies that gauge market developments correctly. It remains to be seen whether the Bristol & West has what it takes to remain independent and prosper in the new financial age; the Society's management believes that it does.

NOTES

1. The author would like to thank all those at the Bristol & West who helped in the preparation of this chapter. Staff of the Corporate Information and Analysis Department, particularly John Jennings-Chick, Geoff Wells, Ken Thomasson and Sean Duggan, were a major source of ideas and information on building society and financial sector matters. Senior managers of the society provided the backing needed for the project to succeed. They also provided insights into the recent history of the Bristol & West which could never have been gleaned through inspection of the documentary evidence alone. Coversations with Mr R.M. Coverdale, Mr B. Sims and Mr R.W. Linden were especially valuable in this regard. Above all, the author is indebted to Mr Andrew Breach, President of the Bristol & West, who in a long interview revealed much of the thinking behind the expansion of the society in the last forty years.

The main documentary sources consulted were Board Minute Books covering the period 1945–68 and Annual Reports and Accounts, 1919–87. In the notes which follow, Bristol & West is shortened to B.& W., Board Minute Book is referenced as BMB and Annual Report and Accounts as ARA. Records held by the Corporate Information and Analysis department are referenced as CIA. All other records of the society are held by the archives section.

2. A useful summary of the main provisions of the Building Societies Act of 1986 is provided in R. Vanderwindt and S. Scott, *An Introduction to the Building Societies Act of 1986* (Ware, 1986).

3. The early history of building societies is a subject that would repay further research. The account given here, and much of the later background on the building societies movement, is drawn from the following: H. Ashworth, *The Building Societies Story* (1980). M. Boddy, *The Building Societies* (1980). M. Boleat, *The Building Society Industry* (2nd edn. 1986). E.J. Cleary, *The Building Society Movement* (1965). S.J. Price, *Building Societies: their Origin and History* (1958).

4. Boddy, *Building Societies*, p.6.

5. Ibid., p.7.

6. Boleat, *Introduction to Building Societies*, p.2.

7. The early history of the Bristol & West is outlined in C.J. Lowe, *The Building Society Movement: a Half Century Record with special reference to the Bristol, West of England and South Wales Permanent Building Society* (Bristol, 1901).

8. Lowe, *A Half Century Record*, p.34.

9. Ibid., p.35.

10. Ibid., p.67.

11. Ibid., p.96.

12. Ibid., p.68.

13. Ibid., p.112.

14. Ibid., p.103.

15. Mark Whitwill Snr (1826–1903) was a director from 1857 to 1903. His firm was heavily involved in shipping, shipbuilding and repair, the docks and transport. He was a J.P. and for a time chairman of the Bristol School Board. Sir Frank Wills (1852–1932) was a director from 1897 to 1932. He was an architect of some note, and was responsible for the Wills tobacco factory in East Street, Bedminster, opened in 1886. He served as Lord Mayor of Bristol in 1911.

16. B.& W., ARA, 1919, p.6.

17. B.& W., ARA, 1919, p.14.

18. Copies of these and other advertising brochures are held at B.& W., CIA.

19. B.& W., CIA, *How to Own Your Home*, p.4.

20. A useful short account of the growth of the building society movement between the wars given in G. Davies, *Building Societies and their Branches* (1981), pp.41–50.

21. Boddy, *Building Societies*, p.154.

22. The argument developed here was first advanced in J. Humphries, 'Inter-War House Building, Cheap Money and the Building Societies: the Housing Boom Revisited', *Business History*, XXIX (1987), pp.325–45.

23. There are useful histories of the Halifax, Abbey Road/National and Woolwich societies: O.R. Hobson, *A Hundred Years of the Halifax* (1953). C. Brooks, *The First Hundred Years: the Woolwich* (1947). H. Bellman, *Bricks and Mortals* (1949).

24. Hobson, *A Hundred Years*, pp.90–114. See also E.J. Cleary, 'Sir Enoch Hill' in D.J. Jeremy, ed. *Dictionary of Business Biography*, vol.III (1985).

25. For an excellent summary of Bellman's career, see E.J. Cleary, 'Sir Charles Harold Bellman' in Jeremy, ed. *Dictionary of Business Biography*, vol.I (1984).

26. Price, *Building Societies*, pp.407–438. See also E.J. Cleary, 'Sir Robert Bruce Wycherley' in Jeremy, ed. *Dictionary of Business Biography*, vol.V (1986).

27. E.C.L. Butler, *History of the Building Societies Institute* (1979), pp.11–47.

28. Hobson, *A Hundred Years*, pp.100–13. Bellman, *Bricks and Mortals*, pp.119–31.

29. See especially, B.& W., ARA, 1930 and 1936.

30. Bellman, *Bricks and Mortals*, pp.132–4.

31. Building Societies Association, *Building Societies Year Book* (1986), pp.131–5.

32. S. Duggan, 'Banks and Building Societies: the Competitive Environment in the Retail Savings Market' (unpublished report, B.& W., CIA, 1987), diagram 2.1.

33. B.& W., BMB 29, 22 Feb. 1945.

34. B.& W., BMB 29, 4 June 1946.

35. B.& W., BMB 29, 25 April 1946.

36. B.& W., BMB 31, 22 Nov. 1951.

37. B.& W., ARA, 1945 and 1950.

38. B.& W., BMB 29, 11 Oct. 1945.

39. The general comments on policy made in this paragraph and others are based on a close reading of board minutes and annual reports and accounts. Confirmation has been provided in interviews with Mr Andrew Breach and other long-serving officers of the society.

40. Notes of interview with Andrew Breach. A brief sketch of Mr Breach's early career is given in M. Braham, 'Man in the News: Breach the Innovator', *Western Mail*, 12 March 1969.

41. B.& W., BMB 29, 22 May 1947.

42. The account given in this chapter of Andrew Breach's career with the Bristol & West is based on documentary sources such as board minutes and papers, his writings in the financial press, and interviews with Mr Breach and some of his closest colleagues.

43. Notes of interview between Andrew Breach and the author.

44. Ibid.

45. B.& W., BMB 31, 25 June and 16 July 1953.

46. B.& W., BMB 31, 16 Oct. 1952.

47. B.& W., BMB 31, 6 Nov. 1952.

48. B.& W., BMB 31, 28 May 1953.

49. B.& W., BMB 32, 1 Dec. 1955.

50. Notes of interview between Andrew Breach and the author.

51. B.& W., BMB 32, 1 Dec. 1955.

52. These figures are calculated from data in relevant annual reports. The total asset figures for societies taken over have been totalled for each period, and are expressed as percentages of relevant growth figures (total assets in final year minus total assets in first year).

53. This section of the chapter has benefited from notes prepared by Mr R.M. Coverdale on 'Typical Reasons for Non-Strategic Mergers'. The author has also examined merger documents, including board minutes, of various societies taken over by the Bristol & West. These papers are held in the Bristol & West archives.

54. B.& W. Archives, Minute Book of the British Workmen & General Building Society, 22 Dec. 1954. The minute book includes a letter from Andrew Breach giving full details of the takeover, dated 14 Dec. 1954.

55. B.& W. Archives, Letter signed by the chairman of the British Workmen, Bertram C. Barber, sent to all members of the society, dated 8 Feb. 1955. Of the members who voted, 2,911 were in favour of the merger and 155 were against.

56. B.& W. Archives, Minute Book of the Shepton Mallet Building Society, 8 Oct. 1959.

57. B.& W., BMB 32, 12 March 1957.

58. B.& W., BMB 33, 3 Jan. 1967.

59. B.& W., BMB 32, 15 March 1960.

60. B.& W., BMB 33, 19 Nov. 1963.

61. Notes of interview between Andrew Breach and the author.

62. B.& W., CIA, J.P. Jennings-Chick, 'Annual Return Analysis, 1985: the Top 15 Societies' (internal report, 1986). Table 8 of this report relates to properties in possession or over 12 monthly payments in arrear. The value of mortgages on such properties are given as a percentage of total mortgages and total mortgage assets respectively.

63. See, for example, A. Breach, 'The Property-Owning Democracy', Investors' Guardian, 17 Nov. 1961.

64. B.& W. Archive, typescript of an interview between a local journalist, Mr Walters, and Andrew Breach. This is undated but details in the document date it to 1970.

65. See, for example, Breach's articles in the Statist, 27 April 1965 and 25 April 1966.

66. See, for example, A. Breach, 'Liquidity and Reserve Ratios', Investors' Guardian, 19 Nov. 1965. Idem, 'Sensitivity to Interest Rate Changes', Investors' Guardian, 17 Nov. 1967.

67. B.& W., ARA, 1960 and 1970.

68. B.& W., BMB 32, 15 Nov. 1960.

69. B.& W., BMB 33, 17 Aug. 1965.

70. These quotations are drawn, in order, from articles in the following: Sunday Telegraph, 9 March 1969. Evening Standard, 6 March 1969. Oldham Evening Chronicle, 13 March 1969. Those describing Breach are from the Western Mail, 12 March 1969.

71. B.& W., BMB 32 and 33, 17 Feb. 1959; 9 May 1961; 12 March 1963.

72. B.& W., BMB 31, 6 Nov. 1952.

73. B.& W., BMB 33, 17 Aug. 1965.

74. B.& W., BMB 33, 6 Jan. 1965.

75. B.& W., ARA, 1975.

76. B.& W., CIA, Annual Return to Chief Registrar of Friendly Societies for the year ended 31 Dec. 1985 (form AR 11).

77. B.& W., BMB 33, 21 Sept. 1965 and 26 April 1966.

78. B.& W., BMB 33, 17 Sept. 1963.

79. *Bristol Evening Post, Hold the Front Page: the History of the Evening Post* (Bristol, 1982), p.48.

80. P. Barnes, *Building Societies: the Myth of Mutuality* (1984) puts the case against the building societies most sharply. A more measured appraisal is provided by T.J. Gough, *The Economics of Building Societies* (1982). On concentration and the multiplication of branches, see G. Davies, *Building Societies and Their Branches* (1981).

Index